INTEGRATING THE ORGANIZATION

INTEGRATING THE ORGANIZATION

A SOCIAL PSYCHOLOGICAL ANALYSIS

EDITED BY *Howard L. Fromkin*
AND *John J. Sherwood*

14409

THE FREE PRESS
A Division of Macmillan Publishing Co., Inc.
NEW YORK

Collier Macmillan Publishers
LONDON

0538929

Copyright © 1974 by The Free Press

A Division of Macmillan Publishing Co., Inc.

All rights reserved. No part of this book may be reproduced or transmitted in any form or by any means, electronic or mechanical, including photocopying, recording, or by any information storage and retrieval system, without permission in writing from the Publisher.

The Free Press
A Division of Macmillan Publishing Co., Inc.
866 Third Avenue, New York, N.Y. 10022

Collier–Macmillan Canada Ltd.

Library of Congress Catalog Card Number: 73-21306

Printed in the United States of America

printing number
1 2 3 4 5 6 7 8 9 10

Library of Congress Cataloging in Publication Data

Fromkin, Howard L   date
    Integrating the organization.

    1. Minorities--Employment. 2. Personnel management.
I. Sherwood, John J., date   joint author.
II. Title. [DNLM: 1. Negroes. 2. Prejudice.
3. Race relations. 4. Psychology, Social. E185.8
F931i]
HF5549.5.M5F76   658.3   73-21306
ISBN 0-02-910920-5

Contents

14409

0538929

Foreword

If the Zeitgeist of the early 1960s dictated optimism about the successful integration of minority groups into American life, the early 1970s have emerged as a time of apathy, if not downright pessimism. The legality of crosstown busing to achieve racial integration is now in jeopardy, and public schools are becoming resegregated. The United States government's Civil Rights Commission is relatively dormant. Recent administrative reorganization may mean that training programs would be curtailed and relegated to state governments through revenue sharing. These Federal cuts have also caused the termination of a large program to hire hard-core unemployed for public service jobs and have fragmented the functions of the now defunct Office of Economic Opportunity into other agencies. For the time being at least (and for just how long?) the United States government has relegated responsibility for one of our nation's greatest needs.

Under these conditions, it is imperative that we increase our level of commitment and escalate contribution of our own resources and skills to the seeking of solutions. *Integrating the Organization: A Social Psychological Analysis* is a responsible attack on one of our national goals—equal rights for all. Its authors recognize that behavioral scientists and business people must take the initiative if the civil rights movement is to attain its goal of providing a meaningful life for all American citizens. *Integrating the Organization* is a useful tool for developing greater communication between the researcher and the manager. While each chapter is not equally balanced between reporting findings and spelling out applications, both goals are admirably met, and the book contains much of value for both types of readers. The academic social psychologist is provided thorough reviews of the literature on prejudice, on personality characteristics of minority groups, on person perception, and other relevant topics. The factory owner, the plant manager, or the company personnel officer will find that chapter authors have taken great care to spell out implications of research findings. Its concluding chapter—a hard-hitting one by a black psychologist—proposes a new strategy for achieving racial justice. *Integrating the Organization* is a unique combination of responsible scholarship and bold interpretation.

Most chapters concentrate on the goal of integrating blacks into organizations, most of which—according to the Preface—"remain racist." The book's concentration on the black example has both strengths and weaknesses. We recognize that more data and knowledge are available about blacks than any other social or ethnic minority in America. The discrimination toward blacks and some of its effects upon society are recognized by even the most insensitive among us, and we share little optimism that the problem will soon be "solved." But the problems and needs of other minorities need to be studied, too—not only racial and ethnic groups, but also women and members of what social scientists have always insensitively called "the lower class." In the early 1970s sexism has joined with racism as the source of protest, and I expect that "classism"—if that becomes the term—will justifiably share this concern in the near future. While *Integrating the Organization* devotes less attention to sexism, the challenge of creating an organization free of social-class discrimination is faced.

The empirically oriented social psychologist is a child of this century alone. While it is currently fashionable to say that this fast-growing child has boasted of more accomplishments than it has achieved, there are signs of growth from one stage to another. Social psychology originally concerned itself with *the individual* as its unit of study. Kurt Lewin in the 1930s directed the field to explorations and analyses of *groups* as organized units of behavior. Now social psychology has broadened its concern to the study of *large organizations* and *communities.* How can we make cities more livable? Can the deleterious effects of an urbanized environment be controlled? Can life become more satisfying for factory workers if assembly line procedures are replaced by other working structures? Will communication between races facilitate understanding and cooperation? *Integrating the Organization: A Social Psychological Analysis* provides a spark of optimism as researchers and leaders of organizations share in the search for answers.

LAWRENCE S. WRIGHTSMAN
George Peabody College for Teachers

Preface

"Jim put the quarter under the hair ball, and got down and listened again. This time he said the hair ball was all right. He said it would tell my whole fortune if I wanted it to. I says, go on. So the hair ball talked to Jim, and Jim told it to me." [*Editors' note*: This is a passage from *The Adventures of Huckleberry Finn*, published by Samuel L. Clemens in 1884, describing the American black of that day as "nigger Jim"—obsequious and foot shuffling, uneducated and stupid, superstitious, lazy, and happy-go-lucky.] Jim continues:

> Ye ole father doan' know yit what he's a-gwyne to do. Sometimes he spec he'll go 'way, en den ag'in he spec he'll stay. De bes' way is to res' easy en let de ole man take his own way. Dey's two angels hoverin' roun' 'bout him. One uv 'em is white en shiny, en t'other one is black. De white one gits him to go right a little while, den de black one sail in en bust it all up. A body can't tell yit which one gwyne to fetch him at de las'. But you is all right. You gwyne to have considable trouble in yo' life, en considable joy. Sometimes you gwyne to git hurt, en sometimes you gwyne to git sick; but every time you's gwyne to git well ag'in. Dey's two gals flyin' 'bout you in yo' life. One uv 'em's light en t'other one is dark. One is rich en t'other is po'. You's gwyne to marry de po' one fust en de rich one by en by. You wants to keep 'way fum de water as much as you kin, en don't run no resk, 'kase it's down in de bills dat you's gwyne to git hung. °

This passage seems as far removed from today as Elizabethan English— a quaint, dead language spoken by fools, soothsayers, and noblemen. The day that blacks are willing to behave as nigger Jim has passed. The day that society can afford to ignore the wealth of resources of black people, or to relegate these resources to menial or dirty work, has also passed. The day that any people can consciously treat others as nigger Jims has long passed. Yet, the organizations of

---

°Copyright, 1884, by Samuel L. Clemens; copyright, 1948, by Grosset & Dunlap, Inc., New York. *The Adventures of Huckleberry Finn*, by Mark Twain.

American society are not integrated. At this time, most organizations remain racist. This describes business and industrial organizations, educational and other service organizations (such as the church and the military), and, of course, voluntary organizations as well.

In some organizations racism takes the clear and simple form of exclusion of minority persons. Other organizations are rascist insofar as blacks and other minorities play minor roles in terms of power, income, status, and skill. Other organizations have a large layer of minority employees at the very bottom of a tall hierarchy.

This book is designed to assist organizations to move toward fuller integration both for humanistic reasons and to utilize more fully the potential resources of minority people.

While the focus is often on blacks both because of their visibility and because of their leadership in civil rights movements of recent years, our intention is that the ideas of this book be used to assist *any* organization integrate *any* minority members.

Our interest in this project is several-fold. We would like to build a bridge of some significance between the research and theory of the social scientist and the world of action of the organizational administrator. We would like, in addition, to stimulate experimental research in both laboratory and field varieties which deals directly with this problem. It sometimes seems as if many organizations are waving "equal opportunity flags". . . fulfilling quotas, yet offering little more than tokenism. To the extent that this is accurate, one might ask what help the research of the psychologist and sociologist has been. In order to answer this question, contributions have been invited from some people whom we believe can generalize from existing theories to the specific problems of integrating organizations.

Each chapter covers a different problem area, e.g., leadership—the black in the supervisory role, and the black as subordinate. The chapters approach the problems of integrating organizations in heuristic and adventuresome ways. Interesting and testable propositions are derived—which it is hoped will lead to innovative social research and social action.

We have placed short, introductory statements in front of each chapter. Our summaries-as-introductions have, of course, left out a lot of the implications for the manager in each chapter. It is our feeling that most of the ideas for managers in this book are best understood in the context of the research and theory offered by each author. Most of the data presented were not gathered with the organizational decision maker in mind, and they need to be stretched with speculation to be made relevant to problems of integrating organizations. The administrator should immerse himself fully in this process with each author. The chapters also contain many ideas for further research which the administrator may wish to advocate and support within his own organization.

While we are, for the most part, delighted by the way our research colleagues responded to our request that they give some of their time and their concern to issues of integrating organizations, we are also disappointed by the data-centered myopia we found among some social science research scholars who are unwilling or unable to take the conceptual leaps necessary to move science and to inspire men.

This book is the product of a very strong group of scientists who were willing to step forward and take a stand on one of the most important problems facing any people. In the first chapter, Howard L. Fromkin analyzes the *social psychological research on race relations,* and he draws implications for integration of organizations. Fromkin begins by distinguishing between prejudice and discrimination. Within this distinction, he then discusses the antecedents and consequences of prejudice as attitudinal phenomena in relation to problems of integrating the organization. Several policy suggestions are based upon extrapolations from research on prejudice and unfavorable interracial attitudes. Fromkin's chapter discusses the social foundations of prejudice and discrimination. An extensive discussion of the roles of cultural norms, opinion leaders, and reference groups shows how the organization, as a subculture, can be designed to inhibit the kind of racial behavior and conflict which occurs within the larger society. Fromkin describes how prejudice and discrimination are governed primarily by conformity to prevailing social norms. He explains the social influence mechanisms which control these social norms and how these mechanisms can be modified within the organization to avoid racial conflict. Fromkin's review of the research literature also identifies numerous personal and situational variables which act as constraints against the translation of prejudice into discriminatory behavior, and which can be recognized and modified in exchange for more friendly and productive race relations. Fromkin also suggests how the organization can facilitate integration and gain wider access to valuable segments of the labor force by providing greater educational and occupational opportunities to minority peoples and by providing special training programs for those who are to supervise minority persons.

Fromkin describes organizational integration as following a sequence of four stages, wherein each stage may terminate with a potential change in prejudice and discrimination. Such a model can be used by an organization to plan productively for the future or retroactively to gain insights into past and present problems of race relations within the organization. A number of variables are introduced which may be altered by the organization to reduce the degree of racial conflict—variables such as organizational sanctions, participative management, racial composition of work groups, social threat, status, inconsistency, competition and economic threat, and power differentials.

The second chapter is by Marvin D. Dunnette, who discusses three main issues concerning *employment of minorities.* The first issue is differentiation versus unfair discrimination. Differentiation involves identifying those individuals who possess attributes well suited for certain job situations or for certain specialized training programs. In contrast, unfair discrimination occurs when a higher proportion of minority members are rejected who, if placed in the job, could have been successful. Thus, Dunnette calls for action on two counts—to end unfair discrimination and to differentiate among all members of the community, including minority members, in an attempt to match people to jobs. Second, Dunnette points out the importance of individualizing the personnel decision processes, especially in relation to minority peoples. He claims the thrust of personnel decisions should be toward individualized prediction strategies in which each candidate's particular merits and shortcomings are examined in relation to their meaning for all possible personnel actions. Dunnette provides a model for decisions in the employment process to solve the dilemma of the personnel executive as he faces persons differing in such factors as education, sex, race, degree of cultural advantage, etc.

Third, Dunnette identifies some special problems involved in conducting useful validity studies for predictors of job success by minority group members and offers some methodological steps which are likely to give useful results in these validation investigations. Finally, an interesting hypothetical model is offered which estimates costs likely to be incurred by decision errors unfairly rejecting minority peoples.

Avner M. Porat and Edward C. Ryterband concern themselves with problems of *occupational choice*. Their chapter begins with a discussion of the current status of blacks in the labor mainstream. Labor statistics for 1970 demonstrate that a high proportion of employed blacks occupy lower-level jobs, mainly unskilled work. Porat and Ryterband discuss current data and see needs for future data in three key areas related to occupations. First, they show how personal characteristics of minority persons affect occupational choice and performance. Second, there is an examination of the "real" and "perceived" characteristics of the environment which allow or prevent the achievement of equality in career development opportunities. Third, these authors examine how both environmental and personal factors constrain career choices of minority group members. Porat and Ryterband cite data showing very little difference between the occupational aspirations of blacks and whites—it is only their expectancy of obtaining the chosen occupation or level of attainment which is considerably lower for blacks.

Under environmental constraints, the authors point to poor educational opportunities as inhibiting career development and argue for compensatory education. They also cite the need for business and industry to contribute to the educational process within communities in order to provide the manpower they will need in the future. They point out constraints which appear in organizations and professional societies which seem to limit blacks' expectancies of success. Furthermore, they provide data showing that low expectancies for income by blacks are certainly very realistic at this time. The authors also provide a section on measurement issues and suggest some problems in assessing abilities of blacks. They conclude that the main opportunities for minority peoples lie in developing a solid economic and occupational base within their own racial or ethnic group. They suggest a need for programs which are designed to encourage minority persons to enter those occupations in which they are underrepresented today, in order to develop and staff the occupations needed within their own community.

Lowell W. Hellervik introduces problems of *training the disadvantaged* minority person and discusses some hard-core hiring programs. He notes some factors which seem to reduce the successfulness of hard-core hiring programs, and he also presents a survey of training practices which have been used for minority peoples. Hellervik then raises the interesting issue of providing training for the co-workers and supervisors of minority persons. He describes some general training needs of the disadvantaged worker and offers evidence to support his suggestions.

Hellervik points out the need to focus on *behavior* change, rather than worrying about the attitudes of workers. He presents an intriguing, creative, and ingenuous strategy for behavior change based on Skinnerian principles. This set of principles of behavior modification are then directly applied to the training of disadvantaged employees. Hellervik presents an interesting discussion of rewards, or in this case, "reinforcers," which are likely to be effective with newly hired disadvantaged persons. Hellervik also suggests that building social support systems helps the hard-core adjust to work. The five main elements of these support systems are organizational involvement, pretraining preparation, training support, job linkage, and follow-up procedures.

Irwin Katz writes about *black culture and personality*. He attacks the currently popular theme that minority groups and their characteristic poverty create cultural norms and personality traits which make it difficult for them to respond to expanding economic opportunities. In essence, he attacks the view that there are cultural and personality explanations for poverty. Katz reviews recent research on lower-class life styles, with appropriate attention to the psychosocial development of the child who grows up in the slums. He questions both the descriptive accuracy and the generalizability of prior research accounts of ghetto life. In addition, Katz questions whether or not the apparent differences between ghetto and mainstream behavior reflect differences in socially transmitted values, beliefs, and norms. He contends, instead, they reflect the individual's functional adaptation to different sets of situational factors. Particularly interesting is Katz's discussion of the social world of the black male as it affects, and is affected by, his job experiences. Many of the most basic and important personality questions about the disadvantaged have not yet received even tentative answers. He finds little support for the "personality deficit" view in spite of its wide acceptance. His discussion of blacks' personalities is directed toward personality traits that are believed to affect one's capacity for achievement in modern industrial society.

Katz notes that the bulk of previous research on black subculture dealt with an extremely deprived underclass which simply does not describe a substantial majority of today's black male adults. The decade of the 1960s saw dramatic shifts in wages, salaries, employment, and educational level of young blacks. Katz suggests that culture and personality traits are now less important factors in job adjustment than objective features of the job itself. The major cause for job termination by marginal workers appears to be the poor quality of working conditions in the positions to which these hard-core unemployed were assigned.

In addition, it is suggested that the pessimism and distrust expressed by hard-core workers, which are often well founded in their experience, are likely to be more significant factors than personality and culture in determining their performance and job tenure. Katz concludes with several policy recommendations concerning the number of black employees placed in jobs at various status levels and some suggestions about supervisors of one's own race and the nature of rewards. In addition, Katz sees a need for organizations to contribute to improving the community conditions of the poor, i.e., housing, quality of education, and health and welfare programs at national, state, and local levels.

The chapter by Robert M. Guion and Patricia Cain Smith deals with *motivation*. Guion and Smith treat motivation as task related with goal-setting characteristics. They discuss factors which influence goal setting, particularly among the disadvantaged. For example, they cite evidence which suggests that organizations would find advantage in offering nutritional supplements to employees. They also discuss the need for pleasant stimulation in the work setting. Guion and Smith find the concept of expectancies useful in understanding motivations of minorities. Then they offer some characteristic expectancies of minority group members and suggest how the organization might respond. They see the need to disconfirm expectancies of failure and to build expectancies of success by providing early tasks which are obtainable with clear signs of completion.

Guion and Smith also consider the rewards of jobs in relation to the idiosyncratic needs of minority group members. High job involvement is likely to occur where there are rewards for completion of meaningful units of work. They provide data which show the need both for confidence training and for suitable incentives which will increase the self-confidence of minority persons. They also discuss achievement and fear of failure in relation to goal setting by minority people. Here they point to the usefulness of tangible rewards which are related to goal-setting activity, especially during training periods.

The chapter by Harry C. Triandis is concerned with *interracial person perception*. It attempts to answer such questions as, "How do people see each other and how does this affect the way they behave toward each other?" "What determines the different ways we see other people?" "What are the consequences of such perceptions?" "What are the implications of differences in perception for organizational functioning?" These questions are answered in terms of their implications for interracial behavior. The discussion focuses on three kinds of responses individuals make to interpersonal stimuli. Attributive responses refer to inferences one makes about the attributes of another person; affective responses refer to the particular way you behave when you are with the other person. Triandis examines the determinants of such responses in situations when the two persons are black and white. He also talks about the effects of stereotyping and the inferior judgmental processes which characterize stereotyping, such as selective distortion, absolutism, and overstressing the similarity among members of the stereotyped group.

Triandis presents an interesting discussion of the black ghetto culture and relates the characteristics he finds there to needs for changing the structure of organizations. His analysis of interracial person perception contains many statements posed in the form of research problems. He concludes with a section on changing the organization in which suggestions are presented which the organization can use in selection and training of black employees. For example, Triandis suggests that great care must be taken in matching the black employee's ability and training with the difficulty of the job. Training of white employees could be directed toward changing basic defense mechanisms which are often employed to feed their prejudice. Triandis also offers ideas about a court system within the organization, which allows blacks and whites special hearings in relation to interracial problems.

Lyman W. Porter views *interracial communication* as a major problem facing organizations which are attempting to integrate. He asserts that unless an organization can develop a work environment that can maintain and foster adequate information exchange, the skills of individual members of an interracial work force will be underutilized. This underutilizaton leads to profound dissatisfaction among employees. Porter analyzes problems of communication with different racial mixes. He describes some ways to address these complex problems, and he identifies many factors which influence comprehension and accuracy in interpersonal communication between persons of different races. He then draws implications for organizational structure and training. For example, Porter's analysis suggests that one critical element is an opportunity for persons to learn the value in understanding communications from the other race. There needs to be a chance to observe things such as expertise, good intentions, and attitude similarities that can lead to attraction to and trust in a communicator of another race—especially when these biracial workers hold more or less common attitudes toward relevant aspects of the work environment, such as the nature and value of the tasks themselves, the quality of the boss, the fairness of the organization, and the like. He also suggests that communication difficulties might be reduced by organizations adopting more decentralized communication networks, and he discusses differences between vertical and horizontal communication as they are affected by biracial factors. Porter then speculates about the effects of various proportions or mixes of different race members in a work group and the effects of this factor upon the accuracy of vertical communication. Last, Porter suggests a number of specific areas where research would be very useful.

The chapter by Donald C. King and Bernard M. Bass examines *leadership, power, and influence*. They support recent data showing the absence of blacks in leadership positions in industry, and they go on to offer an interesting set of theoretical propositions dealing with the obvious resistance to integration in supervisory ranks. They suggest there is a hierarchy of concern in the employment history of minority people in an organization. The first concern is simply entry into the organization—getting jobs. Once entry has been established in sufficient number, the concern shifts to skilled jobs. Once access to skilled jobs has been achieved, the concern is movement into managerial positions. King and

Bass provide some evidence which supports their model and which shows the current demand is for skilled jobs and managerial positions. They then discuss a number of factors affecting the movement of minorities into management.

King and Bass also look at race in leader–subordinate relations, and they discuss variables which appear to influence the effectiveness of different racial mixes of superior and subordinate. They also suggest some problems that black leaders are likely to encounter. Many of their speculations are posed as hypotheses and are easy to test. These hypotheses should generate some useful research. Bass and King call attention to a number of problems which may arise for a white supervisor with black subordinates, and they suggest factors which enhance or inhibit conflict in such situations. This chapter also contains some methods and techniques for identifying black supervisors who have leadership potential. Bass and King note differences in management style between black and white supervisors. They conclude with a brief discussion of some avenues for changing the racial mix in leadership roles of organizations.

The chapter by Ord Elliott and Donald D. Penner attempts to tie problems of integrating the organization into the *societal fabric* within which the organization resides. They discuss the role of social structure as it affects the degree of conflict which accompanies organizational integration. The chapter describes socioeconomic variables and other normative characteristics of black and white groups, such as socioeconomic status, occupational level, and educational level. Elliott and Penner show how these factors contribute to the black's accepting particular roles and behaving in accordance with associated norms. Furthermore, the chapter suggests how an organization may decrease or increase role conflict. Lastly, they point out how organizations can respond and be agents to change those social structures which inhibit the full development and optimal performance of minority people.

James A. Green and Harold B. Gerard describe a large-scale, longitudinal *field study of school desegregation*. Examination of the process of school desegregation enables the reader to get a picture of the stresses and strains and benefits which may accrue from mixing people from different backgrounds. Green and Gerard discuss some implications of their study, suggesting that organizations need to be flexible and to make changes both before desegregation and after desegregation. They present findings that minority members tend to separate into their own ethnic group and develop a strong sense of ethnic identity in the initial uncertainties of desegregation. Most of the Green and Gerard discussion centers around the development of racial awareness, self-esteem, and self-confidence.

Howard L. Fromkin and Thomas M. Ostrom present solutions to *problems encountered in research* on questions of integrating organizations. They note the need for direct experimentation with integrating organizations, and they point out the clear absence of such data to guide us today. The lack of field research on problems of integration and the wealth of laboratory experimentation on race relations suggest the need at this point for organizations to use the available laboratory data. The Fromkin and Ostrom chapter provides a novel perspective which allows organizations to use the available laboratory findings and generalize from them to organizational problems. The chapter also presents a discussion of those variables which inhibit and those which facilitate the translation of data into practice. The claim that laboratory experimentation is artificial and invalid for problems of the "real world" is challenged. Instead, the concept of boundary variable is offered to assist the administrator in bringing laboratory data to bear on his own organizational problems. A number of examples of how this perspective can be used are presented. They focus on the translation of specific laboratory findings on race to problems of integrating organizations. For example, research on the contact hypothesis is reviewed, and findings about frequency of contact between persons of different races and the attraction between them which results are used to suggest methods of integrating an organization and constituting interracial work groups.

Robert W. Terry of the Detroit Industrial Mission has recently written, ". . . to be white is to be deeply confused or to be white means to be in charge without much thought of what it means to be white at all." The final chapter of this book is written by a black social scientist. Dalmas A. Taylor offers a perspective on integrating organizations that neither the white social scientist nor the white administrator can ever experience.

It is the hope of the editors that the thoughts in this book will give those with power in organizations further understanding and insight into the issues, dilemmas, and problems of integrating an organization. But more than that, it is also our hope that with greater clarity will come more thinking about strategies for introducing change into organizations and a sharper focus to the goals of these change efforts.

All proceeds from the sale of this book are to go to the Society for the Psychological Study of Social Issues as seed money for research focusing on problems of integrating organizations.

We gratefully acknowledge the financial support and the continued encouragement we received from Valerie H. Webb and Jerome W. Blood of The Free Press and from Dean John S. Day of the Krannert Graduate School of Industrial Administration here at Purdue University.

HOWARD L. FROMKIN
JOHN J. SHERWOOD
Krannert Graduate School of Industrial Administration
Purdue University

The Editors

Howard L. Fromkin (Ph.D., Ohio State University, 1968) is Associate Professor of Social Psychology and Administrative Sciences and Chairman of the Department of Administrative Sciences at Purdue University. He has authored and coauthored articles in professional journals and chapters in the *Handbook of Industrial and Organizational Psychology*, edited by Marvin Dunnette, and *Social Influence*, edited by James Tedeschi. He is associate editor of the *Journal of Applied Social Psychology* and consulting editor of *Organizational Behavior and Human Performance*.

John J. Sherwood (Ph.D., University of Michigan, 1962) is Professor of Social Psychology and Administrative Sciences in the Krannert Graduate School of Industrial Administration at Purdue University. His teaching and research interests focus on organization development and change. He is also interested in problems of individual change. He has held appointments at Harvard University, Carleton College, and the University of Michigan. Dr. Sherwood is a frequent contributor to professional journals and has coedited *The Study of Attitude Change* with R. V. Wagner.

Contributors

Bernard M. Bass (Ph.D., Ohio State University, 1949) is Professor of Management, Professor of Psychology, and Director of the Management Research Center, The University of Rochester. He has also taught at the University of California, Berkeley, the Instituto Estudios Superiores de las Empresas, Barcelona, and Louisiana State University, and has lectured at Yale, Pennsylvania, Illinois, Michigan, M.I.T., Ohio State, UCLA, Oregon, and abroad. He is consulting editor of *Organizational Behavior and Human Performance,* the *Journal of Applied Psychology,* the *European Journal of Training,* and the *Journal of Cross-Cultural Society* and is the author of several books and articles.

Marvin D. Dunnette (Ph.D., University of Minnesota, 1954) holds a joint appointment as Professor of Psychology and Industrial Relations at the University of Minnesota. Prior to his appointment, Dr. Dunnette was Manager of Personnel Research for the Minnesota Mining and Manufacturing Company (3M). He is the author of numerous journal articles and books in the fields of industrial and organizational psychology and personnel management.

Ord Elliott is an organization development consultant with University Associates. He graduated from Princeton University in 1966 with an A.B. in English. After a three-year tour with the U.S. Marine Corps, which included duty in Vietnam as a rifle platoon commander, he entered a graduate program in organizational behavior at Purdue University; currently he is a doctoral candidate there. His most recent research has been in the area of community interorganizational relations with particular focus on the effectiveness of Youth Service Bureaus. Elliott's professional interests and expertise include teaching organizational behavior, action research on the community level, planned organizational change, and laboratory training.

Harold B. Gerard (Ph.D., University of Michigan, 1952) is Professor of Psychology at the University of California, Los Angeles. Prior to his appointment, he was a Fulbright Scholar at the University of Nijmegen, The Netherlands, and has served as a member of the Technical Staff at Bell Telephone Laboratories. He has also taught at the University of California, Riverside.

James A. Green (Ph.D., University of Colorado, 1967) is an Assistant Research Psychologist and Lecturer at the University of California, Los Angeles. Dr. Green has had major responsibility for collecting and analyzing data from the Riverside School Study, which was a longitudinal study of desegregation in the public schools of Riverside, California. He has contributed to several professional journals and is helping to complete a monograph on the desegregation study.

Robert M. Guion (Ph.D., Purdue University, 1952) teaches at Bowling Green State University. He has previously taught at the University of California, Berkeley, and the University of New Mexico and worked with the Personnel Services Department of the State of Hawaii and the Educational Testing Service. He is the author of *Personnel Testing* (1965) and numerous articles in professional journals.

Lowell W. Hellervik (Ph.D., Minnesota, 1968) is the Executive Vice President of Personnel Decisions, Inc. Earlier he had extensive counseling experience in the Counseling Psychology Service at the Minneapolis Veterans' Hospital and at the University of Minnesota Laboratory School. He has had broad experience in the appraisal of management and sales applicants and has worked on a number of special industrial projects involving studies of organizational stress, communications effectiveness, manpower counseling, integrating the disadvantaged into an organization, and counseling and group relations.

Irwin Katz (Ph.D., Stanford University, 1949) is Professor of Psychology at the Graduate Center of the City University of New York. He has also taught at the University of Michigan, New York University, and the University of Buffalo. He has been a consultant to the United States Commission on Civil Rights and to the United States Office of Education. In addition to many articles and reviews, his publications include *Social Class, Race, and Psychological Development* (with Martin Deutsch and Arthur Jensen), *Race and the Social Sciences* (with Patricia Gurin), and *Conflict and Harmony in an Adolescent Interracial Group.*

Donald C. King (Ph.D., Purdue University, 1957) is currently Professor of Administrative Sciences and Psychology in the Krannert Graduate School of Industrial Administration at Purdue. He has served as a Ford Foundation consultant in the U.A.R. and as an Assistant Dean of the graduate school and director of the graduate program in industrial administration at Purdue. He is the author or coauthor of approximately thirty professional articles and papers.

Thomas M. Ostrom (Ph.D., University of North Carolina, 1964) is currently Professor of Psychology at Ohio State University. He has done research in the areas of attitude theory, attitude measurement, and applications of social psychology and has coedited

Psychological Foundations of Attitudes. Professor Ostrom is a frequent contributor to various journals.

Donald D. Penner (Ph.D., Purdue University, 1966) is Professor of Behavioral Science at the U.S. Army War College at Carlisle Barracks, Pennsylvania. He has previously taught at Iowa State University, the University of North Carolina at Greensboro, and Guilford College. Professor Penner publishes primarily in the areas of cognitive dissonance, theory leadership, and international relations, and his most recent publications include two major leadership studies for the U.S. Army.

Avner M. Porat (Ph.D., University of Pittsburgh, 1968) is the Manager of Business and Organization Development, Midwest Division of Hay Associates, a management consulting firm. Prior to joining Hay Associates in 1970, he was an assistant professor and research associate at the University of Rochester and Pittsburgh, conducting research and consulting in the areas of organizational behavior, executive development, and planning and computer applications for management. Dr. Porat is the author or coauthor of over twenty articles and book chapters on the subjects of management development, decision making, data processing, minority group development, and banking.

Lyman Porter (Ph.D., Yale University, 1956) is Dean of the Graduate School of Administration and Professor of Administration and Psychology at the University of California, Irvine. He has previously taught at the University of California, Berkeley, and at Yale University. Professor Porter has coauthored *Managerial Thinking: An International Study* and *Managerial Attitudes and Performance* and has published widely in such journals as *Personnel Psychology, Journal of Applied Psychology, Industrial Relations,* and *Harvard Business Review.*

Edward C. Ryterband (Ph.D., Purdue University, 1965) is Director of Organization Development with Edward N. Hay and Associates, a Management Consulting firm in Philadelphia. Prior to becoming a Hay consultant, he taught at the Graduate School of Management at the University of Rochester and consulted for INSTAD, Limited, a Rochester consulting firm. Dr. Ryterband is the coauthor of a forthcoming book, *Organizational Psychology,* and a contributor to a number of books including *Management for Accomplishment,* and *Work in the Year 2000.*

Patricia Cain Smith (Ph.D., Cornell University, 1942) is Professor of Psychology at Bowling Green State University and supervising consultant for Cain Smith Associates. She has previously taught at Cornell University and served as supervising consultant for Kurt Salmon Associates. Professor Smith has coauthored *Principles of Industrial Psychology* with T. A. Ryan and *Satisfaction in Work and Retirement* with L. Kendall and has contributed numerous articles to various journals.

Dalmus A. Taylor (Ph.D., University of Delaware, 1965) is Professor of Psychology at the University of Maryland. Prior to his appointment, he was chairman of the Department of Psychology at Federal City College. Professor Taylor is an experimental social psychologist with interests in small groups, person perception, and interpersonal attraction and has authored numerous journal articles in these fields.

Harry C. Triandis (Ph.D., Cornell University, 1958) is Professor of Psychology at the University of Illinois. He is the author of *Attitude and Attitude Change* and *The Analysis of Subjective Culture* and is a frequent contributor to the *Journal of Abnormal Psychology, Journal of Personality and Social Psychology, Sociometry, Human Relations, and Journal of Applied Psychology*. In addition, Professor Triandis serves on the editorial boards of several of these and other journals.

CHAPTER ONE

A Social Psychological Analysis of Organizational Integration

Howard L. Fromkin

INTRODUCTION BY THE EDITORS

Prejudice and discrimination are proposed by Fromkin as two major barriers to successful integration. Their individual, social, and situational foundations are discussed. "Prejudice" is defined as an unfavorable ethnic attitude which is composed of relatively stable stereotypic beliefs, biased perceptions, and predominantly negative reaction tendencies toward members of a particular ethnic group. "Discrimination" is defined as unfriendly behavior toward a target person who is selected only by virtue of his membership in an ethnic group, without regard for individual differences among members of the ethnic group. That is, unfriendly behavior is aroused by racial characteristics of the target person which are irrelevant to the requirements of the situation. Fromkin reviews the theory and research surrounding the assumption that prejudice always leads to discrimination. The findings reveal prejudicial attitudes compete with other individual, social, and situational forces to determine whether discrimination takes place. The chapter is devoted to an exposition of the forces, including prejudice, which enhance and inhibit the expression of discrimination within organizational settings.

The author gratefully acknowledges the comments of John J. Sherwood and Donald King on an earlier draft of this paper. Preparation of this paper was supported, in part, by grants from the Criminal Justice Planning Agency.

Fromkin reviews the literature on the social origins of prejudice and discrimination as they occur within society. Both prejudice and discrimination are based primarily in cultural norms, opinion leaders, mass media, and reference groups. The mass media, directly or indirectly, serve as a communication link in the process of transmission of cultural norms. Opinion leaders mediate the mass media influence by selectively screening and transmitting filtered information to help perpetuate cultural norms. They also serve as models who demonstrate which behavior is appropriate and which attitudes are deemed correct. Reference groups operate as anchors and enforcers of prejudice and discrimination. Although organizations continuously interact with and are dependent upon the larger society of which they are a part, they are also a microsociety which can maintain different cultural norms. Fromkin suggests that prejudices and discrimination can be reduced within an organization by the same mechanisms of social influence which foster them in the external environment. For example, organizations can set policy and provide sanctions to support humanistic norms and nondiscriminatory behavior patterns within the subculture of organizational life. The identification and support of opinion leaders within the organization can be a potent force for the reduction of prejudice and discrimination. Fromkin describes several techniques to map the informal communication structure of the organization and to identify opinion leaders. Procedures of norm maintenance and monitoring are described to support desired organizational norms and opinion leaders. Fromkin recommends that integration can often occur with less conflict when the formal (e.g., management) and the informal (e.g., opinion leaders) leadership subscribe to humanistic norms and publicly support integration. He concludes that the absence of any real opportunities for entrance or advancement by blacks and the stereotypic attitudes of white industrial leaders are a greater impediment to successful integration than are the cultural norms of the external society. Fromkin also discusses the role of prejudicial attitudes as potent forces supporting discrimination and describes different attitude-change techniques which may reduce the degree of prejudice within an organization.

Fromkin also reviews the theory and research, identifying more than thirty situational variables which likely determine whether or not interracial contact will result in the reduction of prejudice and discrimination within the organization. The major variables are organized into a conceptual scheme of orderly and continuous sequences of events which correspond to the temporal stages of organizational integration: the pre-proximity stage, the proximity stage, the interaction stage, and the post-interaction stage. These stages are described in ways that permit administrators to decide which stage is most descriptive of their present state, and then to use the model proactively and/ or retroactively to gain insight into the past, present, or future problems of race relations within their organization.

The pre-proximity stage is concerned with attitudes prior to integration. There is substantial evidence that interracial conflict during later stages is dependent upon the degree of institutional support for integration which is developed during this early stage. Both official policy and an atmosphere of general agreement among significant persons within the organization are basic ingredients of institutional support. It is suggested that the more agreement and acceptance of this new policy, the more likely employees will be provided with relevant information which will also help them accept the new policy. The advantages of this approach and several techniques to initiate it are also discussed. Furthermore, interracial outcomes in later stages are more positive when they occur under positive sanctions for friendly racial contact and negative sanctions for unfriendly racial contact and also under conditions of a high degree of "regulation potential." Regulation potential is the degree to which deviations from desired and expected behavior are visible to those persons who can be expected to punish deviations.

The proximity stage begins when the initial contact occurs among co-workers of different races in the organizational setting. Fromkin describes a number of variables which are potential determinants of discriminaion. For example, the more minority newcomers threaten the status or power of their co-workers, the more negative interracial contact is likely to be. A number of features of job assignment and design are discussed in relation to these variables.

The interaction stage begins with the development of interracial communication and personal relationships. Research demonstrates the importance of variables which influence the potential for acquaintance, such as spatial proximity and frequency and duration of interracial contact. Conflict will be reduced to the extent that meaningful communication occurs and personal relationships develop during this stage. The post-interaction stage involves more extensive elaboration of the above features of the integrated organizational environment.

Fromkin concludes with a discussion of how the survival of modern organizations is dependent, in part, upon their capacity to respond to current social problems, such as the successful integration of minority members of society. This objective can only be accomplished by providing them with real opportunities for achievement, recognition, and advancement into all managerial levels.

Most theories of race relations reflect one of two broad approaches to the dynamics of prejudice and discrimination. One approach stresses *social determinants* and the other emphasizes *forces within the individual*. This distinction is often misleading because both social and psychological forces intersect in the history of an individual. The sociocultural milieu (e.g., social learning) often affects the individual's psychological development. In general, interracial behavior represents an intricate interdependence of social and psychological causation. It is frequently impractical, if not impossible, to determine which is the primary or first cause in any given situation. In this chapter, it is assumed that "prejudice" (e.g., attitude) and "discrimination" (e.g., behavior) are two major obstacles to conflict-free integration of organizations. Furthermore, it is assumed that elimination of these barriers requires an understanding of their genesis.

Accordingly, this chapter begins with a definition and discussion of the interrelationship between prejudice and discrimination. A discussion of the social foundations of prejudice and discrimination is organized into two general classes of determinants—individual foundations and situational foundations. Although these two classes of variables are likely to interact in a complex manner to determine prejudice and discrimination, they are discussed separately to ease exposition. Some *individual* determinants of discriminatory behavior are personality factors (e.g., authoritarianism, dogmatism, etc.), motivational factors (e.g., aggression, status consciousness, etc.), demographic factors (e.g., social class, education, etc.), and attitudinal factors (e.g., stereotypic beliefs, etc.). *Social* determinants include cultural norms, mass media, opinion leaders, and reference group phenomena. *Situational* determinants include the nature and degree of social threat invoked by minority members, characteristics and behavior of the black stimulus person, and the nature of interracial contact and so forth.

It is assumed that the dynamics of integration are not unique to any one kind of organizational setting—industrial, military, or otherwise. Thus, gaps between theory or evidence of race relations and organizational application are filled by extrapolation (cf. Fromkin and Ostrom, 1972, in this volume) and supplemented by speculation whenever necessary. An attempt is made in this chapter to be selective in order to avoid overlap with the contents of other chapters in this volume. The chapter falls short of an encyclopedic list, because theory and research on race relations has yet to uncover all the determinants or to unravel the complexity of their relationships. Fortunately, a number of studies have advanced theory far enough to identify many of the relevant factors.

PREJUDICE AND DISCRIMINATION

Definitions and Relationships

The origin of social psychology's interest in ethnic relations may be traced historically to the study of interracial attitudes (Bogodus, 1925; Thomas and Znaniecki, 1918). This original association between the study of attitudes and race relations continued, and, as a result, the vast majority of social psychological theory and research on race relations is preoccupied with the antecedents and consequences of racial *attitudes*. Current knowledge concerning the dynamics of interracial attitudes has also benefited from a cross-fertilizing relationship with the study of attitudes in general. Much less attention has been given to how people actually behave with members of other races.

PREJUDICE. Although there is a plethora of definitions of the construct "attitude" (cf. Allport, 1935; Greenwald, 1968; Ostrom, 1968), some degree of convergence occurs upon a limited number of common themes. For example, any broad summary statement would suggest that "attitude" is a construct which refers to "a learned readiness to respond" to a stimulus object, a potential response which consists of cognitive, affective, and conative components (Chein, 1951; Fishbein, 1966; Hovland and Rosenberg, 1960; Insko and Schopler, 1967; Kothandapandi, 1971; Kramer, 1949; Ostrom, 1969; Rosenberg, 1960a, 1960b; Smith, Bruner and White, 1956). The *cognitive component* of attitudes consists of a number of interrelated beliefs which all refer to the same specific object or person, etc. For example, many persons believe that eating spinach will increase their strength or that housing values will depreciate if blacks move into their neighborhood. The origin of beliefs is a product of a person's direct or indirect (parents, teachers, journalists, etc.) experiences with the object and a number of rational–irrational processes within the individual. The *affective component* of attitudes refers to the person's favorable or un-favorable feelings toward a particular stimulus object or person, i.e., the degree to which an object or person is positively or negatively evaluated. For example, a person may like or dislike spinach. The *conative* or *action component* refers to the person's behavioral intent with regard to the stimulus object, i.e., the probability that the person would *perform* a specific set of behaviors which are relevant to the attitude object. Presumably, when a person has a favorable attitude toward a given stimulus, he will *intend* to act positively toward it. For instance, a person who has a favorable attitude toward spinach will intend to purchase, cook, and eat the spinach—unless other circumstances prevent him from doing so. Thus, attitudes (including conative components) are distinct from overt behavior. The few studies of the components of ethnic attitudes suggest that the cognitive or belief component is the most susceptible to change and the different components may require different methods to produce attitude change (Katz and Stotland, 1959; Mann, 1960; Merz and Pearlin, 1957).

Presumably then, a person who holds a very favorable attitude toward a stimulus object will, under some circumstances, respond more positively to-ward that object than a person who holds a very unfavorable attitude. *Inter-racial attitudes* involve potential responses to specific kinds of stimuli—namely, persons who are members of the same or different ethnic groups. An *ethnic group* refers to ". . . a collection of people considered both by themselves and by other people to have in common one or more of the following characteristics: (1) religion, (2) racial origin (as indicated by readily identifiable physical features), (3) national origin, or (4) language or cultural tradition" (Harding, Proshansky, Kutner and Chein, 1969, p. 3; Tumin, 1964). An *ethnic attitude*, then, refers to an attitude which ". . . a person has toward some or all members of an ethnic group, provided that the attitude is influenced to some degree by knowledge (or presumed knowledge) of the other group membership" (Harding, Kutner, Proshansky and Chein, 1954, p. 1022; Harding, Proshansky, Kutner and Chein, 1969, p. 3).

According to the present perspective, "prejudice" will refer to an *unfavorable* ethnic attitude[1] which is associated with relatively stable stereotypic beliefs, biased perceptions, and a number of inaccurate expectations about and predominantly negative reaction tendencies toward members of a particular ethnic group.[2] A compendium of unfavorable beliefs about members of various ethnic groups is generally viewed as a central component of a prejudicial attitude (Allport, 1954; Harding, Kutner, Proshansky and Chein, 1954; Harding, Proshansky, Kutner and Chein, 1969; LaViolette and Silvert, 1951; Secord, 1959; Secord and Backman, 1964; Simpson and Yinger, 1965; Vinacke, 1957). In addition, one generally finds a high degree of trait attribution to *all* members of particular ethnic groups without regard for potential individual differences. These *generalized* impressions[3] are held by large numbers of individuals who have varying degrees of personal contact with members of the ethnic groups.

When such beliefs are simple, inadequately founded, or at least partially inaccurate, and held with a great deal of confidence by large numbers of individuals, the beliefs are referred to as "stereotypes" (Lippman, 1922). At present, there is some ambiguity and dissent regarding the nature of stereotypes (cf. Brigham, 1971). Most conceptualizations focus upon the validity of stereotypic generalizations (Campbell, 1967; Rokeach, 1968a; Saenger and Flowerman, 1954; Secord, 1959; Sherif and Sherif, 1969; Simpson and Yinger, 1965) or the intrapersonal characteristics of the "stereotyper" (Brown, 1965; Campbell, 1967). The pioneer study of stereotypes by Katz and Braly (1933, 1935) found that "superstitious," "lazy," and "happy-go-lucky" were the three traits most frequently ascribed to blacks by white college students at Princeton University. More recent research reveals some modification in black stereotypes. For example, the data of Gilbert (1951) and Karlins, Coffman, and Walters (1969) show a consistent trend toward more favorable characterization of blacks among successive generations of Princeton college students. Comparison of the Katz and Braly (1933) and the Karlins, Thomas, and Walters (1969) data reveals that: the number of students checking "superstitious' declined from 85 percent to 13 percent; the number of students checking "lazy" declined from 75 percent to 26 percent; the number of students checking "ignorant"

---

[1] The definition includes any or all of the above mentioned cognitive, affective, and conative components.

[2] Prejudicial attitudes may be manifest either (Allport, 1954) as an unfavorable response bias (e.g., "hate prejudice") or as a favorable response bias (e.g., "love prejudice"). Recent research found a higher proportion of "love prejudice" than "hate prejudice" among three samples of college students and one general sample of adults in the Boston area (Schuman and Harding, 1964).

[3] Without raising the rather complex issue of the "truth" value of such beliefs, it is merely noted that derogatory stereotypes are a central component of the present use of the term "prejudice" (Campbell, 1967; Prothro and Melikian, 1955; Triandis and Vassiliou, 1967; Vinacke, 1956).

declined from 38 percent to 11 percent; and the number of students checking "stupid" declined from 22 percent to 4 percent. Similarly, Bayton, McAlister, and Hamer (1956) found that *lower-class* blacks were most frequently labeled as "superstitious," "lazy," "dirty," "ignorant," and "happy-go-lucky." In contrast, *upper-class* blacks were not characterized by any of the above traits; instead, upper-class blacks were described as "intelligent," "ambitious," "industrious," and "neat." Thus, the negative belief components of stereotyping may vary more as a function of perceived "social class" than as a function of race. Hyman (1969, p. 10) also notes a more subtle but related change in stereotyping: subjects report greater apprehension for the labeling task and are reluctant to make broad generalizations when applying the traits to all members of a particular race. Hyman (1969, 12–13) generalizes optimistically from the above data and suggests that the rising number of blacks in the American class structure will be associated with increased favorability of white attitudes toward blacks. In spite of shared optimism (e.g., Bettelheim and Janowitz, 1950; Secord and Backman, 1964) regarding the positive effects of improved perceptions of black and other ethnic groups, some caution seems warranted. For instance, it is difficult to determine if the above decline in negative stereotyping represents actual attitude change or simply greater conformity to the current norm of depicting oneself as a "liberal" college student (Linn, 1965). Second, the waning of stereotypes was found in a broadly educated younger generation (e.g., college students). The norm and population are atypical to the population of most organizations.

PREJUDICE AND BEHAVIOR. The attention given to the study of attitudes[4] rests on the psychological assumption that attitudes are determinants of social behavior (Cohen, 1964, pp. 137–138). While prejudicial attitudes are likely to exert a significant influence upon behavior, they share certain dynamic properties with other attitudes. Most notable of these overlapping properties is the failure of attitudes to predict behavior "reliably" (cf. reviews by Campbell, 1963; Festinger, 1964a; Fishbein, 1966, 1967; Rokeach, 1966; Wicker, 1969). Similarly, investigations of the relationship between attitudes and behavior in job settings rarely obtains more than slight and nonsignificant relationships between job attitudes and job performance (cf. reviews by Herzberg, Peterson and Capwell, 1957; Vroom, 1964). The assumption that attitudes are precursors of behavior implies that unfavorable attitudes toward blacks will evoke rejecting or hostile behavior toward them. However, the veridicality of this assumption has been frequently questioned by empirical evidence to the contrary (cf. reviews by Harding, Proshansky, Kutner and Chein, 1969; Hyman, 1969; Insko and Schopler, 1967; Katz, 1970).

Most studies of race relations find that even strong prejudicial attitudes result in discriminatory behavior only in a relatively few interracial contact situations. For example, an often-cited study by La Piere (1934) found little

[4] The study of attitudes is also technologically seductive, because they are relatively easy to measure and are relatively easy to correlate with other variables.

relationship between the overt behavior of restaurant and hotel personnel toward a Chinese man and woman and subsequent written requests for reservations. The couple were denied service only once when they appeared in person at the restaurants and hotels, but over 90 percent of the 128 proprietors responded by mail that they would *not* serve Chinese. In spite of methodological difficulties with La Piere's procedures, a similar study with a black woman (Kutner, Wilkins and Yarrow, 1952) replicated the discrepancy between attitudes and behavior.

More recent research also failed to demonstrate any kind of simple relationship between interracial attitudes and behavior. Self-report measures of attitudes toward blacks were examined in relation to: verbal commitments to be photographed with them (Defleur and Westie, 1958; Green, 1969; Linn, 1965); verbal commitments to discussions of racial problems with blacks and actual behavior during the discussion (Fendrich, 1967); verbal commitments to engage in behaviors which either maintained white status superiority over blacks or which reduced white status superiority over them (Warner and Defleur, 1969); signing a petition which advocated abolishing discrimination against Negroes in employment situations (Kamenetsky, Burgess and Rowan, 1956). With the exception of the studies by Fendrich (1967), Green (1969), and Kamenetsky, Burgess and Rowan (1956), which measure behavior prior to the measurement attitudes (cf. a discussion by Wicker, 1969, p. 65), the data show very little correspondence between interracial attitudes and interracial behavior. Occasionally some reversals of the expected attitude–behavior relationship are revealed.

In light of the failure of most studies to show a relationship between prejudicial attitudes and discriminatory behavior, it seems reasonable to assume *either* that prejudicial attitudes do not cause discriminatory behavior *or* that they compete with other forces to determine when such attitudes are inhibited or openly expressed. The latter explanation seems to be more suited to the data on race relations.[5] For example, Hyman (1969) calls attention to the narrow range of situations in which the attitude–behavior relationship has been examined—all of which were economic in nature, e.g., interracial behavior in hotel room rental (La Piere, 1934) or department store sales (Harding and Hogrefe, 1952). Similarly, following a review of relevant literature, Harding, Proshansky, Kutner and Chein (1969, p. 43) conclude:

> Studies showing no correlation between ethnic attitudes and intergroup behavior have nearly always involved either (1) behavior that was so strongly determined by other factors that it did not vary from individual to individual in the situation studied (for example, white landlords bound by a restrictive covenant not to sell to Negroes; or white workers required by union and company policy to work

[5] A more subtle reason the foregoing studies do not find a stronger relationship between racial attitudes and social action is that *behavior* is frequently the cause of attitudes (cf. Festinger, 1964, and "Attitude Change: Role Playing" below). Thus, attitudes and behavior may mutually support each other by alternating in a causal chain in which the primary cause tends to shift continuously between any two points in time.

under Negro supervisors); or else (2) relationships of very brief duration, such as renting or buying from one sales clerk rather than another (Kutner, Wilkins & Yarrow, 1952; La Piere, 1934; Minard, 1953; Saenger & Gilbert, 1950). One exception to this generalization is a study by Wolf (1957) in which there appeared to be no relationship between attitude toward Negroes among white homeowners and the speed with which they moved out of a neighborhood changing from white to Negro occupancy (p. 43).

The most frequent situation where these ethnic attitudes influence intergroup behavior, in combination with other factors, is that of friendly association in apartment settings (Williams, 1964; Wilner, Walkley and Cook, 1952) or behavior toward co-workers in industrial settings (Hughes and Hughes, 1952; Schuman and Harding, 1963).

The above findings do not weaken the importance of attitude research. Instead, they compel the adoption of a more complex perspective. Namely, there are a large number of personal and situational variables (discussed below) which may interact with attitudes to determine overt behavior at any given point in time. The inconsistency between attitudes and behavior shown in the foregoing research contains important implications for the study of intergroup relations. First, research is needed to examine the relative potency of personal and situation variables in competition with racial attitudes as determinants of intergroup behavior. Second, to the extent that interracial behavior can be influenced by variables other than attitudes, any conceptual framework should separate these variables from attitudes. Interracial behavior should be a uniquely defined focus of research. At the very least, the identification of other determinants of behavior will be greatly facilitated by separating conceptually prejudicial attitudes from overt acts of intergroup behavior.

DISCRIMINATION. Application of the above implications requires a distinction between interracial attitudes and interracial behavior. In particular, the term "prejudice" was defined as an unfavorable ethnic attitude which is associated with a number of relatively stable stereotypic beliefs, biased perceptions, and inaccurate expectations about and predominantly negative reaction tendencies toward members of a particular ethnic group. Interracial behavior may include friendly or unfriendly acts toward minority group members. Unfriendly interpersonal acts vary from simple verbal abuse to physical aggression and include more subtle forms of demeaning actions such as indifference, avoidance, and exaggerated ingratiation. "Discrimination" refers to unfriendly behavior toward a target person who is selected only by virtue of his membership in an ethnic group, without regard for individual differences among members of the ethnic group, i.e., when behavior is aroused by racial characteristics of the target person, which are irrelevant to the requirements of the situations.

SUMMARY. The most satisfactory generalization to be drawn from the foregoing review of the literature is that there is a general primacy of personal and situational variables which can act as constraints against the translation of prejudicial attitudes into discriminatory behavior (cf. Hyman, 1969). Given the present state of knowledge, an exhaustive list of personal and situational variables is impractical and perhaps impossible at the present time. A number of "important" variables are identified in excellent summaries by Cook (1969), Fishbein (1967), Insko and Schopler (1967), Katz and Gurin (1969), and Wicker (1969). Many of the variables which can enhance the possibility that prejudicial attitudes will be manifest in discriminatory behavior are organized in tabular form (see Table 1–1 on p. 26). However, many variables can produce discrimination without corresponding prejudicial attitudes. As couched in the broader perspective of this chapter, both kinds of variables are discussed without distinction throughout the remaining sections.

SOCIAL FOUNDATIONS OF PREJUDICE AND DISCRIMINATION

Most social scientists agree that prejudice and discrimination are learned as a result of experience in the social environment rather than inherited. In order to better understand the dynamics of discrimination and reduce the potential for interracial conflict during integration, it is necessary to examine the social foundations of prejudice and discrimination. They are founded primarily in the cultural norms, opinion leaders, mass media, and reference groups which are significant attributes of society. The cultural norms prescribe the "appropriate" ideology and values. The mass media provide direct and indirect symbolic representations of the ideology, and opinion leaders are the "gatekeepers" of the ideology. The groups, (e.g., family, social, recreational, religious, work etc.) which constitute the fabric or structure of society, are the mechanisms by which the norms are translated into everyday practice.

Cultural Norms

Sociologists have noted that in spite of different economic, cultural historical, political, and psychological backgrounds, "outgroups" such as blacks, Jews, and other minorities are the target of prejudice and discrimination. It appears that members of society construct a subjective social order which is based upon group membership. The broadest categorization is "we" versus "they," or "ingroups" versus "outgroups." This process of social stratification often results in hostile competitive relationships between groups and also contains prescriptions concerning appropriate forms in ingroup behavior. These prescriptions or *social norms* are the individual's expectations of how others expect him to behave and his expectations of how other people will behave in a given social situation. Behavioral adherence to the norms depends primarily upon the perceived relevance of a particular situation to the specific set of expectations and the existence of positive sanctions for compliance and negative sanctions for deviation from these norms. In general, when social norms are perceived as relevant to the situation, individuals usually behave in accordance with norm prescriptions.

According to Tajfel (1970), a "generic norm" of behavior emerges from this process. Tajfel reports a series of experiments which document a general "outgroup discrimination" and provide convincing evidence for the existence of a generic norm of behavior toward outgroups. Tajfel (1970, p. 99) also describes some interesting consequences of this norm.

> First, discrimination against an outgroup can occur in the absence of any self interest benefits to be derived from discriminating against the outgroup. Second, discriminatory behavior can occur in the absence of previously prejudicial attitudes or dislike of the outgroup. Third, the generic norm may produce behavior toward the outgroup before any prejudice or hostility have been formed.

Thus, cultural norms are potentially more powerful determinants of discrimination than prejudice because cultural norms are not merely shared attitudes, but expectations that behavior which is consistent with the norms will result in prized rewards (e.g., group approval and acceptance) and behavior which is inconsistent with the norms will result in punishment (e.g., group disapproval and rejection).

Cultural norms can be manifest indirectly with symbolic referents within the social structures of society. For example, Clark (1963, 1972) notes that *segregated* churches, schools, recreational facilities, and residential communities represent the norm of prejudice and discrimination. They serve as a designation of "what is proper behavior" and increase the probability that prejudice will be expressed as discrimination in those communities. Some of the largest social fraternities and business men's clubs are currently attempting to retain their charter restrictions against black membership (cf. data collected by Powell, 1969). Yet, organizations must accept the social responsibility of desegregation and thereby reduce the number of symbolic sanctions for prejudice and discrimination. Indeed, organizations can set policy and provide sanctions to develop equalitarian norms at least within the subculture of organizational life. But beyond that, organizations can establish norms that permeate the community.

Although organizations continuously interact with and are dependent upon the larger society, they are in many ways an *independent* subsystem or microsociety. Witness, for example, the findings which show differences between behavior toward blacks within work settings and behavior toward blacks outside of the work setting. Amiable interracial relations on the job did not generalize to nonwork settings (Gundlach, 1956; Minard, 1952; Saenger and Gilbert, 1950) or to other kinds of interpersonal relationships (Harding and Hogrefe, 1952). Organizations can support norms which differ from those which govern behavior in the larger society (Schein, 1968, 1971). Several studies have shown that interracial contact "sanctioned" by institutional support reduces interracial conflict and increases favorability of interracial attitudes within the community (Brophy, 1946; James, 1955; Wilner, Walkley and Cook, 1952; Yarrow, Campbell and Yarrow, 1958). The effect of a "community" social norm supported by "authority" is demonstrated dramatically in the housing study by Deutsch and Collins (1951), where the social norm of "friendly interracial relations" and the official policy of the housing authority substantially contributed to positive interpersonal relations among different race residents. Thus, establishing norms favoring friendly intergroup relations within an organization can reduce interracial conflict within the organization. It is important to realize that equalitarian norms and corresponding nondiscriminatory practices *within the organization* can initiate potent forces opposing the maintenance of prejudicial and discriminatory norms in the larger society.

In addition to the symbolic impact of segregated organizations, cultural norms and prejudice can be communicated more directly by the mass media and opinion leaders.

Mass Media

The mass media participate in this social influence process by omission of reference to blacks, or by direct or symbolic representation of blacks in subordinate positions in the social class hierarchy, and thereby contribute to unfavorable stereotyping. Recently, the mass media representation of blacks is rapidly changing toward a more favorable portrayal (Hyman, 1969, p. 8). For example, Larrick's (1965) survey of seventy publishers of more than 5,000 children's books in 1962, 1963, and 1964 revealed that less than 7 percent of the books included any representation of one black or more. At the same time, most publishers reported that they were taking steps to achieve a more balanced representation of minority members. Similarly, Gast's (1967) analysis of forty-two recent children's fiction books found ". . . a general absence of negative stereotyping, an absence of Negro occupational stereotyping, and also a general tendency to portray Negroes as the only ethnic minority obtaining higher education and attending college." Hyman (1969, p. 40) also describes the increment in television appearances of blacks found in television monitoring studies between 1962 and 1964. However, the absolute rate of appearance of blacks on television in 1966 was minimal, with blacks only appearing in 5 percent of commercials accompanying sports programs (Plotkin, 1967). Most recently, there has been a substantial increase in the number of black television programs.

Opinion Leaders

Critical examinations of the relatively minor social influence exerted by the mass media has led to identification of the "two-step" flow of communication (Katz, 1957). The mass media itself seems to be, at best, a necessary but insufficient first step in the process of social influence. The second step requires "opinion leaders" or family members, friends, teachers, and acquaintances, who selectively screen the flow of information from the mass media and transmit the filtered information to the public. Two studies found that the general public's opinions about marketing, public affairs, fashions, movie selection (Katz and Lazersfeld, 1955), and doctors' decisions about the adoption of new drugs (Menzel and Katz, 1956) were more influenced by personal contacts than by the mass media. Of particular interest is the finding that the source of this influence was not merely random persons within the subjects' environment. Instead, the influence is concentrated among a few individuals within each social group. For example, opinions about household marketing matters were most influenced by older women with large families, and opinions about fashions and movie selection were most influenced by young unmarried women. Thus, opinion leaders serve as mediators of social influence between general sources of information and members of the general public. A study of integrated housing projects by Wolf (1957) found that the residents depended upon the views and behavior of significant others to help them decide if their neighborhood was becoming "undesirable" because of the influx of black home owners. Wolf identified a wide variety of opinion leaders, such as realtors, lending and government insurance agencies, social, religious, and commercial establishments, public school staffs, property owners' associations, and informal experts who had similar previous experiences. Their opinions were valued only in the limited area of prescriptions about the segregation of residential areas.

It is likely that opinion leaders also mediate (or occasionally originate) information and influence opinions about interpersonal relationships in other settings such as work environments. More importantly, opinion leaders do more than transmit information to the general population. They also help create and perpetuate the social norms of the community; that is, they serve as *models* who demonstrate which behaviors are appropriate and which attitudes are correct. Accordingly, the process of bringing about social change in an organization is often analogous to the two-step flow of information. Opinion leaders provide one important mediating link between an external force for change and a modification of the behaviors and attitudes within the organization at large (Bem, 1970, p. 77). Therefore, the identification and support of opinion leaders seems to provide a potent force for the reduction of prejudice and discrimination within the organization. A number of techniques are available to map the informal social structure of organizations and identify opinion leaders for these purposes (Dalton, 1959; Jacoby, 1968; Melcher and Beller, 1967).

Reference Groups

The problem is further complicated because the social norms governing attitudes and behavior in general are anchored *not only* in the behavior of opinion leaders but also in the subgroups to which most people belong. Almost all group life (e.g., family, social, recreational, work) is characterized by implicit or explicit sets of beliefs, attitudes, values, and behaviors which are deemed appropriate for the members. The phrase "reference group," coined by Hyman (1942), refers to situations in which a given individual defines his own status by comparison with some groups of individuals—i.e., his "reference group." More recently, the term has been extended to denote any group (e.g., family, religious, recreational, work, social, etc.) which "shapes" or "anchors" a person's attitudes (Cartwright and Zander, 1968, p. 53). The dynamics of group membership account for a substantial portion of the formation and maintenance of attitudes and behavior (Hyman and Singer, 1968; Merton, 1957; Siegel and Siegel, 1957; Strauss, 1959; Turner, 1955)—including the support of prejudicial attitudes and the steering of discriminatory behavior (Hyman, 1969; Parker and Kleiner, 1964; Noel, 1964).

PRIMARY REFERENCE GROUPS. The wellsprings of values, attitudes, beliefs, and behavioral prescriptions reside in the parental socialization of the children (Inkeles, 1955). A substantial body of evidence demonstrates that prejudicial dispositions and discrimination originate in the primary reference group, that is, the family. This process of ethnic attitude and belief transmission from parents to children has been frequently documented (Bird, Monachesi and Burdick 1952; Quinn, 1954; Schaffer and Schaffer, 1958; Williams, 1964). Prejudicial attitudes and "interracial rules of conduct" can be communicated overtly with direct instruction "not to play with them." This dictum is frequently reinforced by means of disciplinary practices which vary from harsh physical punishment for playing with blacks (Horowitz and Horowitz, 1938) to subtle withholding of love and other physiological rewards in response to deviation from parental beliefs that "those children are not nice." Other, more subtle, mechanisms inculcate prejudicial attitudes and discriminatory behavior. For example, the use of hostile descriptions and stereotypes to explain racial differences to children (e.g., Radke-Yarrow, Trager and Miller, 1952) is often sufficient. Similarly, indirect communication occurs when children overhear parental beratement or derogation of blacks. The latter frequently occurs when parents need a "scapegoat" to blame for their personal troubles and problems.

Studies of white school children (Goodman, 1952) found racial awareness emerging in children of four years or older. The "ethnic orientation" (i.e., the rudiments of attitudes) of 24 percent of these children was characterized by a high awareness of the unfavorable social implications of racial characteristics and by some hostility toward blacks in 33 percent of the children. Beliefs related to the concept of black generalized to all representatives of the minority group with increasing age (Allport, 1954).

Ethnic attitudes develop from the use of words without generality or full comprehension of their meaning to a highly differentiated and integrated (e.g., Harding, Proshansky, Kutner and Chein, 1969, pp. 22–24), stabilized and generalized (Allport, 1954) composite of beliefs, feelings, and behavioral tendencies which crystallize in most children during early adolescence. Ros-now (1972) discusses the development of prejudice within Triandis's (1971) more general framework, which describes the four stages of attitude development. A recent study of white and Oriental children by Epstein and Komorita (1965) found that prejudicial attitudes toward social class, rather than color, are learned early in life. Several researchers report the generalized nature and greater intensity of prejudicial attitudes toward blacks (e.g., Frenkel-Brunswik and Havel, 1953, Trager and Yarrow, 1952). If this prepotency of social class prejudice generalizes to blacks, and there is reason to believe that it does (Hyman, 1969), it may be assumed that white children learn to respond unfavorably to lower-class persons and associate the concept "black" with positions of lower social class. Although formulated by age fourteen in most children, ethnic attitudes are susceptible to some modification by a variety of social influences (cf. Harding, Kutner, Proshansky and Chein, 1954, pp. 1034-37; Hraba and Grant, 1970; Karlins, Coffman and Walters, 1969; Minard, 1952; Rosnow, 1972).

Valien (reported in Hyman, 1969) found that high school students were able to report accurately their parents' attitudes and beliefs regarding desegregation. Allport and Kramer (1946) found a higher proportion of prejudiced than unprejudiced college students adopting their parents' racial attitudes. While it seems reasonable to assume that the attitudes and behavior prescriptions reflect those of the parent, it does not necessarily follow that unfavorable ethnic attitudes are communicated only by parents with "prejudicial" attitudes. William's (1964, p. 100) study of segregated and integrated housing suggests that prejudicial *behavior* may not reflect a prejudicial *attitude* as much as it denotes ". . . a generalized timidity and feeling of awkwardness in coping with unfamiliar situations and unknown people." The unprejudiced parent may not be aware of how to socialize his children for a relationship which is completely unknown in his experience (Hyman, 1969). Whatever the dynamics, it is very clear that for some individuals, prejudice and/or discrimination stem from parental mandate or observations of parental attitudes and behavior.

SECONDARY REFERENCE GROUPS. As children grow older and widen their circle of activities and interpersonal relationships, their group membership expands beyond the family to educational, recreational, and occupational groups. Parents lose some of their influence as primary agents of socialization to peers who are members of these secondary reference groups. Such secondary reference groups shape attitudes and behavior by exerting either or both "normative influence" and "comparative influence" (Kelley, 1952). According to Kelley (1952, p. 413) ". . . a group functions as a normative reference group for a person to the extent that its evaluations of him are based upon the degree of his conformity to certain standards of behavior or attitude and to the extent that the delivery of rewards or punishments is conditional upon these evaluations." Studies of group pressures toward uniformity of attitudes and behavior found that communication tended to be directed more toward persons who deviate from the group norm than other members—especially in relatively cohesive groups or groups characterized by high interpersonal attraction among the members (Gerard, 1954; Lott and Lott, 1965). Other studies demonstrate the low tolerance for and greater rejection of deviants characterized by relatively high intermember attraction (Emerson, 1954; Festinger, Gerard, Hymovitch, Kelley and Raven, 1952; Schachter, 1951; Schachter, Nuttin, DeMonchaux, Maucorps, Osmer, Dyiijker, Rommetvelt and Israel, 1954). Therefore, when continued membership in a particular group is desired, anticipation of loss of membership is a potent group force for inducing members to ascribe, at least publicly, to a uniform set of prejudicial beliefs and discriminatory behaviors.

The second function or "comparison function" of reference groups is to provide an evaluative frame of reference for the members' attitudes and behavior: ". . . a group functions as a comparison reference group for an individual to the extent that the behavior, attitudes, circumstances, or other characteristics of its members represent standards or comparison points which he uses in making judgments regarding the validity of his attitudes and behavior" (Kelley, 1952, p. 413). Festinger and his colleagues examine the processes of social comparison (Festinger, 1954; Latané, 1966). Social communication, the means by which individuals compare their opinions with others to validate them against the standards of social reality, is greater in highly cohesive groups (Festinger, 1950). The greater the attractiveness of the group to its membership, the more important group norms become as a standard of comparison for attitudes and opinions. The amount of opinion change toward uniformity with group norms is a function of the magnitude of the forces acting upon an individual member to remain in the group or the attractiveness of the group members and activities (Festinger, 1954).

The comparison function of reference groups for maintaining group norms when challenged by an external source is strikingly demonstrated in several studies. For example, Kelley and Volkart (1952) found that young boys who valued their membership in the Boy Scouts showed the least change in the favorability of their attitudes toward scouting activities following an adult's speech which was critical of the scouting emphasis on woodcraft and other camping activities. A convincing study by Kelley and Woodruff (1956) indicates that when a reference group changes its position, the membership follows suit. A group of student teachers at a progressive teachers college listened to a tape-recorded speech which advocated return to more traditional methods of teaching. The speech was interrupted seven times by applause allegedly emanating from the audience attending the speech. Half the student teachers were told that the audience was composed of members of their own college and the remaining half of the students were informed that the audience was composed of local people from the town in which the school was located. Greater attitude change favoring the "traditional" methods occurred in students who believed that the applause was from members of their own group (their reference group) than in students who believed the applause was from members of the town. Thus, reference group norms constitute one determinant of the formation and/or maintenance of prejudicial attitudes and discriminatory behavior by providing a "yardstick" against which to measure or compare and evaluate such attitudes and behavior. In sum, there is evidence to suggest that the individual is more likely to acquire prejudicial attitudes and discriminatory behavior patterns in response to social pressure from a particular reference group when he is strongly attracted toward membership in the group (cf. a review in Cartwright and Zander, 1968, p. 53). The two forms of group influence, normative and comparative, are even more pervasive since they have been shown to extend to *nonmembers* who *aspire* to group membership either in actuality or by identification.

SOME IMPLICATIONS. The *first position* being developed here is that although attitudes and behavior are determined by a number of historical, sociological, and psychological determinants, prejudice and discrimination are governed *primarily* by conformity to prevailing social norms which appear to be mediated by the social influence mechanisms described above. A prominent alternative position is that anti-black sentiments are directly attributable to the personality characteristics of persons with prejudicial attitudes. More specifically, the latter position claims that there are many unconscious reasons for unfavorable ethnic attitudes—many of which characterize an "authoritarian personality" (Adorno, Frenkel-Brunswik, Levenson and Sanford, 1950). It is clear that the above two ". . . diagnoses of the problem generate different prescriptions for change, one emphasizing maximum expansion of the opportunity structure and the other calling for a mixture of structural and psychological rehabilitation" (Katz and Gurin, 1969, p. 361). An important implication of the "social norm" position is that prejudice and discrimination may be reduced by changing social norms via the above mechanisms of social influence. An important contrasting implication of the "personality" position is that the reduction of prejudice and discrimination requires extensive psychotherapy.

Although the personality approach must remain a plausible explanation for some individuals, extensive theoretical and methodological problems relegate his position to one of secondary importance (Hyman and Sheatsley, 1954). In contrast, the greater preponderance of research supports the conformity position (Pettigrew, 1959; Rose, 1956; Schlesinger, 1957). For example, a study by Pettigrew (1969) tested both the authoritarian and conformity theories of prejudice and found stronger support for the conformity notion. Therefore, it seems reasonable to suggest that integration could often be institutionalized with less conflict when the formal (e.g., management) and informal (work group) opinion leaders, who set and/or transmit a norm of prejudice, are persuaded to support integration publicly. The identification of opinion leaders for this role must recognize that the magnitude of any given opinion leader is restricted to particular issues and populations. Other procedures of norm maintenance (Jackson, 1959) and monitoring may be instituted (described below) to support the positions of opinion leaders. At the very least, the magnitude of the problem is reduced from the necessity of changing the personalities of the organizational community to changing the beliefs of a relatively few opinion leaders and the related norms which support prejudice.

The *second position* of this chapter is that a major impediment to the assimilation of blacks into American organizations is the absence of any *real opportunities* for entrance or advancement (Dunnette, 1972, in this volume; Hellervik, 1972, in this volume; Powell, 1969). More specifically, it appears that the barriers to such opportunities reside in the stereotypic beliefs and attitudes of white industrial leaders. An opposite position is that the stereotypic beliefs are "true," i.e., the belief that even if all obstacles were eliminated, performance capacities of blacks are handicapped by unique and enduring attitudes, values, habits, or personal characteristics which are firmly rooted in the unique early black experiences. Furthermore, it is usually proposed that these incapacities are inimical to success in today's industrial society.

The latter approach to the problem is based on a composite of stereotypic beliefs about blacks. These beliefs perpetuate an inaccurate portrait of the black as a person with enduring personality liabilities acquired during early experiences with impoverished family resources which set him apart with "immutable performance limitations." The recent accumulation of evidence seems to suggest that these beliefs are couched in rather tenuous and equivocal findings (cf. Elliott, 1972, in this volume; Katz, 1972, in this volume). Many of these studies contain a host of methodological inadequacies (cf. reviews by Katz, 1972, in this volume; Katz and Gurin, 1969, pp. 631–636). For example, failure to control for socioeconomic variables ignores recent evidence showing the importance of social class (Hyman, 1969; Katz and Gurin, 1969). Similarly, failure to control for conditions such as race of experimenter (e.g., Sattler, 1970) or race of tester (Katz, 1970) ignores critical variables which prevailed in the situations where performance of blacks was examined. Such methodological problems leave little strong support for the black "personality deficit" notion (cf. a chapter by Katz, 1972, in this volume).

More specifically, expectations of black performance on a variety of tasks are frequently based on the belief that the black personality is characterized by low self-esteem, poor achievement orientation, low sense of fate control, and so forth. Yet the findings are quite equivocal (cf. reviews by Katz, 1967; Katz, 1972, in this volume; Katz and Cohen, 1962; Pettigrew, 1969; Porat and Ryterband, 1972, in this volume; Proshansky and Newton, 1968). There is at least one invidious effect of such inaccurate beliefs which is usually unrecognized. The ascription of traits of "inferiority" to blacks tends to "... create in the victim those very traits of 'inferiority' that it ascribes to him" (Katz, 1968, p. 175). Common stereotypes of black poor ability and apathy can operate as "self-fulfilling prophecies" (Merton, 1948) which cause blacks to behave that way. A series of studies demonstrate dramatically how teacher expectations about pupils' performance can serve as a determinant of their performance (Rosenthal and Jacobsen, 1968a). An industrial study by Jastrow (reported in Rosenthal and Jacobsen, 1968b) found that clerks who were informed that their work with a new machine would be quite demanding became exhausted with 700 cards per day. In contrast, a new group of clerks, who did not have these expectations, began by producing three times that number without emotional ill effects. Similar evidence for the operation of self-fulfilling prophecy in industry was found by Bavelas (reported in Rosenthal and Jacobsen, 1968b). After female applicants took tests of intelligence and finger dexterity for job evaluation, their foremen were told that some women scored high and others low in the test. This information was *not* related to actual test scores. Later, foremen evaluations and actual productions records showed that more favorable evaluations were obtained by women alleged to have higher test scores. More striking is the finding that *objective* production records of workers were in agreement with foremen's (falsely based) expectations. The actual test scores (not revealed to foremen) showed no relationship to either the foremen's subsequent evaluations or to the objective production records. It seems that, *contrary to popular belief, traits commonly ascribed to blacks are more influenced by the perception of opportunity for achievement within the immediate integrated environment than by personality traits (Katz and Gurin, 1969, pp. 364–365). In light of the above evidence, it appears that the organization can facilitate integration and gain access to a valuable labor force by providing greater educational and occupational opportunities to blacks and by providing special training programs for their supervisors and foremen.*

PSYCHOLOGICAL FORCES

The broadest interpretation of psychological forces includes a vast number of demographic and cognitive variables such as personality traits (Adorno, Frenkel-Brunswik, Levinson and Sanford, 1950; Amir, 1969, p. 335; Eisenman, 1965; Mussen, 1950; Rokeach, 1960; Williams, 1964) and attitudes (e.g., prejudice). Since it is unlikely that an organization can or "should" tamper with the personalities of its members or employees, changes in attitudes are discussed below.

Prejudice and Attitude Change

A number of writers have identified dimensions of attitudes which increase the likelihood that prejudice will lead to discrimination. For example, the centrality and generality of prejudicial attitudes in the individual's total attitude structure, the direction and intensity of the prejudicial attitude, and the defensive function of the prejudicial attitude and four characteristics which increase the probability that prejudicial attitudes will be overtly manifest in discriminatory behavior during interracial contact (Amir, 1969, pp. 335–337; Katz and Gurin, 1969; Selltiz and Cook, 1962). Others emphasize the relative strength of prejudicial attitudes in competition with other countervailing tendencies (e.g., motives) which conflict with the desire to discriminate (Hyman, 1969; Insko and Schopler, 1967; Katz, 1970). Although prejudice does not invariably result in discrimination, prejudicial attitudes operate as powerful predispositional forces in interaction with situational factors. Consequently, the application of techniques of persuasion and attitude change toward the amelioration of prejudice may eliminate one principle component of the pressures responsible for discrimination. A large body of theory and research exists on persuasion and attitude change. Unfortunately, this literature is replete with theoretical controversy, unintegrated, and *rarely focuses upon racial attitudes.* Considering the importance of prejudice, this deficiency requires immediate and concentrated research attention. A *tour de force* of persuasion and attitude change literature would provide some justification for optimistic discovery of useful studies. At the very least, the findings provide a foundation from which ideas can be drawn to suggest techniques which may reduce prejudice in organizational settings.

Forced Compliance: Role Playing

During the last two decades of attitude research, attention has been drawn to the effectiveness of techniques which induce subjects to *engage in action which is inconsisent with their private beliefs or attitudes.* The implications of this research are significant. For example, the study of forced compliance produces important data regarding the psychological consequences of requiring changes in *public behavior* (e.g., integration) by legislation or organizational policy.

Experimental studies have examined the effects of a number of techniques for producing forced compliance and attitude change. One such technique, "role playing," requires subjects to behave (e.g., write an essay or deliver a speech) in a manner which is either consonant or dissonant with their private beliefs or attitudes. The early research found that role-playing subjects who actively participated in the persuasive process by improvising a counterattitudinal communication changed their attitudes toward these issues more than subjects who participated passively by listening (Janis and King, 1954) or by oral reading or silent reading (King and Janis, 1956). These findings were confirmed in a large number of studies using a large number of different attitude issues (cf. reviews by Elms, 1967, 1969; Insko, 1967, pp. 15–18, 219–244; McGuire, 1966, pp. 492–498). However, only one experiment studied the effects of role playing upon racial attitudes. Culbertson (1957) used a psychodrama context to examine attitude change among subjects who were not extremely pro-black. Subjects were given three minutes to prepare a speech which advocated and defended a particular pro-integration theme. Attitudes toward blacks became more favorable for participants than for observers of the psychodrama. The only study which failed to show a significant effect of role playing (Stanley and Klausmeier, 1957) found that subjects whose performance was rated "unconvincing" were least persuaded by their counterattitudinal advocacy. This finding suggests that "sincerity" or "zestful" involvement (Aronson, 1966) is one important mediator of the counterattitudinal advocacy processes. It seems the person must be actively involved in the role playing before active participation will produce greater attitude change than mere passive exposure to information (McGuire, 1966).

INCENTIVES FOR ROLE PLAYING. Since counterattitudinal advocacy produces attitude change, it is important to determine what factors will induce persons to engage in such attitude discrepant behavior. Various kinds of rewards have been examined as incentives to induce persons to advocate publicly a point of view which is privately unacceptable to them. Social approval (Scott, 1957; Wallace, 1966), cash prizes (Scott, 1959), and course grades (Bostrom, Vlandis and Rosenbaum, 1961) were found to produce attitude change following counterattitudinal advocacy on a wide variety of attitude issues—none of which were racial in nature. Furthermore, it cannot be determined by this research whether the effects of these incentives are due to reward or to a reduction in the discomfort due to inconsistency.

MAGNITUDE OF REWARD. An experiment by Festinger and Carlsmith (1959) paid subjects $1 or $20 to play the role of an experimental assistant and to "lie" by informing other waiting subjects that a dull, boring task was "enjoyable" and "interesting." The data reveal that forced compliance produced by a small reward (e.g., $1) affected greater attitude change (e.g., perception of the task as enjoyable and interesting) than that produced by a large reward (e.g., $20). This study served as a primogenitor of several theoretical controversies and a long line of research with relevance to the present application of improvisation and role playing. A major question concerns the dynamics underlying the relationship between the magnitude of incentive and the effects of counterattitudinal advocacy. Dissonance theory (Aronson, 1966; Brehm, 1965; Brehm and Cohen, 1962; Festinger, 1957, 1964b), reinforcement theory (Elms and Janis, 1965; Hovland, Janis and Kelley, 1953, p. 11; Janis, 1959; Janis and Gilmore, 1965, p. 18; Janis and King, 1954), and self-perception theory (Bem, 1965, 1967a, 1967b, 1968) are competing for the honors of unequivocally explaining all the relevant data. However, "at present no existing hypothesis appears to completely systematize all of the existing literature" (Insko, 1967, p. 244). It is more likely that resolution will occur, as in other issues (Aronson, 1966; Fromkin, 1968a; Lott, 1963), with predictions from many theories being simultaneously valid within different boundary conditions. That is, the theories will compliment one another in the explanation of attitudinal phenomena. Instead of becoming encumbered by partisan theoretical controversy, this approach tends more toward oversimplification and a nontheoretical presentation of the operational conditions which have been empirically demonstrated to produce attitude change following counterattitudinal advocacy.

A *large* financial incentive for counterattitudinal advocacy will produce greater attitude change than a small incentive when: (a) the financial incentive (e.g., $5)[6] is offered for written anonymous counterattitudinal essays (Carlsmith, Collins and Helmreich, 1966); (b) the financial incentive (e.g., $10) is offered by a "favorable sponsor" such as a private research firm hired by the U.S. Department of State compared with a private research firm hired by the Soviet Embassy (Elms and Janis, 1965); (c) the financial incentive ($2.50) is paid *after* persons have committed themselves to write the counterattitudinal essay (Jones and Cooper, 1966). The mechanisms mediating the greater effectiveness of large rewards are not fully understood and have been labeled "self-examination set" (Rosenberg, 1966), "process set" (Helmreich and Collins, 1968), and "biased scanning" (Janis and Gilmore, 1965). These views share emphasis on subjects' attentiveness and responsiveness to the logic and merit of their self-generated attitude discrepant arguments. For example, Rosenberg (1965, p. 39) proposes that the development or elaboration of arguments which oppose one's own attitude evoke processes of interattitudinal consistency. Some of these *new* counterattitudinal arguments (e.g., favoring integration) are inconsistent with and more persuasive than old consonant arguments (e.g., favoring segregation). This inconsistency is resolved by suppression of the old arguments and attitude and changing one's attitudes to be in concert with the new arguments. A similar reinforcement view (e.g., Janis and Gilmore, 1965) proposes that large financial incentives promote "biased scanning" of only evidence which favors the counterattitudinal position and thereby leads to greater acceptance of the opposing attitude.

A *small* financial incentive for counterattitudinal advocacy will produce greater attitude change than a large reward when: (a) a small reward (50 cents)[7] is offered for counterattitudinal advocacy which is public, oral, and in a face-to-face situation (Carlsmith, Collins, and Helmreich, 1966); (b) the small reward (50 cents) is offered prior to agreement to write an attitude discrepant essay (Jones and Cooper, 1966); (c) people perceive that they are "free" to refuse to write the counterattitudinal essay (Brehm, 1965; Linder, Cooper and Jones, 1967); (d) there is only commitment to advocacy without actually carrying it out (McGuire, 1966; Rosenberg, 1965, p. 39); (e) the larger reward

---

[6] The monetary values in parentheses are the actual incentives used in the particular studies. Application to organizations may require some preliminary data collection to determine the equivalent magnitude of incentive which is most relevant in the organizational setting.

[7] See note 6 above.

($5) is viewed as a bribe under conditions which arouse "evaluation apprehension" (Rosenberg, 1965), suspicion, or incredulity (Chapanis and Chapanis, 1964). The most parsimonious explanation for the inverse relationship between the magnitude of reward and the effects of counterattitudinal advocacy is dissonance theory (Brehm and Cohen, 1962; Festinger, 1957, 1962). The most cogent description of the dissonance dynamics of role playing is presently by Cohen (1964, pp. 82–83):

> If a person is led to express outwardly an attitude which is discrepant from his actual private attitude, a state of dissonance results. Since the behavior is fixed, dissonance in such a setting can be reduced by changing one's attitude so that it becomes consistent with the behavior one has engaged in publicly. There is no dissonance remaining because private attitude and private expression are now consistent with each other.

Bem's self-perception view (cf. Bem, 1965, 1967a, 1967b, 1968; Bem and McConnell, 1970) is one of the most controversial alternative explanations (cf. Brehm, 1965; Chapanis and Chapanis, 1964; Elms, 1967; Rosenberg, 1965, 1966; Silverman, 1964) of the *small-reward effect* and is not without opposition (cf. Dillehay and Clayton, 1970; Jones, Linder, Kiesler, Zanna and Brehm, 1968; Mills, 1967; Piliavin, Piliavin, Loewenton, McCauley and Hammond, 1969).

Other alternative explanations of the small-reward effect are not mutually exclusive. The various proponents of incredulity (Chapanis and Chapanis, 1964), evaluation apprehension (Rosenberg, 1965), and "duplicity set" (Rosenberg, 1966), seem to fit "incentive theory's" more general statement regarding the conditions under which large rewards operate as cues for the arousal of emotional responses (e.g., anxiety) which interfere with the attitude change processes. It is proposed that incentives produce greater counterattitudinal advocacy effects when the large rewards arouse suspicion regarding the motives of the source of reward (cf. Elms and Janis, 1965; Janis and Gilmore, 1965) or when the large reward is viewed as a "bribe" under conditions which arouse "evaluation apprehension" (cf. Rosenberg, 1965, 1969), feelings of guilt (Janis and Gilmore, 1965, p. 26; Rosenberg, 1966), suspicion, or incredulity (Chapanis and Chapanis, 1964). Similarly, a *large-reward effect* can be expected when subjects are anxiously aware that their counterattitudinal advocacy is a conscious attempt to deceive others (e.g., a "duplicity set," Rosenberg, 1966, p. 4) or when subjects expect that their essays would be used to persuade someone, likely a peer, about a position which they, the subjects, do not believe to be true (e.g., a "consequence set," Helmreich and Collins, 1968).

Examination of the characteristics of any given situation may reveal which conditions, e.g., small or large reward, may be present or introduced into an organization to reduce prejudice during the early stages of integration (see "Pre-proximity" and "Proximity" stages below).

Value Consistency

Rokeach's (1968a, 1971) theory and research on values and attitudes provides an alternative technique for producing enduring changes in prejudice and discrimination. Rokeach (1968a) distinguishes between organized systems of interrelated beliefs (e.g., attitudes) and desirable end states of existence (i.e., terminal values) and modes of behavior (e.g., instrumental values). Values are proposed as the more stable determinant of attitudes and behavior. Although Rokeach's focus is upon the dynamics of change which are aroused when a person's own behavior becomes a source of *self-dissatisfaction*, his experimental procedures may be readily adapted to organizational settings during the early stages of integration.

First, white members of the organization are asked to *rank* in order of importance eighteen terminal values (e.g., a comfortable life, equality, freedom, happiness, etc.) in order of importance and also to *write* their position toward civil rights demonstrations. Second, members are shown a table showing the average rankings of these eighteen values allegedly made by their peers. A discrepancy between two values, equality and freedom, is the focus of attention. These fictitious data reveal that *freedom* received an average rank of first, while in contrast, *equality* received an average rank of eleventh. Next, the group leader interprets this discrepancy to mean that the members are more interested in their "personal freedom" than in the freedom of others. Fourth, according to Rokeach (1968a, 1971) self-dissatisfaction is increased when the members compare their own rankings with the fictitious rankings of their peers. Fifth, further to enhance this process of self-dissatisfaction, members are asked to rate the extent of their sympathy with civil rights demonstrations and examine a second table which shows a fictitious highly significant relationship between valuation of "equality" and attitudes favoring civil rights demonstrations. Sixth, to complete this negative self-confrontation, group members read a fictitious interpretation which suggests that those members who oppose civil rights are self-centered in relation to their freedom. Last, members once again compare their rankings of freedom and equality with their own position on the civil rights issue with the findings in the second table. The reiterative procedures of negative self-confrontation heighten awareness of the major inconsistency in value–attitude systems which can produce enduring change in attitudes and behavior.

Rokeach's procedures have produced some of the most powerful and enduring changes in attitudes and behavior reported in the literature. While control groups remain unchanged from their pre-test rankings, the induction of self-dissatisfaction in experimental groups produced highly significant changes in values and attitudes which endured three to five months (Rokeach, 1968b, 1968c) and fifteen to seventeen months (Rokeach, 1971) after the experiments. Even more striking are the findings that subjects' behavior paralleled the above changes in attitudes. Responses to a letter from the NAACP soliciting a $1 membership fee and enrollment in ethnic relations courses were greater for experimental groups when measured three to five months and fifteen to seventeen months after the experiments. Supplementary findings suggest that the degree of self-dissatisfaction mediated the above changes in attitudes and behavior.

ORGANIZATION INTEGRATION

Disappointment with the failure of "single-factor" theories (e.g., attitudes) reliably to predict discriminatory behavior has diverted attention away from psychological forces toward the study of situational determinants other than prejudice. An early forecast that interracial *contact,* in and of itself, reduces prejudice and discrimination (Allport, 1954; Williams, 1947) has recently been rejuvenated (Amir, 1969; Cook, 1969; Katz, 1970; Pettigrew, 1969). Recent research demonstrates that this hypothesis is optimistically simple: the reduction in prejudice and discrimination which may accompany contact with blacks is limited to specific kinds of interracial contacts, experiences, and settings. A fortuitous by-product of this research is the identification of more than thirty significant variables (Amir, 1969; Cook, 1969; Williams, 1964). In addition to personal and social variables, the more potent situational factors which reflect the complexity of interracial contact situations are shown in Table 1–1 below. Some of these variables are developed in detail below as examples of their application to organizations. They are, in part, a composite of two other conceptual frameworks (Cook, 1969; Katz and Gurin, 1969). There is no attempt to examine potential distinctions between or retain original meanings from the variable categories of either of the frameworks. Some variables are excluded from the following perspective to avoid overlap among instances when different labels are appended to the same variables. Other variables are excluded because they affect discrimination only indirectly by influencing one or more of the other important variables.

The vast majority of the previously mentioned variables are creatively integrated in Cook's (1969) recent analysis of *unintended* racial contact. Cook's (1969) descriptive model synthesizes the interrelationships between variables which influence prejudice and discrimination into an orderly pattern of events which follow a temporal sequence of four stages, i.e., "pre-proximity stage," "proximity stage," "interaction stage," and "post-interaction stage." Each stage terminates with a potential change in prejudice and discrimination. Although each stage is described as a discrete step, the four stages are continuous and the variables which affect behavior in any one stage may interact progressively with variables in later stages. For example, the frequency and duration of interracial contact in the proximity stage affects the degree of intimacy of interracial relationships in the interaction stage. The processes of organizational

Table 1–1 *Examples of Factors Affecting Outcome of Interracial Contact*

PSYCHOLOGICAL VARIABLES			AROUSAL POTENTIAL[a]	REGULATION POTENTIAL[b]
				Characteristics of Context of Contact Situation
Attributes of Minority Group Members	*Attributes of Majority Group Members*	*Characteristics of Contact Situation*	*Characteristics of Racial Interaction*	*Characteristics of Context of Contact Situation*
Confirmation or Disconfirmation of Stereotypes	Intensity of Racial Attitudes	Physical Proximity	Status Threat	Implication of Interracial Association for Social Acceptance
Valued Traits	Direction (Favorable or Unfavorable) of Racial Attitudes	Frequency and Duration of Contact	Economic Threat	
Similarity of Beliefs			Power Threat	
			Proportion of Minority Members	Expectations of Accepted Authority Figures Who Are Source of Material Rewards and Punishments and Approval/ Disapproval
Relative Status	Centrality of Racial Attitudes			
	Specificity-Generality of Racial Attitudes		Cooperation-Competition	
			Interdependence–Independence	
	Relationship Between Racial Attitudes and Other Competing Attitudes or Values and Behavior		Commonality of Goals	
			Intimacy of Relationships	
	Defensive Function of Racial Attitudes		Direction and Strength of Peer Group Norms Toward Interracial Association	
	Motivation and Competing Motives (e.g., Approval, Achievement, Affiliation, etc.)			
	Personality (e.g., Self-esteem, Ego-defense, etc.)			

[a] Arousal potential refers to the amount of threats to a person's security that exists in a particular interracial contact situation (Katz and Gurin, 1969).
[b] Regulation potential refers to the extent to which behavior in a given situation is capable of being socially controlled by virtue of its visibility and the possibility of applying positive or negative sanctions (Katz and Gurin, 1969).

integration can be similarly classified according to a number of stages which follow an orderly temporal sequence. In order to apply the above theory and research of social psychology to organizational settings, the following analysis extrapolates liberally from Cook's four stage schema.[8] It is recognized that most organizations are in one of the later stages of integration. However, all of the stages are described so that organizations can decide which stage is most representative of their present state. Accordingly, the model may be used proactively or retroactively to gain insight into past, present, or future problems of race relations within the organization.

There are a number of procedures which an organization can adopt to reduce prejudice and discrimination during each of these stages. The strategies, discussed below, are based upon extrapolations from a variation of research methods applied to a wide variety of settings. Yet the careful application of these data-based suggestions (Fromkin and Ostrom, 1972, in this volume) seems a wiser strategy than the current state of *indolence*. Redundant warnings about the sources of data are avoided. Instead, references are provided for the reader who is interested in securing his own interpretations. Perhaps the ideal solution is for the organization to employ a program of modest experimentation with some suggestions found in this volume and to evaluate their effectiveness (Campbell, 1969; Jacobson, Kahn, Mann and Morse, 1951; Seashore, 1964).

Pre-proximity Stage

At some point in the history of the organization, a decision is made to integrate, i.e., to hire minority group members. These decisions are often affirmed at the upper levels of management and may occur as a result of social, economic, or personal pressures. The pre-proximity period is the time prior to integration, i.e., prior to organizational contact with minority newcomers. During this time, a number of personal and environmental factors may have a decisive influence upon the favorability of organizational members' responses to impending integration and minority newcomers. For example, the individual's economic need, expected rewards (e.g., salary inducements) or costs (e.g., salary loss), and job market conditions (e.g., availability of other more attractive job situations) may determine his decision to remain or leave the impending integration.

REGULATION POTENTIAL. Awareness of explicit negative sanctions is a fundamental precondition for the control of prejudice and discrimination in organizational settings. However, interracial contact situations will also vary

---

[8] In many instances, the original meaning is lost in the translation. For example, there is no attempt to restrict the application only to situations of unintended racial contact. Furthermore, the first stage, "pre-proximity," merely antedates the more crucial remaining stages in Cook's analysis, while in contrast, the pre-proximity stage is a critical stage in the view of organizational integration presented here.

according to the degree of "regulation potential" (Katz and Gurin, 1969) or the extent to which deviations from the sanctions are potentially visible to other persons who can be expected to punish such deviations (cf. King and Bass, 1972, in this volume). For example, prejudice and/or discrimination are not likely to be expressed when public deviation will result in punishing consequences to the individual. Conversely, prejudicial and/or discriminatory acts can occur when they may be privately expressed or when they result in positive consequences. In the latter instance, discrimination may occur in the absence of prejudice.

The outcomes of interracial contacts *during the latter stages* will be more positive when they occur under the aegis of organizational sanctions which favor friendly race relations and a high degree of regulation potential for these sanctions.

ORGANIZATIONAL SANCTIONS.   Institutional support has been observed as (a) *law or "official policy,"* within the larger context of the organization, which is set by an authority who is accepted by the membership, or (b) a *social atmosphere* of general agreement among significant persons in the immediate biracial work group. Evidence for the reduction of prejudice and discrimination which accompany interracial contact under conditions of favorable institutional support is found in Deutsch and Collins (1951); James (1955); Wilner, Walkley and Cook (1952); and Yarrow, Campbell and Yarrow (1958). Industrial studies found less discrimination in plants integrated with top management and union sanctions than in plants without such sanctions (Haas and Fleming, 1946; Hope, 1952; London and Hammett, 1954; Powell, 1969). For instance, reports of discrimination were reduced by more than 50 percent (i.e., less than 15 percent of employees observed discrimination) in plants where top management and union officials implemented a formal nondiscrimination policy in concert with: (a) a training program to acquaint supervisors of nondiscrimination policy, (b) communications which informed new employees of the nondiscrimination policy, (c) the employment of blacks in the employment office, and (d) program whereby the management could periodically monitor the effectiveness of the policy (London and Hammett, 1954). Similarly, a study of union officials found that blacks did not advance in local unions without the support of the white union leadership (Kornhauser, 1952). Recent evidence shows that resistance against hiring blacks and accepting black co-workers is also related to the degree of support expected from subordinates (Eidson, 1968; Morgan, Blonsky and Rosen, 1969; Strauss, 1967).

Although it is difficult to separate the effects of "authority" from general "social atmosphere" (because authority is one source of social atmosphere), it is likely that sanctions for interracial contact from either source can independently produce friendlier race relations. A second level of organizational sanctions for improving race relations is the potential social support in cohesive work groups where beliefs favoring interracial association are a "norm" or are expected. The degree of influence exerted by this social atmosphere depends upon the extent to which there are similar beliefs among the white peer group and the degree of cohesion or mutual admiration and respect among the white peer group. When shared beliefs and valued social traits are prevalent, the peer group becomes a potent source of social rewards and punishments such as approval and rejection. In the context of a social atmosphere which is favorable toward integration, the anticipation of negative consequences like rejection for deviation from norms favoring equalitarian attitudes is a powerful deterrent to prejudice and discrimination.

In order to increase the potential for amiable race relations, the organization may take advantage of opportunities to garnish support for organizational sanctions during the pre-proximity period prior to interracial contact. Most organizations implement the "new policy of integration" slowly and in minimal fashion, without fanfare or announcement to the organizational membership. In other instances, the "new policy of recruiting and hiring minority members" is unobtrusively announced via a formal memo or letter to members. Such rudimentary procedures may be standard practice for any new policy or may be an intentional attempt to obfuscate the issue in order to avoid anticipated disruption. An alternative strategy is to allow employees to participate in the decision-making process before the policy is "set." The above practices have different effects upon employee attitudes toward and subsequent resistance to integration. Most persons' (prejudicial or unprejudicial) attitudes toward blacks contain a constellation of different beliefs about integration. Some of these beliefs will be ill-founded and unfavorable, i.e., expectations about some negative consequences of integration.

The procedures of employee decision making offer several distinct advantages to the organization. *They can serve as a vehicle to identify unfavorable beliefs about integration. They provide an opportunity for employees to discover evidence which dispels invalid beliefs about integration. They serve as a platform from which the organization can take steps to ensure that potential negative consequences do not result from integration. Most important, however, are the enduring effects of group decision making upon the acceptance of new beliefs and practices.* The seminal notions and research of Kurt Lewin and his associates (Lewin, Lippitt and White, 1939; Lewin, 1947; French and Marrow, 1945) clearly delineate the decreased resistance to new ideas which occurs when employees have an opportunity to participate in decisions which directly affect their organizational life. For example, the Lewin food studies showed that group decision methods were more effective than lectures inducing women to adopt new food habits (Lewin, 1947; Radke and Klisurich, 1947; Simmons, 1954).

The basic procedures used by Lewin and his colleagues can be easily adapted to changing unfavorable stereotypes toward blacks and integration (cf. French and Marrow, 1945). The rather simple procedures involve meetings with small groups of workers (including opinion leaders) who are likely to

14409

0538929

have direct on-the-job contact with the minority newcomers. The agenda of these meetings include informal discussion of expected difficulties and advantages and disadvantages of integration. The meetings are also a valuable forum for two-way communication between management and the worker concerning real and false expectations about organizational and individual implications of integration. In the event of unsettled issues, several employees from the group can be charged with a fact-finding mission with the resources of the larger organization as support. The issues are more likely to be resolved to the workers' satisfaction because the results of their *own* research are more likely to be trusted and accepted by them. It is important to note that when the workers participate in such a program to discover the facts about their own beliefs, the findings serve *only* as a necessary but insufficient stimulus for acceptance of organizational innovation. The second and crucial step is allowing each worker to reach his own decision and vote recommending the procedures by which integration is to occur.[9] Information alone concerning the favorable outcomes of integration will not suffice to change unfavorable beliefs and produce acceptance of integration. The above process of decision making, ". . . which takes only a few minutes, is able to affect conduct for many months to come. The decision seems to have a 'freezing' effect which is partly due to the individual's tendency to 'stick to his decision' and partly to the commitment to the group" (Marrow, 1969, p. 144).

Current applications of employee participation notions provide support, albeit inconclusive, for Lewin's earlier contention that participative management leads to greater organizational efficiency (Bennis, 1966; Bennis, Benne and Chin, 1961; Bucklow, 1966; Fleishman, 1965; French, Israel and Aas, 1960; Gomberg, 1966a, 1966b; Katz and Kahn, 1966; Leavitt, 1964b; Likert, 1961; Lowin, 1968; Marrow, 1966; McMurry, 1958; Morse and Reimer, 1956; Schein and Bennis, 1965; Seashore and Bowers, 1970; Tannenbaum, 1966; Vroom, 1960; Wilensky, 1957). Much of the current controversy may be attributed to differences in interpretation of the terms "participation" (Strauss, 1963) and "efficiency" (Vroom, 1969, pp. 227–240). Of the three criteria used to evaluate "efficiency"—decision quality, decision time, and decision execution —the evidence is most controversial regarding the effects of participation on decision quality and decision time. The decision-quality issue focuses upon the quality of group versus individual solutions to complex problems (Lorge, Fox, Davitz and Brenner, 1958). Given the nature of the solutions, the data obtained for this criterion are largely irrelevant to the present application. In relation to the decision-time criterion, it is true that the procedures of management by participation may require a greater investment of man-hours than autocratic declaration of new policy. Yet, the long-range advantages of implementing new policy by means of employee decision making surely warrant the investment of time for important policies such as integration.

---

[9] It is important that management engage in participation strategies with a commitment to consider seriously and act upon, where possible, any suggestions put forth by the group.

The findings on the third criterion, acceptance of and action upon decisions, are less in dispute. Research reveals that group decision making substantially increases employee willingness to accept new production goals (Bavelas in French, 1950; Lawrence and Smith, 1955; Morse and Reimer, 1956), new merit rating practices (Levine and Butler, 1952), new production methods (Coch and French, 1948) and new policies regarding the employment of women over thirty years of age (French and Marrow, 1945). It is interesting to note that even the mere *perception* of group participation may be as *strong* a force as direct participation in decision making for the acceptance of organizational change (Fleishman, 1965, p. 266). These findings also show that group decision making is most likely to enhance employee willingness to engage in a particular action in situations where there is a high degree of group consensus that the action is desirable (cf. Bennett, 1955) and where the leaders are trained in the principles of conducting the meetings (Maier, 1950, 1953, 1963; Maier and Hoffman, 1960).

The group discussion and lecture methods of introducing organizational change differ on a large number of dimensions (Lorge, Fox, Davitz and Brenner, 1958; Vroom, 1969). Unfortunately, it has not been determined which of these differences contribute to greater acceptance of innovation produced by participation. Similarly, the dynamics of group decision making are not yet fully understood. In spite of partisan controversy, the customary procedures, described above, circumscribe an intricate complexity of issues. For example, participation in decision making may produce greater acceptance of decisions because group members tend to achieve a greater understanding of their decision (Bass and Leavitt, 1963), tend to become more "ego-involved" in their decisions (Vroom, 1960), or tend to value their decisions more because of post-decision "dissonance" (Vroom, 1969, p. 237). At the same time, the motivational consequences of participation are also produced by group forces which are generated by group cohesion and adherence to group norms (Coch and French, 1948; Likert, 1961; Maier, 1963; Marrow, 1969, pp. 141–152).

Further research is required to determine the exact nature of the dynamics underlying the processes of participation and acceptance and more clearly to delineate the organizational conditions under which participation will increase acceptance of organization innovation (cf. Lowin, 1968). Whatever the exact nature of the interaction between forces within the individual and forces within the groups, *group discussion* and *decision making* are two principal components (cf. Bennett, 1955).

The pre-proximity stage terminates with actions which commit the individual members of the organization to leave or remain in a desegregated setting. Desirable outcomes of interracial contact are most likely to occur under a state of institutional sanctions and high degrees of regulation potential. It is clear that, in contrast to decisions made *for* employees *by others*, even a slight degree of employee participation increases acceptance of institutional norms and is a most effective method of confronting unfavorable beliefs toward integration. A second by-product of these procedures of employee decision making is the heightening of cohesion in peer groups which are characterized by beliefs favoring integration. Observations of the positive or negative reactions of co-workers toward minority group members is a significant incentive for compliance by other persons in the setting. Thus, the peer group becomes a potential ally with powerful social rewards for compliance (e.g., approval) and social punishments (e.g., rejection) for deviations from norms of equalitarian attitudes and behavior. These norms are more powerful in the organizational setting than any opposing forces from the larger society.

Proximity Stage

The second, "proximity," stage begins when the initial contact occurs among different race co-workers in the organizational setting. There are a number of potential determinants of the degree of prejudice and/or discrimination which develops during this period. The degrees of arousal potential or social threat (e.g., status, competition, power) evoked by minority members are primary influences on the outcomes of interracial contact during this period. In turn, the absolute number and percentage of minority members in the organization and in the primary work groups exerts a significant influence upon the nature and dynamics of social threat. Furthermore, the positive or negative emotion associated with interracial contact during this period may result from confirmation (or lack of confirmation) of anticipated (or unanticipated) consequences of integration. The termination of this period is characterized by a potential for two general kinds of interpersonal relationships during the following "interaction" stage. That is, the outcomes of contact between different race co-workers can lead to more personal interracial relationships or *ex post facto* segregation into "racial islands" within work groups as well as within the larger organization.

AROUSAL POTENTIAL.   Many characteristics of interracial contact situations may enhance the tendency for prejudice to be manifest in discrimination or for discriminatory behavior in the absence of prejudicial attitudes. The identification of these characteristic features permits the examination of interracial contact situations according to their degree of "arousal potential," i.e., *the potential to arouse prejudice and discrimination* (Katz and Gurin, 1969, pp. 371–374). For example, arousal potential is high when racial features of the situation exist which constitute an actual or perceived *social threat* to the individual's security. In the most general sense, social threat refers to events or characteristics of the social situation which tend to elicit fearful or anxiety-provoking expectations. Such may be the case when the situation demands more intimate relationships between members of different races than is acceptable by "strictly defined role behavior" or when the acquisition of valued outcomes (ego or economic rewards) is expected to be jeopardized by the relative status or power of different race co-workers (Katz, 1970, p. 73).

The degree of social threat may be a function of the extent to which features of the organization are similar to other situations which have a history of racial conflict and hostility. Thus, social threat can be aroused when characteristics of the organizational contact situation are similar to other situations in which the members previously experienced interracial conflict and hostility (Katz, 1968). Similarly, the degree of novelty which characterizes the interracial contact situation may arouse social threat. A novel situation may fail to provide the behavioral prescriptions of what is "appropriate" interracial behavior. In such instances, individuals may avoid any contact in fear of violating unknown social taboos. The organization can attenuate the latter threat by "facilitating" the establishment of behavioral "norms" which favor friendly interracial relations and cooperation (see "Pre-proximity Stage" above).

Blalock's (1967) comprehensive review of relevant theory and research suggests that whites can experience three major types of social threat in interracial contact situations—status, competition, and power.[10] Blalock finds evidence confirming ninety-seven propositions which reflect the unique dynamics and consequences of each of these types of social threat. Status, competition, and power are only briefly discussed below to generate some organizational prescriptions without regard for potential differences in the dynamics.

STATUS. Of the multitudinal forms of discriminatory behavior, avoidance of blacks in socially equal situations is the most subtle, and perhaps most invidious, barrier to integration.[11] As mentioned earlier, avoidance of minority members may be rejection of lower-class or -status persons rather than (or in addition to) rejection of outgroup members. The general tendency to discriminate habitually on the basis of status concerns, i.e., reject lower-status persons regardless of their race or religion, etc., refers to "status consciousness." Blalock (1967) defines "status consciousness" as a personal attribute which is inferred when status differences between several individuals result in avoidance behavior on the part of higher-status persons and deference on the part of the lower-status persons. There are few direct empirical studies of the relative importance of status factors in race relations (Blalock, 1969; Turner, 1952; Westie, 1952; Westie and Howard, 1954; Westie and Westie, 1957; Williams,

---

[10] The degree of perceived belief disparity between people of different races may also be a potential source of social threat (Katz, 1970). This variable is reviewed in the Fromkin and Ostrom (1972) chapter in this volume. In sum, white perceptions of the degree of belief similarity with blacks appears to be a more important determinant of *nonintimate* behavioral intentions than racial dissimilarity (Rokeach and Mezei, 1966). In contrast, racial dissimilarity appears to be a more important determinant of *intimate* behavioral intentions than belief dissimilarity (Triandis and Davis, 1965). Earlier studies show that white college students in general expect some degree of belief dissimilarity between themselves and black college students (Byrne and McGrath, 1964; Byrne and Wong, 1962; Stein, Hardyck and Smith, 1965), and subjects with highly prejudicial attitudes, in the absence of contradictory information, expect high degrees of belief dissimilarity between themselves and blacks (Byrne and Wong, 1962; Stein, Hardyck and Smith, 1965). More recent research suggests that the magnitude of belief dissimilarity which white college students in general perceive between themselves and black college students may be waning (Fromkin, Dipboye and Pyle, 1972; Fromkin, Klimoski and Flanagan, 1972).

[11] Rejection of black co-workers is also a powerful determinant of low black performance in biracial work situations (Katz, 1968, 1970; Proshansky and Newton, 1968).

1964). For example, Blalock (1959) examined seven dimensions of status consciousness and found that only "social distance" was related to prejudice and self-reported contact with blacks. The social-distance factor consisted of subjects' reports of the degree of intimacy permitted with low-status persons. This study distinguishes interracial contact situations which require face-to-face interactions from relationships of a less intimate and more general nature.

"Status consciousness" leads to discriminatory behavior in interaction with other situational variables such as degree of intimacy and visibility of the interracial contact. Indeed, Blalock (1967) suggests that some forms of interracial contact are strictly taboo for most individuals regardless of their level of status consciousness. For these types of contact, conformity to prevailing cultural norms is a more appropriate explanation than expected status loss.[12] Although it is particularly difficult to draw precisely the line of demarcation where permissible contact ends and prohibited contact begins, considerable research has shown that *the degree and nature of intimacy* is a relevant dimension (see discussion of "intimacy" below). For example, interracial marriage and sexual behavior are generally unacceptable forms of social contact, and less intimate kinds of contact which occur in work environments are acceptable in the absence of negative sanctions in the formal or informal organizational context.

More generally, status differences can lead to discrimination, in lieu of status consciousness, when negative outcomes are perceived to be a consequence of association with low-status persons. For example, one negative outcome is the expectation of *status loss* and subsequent peer rejection which is thought to result from contact with minority members in many situations.[13] Several variables which may contribute to expectations of status loss in organizational settings can be selected from Blalock's (1967) more complete analysis. First, expectations of status loss through interracial contact are salient to the degree that the individual's status is determined by his social contacts. Second, expected status loss is a relative function of the average status of the black and white members of the organization. One hypothesis is that status loss can be expected to increase with increments in the magnitude of status gap between the different race members of the organization. Third, expectations of status

---

[12] There are two exceptions to this hypothesis. First, a highly prejudiced person is more likely to subscribe to the belief that blacks are "lower-class citizens" and that association with blacks results in status loss. Thus, interracial contact situations which impel expectations of status loss enhance the likelihood that prejudice leads to discriminatory behavior such as avoidance of blacks. Second, and at the same time, in the absence of prejudicial attitudes, persons with high status consciousness also attribute status loss to interracial contact and therefore, discriminate against blacks.

[13] If expected status loss is a frequent determinant of discrimination, then "deep-seated personality explanations" become a relatively less important explanation. An important implication is that as the identification of more situational determinants of discrimination increases, like conformity to norms and expected status loss, then attempts to reduce discrimination may be directed toward regulation of the appropriate social mechanisms via the relatively easy modification of organizational structure. That is, it is usually easier to change an organization than to change a personality or attitudes (Triandis and Malpass, 1971).

loss are heightened as the interracial contact becomes more public or visible to other persons. Fourth, the percentage of minority members and the degree of racial heterogeneity of the entire organization affects expectations of status loss due to association with blacks. Another hypothesis is that when the number of black members represents a substantial proportion of a *racially heterogeneous organization,* expected status loss due to interracial contact should be at a minimum.

Research suggests that racial tensions decrease when minority members occupy positions equal in status to the majority members within the contact situation. For example, the Harding and Hogrefe (1952, p. 27) study of white and black department store personnel found that equal status work contacts increased willingness to work with blacks but did not increase willingness to enter into *other kinds* of relationships with them. Studies of equal status contacts employ a great variety of definitions of status, such as job responsibilities or job titles within a work situation (Harding and Hogrefe, 1962); occupational status (MacKenzie, 1948); intelligence, skill level and socioeconomic status (Watson, 1950); and educational level (Mannheimer and Williams, 1949). However, the relative potency of each of these definitions vis-à-vis the favorability of interracial attitudes and the potential unique dynamics of each of the definitions of status require further research.

The evidence showing *favorable* effects of contact with high-status representatives of minority groups was obtained in a *small* number of *early* studies. The positive relationship between degree of status and favorability of attitude toward minority group members was not without some contradictory findings (cf. review by Amir, 1969, pp. 327–328). These studies involved students' visits to a black hospital and observation of a black surgeon (Young, 1932) and visits to homes of prominent black families (Smith, 1943). The contacts with high-status blacks were extremely transitory, low in acquaintance potential, and low in intimacy and involvement. Therefore, the findings should not be generalized to work-group situations without much caution. Further research is required to determine the contemporary effects of this important variable in settings comparable to work environments. It is likely that the dynamics of high-status contact are very different within a work-group situation. For example, contact with high-status blacks in more intimate and static work-group situations may arouse fear of status loss or competition in *low*-status white workers (cf. Winder, 1952) and result in hostility toward instead of approval of black co-workers.

As discussed above, an important characteristic of the contact situation is the relative status of white and black co-workers. This variable is of special importance, because it is the relative status *within the contact situation* rather than more general characteristics of socioeconomic and educational status which can reduce prejudice and discrimination. Although intelligence, educational level, skill level, and some dimensions of status may be varied through selection, placement (cf. Dunnette, 1972, in this volume), and training (cf. Hellervik, 1972, in this volume), it seems easier to assign equal status to different race co-workers on the basis of dimensions which are more relevant to the specific contact situation, i.e., on the basis of roles and positions within the organizational structure.

COMPETITION AND ECONOMIC THREAT.   Social psychological research on group dynamics shows that interracial antagonism is reduced in biracial groups by several interacting characteristics which seem to foster *cooperative* relationships among different race group members. First, cooperative biracial group life is facilitated by group norms which favor joint participation (Sherif and Sherif, 1953) and "shared"-objective group goals which require interdependent action in an equalitarian environment (Allport, 1954; Amir, 1969; Burnstein and McRae, 1962; Fromkin, Klimoski and Flanagan, 1972; Sherif, 1958)—especially when the group goals take precedence over the members' personal concerns (Sherif, 1966, pp. 146–147). The establishment of interdependence within biracial work groups requires highly appealing *group* goals which cannot be obtained by members of either racial group without the combined efforts of members of the other racial group (Sherif and Sherif, 1953; Sherif, 1966). Second, the cooperative effects of the above group structures are enhanced when the different race group members receive equal shares of the reward for successful task performance (Katz, Goldston and Benjamin, 1958; Lott and Lott, 1965). Some contradictory findings warrant caution against the oversimplification of the shared-goal hypothesis (Katz, 1970, p. 93). Most discussions fail to take into account the cognitive predispositions of the different race co-actors. Prejudice and assumptions about other members' motives may mediate the relationship between shared goals and cooperation. An insightful and heuristic application of the Jones and Davis (1965) attributional analysis, particularly status, to the shared-goal hypothesis is provided by Katz (1970, pp. 93–100).

In contrast, discrimination may be fostered by economic elites to preserve their dominant position in situations of genuine competition for scarce economic or social resources. This form of *economic* discrimination, in contrast to *ideological* discrimination, is most likely to occur in situations of economic self-interest when two or more members of different races are competing for the same scarce resources and the success of one person or group implies probable loss by the other person or group.

Some predictions about the occurrence of social threat due to economic competition[14] may be extrapolated from Blalock's (1967) insightful analysis of early settler and pre-industrial economies and also race relations in professional sports. For example, intergroup competition and overt conflict are likely to occur in organizations when there is (1) objective competition for scarce and valued outcomes, and when there are (2) no satisfactory alternative means to attain a livelihood. In larger organizations, third-party powers can

---

[14] *Competition* may reduce interracial hostility in situations when *both* groups perceive a common third party as a competitor (Sherif, 1966), such as the interracial bond which develops among different race members of a professional athletic team when competing with other teams (Blalock, 1967).

provide only a weak deterrent authority because of either "psychological" or actual physical distance from the source of conflict. The latter "distance" problem may be vitiated, in part, by the organizational court systems recommended in the Triandis (1972) chapter of this volume.

Competition and overt conflict can be reduced when blacks possess two kinds of *compensatory resources* in organizational settings. The first, "competitive resources," are unique skills which blacks (or any minority) can contribute to successful job performance. Conflict can be reduced by appropriate selection and placement techniques (cf. Dunnette, 1972, in. this volume) and/or by appropriate training (cf. Hellervik, 1972, in this volume). "To the degree that high individual performance works to the advantage of other members of the work group who share the rewards of high performance, the higher the positive correlation between performance and status within the group, the lower the degree of minority discrimination" (Blalock, 1967, p. 98). For example, an experiment by Fromkin, Klimoski and Flanagan (1971) found that the magnitude of acceptance of highly competent black newcomers into work groups was equal to the magnitude of acceptance for highly competent white newcomers. The second, "pressure resources," is the capacity of minority members to punish employers for discriminatory practices or failing to control discriminatory behavior within the organization. Such pressures include the potential to threaten the organization with loss of minority customers and government contracts or the initiation of public censure, etc. At this time, the rapid increase in the number of black organizations, recent Federal government legislation, and public support constitutes a potential deterrent to discrimination against blacks and other minorities.

POWER. Many social scientists conceive of interethnic relations as power struggles and believe that prejudice cannot be transformed into effective discriminatory practices without the power to support such practices (Allport, 1954, p. 55; Blalock, 1967, p. 111; DeFleur and Westie, 1958, pp. 667–672; LaPiere, 1934, pp. 230–237; Merton, 1957, ch. 11; Williams, 1964, ch. 9). However, relatively little is known about the different kinds of power available to minority members and the different consequences which would arise from minority use of power within organizations. It is likely that the percentage of minority workers within the organization is a strong base of power which has not been examined.

Interaction Stage

The third, or "interaction," stage begins with the development of interracial communication and personal relationships. Relationships between different race members of an organization can vary from personal and intimate to casual and superficial. Interracial contacts during this stage may extend beyond work settings to other activities, such as company bowling or basketball teams. Given the other conditions described in previous stages, such as approval from co-workers and successful work-group performance, the development of close personal relationships between different race co-workers during this period leads to long-range friendly race relations within the organization.

ACQUAINTANCE POTENTIAL. The importance of acquaintance potential (Cook, 1962, p. 75) has been frequently documented in many contact situations. This variable, in general, refers to spatial proximity and to frequency and duration of opportunities for racial contact. For example, interracial encounters may occur on a crowded bus or may occur during operation of two drill presses which are situated in close proximity to each other. The latter affords greater opportunities for interracial communication. The evidence suggests that high levels of acquaintance potential, particularly frequency of contact, does not invariably lead to a reduction in prejudice (Deutsch and Collins, 1951; Kelman, 1962; Wilner, Walkley and Cook, 1952; Saenger, 1953; Schild, 1962; Selltiz and Cook, 1962). Proximity seems to be a necessary but insufficient condition for the fostering of favorable interracial attitudes (Wilner, Walkley and Cook, 1955). Although the majority of these studies examined acquaintance potential in nonwork environments, encouragement for organizational integration is found in a large-scale study which showed that work-group situations provide the most opportunities while neighborhood and voluntary organizational settings provide the fewest opportunities, for contacts which lead to a reduction in prejudice (Williams, 1964). In sum, it appears that acquaintance potential (e.g., spatial proximity, frequency and duration of contact) is important because it provides an opportunity for continuous interracial contact. Given the presence of other variables (described above), acquaintance potential can serve as a catalyst for more intimate and personal relationships. The rather obvious implication is that work-group composition and job design should reflect high levels of acquaintance potential.

INTIMACY OF RELATIONSHIPS. If close proximity and high frequency (and/or duration) of contact strengthens as well as weakens prejudice, then closer inspection and search for interacting variables is warranted.[15] Contact may produce interpersonal relationships which vary from very casual and superficial to more intimate and ego-involving relationships. Intimacy refers to the nature of conversation and information exchange between members of different races.[16] When information is personal or intimate and in sufficient detail, whites discover new information about minorities which tends to dispel negative stereotypes and illuminate interpersonal similarities. As a result, mem-

[15] Cook (1962, 1963) notes an important distinction between characteristics of the *contact situation* (i.e., proximity and frequency of contact) and characteristics of the *transpiring interaction* (i.e., intimacy). One source of conceptual confusion between the two categories is the problem that both proximity and frequency of contact are characteristics of the contact situation which exert a decisive influence both upon the amount of contact and upon the degree of intimacy (cf. Amir, 1969).

[16] A more detailed account of the perceptual and communication dynamics of such interactions is found in Triandis (1972, in this volume) and Porter (1972, in this volume) respectively.

bers of minority and majority groups tend to know each other as individuals rather than as "whites" and "blacks." Several features of the contact situation, e.g., acquaintance potential, relative status, and intensive joint participation (Schild, 1962) in involving activities (Kelman, 1962) facilitate the above process of individuation. In contrast to casual encounters, other contact situations foster intimate and personal interracial relationships, with continuous opportunities for serious dialogue and processes of individuation (cf. Fromkin, 1968b, 1970, 1971, 1972; Zimbardo, 1969), and reduce prejudice and discrimination via the eradication of negative stereotypes and the uncovering of attraction-producing similarities (cf. Deutsch and Collins, 1951; Meer and Freedman, 1966; Stouffer, Lumsdaine, Lumsdaine, Williams, Smith, Janis, Star and Cottrell, 1949; Wilner, Walkley and Cook, 1952; Yarrow, Campbell and Yarrow, 1958). The interaction stage terminates with the establishment of feelings of "liking" (or disliking) and "respect" (or disrespect) for minority members in the contact situation. Such intimacy accrues long-range benefits to the organization and the larger society, because

> One of the clearest findings of studies of the relation between intergroup contact and attitude change is that, while individuals rather quickly come to accept and even approve of association with members of another social group in situations of the type where they have experienced such association, this approval is not likely to be generalized to other situations *unless* the individuals have quite close personal relationships with members of the other group (Cook, 1963, p. 41–42, italics added).

The Postinteraction Stage

The "post-interaction" stage involves more extensive elaboration of the above racial features of the integrated organizational environment. One defining characteristic of this stage is that the particular attitudes and behavior patterns which developed in relation to specific minority members in the contact situation generalize to other minority members. That is, members respond to minority members as a class. These generalized new responses differ in intensity (e.g., moderately favorable or strongly favorable) or in direction (favorable or unfavorable) from the pre-proximity stage and are determined by the *interaction* of prior experiences in the integrated environment during the first three stages.

QUOD ERAT DEMONSTRANDUM

"To link knowledge with application is admittedly a difficult task. But industry has found that science is ultimately the most effective means of understanding and meeting its human problems" (Marrow, 1964, p. 20). This chapter applies the wisdom of the social sciences to one of the most pressing of contemporary problems, namely race relations in organizations. The survival of modern organizations is dependent, in part, upon their capacity to respond to current social problems, such as the working integration of minority members. Prejudice and discrimination are two distinct and formidable sources of interracial conflict which frequently accompany integration. In contrast to the personality deficiency view, there is compelling evidence that prejudice and discrimination are governed primarily by conformity to prevailing cultural norms in the larger society. Consequently, prejudice and discrimination can be changed by social mechanisms, such as mass media, and pressures from opinion leaders and reference groups. There is also evidence that, when these same social mechanisms are institutionalized, as described in this chapter, equalitarian norms within organizations are stronger than the norms which govern behavior in the larger society. In lieu of perpetuating a static state of indifference, socially responsible organizations can provide a powerful model of negative sanctions for prejudice and discrimination, and thereby exert a positive influence far beyond their organizational boundaries into the external community.

The foremost barrier to the integration of minority members into organizations is a morass of inaccurate beliefs commonly held by white leaders. These ill-founded beliefs about black performance limitations not only inhibit the hiring of blacks, but are also responsible for pernicious self-fulfilling prophecies inside the organization. At the same time, research shows the major impediment to adequate black performance in organizations is the absence of any real opportunities for achievement, recognition, or advancement to managerial levels. The review of literature in this chapter identifies situational variables which act as constraints against the expression of prejudice and discrimination. These variables are relatively easy to modify in an organizational context in exchange for friendly and productive race relations. They are presented within a temporal framework which organizes the process of integration into four stages. The organization can use this information either retroactively or proactively, depending upon its present stage of integration. At the very least, even the most diffident leadership can modestly initiate integration with real educational and occupational opportunities for minority members. The long-range success of organizational integration requires commitment and personal surveillance by top management. It also requires an ongoing program of evaluative research.

REFERENCES

Adorno, T. W., Frenkel-Brunswik, E., Levinson, D. J., and Sanford, R. N. *The authoritarian personality.* New York: Harper, 1950.

Allport, G. W. Attitudes. In C. A. Murchison (ed.), *A handbook of social psychology.* Worcester, Mass.: Clark University Press, 1935, pp. 798–844.

Allport, G. W. *The nature of prejudice*. Cambridge, Mass.: Addison-Wesley, 1954.

Allport, G. W. Prejudice: A problem in psychological and social causation. *Journal of Social Issues*, 1964, Supplement No. 4.

Allport, G. W., and Kramer, B. M. Some roots of prejudice. *Journal of Psychology*, 1946, *22*, 9–39.

Amir, Y. Contact hypothesis in ethnic relations. *Psychological Bulletin*, 1969, *71*, 319–342.

Aronson, E. The psychology of insufficient justification: An analysis of some conflicting data. In S. Feldman (ed.), *Cognitive consistency*. New York: Academic Press, 1966, pp. 115–133.

Bayton, J. A., McAlister, L. B., and Hamer, J. Race–class stereotypes. *Journal of Negro Education*, 1956, *XXV*, 75–78.

Bass, B. M., and Leavitt, H. J. Some experiments in planning and operating. *Management Science*, 1963, *9*, 574–585.

Bem, D. J. An experimental analysis of self-persuasion. *Journal of Experimental Social Psychology*, 1965, *1*, 199–218.

Bem, D. J. Self-perception: An alternative interpretation of cognitive dissonance phenomena. *Psychological Review*, 1967, *74*, 183–200. (a)

Bem, D. J. A reply to Judson Mills. *Psychological Review*, 1967, *74*, 536–537. (b)

Bem, D. J. Self-perception: The dependent variable of human performance. *Organizational Behavior and Human Performance*, 1967, *2*, 105–121. (c)

Bem, D. J. The epistemological status of interpersonal simulations: A reply to Jones, Linder, Kiesler, Zanna, and Brehm. *Journal of Experimental Social Psychology*, 1968, *4*, 270–274.

Bem, D. J. *Beliefs, attitudes, and human affairs*. Belmont, Calif.: Brooks/Cole, 1970.

Bem, D. J., and McConnell, H. K. Testing the self-perception explanation of dissonance phenomena: On the salience of premanipulation attitudes. *Journal of Personality and Social Psychology*, 1970, *14*, 23–31.

Bennett, E. B. Discussion, decision, commitment, and consensus in group decision. *Human Relations*, 1955, *8*, 251–273.

Bennis, W. G. When democracy works. *Trans-Action*, 1966, *3*, 35–36.

Bennis, W. G., Benne, K. D., and Chin, R. (eds.), *The planning of change*. New York: Holt, 1961.

Bettelheim, B., and Janowitz, M. *Dynamics of prejudice*. New York: Harper, 1950.

Bird, C., Monachesi, E., and Burdick, H. Studies of group tensions: III, The effect of parental discouragement of play activities upon the attitudes of white children toward Negroes. *Child Development*, 1952, *XXIII*, 295–306.

Black, P., and Atkins, R. D. Conformity versus prejudice as exemplified in Negro-white relations in the south: Some methodological considerations. *Journal of Psychology*, 1950, *30*, 109–121.

Blalock, H. M. Status consciousness: A dimensional analysis. *Social Forces*, 1959, *37*, 243–248.

Blalock, H. M., Jr. *Toward a theory of minority-group relations*. New York: Wiley, 1967.

Bogardus, E. S. Social distance and its origins. *Journal of Applied Psychology*, 1925, *9*, 216–226.

Bostrom, R. N., Vlandis, J. W., and Rosenbaum, M. E. Grades as reinforcing contingencies and attitude change. *Journal of Educational Psychology*, 1961, *52*, 112–115.

Brehm, J. W. Comment on counter-norm attitudes induced by consonant versus dissonant conditions of role-playing. *Journal of Experimental Research in Personality*, 1965, *1*, 61–64.

Brehm, J. W., and Cohen, A. R. *Explorations in cognitive dissonance*. New York: Wiley, 1962.

Brigham, J. C. Ethnic stereotypes. *Psychological Bulletin*, 1971, *76*, 15–38.

Brooks, L. M. Racial distance as affected by education. *Sociology and Social Research*, 1936, *XXI*.

Brophy, I. N. The luxury of anti-Negro prejudice. *Public Opinion Quarterly*, 1946, *9*, 456–466.

Brown, R. *Social psychology*. New York: Free Press, 1965.

Bucklow, M. The new role for the work group. *Administrative Sciences Quarterly*, 1966, *11*, 59–78.

Burnstein, E., and McRae, A. Some effects of shared threat and prejudice in racially mixed groups. *Journal of Abnormal and Social Psychology*, 1962, *64*, 257–263.

Byrne, D., and McGraw, C. Interpersonal attraction toward Negroes. *Human Relations*, 1964, *17*, 201–213.

Byrne, D., and Wong, T. J. Racial prejudice, interpersonal attraction, and assumed dissimilarity of attitudes. *Journal of Abnormal and Social Psychology*, 1962, *65*, 246–253.

Campbell, D. T. Social attitudes and other acquired behavioral dispositions. In S. Koch (ed.), *Psychology: A study of a science*, Vol. 6. New York: McGraw- Hill, 1963, pp. 94–172.

Campbell, D. T. Stereotypes and the perception of group differences. *American Psychologist*, 1967, *22*, 817–829.

Campbell, D. T. Reforms as experiments. *American Psychologist*, 1969, *24*, 409–429.

Carlsmith, J. M., Collins, B. E., and Helmreich, R. K. Studies in forced compliance on attitude change produced by face-to-face role playing and anonymous essay writing. *Journal of Personality and Social Psychology*, 1966, *4*, 1–13.

Carlson, E. R. Attitude change through modification of attitude structure. *Journal of Abnormal Social Psychology*, 1956, *52*, 254–261.

Cartwright, D., and Zander, A. *Group dynamics: Research and theory*, 3rd. ed. New York: Harper, 1968.

Chapanis, N., and Chapanis, A. C. Cognitive dissonance: Five years later. *Psychological Bulletin*, 1964, *61*, 1–22.

Chein, I. Notes on a framework for the measurement of discrimination and prejudice. In M. Jahoda, M. Deutsch, and S. W. Cook. *Research methods in social relations*, Vol. 1. New York: Dryden, 1951, pp. 382–390.

Clark, K. B. *Prejudice and your child*, 2nd ed. New York: Beacon House, Inc., 1963.

Clark, K. B. A psychologist looks at discrimination patterns. *The MBA*, 1972, *6*, 33–34.

Coch, L., and French, J. R. P., Jr. Overcoming resistance to change. *Human Relations*, 1948, *1*, 512–533.

Cohen, A. R. *Attitude change and social influence*. New York: Basic Books, 1964.

Cohen, M. White students' reactions to the test performance of Negroes. Unpublished doctoral dissertation, New York University, 1965.

Cook, S. Desegregation: A psychological analysis. *American Psychologist*, 1957, *12*, 1–13.

Cook, S. W. The systematic analysis of socially significant events: A strategy for social research. *Journal of Social Issues*, 1962, *18*, 66–84.

Cook, S. W. Desegregation: A psychological analysis. In W. W. Chapters, Jr., and N. L. Gage (eds.), *Readings in the social psychology of education*. Boston: Allyn and Bacon, 1963.

Cook, S. W. Motives in a conceptual analysis of attitude-related behavior. In W. J. Arnold and D. Levine (eds.), *Nebraska symposium on motivation*. Lincoln, Neb.: University of Nebraska Press, 1969, 179–231.

Cook, S. W., and Selltiz, C. A multiple-indicator approach to attitude measurement. *Psychological Bulletin*, 1964, *62*, 36–55.

Cross, T. L. *Black capitalism: Strategy for business in the ghetto*. Boston: Atheneum, 1971.

Culbertson, F. M. Modification of emotionally-held attitude through role-playing. *Journal of Abnormal and Social Psychology,* 1957, *54,* 230–233.

Dalton, M. *Men who manage.* New York: Wiley, 1959.

Dean, J. P., and Rosen, A. with the assistance of R. B. Johnson. *A manual of inter-group relations.* Chicago: University of Chicago Press, 1955.

DeFleur, M., and Westie, F. Verbal attitudes and overt acts: An experiment on the salience of attitudes. *American Sociological Review,* 1958, *23,* 667–673.

DeFriese, G. H., and Ford, W. S. Open occupancy—what whites say, and what they do. *Trans-Action,* 1968, *5,* 53–56.

Deutsch, M., and Collins, M. E. *Interracial housing: A psychological evaluation of a social experiment.* Minneapolis: University of Minnesota Press, 1951.

Deutsch, M., Katz, I., and Jensen, A. R. (eds.) *Social class, race, and psychological development.* New York: Holt, 1968.

Dillehay, R. C., and Clayton, M. L. Forced compliance studies, cognitive dissonance, and self perception theory. *Journal of Experimental Social Psychology,* 1970, *6,* 458–465.

Dittes, J. E., and Kelley, H. H. Effects of different conditions of acceptance upon conformity to group norms. *Journal of Abnormal and Social Psychology,* 1956, *53,* 100–107.

Dunnette, M. D., Campbell, J. P., and Jaastad, K. The effect of group participation on brainstorming effectiveness for two industrial samples. *Journal of Applied Psychology,* 1963, *47,* 30–37.

Eidson, B. K. Major employers and their manpower policies. In *Supplemental Studies for the National Advisory Commission on Civil Disorders.* Washington, D.C.: U.S. Government Printing Office, 1968, 115–123.

Eisenman, R. Reducing prejudice by Negro-white contacts. *Journal of Negro Education,* 1965, *34,* 461–462.

Eldersveld, S. J., and Dodge, R. W. Personal contact or mail propaganda? An experiment in voting turnout and attitude change. In D. Katz, D. Cartwright, S. J. Eldersveld, and A. McLung Lee (eds.), *Public opinion and propaganda.* New York: Dryden Press, 1954, pp. 532–542.

Elms, A. C. Role playing, incentive, and dissonance. *Psychological Bulletin,* 1967, *68,* 132–148.

Elms, A. C. *Role playing, rewards, and attitude change.* New York: Van Nostrand, 1969.

Elms, A. C., and Janis, I. L. Counter-norm attitudes induced by consonant versus dissonant conditions of role-playing. *Journal of Experimental Research in Personality,* 1965, *1,* 50–60.

Emerson, R. M. Deviation and rejection. An experimental replication. *American Sociological Review,* 1954, *19,* 688–693.

Epstein, R., and Komorita, S. S. Parental discipline, stimulus characteristics of outgroups, and social distance in children. *Journal of Personality and Social Psychology,* 1965, *2,* 416–420.

Fendich, J. M. A study of the association among verbal attitudes, commitment, and overt behavior in different experimental situations. *Social Forces,* 1967, *45,* 347–355.

Festinger, L. Informal social communication. *Psychological Review,* 1950, *57,* 271–282.

Festinger, L. A theory of social comparison processes. *Human Relations,* 1954, *7,* 117–140.

Festinger, L. *A theory of cognitive dissonance.* Evanston, Ill.: Row, Peterson, 1957.

Festinger, L. Behavioral support for opinion change. *Public Opinion Quarterly,* 1964, *28,* 404–417. (a)

Festinger, L. *Conflict, decision and dissonance.* Stanford, Calif.: Stanford University Press, 1964. (b)

Festinger, L., and Carlsmith, J. M. Cognitive consequences of forced compliance. *Journal of Abnormal Social Psychology,* 1959, *58,* 203–210.

Festinger, L., Schachter, S., and Back, K. *Social pressures in informal groups.* New York: Harper, 1950.

Festinger, L., Gerard, H. B., Hymovitch, B., Kelley, H. H., and Raven, B. The influence process in the presence of extreme deviates. *Human Relations,* 1952, *5,* 327–346.

Fishbein, M. The relationship between beliefs, attitudes, and behavior. In S. Feldman (ed.), *Cognitive consistency: Motivational antecedents and behavioral consequences.* New York: Academic Press, 1966, pp. 199–223.

Fishbein, M. Attitude and the prediction of behavior. In M. Fishbein (ed.), *Readings in attitude theory and measurement.* New York: Wiley, 1967.

Fleishman, E. A. Attitude versus skill factors in work group productivity. *Personnel Psychology,* 1965, *18,* 253–266.

French, J. R. P., Jr. Field experiments: Changing group productivity. In J. G. Miller (ed.), *Experiments in social process: A symposium on social psychology.* New York: McGraw-Hill, 1950, 79–96.

French, J. R. P., Jr., and Marrow, A. J. Changing a stereotype in industry. *Journal of Social Issues,* 1945.

French, J. R. P., Jr., Israel, J., and Aas, D. An experiment on participation in a Norwegian factory. *Human Relations,* 1960, *13,* 3–19.

Frenkel-Brunswick, E., and Havel, J. Prejudice in the interviews of children: Attitudes toward minority groups. *Journal of Genetic Psychology,* 1953, *82,* 91–136.

Fromkin, H. L. Effort and attractiveness: Predictions of reinforcement theory versus predictions of dissonance theory. *Journal of Personality and Social Psychology,* 1968, *9,* 347–352. (a)

Fromkin, H. L. Affective and valuational consequences of self-perceived uniqueness deprivation. Unpublished doctoral dissertation, Ohio State University, 1968. (b)

Fromkin, H. L. The effects of experimentally aroused feelings of undistinctiveness upon valuation of scarce and novel experiences. *Journal of Personality and Social Psychology,* 1970, *16,* 521–529.

Fromkin, H. L. Reversal of the attitude similarity-attraction effect by uniqueness deprivation. Paper presented at the Midwestern Psychological Association Convention, Detroit, May 1971.

Fromkin, H. L., Klimoski, R. J., and Flanagan, M. F. Race and task competency as determinants of newcomer acceptance in work groups. *Organizational Behavior and Human Performance,* 1972, *7,* 25–42.

Fromkin, H. L. Feelings of interpersonal undistinctiveness: An unpleasant affective state. *Journal of Experimental Research in Personality,* 1972.

Fromkin, H. L. Dipboye, R. L., and Pyle, M. Reversal of the attitude similarity-attraction effect by uniqueness deprivation. Institute for research in the behavioral, economic, and management sciences, Paper No. 344, Purdue University, 1972.

Fromkin, H. L., and Ostrom, T. M. Laboratory research and the organization: Generalizing from lab to life. In H. L. Fromkin and J. J. Sherwood (eds.), *Integrating the Organization.* New York: Free Press, 1974.

Garrison, K. C., Jr. The behavior of clergy on racial integration as related to a childhood socialization factor. *Sociology and Social Research,* 1967, *LI,* 209–219.

Gast, D. Minority Americans in children's literature. *Elementary English,* 1967, *XLIV,* 12–23.

Gerard, H. B. The anchorage of opinions in face-to-face groups. *Human Relations,* 1954, *7,* 313–325.

Gilbert, G. Stereotype persistence and change among college students. *Journal of Abnormal and Social Psychology,* 1951, *46,* 245–254.

Gomberg, W. The trouble with democratic management. *Trans-Action*, 1966, *3*, 30–35. (a)

Gomberg, W. Harwood's "press agentry." *Trans-Action*, 1966, *3*, 35–36. (b)

Goodman, M. E. *Race awareness in young children*. Cambridge, Mass.: Addison-Wesley, 1952.

Green, J. A. Attitudinal and situational determinants of intended behavior toward Negroes. Paper presented at the meeting of the Western Psychological Association, Vancouver, British Columbia, June, 1969.

Greenwald, A. G. On defining attitude and attitude theory. In A. G. Greenwald, T. C. Brock, and T. M. Ostrom (eds.), *The psychological foundations of attitudes*. New York: Academic Press, 1968, pp. 361–388.

Greenwald, A. G. When does role playing produce attitude change? Toward an answer. *Journal of Personality and Social Psychology*, 1970, *16*, 214–219.

Gundlach, R. H. Effects of on the job experience with Negroes upon racial attitudes of white workers in union shops. *Psychological Reports*, 1956, *2*, 67–77.

Guttman, L., and Foa, U. G. Social attitude and an intergroup attitude. *Public Opinion Quarterly*, 1951, *15*, 43–53.

Haas, F. J., and Fleming, G. J. Personnel practices and wartime changes. *The Annals of the American Academy of Political and Social Science*, 1946, *CCXLIV*, 53.

Harding, J., and Hogrefe, R. Attitudes of white department store employees toward Negro co-workers. *Journal of Social Issues*, 1952, *8*, 18–28.

Harding J., Kutner, B., Proshansky, H., and Chein, I. Prejudice and ethnic relations. In G. Lindzey (ed.), *Handbook of Social Psychology*, Vol. 2. Cambridge, Mass: Addison-Wesley, 1954, pp. 1021–1061.

Harding, J., Proshansky, H., Kutner, B., and Chein, I. Prejudice and ethnic relations. In G. Lindzey and E. Aronson (eds.), *Handbook of social psychology*, 2nd ed., Vol. 5. Reading, Mass: Addison-Wesley, 1969, 1–76.

Helmreich, R. L., and Collins, B. E. Studies in forced compliance: Commitment and magnitude of inducement to comply as determinants of opinion change. *Journal of Personality and Social Psychology*, 1968, *10*, 75–81.

Herzberg, F., Peterson, R., and Capwell, D. *Job attitudes: Review of research and opinion*. Pittsburgh: Psychological Service of Pittsburgh, 1957.

Hope, J. Industrial integration of Negroes: The upgrading process. *Human Organization*, 1952, *II*, 5–14.

Horowitz, E. L., and Horowitz, R. Development of social attitudes in children. *Sociometry*, 1938, *1*, 301–338.

Hovland, C. I., and Rosenberg, M. J. (eds.) *Attitude organization and change*. New Haven: Yale University Press, 1960.

Hovland, C. I., Janis, I. L., and Kelley, H. H. *Communication and persuasion*. New Haven: Yale University Press, 1953.

Hraba, J., and Grant, G. Black is beautiful: A reexamination of racial preference and identification. *Journal of Personality and Social Psychology*, 1970, *16*, 398–402.

Hughes, E. C., and Hughes, H. M. *Where people meet: Racial and ethnic frontiers*. Glencoe, Ill.: Free Press, 1952.

Hyman, H. H. The psychology of status. *Archives of Psychology*, 1942, No. 269.

Hyman, H. H. Social psychology and race relations. In I. Katz and P. Gurin (eds.), *Race and the social sciences*. New York: Basic Books, 1969.

Hyman, H. H., and Sheatsley, P. B. The authoritarian personality—a methodological critique. In R. Christie and M. Jahoda (eds.), *Studies in the scope and method of the authoritarian personality*. Glencoe, Ill.: Free Press, 1954, pp. 50–122.

Hyman, H., and Sheatsley, P. Attitudes toward desegregation. *Scientific American*, 1964, *211*, No. 1, 16–23.

Hyman, H. H., and Singer, E. (eds.) *Readings in reference group theory and research*. New York: Free Press, 1968.

Inkeles, A. Social change and social character: The role of parental mediation. *Journal of Social Issues*, 1955, *XI*, 12–23.

Insko, C. A. *Theories of attitude change*. New York: Appleton-Century-Crofts, 1967.

Insko, C. A., and Schopler, J. Triadic inconsistency: A statement of affective-cognitive-conative consistency. *Psychological Review*, 1967, *74*, 361–376.

Jackson, J. M. Reference group processes in a formal organization. *Sociometry*, 1959, *22*, 307–327.

Jacobson, E., Kahn, R. L., Mann, F. C., and Morse, N. C. Research in functioning organizations. *Journal of Social Issues*, 1951, 7, 64–71.

Jacoby, J. Examining the other organization. *Personnel Administration*, 1968, *31*, 36–42.

James, H. E. O. Personal contact in school and change in intergroup attitudes. *International Social Science Bulletin*, 1955, 7, 66–70.

Janis, I. L. Motivational factors in the resolution of decisional conflict. In M. R. Jones (ed.), *Nebraska symposium on motivation*. Lincoln, Neb.: University of Nebraska, 1959, pp. 198–231.

Janis, I. L., and Gilmore, J. B. The influence of incentive conditions on the success of role playing in modifying attitudes. *Journal of Personality and Social Psychology*, 1965, *1*, 17–27.

Janis, I. L., and King, B. T. The influence of role playing in opinion change. *Journal of Abnormal and Social Psychology*, 1954, *49*, 211–218.

Jones, E., and Cooper, J. Incentive magnitude and time of commitment as determinants of cognitive dissonance. Unpublished paper, 1966.

Jones, E. E., and Davis, K. E. From acts to dispositions: The attribution process in person perception. In L. Berkowitz (ed.), *Advances in experimental social psychology*, Vol. 2. New York: Academic Press, 1965, pp. 219–266.

Jones, R. A., Linder, D. E., Kiesler, C. A., Zanna, M., and Brehm, J. W. Internal states or external stimuli: Observers' attitude judgments and the dissonance theory–self persuasion controversy. *Journal of Experimental Social Psychology*, 1968, *4*, 247–269.

Kamenetsky, J., Burgess, G. G., and Rowan, T. The relative effectiveness of four attitude assessment techniques in predicting criterion. *Educational and Psychological Measurement*, 1956, *16*, 187–194.

Karlins, M., Coffman, T. L., and Walters, G. On the fading of social stereotypes: studies in three generations of college students. *Journal of Personality and Social Psychology*, 1969, *13*, 1–16.

Katz, D., and Braly, K. Racial stereotypes in one hundred college students. *Journal of Abnormal and Social Psychology*, 1933, *28*, 280–290.

Katz, D., and Braly, K. W. Racial prejudice and racial stereotypes. *Journal of Abnormal and Social Psychology*, 1935, *30*, 175–193.

Katz, D., and Kahn, R. L. *The social psychology of organizations*. New York: Wiley, 1966.

Katz, D., and Stotland, E. A preliminary statement to a theory of attitude structure and change. In S. Koch (ed.), *Psychology: A study of a science*, Vol. 3. Formulations of the person and the social context. New York: McGraw-Hill, 1959, pp. 423–475.

Katz, E. The two-step flow of communications: An up-to-date report on a hypothesis. *Public Opinion Quarterly*, 1957, *21*, 61–78.

Katz, E., and Lazarsfeld, P. F. *Personal influence*. Glencoe, Ill.: Free Press, 1955.

Katz, I. Some motivational determinants of racial differences in intellectual achievement. *International Journal of Psychology*, 1967, *2*, 1–12.

Katz, I. Social and psychological perspectives: Introduction. In M. Deutsch, I. Katz, A. R. Jensen (eds.), *Social class, race, and psychological development*. New York: Holt, 1968, pp. 175–177.

Katz, I. Factors influencing Negro performance in the desegregated school. In M.

Deutsch, I. Katz, and A. R. Jensen (eds.), *Social class, race, and psychological development.* New York: Holt, 1968, pp. 254–289.

Katz, I. Experimental studies of Negro-white relationships. In L. Berkowitz (ed.), *Advances in experimental social psychology,* Vol. 5. New York: Academic Press, 1970, pp. 71–117.

Katz, I., and Benjamin, L. Effects of white authoritarianism in racial work groups. *Journal of Abnormal and Social Psychology,* 1960, *61,* 448–456.

Katz, I., and Cohen, M. The effects of training Negroes upon cooperative problem solving in bi-racial teams. *Journal of Abnormal and Social Psychology,* 1962, *64,* 319–325.

Katz, I., and Gurin, P. (eds.) *Race and the social sciences.* New York: Basic Books, 1969.

Katz, I., Goldston, J., and Benjamin, L. Behavior and productivity in bi-racial work groups. *Human Relations,* 1958, *11,* 123–141.

Katz, I., and Greenbaum, C. Effects of anxiety, threat, and racial environment on task performance of Negro college students. *Journal of Abnormal and Social Psychology,* 1963, *66,* 562–567.

Katz, I., Roberts, S. O., and Robinson, J. M. Effects of difficulty, race of administrator, and instruction on Negro digit-symbol performance. *Journal of Personality and Social Psychology,* 1965, *2,* 53–59.

Kelley, H. H. Two functions of reference groups. In G. E. Swanson, T. M. Newcomb, and E. L. Hartley (eds.), *Readings in social psychology,* rev. ed. New York: Holt, 1952.

Kelley, H. H., and Volkhart, E. H. The resistance to change of group anchored attitudes. *American Sociological Review,* 1952, *17,* 453–465.

Kelley, H. H., and Woodruff, C. L. Members' reaction to apparent group approval of a counternorm communication. *Journal of Abnormal and Social Psychology,* 1956, *52,* 67–74.

Kelman, H. C. Processes of opinion change. *Public Opinion Quarterly,* 1961, *25,* 57–78.

Kelman, H. C. Changing attitudes through international activities. *Journal of Social Issues,* 1962, *18,* 68–87.

Kelman, H. C., and Pettigrew, T. F. How to understand prejudice. *Commentary,* 1959, *28,* 436–441.

Killian, L. M. The effects of southern white workers on race relations in northern plants. *American Sociological Review,* 1952, *XVII,* 327–331.

Killingsworth, C. C. Jobs and income for Negroes. In I. Katz and Patricia Gurin (eds.), *Race and the social sciences.* New York: Basic Books, 1969.

King, B. T., and Janis, I. L. Comparison of the effectiveness of improvised versus non-improvised role-playing in producing opinion change. *Human Relations,* 1956, *9,* 177–186.

Kornhauser, W. The Negro union official: A study of sponsorship and control. *American Journal of Sociology,* 1952, *57,* 443–452.

Kothandapandi, V. Validation of feeling, belief, and intention to act as three components of attitude and their contribution to prediction of contraceptive behavior. *Journal of Personality and Social Psychology,* 1971, *19,* 321–333.

Kramer, B. M. Dimensions of prejudice. *Journal of Psychology,* 1949, *27,* 389–451.

Kutner, B., Wilkins, C., and Yarrow, P. Verbal attitudes and overt behavior involving racial prejudice. *Journal of Abnormal and Social Psychology,* 1952, *47,* 649–652.

LaPiere, R. Attitude versus action. *Social Forces,* 1934, *13,* 230–237.

Larrick, N. The all-white world of children's books. Paper presented at School Desegregation Training and Research Institute, University of Oregon, 1965.

Latane, B. (ed.) Studies in social comparison. *Journal of Experimental Social Psychology,* 1966, Monograph Supplement 1, 1–115.

LaViolette, F., and Silvert, K. H. A theory of stereotypes. *Social Forces,* 1951, *29,* 237–257.

Lawrence, L. C., and Smith, P. C. Group decision and employee participation. *Journal of Applied Psychology,* 1955, 39, 334–337.

Leavitt, H. J. *Managerial Psychology,* rev. ed. Chicago: University of Chicago Press, 1964, pp. 352–354. (a)

Leavitt, H. J. Applied organizational change in industry. Structural, technical, and human approaches. In W. W. Cooper, H. J. Leavitt, and M. W. Shelly, II (eds.), *New perspectives in organizational research.* New York: Wiley, 1964. (b)

Lee, F. F. The race relations patterns by areas of behavior in a small New England town. *American Sociological Review,* 1954, *19,* 138–143.

Levine, J., and Butler, J. Lecture vs. group discussion in changing behavior. *Journal of Applied Psychology,* 1952, *36,* 29–33.

Lewin, K. Group decision and social change. In T. M. Newcomb and E. L. Hartley (eds.), *Readings in social psychology.* New York: Holt, 1947, pp. 330–344.

Lewin, K. Group decision and social change. In E. E. Maccoby, T. M. Newcomb, and E. L. Hartley (eds.), *Readings in social psychology,* 3rd ed. New York: Holt, 1958, pp. 197–211.

Lewin, K. *Field theory in social science.* New York: Harper, 1951.

Lewin, K., Lippitt, R., and White, R. K. Patterns of aggressive behavior in experimentally created social climates. *Journal of Social Psychology,* 1939, *10,* 271–279.

Likert, R. *New patterns of management.* New York: McGraw-Hill, 1961.

Linder, D. E., Cooper, J., and Jones, E. E. Decision freedom as a determinant of the role of incentive magnitude in attitude change. *Journal of Personality and Social Psychology,* 1967, *6,* 245–254.

Linn, L. S. Verbal attitudes and overt behavior: A study of racial discrimination. *Social Forces,* 1965, *XLIII,* 353–364.

Lippitt, R., and White, R. K. *Autocracy and democracy: An experimental inquiry.* New York: Harper, 1960.

Lippmann, W. *Public Opinion.* New York: Harcourt, 1922.

London, J., and Hammett, R. Impact of company policy upon discrimination. *Sociology and Sociological Research,* 1954, *39,* 88–91.

Lorge, I., Fox, D., Davitz, J., and Brenner, M. A survey of studies contrasting the quality of group performance and individual performance, 1920–1957. *Psychological Bulletin,* 1958, *53,* 337–372.

Lott, A. J., and Lott B. E. Group cohesiveness as interpersonal attraction: A review of the relationships with antecedent and consequent variables. *Psychological Bulletin,* 1965, *64,* 259–302.

Lott, B. E. Secondary reinforcement and effort: Comment on Aronson's "The effect of effort on the attractiveness of rewarded and unrewarded stimuli." *Journal of Abnormal and Social Psychology,* 1963, *67,* 520–522.

Lott, Bernice E., and Lott, A. J. The formation of positive attitudes toward group members. *Journal of Abnormal and Social Psychology,* 1960, *61,* 297–300.

Lowin, A. Participative decision making. A model, literature critique and prescriptions for research. *Organizational Behavior and Human Performance,* 1968, *3,* 68–106.

MacKenzie, B. K. The importance of contact in determining attitudes toward Negroes. *Journal of Abnormal and Social Psychology,* 1948, *XLIII,* 417–441.

Maier, N. R. F. The quality of group decisions as influenced by the discussion leader. *Human Relations,* 1950, *3,* 155–174.

Maier, N. R. F. An experimental test of the effect of training on discussion leadership. *Human Relations,* 1953, *6,* 161–173.

Maier, N. R. F. *Problem-solving discussions and conferences: Leadership methods and skills.* New York: McGraw-Hill, 1963.

Maier, N. R. F., and Hoffman, L. R. Using trained "developmental" discussion leaders to improve further the quality of group decisions. *Journal of Applied Psychology,* 1960, *44,* 247–251.

Malof, M., and Lott, A. J. Ethnocentrism and the acceptance of Negro support in a group pressure situation. *Journal of Abnormal and Social Psychology,* 1962, *65,* 254–258.

Mann, J. H. The effect of interracial contact on sociometric choices and perceptions. *Journal of Social Psychology,* 1959, *50,* 143–152.

Mann, J. H. The differential nature of prejudice reduction. *Journal of Social Psychology,* 1960, *52,* 339–343.

Mannheimer, D., and Williams, R. M., Jr. A note on Negro troops in combat. In S. A. Stouffer, E. A. Suchman, L. C. DeVincy, S. A. Star, and R. M. Williams, Jr. *The American Soldier,* Vol. 1. Princeton: Princeton University Press, 1949.

Marlowe, D., Frager, R., and Nuttall, R. L. Commitment to action taken as a consequence of cognitive dissonance. *Journal of Personality and Social Psychology,* 1965, *2,* 864–868.

Marrow, A. J. Gomberg's "Fantasy." *Trans-Action,* 1966, *3,* 36ff.

Marrow, A. J. *The practical theorist: The life and works of Kurt Lewin.* New York: Basic Books, 1969.

Marrow, A. J. Risks and uncertainties in action research. *Journal of Social Issues,* 1964, *3,* 5–20.

Marrow, A. J., Bowers, D. G., and Seashore, S. E. *Management by participation.* New York: Harper, 1967.

Mayer, A. J. (ed.) Race relations in private housing. *Journal of Social Issues,* 1957, *XIII,* 4.

McGuire, W. J. The nature of attitudes and attitude change. In G. Lindzey and E. Aronson (eds.), *The handbook of social psychology,* 2nd ed., Vol. 3. Reading, Mass.: Addison-Wesley, 1969, pp. 136–314.

McGuire, W. J. Attitudes and opinions. *Annual Review of Psychology,* 1966, *17,* 475–514.

McMurry, R. N. The case for the benevolent autocracy. *Harvard Business Review,* 1958, *36,* 82–90.

Meer, B., and Freedman, E. The impact of Negro neighbours on white house owners. *Social Forces,* 1966, *45,* 11–19.

Melcher, A. J., and Beller, R. Toward a theory of organizational communication: Consideration in channel selection. *Academy of Management Journal,* 1967, *10,* 39–52.

Menzel, H., and Katz, E. Social relations and innovations in the medical profession: The epidemology of a new drug. *Public Opinion Quarterly,* 1956, *19,* 337–352.

Merton, R. K. The self-fulfilling prophecy. *Antioch Review,* 1948, *8,* 193–210.

Merton, R. K. Fact and factitiousness in ethnic opinionnaires. *American Sociological Review,* 1940, *5.*

Merton, R. K. *Social theory and social structure.* Glencoe, Ill.: Free Press, 1957.

Merz, L. E., and Pearlin, L. I. The influence of information on three dimensions of prejudice toward Negroes. *Social Forces,* 1957, *35,* 344–351.

Mills, J. Comment on Bem's "Self-perception: An alternative interpretation of cognitive dissonance phenomena." *Psychological Review,* 1967, *74,* 535.

Minard, R. D. Race relations in the Pocahontas coal field. *Journal of Social Issues,* 1952, *8,* 1.

Morgan, B. S., Blonsky, M. R., and Rosen, H. Employee attitudes toward a hard-core hiring program. American Psychological Association Experimental Publication System, 1969, *2,* 1–16.

Morse, N., and Reimer, E. The experimental change of a major organizational variable. *Journal of Abnormal and Social Psychology,* 1956, *52,* 120–129.

Mussen, P. H. Some personality and social factors related to changes in children's attitudes toward Negroes. *Journal of Abnormal and Social Psychology,* 1950, *45,* 423–441.

Noel, D. L. Group identification among Negroes: An empirical analysis. *Journal of Social Issues,* 1964, *20,* 71–84.

Ostrom, T. M. The emergence of attitude theory: 1930–1950. In A. G. Greenwald, T. C. Brock, and T. M. Ostrom (eds.), *Psychological foundations of attitudes.* New York: Academic Press, 1968, pp. 1–32.

Ostrom, T. M. The relationship between the affective, behavioral and cognitive components of attitude. *Journal of Experimental Social Psychology,* 1969, *5,* 12–30.

Palmore, E. B. The introduction of Negroes into white departments. *Human Organization,* 1955, *14,* 27–28.

Parker, S., and Kleiner, R. J. Status position, mobility, and ethnic identification of the Negro. *Journal of Social Issues,* 1964, 20, 2, 85–102.

Peak, H. and Morrison, H. W. The acceptance of information into attitude structure. *Journal of Abnormal and Social Psychology,* 1958, 57, 127–135.

Pettigrew, T. F. (ed.) Desegregation research in the North and South. *Journal of Social Issues,* 1959, *4.* (a)

Pettigrew, T. F. Regional differences in anti-Negro prejudice. *Journal of Abnormal and Social Psychology,* 1959, *59,* 28–36. (b)

Pettigrew, T. F. Social psychology and desegregation research. *American Psychologist,* 1961, *16,* 105–112.

Pettigrew, T. F. The Negro American personality: Why isn't more known? *Journal of Social Issues,* 1964, *20,* 4–23.

Pettigrew, T. F. Social evaluation theory: Convergences and applications. In D. Levine (ed.), *Nebraska symposium on motivation.* Lincoln, Neb.: University of Nebraska Press, 1967, pp. 241–315.

Pettigrew, T. F. Racially separate or together. *Journal of Social Issues,* 1969, *25,* 43–69.

Piliavin, J. A., Piliavin, I. M., Loewenton, E. P., McCauley, C., and Hammond, P. On observers' reproductions of dissonance effects. The right answers for the wrong reasons? *Journal of Personality and Social Psychology,* 1969, *13,* 98–106.

Plotkin, L. Report on the frequency of appearance of Negroes on televised commercials. New York: City College, mimeo, 1967.

Porier, G. W., and Lott, A. J. Galvanic skin responses and prejudice. *Journal of Personality and Social Psychology,* 1967, *5,* 253–259.

Powell, R. M. *Race, religion, and the promotion of the American executive.* College of Administrative Science Monograph No. AA-3. Columbus, Ohio: The Ohio State University, 1969.

Prentice, N. M. The influence of ethnic attitudes on reasoning about ethnic groups. *Journal of Abnormal and Social Psychology,* 1957, 55, 270–272.

Proshansky, H., and Newton, P. The nature and meaning of Negro self identity. In M. Deutsch, I. Katz, and A. R. Jensen (eds.), *Social class, race, and psychological development.* New York: Holt, 1968, pp. 178–218.

Prothro, E. T., and Melikian, L. H. Studies in stereotypes: V. Familiarity and the kernel of truth hypothesis. *Journal of Social Psychology,* 1955, *41,* 3–10.

Quinn, O. The transmission of racial attitudes toward white southerners. *Social Forces,* 1954, *XXXIII,* 41–47.

Radke, M., and Klisurich, D. Experiments in changing food habits. *Journal of American Dietetic Association,* 1947, *23,* 403–409.

Radke-Yarrow, M., Trager, H. G., and Miller, J. The role of parents in the development of children's ethnic attitudes. *Child Development,* 1952, *XXIII,* 13–53.

Rankin, R. E., and Campbell, D. T. Galvanic skin response to Negro and white experimenters. *Journal of Abnormal and Social Psychology,* 1955, *51,* 30–33.

Rokeach, M. *The open and closed mind.* New York: Basic Books, 1960.

Rokeach, M. Attitude change and behavior change. *Public Opinion Quarterly,* 1966, *30,* 529–550.

Rokeach, M. *Beliefs, attitudes, and values.* San Francisco: Jossey-Bass, 1968. (a)

Rokeach, M. The nature of attitudes. In *International Encyclopedia of the Social Sciences.* New York: Macmillan, 1968. (b)

Rokeach, M. A theory of organization and change within value-attitude systems. *Journal of Social Issues,* 1968, 24, 13–33. (c)

Rokeach, M. Long-range experimental modification of values, attitudes, and behavior. *American Psychologist,* 1971, *26,* 453–459.

Rokeach, M., and Mezei, L. Race and shared belief as factors in social choice. *Science,* 1966, *151,* No. 3707, 167–172.

Rose, A. M. Intergroup relations vs prejudice: Pertinent theory for the study of social change. *Social Problems,* 1956, *4,* 173–176.

Rosenberg, M. J. The conditions and consequences of evaluation apprehension. In R. Rosenthal and R. L. Rosnow (eds.), *Artifact in behavioral research.* New York: Academic Press, 1969, pp. 279–349.

Rosenberg, M. J. Cognitive structure and attitudinal affect. *Journal of Abnormal Social Psychology,* 1956, *53,* 367–372.

Rosenberg, M. J. Cognitive reorganization in response to the hypnotic reversal of attitudinal affect. *Journal of Personality,* 1960, *28,* 39–63.

Rosenberg, M. J. An analysis of affective-cognitive consistency. In M. J. Rosenberg and C. I. Hovland (eds.), *Attitude organization and change.* New Haven, Conn.: Yale University Press, 1960, pp. 15–64.

Rosenberg, M. J. When dissonance fails: On eliminating evaluation apprehension from attitude measurement. *Journal of Personality and Social Psychology,* 1965, *1,* 28–43.

Rosenberg, M. J. Some limits of dissonance: Toward a differentiated view of counter attitudinal performance. In S. Feldman (ed.), *Cognitive consistency.* New York: Academic Press, 1966, pp. 135–170.

Rosenthal, R., and Jacobsen, L. *Pygmalion in the classroom: Teacher expectation and pupil intellectual development.* New York: Holt, 1968. (a)

Rosenthal, R., and Jacobsen, L. Self-fulfilling prophecies in the classroom: Teacher expectations as unintended determinants of pupils' intellectual competence. In M. Deutsch, I. Katz, and A. R. Jensen (eds.), *Social class, race and psychological development.* New York: Holt, 1968, pp. 218–253. (b)

Rosnow, R. L. Poultry and prejudice. *Psychology Today,* 1972, *5,* 53–56.

Saenger, G. *The social psychology of prejudice.* New York: Harper, 1953.

Saenger, G., and Flowerman, S. Stereotypes and prejudicial attitudes. *Human Relations,* 1954, *7,* 217–238.

Saenger, G., and Gilbert, E. Customer reactions to the integration of Negro sales personnel. *International Journal of Opinion and Attitude Research,* 1950, *4,* 57–76.

Sapir, R. A shelter. *Megamot,* 1951, *3,* 8–36.

Sattler, J. M. Racial "experimenter effects" in experimentation, testing, interviewing and psychotherapy. *Psychological Bulletins,* 1970, *73,* 137–160.

Schachter, S. Deviation, rejection, and communication. *Journal of Abnormal and Social Psychology,* 1951, *46,* 190–207.

Schachter, S., Nuttin, J., DeMonchaux, C., Maucorps, P., Osmer, D., Duiijker, H., Rommetvelt, R., and Israel, J. Cross-cultural studies on threat and rejection. *Human Relations,* 1954, *7,* 403–439.

Schaffer, R. C., and Schaffer, A. Socialization and the development of attitudes toward Negroes in Alabama. *Phylon,* 1958, *XIX,* 274–285.

Schein, E. H. Organizational socialization and the profession of management. *Industrial Management Review,* 1968, *9,* 1–6.

Schein, E. H. The individual, the organization, and the career: A conceptual scheme. *Journal of Applied Behavioral Science,* 1971, 7, 401–426.

Schein, E. H., and Bennis, W. G. *Personal and organizational change through group methods: The laboratory approach.* New York: Wiley, 1965.

Schein, E. O. The foreign student, as stranger, learning the norms of the host culture. *Journal of Social Issues,* 1962, *18,* 41–54.

Schlesinger, L. The influence of social communication on ethnic opinions. Paper presented at American Psychological Association Convention, September 1956. In M. M. Tumin, *Segregation and desegregation: A digest of recent research.* New York: Anti-defamation League of B'nai B'rith, 1957, 59.

Schuman, H., and Harding, J. Sympathetic identification with the underdog. *Public Opinion Quarterly,* 1963, 27, 230–241.

Schuman, H., and Harding, J. Prejudice and the norm of rationality. *Sociometry,* 1964, 27, 353–371.

Scott, W. A. Attitude change through reward of verbal behavior. *Journal of Abnormal and Social Psychology,* 1957, 55, 72–75.

Scott, W. A. Attitude change by response reinforcement: replication and extension. *Sociometry,* 1959, *22,* 328–335.

Seashore, S. E. Field experiments with formal organizations. *Human Organization,* 1964, *23,* 164–170.

Seashore, S. E., and Bowers, D. G. Durability of organizational change. *American Psychologist,* 1970, *25,* 227–233.

Secord, P. F. Stereotyping and favorableness in the perception of Negro faces. *Journal of Abnormal and Social Psychology,* 1959, 59, 309–315.

Secord, P. F., and Backman, C. W. *Social psychology.* New York: McGraw-Hill, 1964.

Secord, P. F., Bevan, W., and Katz, B. The Negro stereotype and perceptual accentuation. *Journal of Abnormal and Social Psychology,* 1956, 53, 78–83.

Selltiz, C., and Cook, S. W. Factors influencing attitudes of foreign students toward their host country. *Journal of Social Issues,* 1962, *18,* 7–23.

Sherif, M. Group influences under the formation of norms and attitudes. In T. M. Newcomb and E. L. Hartley (eds.), *Readings in social psychology.* New York: Holt, 1947.

Sherif, M. Superordinate goals in the reduction of intergroup conflict. *American Journal of Sociology,* 1958, 48, 349–356.

Sherif, M. *Group conflict and cooperation.* London: Routledge and Kegan Paul, 1966.

Sherif, M., and Sherif, C. W. *Groups in harmony and tensions: An integration of studies in intergroup relations.* New York: Harper, 1953.

Sherif, M., and Sherif, C. W. *Social psychology.* New York: Harper, 1969.

Siegel, A. E., and Siegel, S. Reference groups, membership groups, and attitude change. *Journal of Abnormal and Social Psychology,* 1957, 55, 360–364.

Silverman, I. In defense of dissonance theory: Reply to Chapanis and Chapanis. *Psychological Bulletin,* 1964, 62, 205–209.

Simmons, W. The group approach to weight reduction: I. A review of the project. *Journal of American Dietetic Association,* 1954, *30,* 437–441.

Simpson, G. E., and Yinger, J. M. *Racial and cultural minorities: An analysis of prejudice and discrimination,* 3rd ed. New York: Harper, 1965.

Smith, E. W., and Dixon, T. R. Verbal conditioning as a function of race of experimenter and prejudice of the subject. *Journal of Experimental Social Psychology,* 1968, *4,* 285–301.

Smith, F. T. *An experiment in modifying attitudes toward the Negro.* New York: Teachers College, Columbia University, 1943.

Smith, M., Bruner, J., and White, R. *Opinions and personality.* New York: Wiley, 1956.

Stanley, J., and Klausmeier, H. Opinion consistency after formal role playing. *Journal of Social Psychology*, 1957, *46*, 11–18.

Stein, D. D. The influence of belief systems on interpersonal preference: A validation study of Rokeach's theory of prejudice. *Psychological Monograph*, general and applied, 1966, 80 (8), 29.

Stein, D., Hardyck, J., and Smith, M. Race and belief: An open and shut case. *Journal of Personality and Social Psychology*, 1965, *1*, 281–289.

Stember, C. H. *Education and attitude change: The effects of schooling on prejudice toward minority groups*. New York: Institute of Human Relations Press, 1961.

Stouffer, S. A., Lumsdaine, A. A., Lumsdaine, M. H., Williams, R. M., Jr., Smith, M. B., Janis, I. L., Star, S. A., and Cottrell, L. S., Jr. *The American soldier*, Vol. 2. Princeton, N.J.: University of Princeton Press, 1949.

Strauss, A. L. *Mirrors and masks: The search for identity*. Glencoe, Ill.: Free Press, 1959.

Strauss, G. Some notes on power equalization. In H. J. Leavitt (ed.), *The social science of organizations*. Englewood Cliffs, N.J. Prentice-Hall, 1963, pp. 39–84.

Strauss, G. How management views its race relations responsibilities. In A. Ross and H. Hill (eds.), *Employment, race and poverty*. New York: Harcourt, 1967, pp. 261–289.

Summers, G. F., and Hammonds, A. D. Effect of racial characteristics of investigator on self-enumerated responses to a Negro prejudice scale. *Social Forces*, 1966, *44*, 515–518.

Tannenbaum, A. S. *Social psychology of the work organization*. San Francisco: Wadsworth, 1966.

Tajfel, H. Experiments in intergroup discrimination. *Scientific American*, 1970, November, 96–102.

Taylor, D. W., Berry, P. C., and Block, C. H. Does group participation when using brainstorming facilitate or inhibit creative thinking. *Administrative Sciences Quarterly*, 1958, *3*, 23–47.

Thistlewaite, D. Attitude and structure as factors in the distortion of reasoning. *Journal of Abnormal and Social Psychology*, 1950, *45*, 442–458.

Thomas, W. I., and Znaniecki, F. *The Polish peasant in Europe and America*, Vol. 1. Boston: Badger, 1918.

Trager, H. G., and Yarrow, M. R. *They learn what they live: Prejudice in young children*. New York: Harper, 1952.

Triandis, H. C. A note on Rokeach's theory of prejudice. *Journal of Abnormal and Social Psychology*, 1961, *62*, 184–186.

Triandis, H. C. Exploratory factors analyses of the behavioral component of social attitudes. *Journal of Abnormal and Social Psychology*, 1964, *68*, 420–430.

Triandis, H. C., and Davis, E. E. Race and belief as determinants of behavioral intentions. *Journal of Personality and Social Psychology*, 1965, *2*, 715–725.

Triandis, H. C. *Attitude and attitude change*. New York: Wiley, 1971.

Triandis, H. C., and Malpass, R. S. Studies of black and white interaction in job settings. *Journal of Applied Social Psychology*, 1971, *1*, 101–117.

Triandis, H. C., and Vassiliou, V. Frequency of contact and stereotyping. *Journal of Personality and Social Psychology*, 1967, *7*, 316–328.

Tumin, M. M. *Segregation and desegregation: A digest of recent research*. New York: Anti-defamation league of B'nai B'rith, 1957.

Tumin, M. *Desegregation: Resistence and readiness*. Princeton, N.J.: Princeton University Press, 1958.

Tumin, M. M. Ethnic group. In J. Gould and W. L. Kolb (eds.), *A dictionary of the social sciences*. New York: Free Press, 1964, pp. 243–244.

Turner, R. H. Foci of discrimination in the employment of nonwhites. *American Journal of Sociology*, 1952, LVIII, 247–256.

Turner, R. H. Reference groups of future-oriented men. *Social Forces,* 1955, *34,* 130–136.

Valien, B. *The St. Louis Story: A study of desegregation.* New York: Anti-defamation League, 1956.

Vinacke, W. E. Explorations in the dynamic process of stereotyping. *Journal of Social Psychology,* 1956, *43,* 105–132.

Vinacke, W. E. Stereotypes as social concepts. *Journal of Social Psychology,* 1957, *46,* 229–243.

Vroom, V. H. *Work and motivation.* New York: Wiley, 1964.

Vroom, V. H. *Some personality determinants of the effects of participation.* Englewood Cliffs, N.J.: Prentice-Hall, 1960.

Vroom, V. H. Industrial social psychology. In G. Lindzey and E. Aronson (eds.), *The handbook of social psychology,* Vol. 5. Reading, Mass.: Addison-Wesley, 1969, pp. 196–268.

Wallace, J. Role reward and dissonance reduction. *Journal of Personality and Social Psychology,* 1966, *3,* 305–312.

Warner, L., and DeFleur, M. L. Attitude as an interactional concept: Social constraint and social distance as intervening variables between attitudes and action. *American Sociological Review,* 1969, *34,* 153–169.

Watson, J. Some social and psychological situations related to change in attitude. *Human Relations,* 1950, *3,* 15–56.

Westie, F. R. Negro-white status differentials and social distance. *American Sociological Review,* 1952, *XVII,* 550–558.

Westie, F. R., and Howard, D. H. Social status differentials and the racial attitude of Negroes. *American Sociological Review,* 1954, *XIX,* 584–591.

Westie, F. R., and Westie, M. L. The social-distance pyramid: Relations between caste and class. *American Journal of Sociology,* 1957, *LXIII,* 190–196.

Wicker, A. W. Attitude versus actions: The relationship of verbal and overt behavioral responses to attitude objects. *Journal of Social Issues,* 1969, *XXV,* 41–78.

Wicker, A. W. An examination of the "other variables" explanation of attitude-behavior inconsistency. *Journal of Personality and Social Psychology,* 1971, *19,* 18–30.

Wilensky, H. L. Human relations in the work place: An appraisal of some recent research. In C. Arensberg, S. Barkin, W. E. Chalmers, H. L. Wilensky, J. C. Worthy, and B. D. Dennis (eds.), *Research in industrial human relations.* New York: Harper, 1957, pp. 25–50.

Williams, R. M., Jr. *The reduction of intergroup tensions.* New York: Social Science Research Council, 1947.

Williams, R. M., Jr. *Strangers next door.* Englewood Cliffs, N.J.: Prentice-Hall, 1964.

Williams, R. M., Jr., and Ryan, M. W. (eds.) *Schools in transition: community experiences in desegregation.* Chapel Hill: University of North Carolina Press, 1954.

Wilner, D. M., Walkley, R. P., and Cook, S. W. Residential proximity and intergroup relations in public housing projects. *Journal of Social Issues,* 1952, *8,* 45–69.

Winder, A. E. White attitudes toward Negro-white interaction in an area of changing racial composition. *American Psychologist,* 1952, *7,* 330–331 (abstract).

Wolf, E. P. The invasion-succession sequence as a self-fulfilling prophecy. *Journal of Social Issues,* 1957, *13,* 7–20.

Yarrow, M. R. (ed.) Interpersonal dynamics in a desegregation process. *Journal of Social Issues,* 1958, *1.*

Yarrow, M. R., Campbell, J. P., and Yarrow, L. J. Acquisition of new norms: A study of racial desegregation. *Journal of Social Issues,* 1958, *14,* 8–28.

Young, D. *American minority peoples: A study in racial and cultural conflicts in the United States.* New York: Harper, 1932.

Zimbardo, P. G. The human choice: Individuation, reason and order, vs. deindividuation, impulse and chaos. Lincoln, Neb.: *Nebraska symposium on motivation,* 1969, *17,* pp. 237–307.

CHAPTER TWO

Personnel Selection and Job Placement of Disadvantaged and Minority Persons: Problems, Issues, and Suggestions

Marvin D. Dunnette

INTRODUCTION BY THE EDITORS

Organizational effectiveness is ultimately dependent upon the degree of match between people and jobs. Personnel selection and placement *is the first crucial step toward achieving integration of man and machine, thereby increasing organizational potency. Unfortunately, executives often erroneously assume that training and development programs, job transfers, and job design are sufficient remedies for lack of early attention to selection and placement. Dunnette argues compellingly that selection and placement should be viewed as integral parts of the total manpower system. As such, personnel decisions must be made with greater awareness of broader purposes of manpower utilization.*

Dunnette draws several important implications of his viewpoint when applied to employment of minority group members. First, he warns the administrator against the dangers of confusing diagnosis or differentiation with

Preparation of this chapter was supported in part by ONR Contract N00014-68-A-0141-0003 and by a behavioral science research grant from the General Electric Foundation.

unfair discrimination. Differentiation among people on the basis of their individual capabilities is central to effective personnel administration—i.e., identification by appraisal methods of those individuals who possess personal attributes which are known to be related to effective performance in a particular training program or a particular job. In contrast, unfair discrimination takes place whenever a higher proportion of minority persons are rejected who if chosen would have the skills or skill potential to do the job successfully. The theme developed throughout this chapter is that differential treatment of minority and nonminority members is advocated when it can be shown to enhance the accuracy (fit) of personnel decisions.

Traditionally, employers concern themselves with errors of selection which involve hiring someone who does not succeed on the job, or select-errors. In order to enhance fuller utilization of our human resources as well as to treat people more humanely, organizations must become more concerned about erroneous selection decisions which are made when persons are rejected who, if hired, could perform a job successfully, or reject-errors. According to Dunnette, "unfair discrimination against a minority member group occurs when a firm's personnel decisions yield a higher proportion of reject-errors for members of the minority group than for members of the nonminority group." An important implication here is that organizations will have to shift their emphasis away from relying solely upon traditional selection models toward vocational guidance and other accommodating strategies which broaden opportunities to persons of all groups. Furthermore, the personnel decision-makers will have to adopt more individualized prediction strategies which focus upon each job candidate's strengths and weaknesses. In this personalized perspective, each candidate's skills are interpreted in relation to all possible personnel actions, e.g., training, job design, etc.

Dunnette describes a workable individualized approach to identify particular subgroups of persons, jobs, and predictors for which different personnel decision rules may apply. The process and related research is shown graphically in Figure 2–1. The flow diagram shows the need for a number of different tracks of personnel decisions which are based upon the person's education and vocational background, psychological testing, individualized training, and so forth. This flow diagram for personnel decisions may, at first glance, seem too idealized and impractical. Dunnette makes the point that most organizations currently employ more elaborate but chaotic programs which closely approximate his model in complexity, but fall far short in utility. Similarities are drawn to a program currently being used by the Civil Service Commission.

The ongoing aim of personnel selection is to assess the usefulness and accuracy of any procedure involved in making personnel decisions. Traditional techniques involve a statistic which shows the validity of the procedure—i.e., relationship between the prediction of job performance and actual job performance. Dunnette presents strong arguments for substituting the concept of utility in place of validity for personnel decisions, and, in particular, for the selection of minority members. Utility involves a concern for the costs related to initiating and implementing personnel selection procedures and costs associated with errors in personnel decisions. He provides a hypothetical example of such costs which does not stray too far from reality. In estimating costs, he includes recruiting, selection and training, etc., and also costs to society such as welfare payments to the unemployed, as well as those costs related to riots by unemployed persons, etc. (see Table 2–2, page 68). When applied to the hiring of employees, this analysis highlights the moral dilemma faced by employers. In essence, it emphasizes the choice of whether or not today's organizations are willing to assume direct responsibility for part of society's problems in optimal utilization of human resources. As implied in other chapters, this may require the organization to look beyond its boundaries for investments in community housing improvement programs or education and vocational programs. The organization may choose to ignore this responsibility, i.e., to depend upon the public sector to absorb the costs of manpower utilization. However, avoidance of the negative economic implications shown in the model requires the organization, at the very least, to encourage legislation to expand and overhaul existing public welfare programs.

Last, Dunnette describes other programs in validating the accuracy of personnel selection procedures. For example, useful validity studies are made difficult by the need to develop accurate measures of job success. Useful guidelines, such as probability charts, which fit Dunnette's individualized decision-making system, are derived from studies of validation procedures for minority employment.

This chapter discusses personnel selection and job placement in the broad context of a decision-making model of the *process* of making decisions about people, jobs, and interactions between people and jobs. Emphasis is placed on the different levels of importance which the organization attaches to various "hits" and "misses" in the matching of people and jobs. We argue for individualizing personnel decisions in order to minimize overall net error in making such decisions. In developing this argument, we discuss and define unfair discrimination and contrast it with methods of diagnosis and valid differentiation. Research results showing differential test validities between blacks and whites are presented and are used to illustrate improved methods for interpreting such results.

First of all, we must consider *why* personnel selection and job placement should be of any concern to an administrator. Why should a top executive ask or wonder about the research findings of personnel selection? How is organizational effectiveness related to the total process of personnel evaluation, selection, and job placement? Why should a company president be persuaded toward being certain that his firm is using the best possible approaches in its selection and its efforts to match placement of people with individual capabilities properly with job requirements?

These matters are considered in the paragraphs immediately below.

PEOPLE DIFFER

At any given time, people differ from one another in many different ways. They differ in appearance. They differ in energy level, strength, and other physiologically related attributes. They differ in a variety of proficiencies. They differ in temperament. And they differ in what they want out of life and in what they want out of a job. Psychology, in its brief history, has learned much about measuring and describing human differences in aptitude, proficiency, temperament, and goal orientation.

JOBS DIFFER

A society, no matter how simple or how complex, can only be sustained by producing goods and services. A world of work develops for their production; and, as societies increase in complexity, the variety of goods and services demanded, produced, and consumed becomes greater and greater. In time, thousands of jobs come to be encompassed by a society's world of work. Tasks necessary for accomplishing these many different jobs vary greatly, and the human qualities demanded by the varying tasks differ greatly from job to job. Planting grain, nurturing its growth, and harvesting it is considerably different from playing a clarinet in an orchestra or from helping an elderly patient use a bedpan. The interface between human variability and job variability has been of major concern to administrators as they have sought to build organizations to produce the best possible goods and services. Similarly, the interface between human variability and job variability has been of major concern to psychologists as they have sought to assure that each individual might use his special attributes in the best way possible for him, so that society, in turn, may be assured that it is effectively developing and using its human resources in a wise and humane manner.

PEOPLE CHANGE AND JOBS CHANGE

People, jobs, and their interactions are not static entities. If they were, the simplistic notion of a "one-shot" matching of men and jobs would have great merit. As it is, however, a number of dynamic processes constantly are under way to alter the nature of any given man–job relationship. Some of the more obvious include:

(1) *Training and development programs.* The purpose of training is to modify employees' knowledge, skills, or attitudes in order to equip them to do their jobs better. At one extreme, if all persons were perfectly modifiable through training, a proper number could merely be recruited and trained to do whatever jobs were available. At the other extreme, if persons were completely unchangeable through training or experience, personnel selection would indeed be a one-shot affair, the *only* way for assuring a proper fit between men and jobs. As it is, of course, a well-designed training program should specify the kinds of personal qualities necessary to enter the program, and a well-designed job placement program should take account of changes which may be induced through training, orientation, and experience on the job.

(2) *Job transfers.* Most firms, large firms in particular, have a great diversity of jobs available. Initial selection errors can often be rectified by adopting a vocational guidance point of view to develop greater flexibility within a firm for arranging job transfers.

(3) *Job design.* Though used rather rarely, jobs may be redesigned to utilize more effectively the special attributes of individuals. At the white-collar and managerial levels, the actual means for achieving job objectives often remain unspecified, allowing each new job incumbent to change the job to fit his own propensities, strengths, weaknesses, or stylized patterns of job behavior. Unfortunately, most rank-and-file jobs have had such opportunities for variation engineered out of them. Nonetheless, jobs may be enlarged, enriched, diminished, or otherwise changed to take better and more individualized account of an employee's special attributes.

(4) *Social environment.* In many instances, *what* a person does in the job may be less important than *how* he does it and, in particular, *who* he does it with. Every job needs to be described not only according to functions performed, but also according to situational and social circumstances surrounding it. Thus, the kind of supervisor a man has can obviously affect his own job competence, as can his co-workers, the customers he has if he's a salesman, or even the expectations developed among others by the way his predecessor did the job. Fine (1967) has labeled as *adaptive* those individual skills relevant to the social context of a job. Adaptive skills, according to Fine, grow out of cultural habit patterns and include such things as response to authority, habits of dress, punctuality and attendance, and respect for and care of property.

PERSONNEL SELECTION AND JOB PLACEMENT: AN OPEN SYSTEM

The above considerations lead us to an obvious and, by now, almost trite conclusion. But, because it seems still to be rather foreign to many industrial settings, I believe it deserves and needs special emphasis. Quite simply, we conclude that the process of personnel selection is a *never-ending* sequence of job placement decisions, embedded in an open system with continual inputs of human, material, and financial resources and outputs of goods and services. It makes no better sense to attach a single decision point to the utilization of an element of the human resource system that it does to argue a single and irrevocable utilization pattern for elements of a firm's material or financial resource system. The process of making personnel decisions cannot be viewed as "just" selection or "just" training or "just" anything else. The process is never ending, including individual diagnosis, possibilities for job design and redesign, specialized training, counseling and vocational guidance, and the removal of organizational constraints standing in the way of employees' exercising their full potential. Judgments about the selection of applicants or the promotion of employees should be made with full awareness, then, of the broader purposes of manpower utilization. The ultimate wisdom or accuracy of selection or promotion decisions needs to be judged not only in terms of traditional validity coefficients, but according to the long-term contributions made by individuals. Thus, if it is known that an individual's capabilities can be enhanced through training, if the job can be changed by design or by other circumstances, or if initial job placement errors can be rectified rather easily through transfers, these *all* act to modify any presumed relationships between individual assessment results and job behavior outcomes; and knowledge about them must be taken into account as an integral part of personnel selection and job placement decisions.

Maslow (1969) has also argued forcefully for dealing with the employment process as a total system of mutually interdependent parts comprised of job analysis, special recruiting efforts, job-related screening, interviewing, testing and validation.

Implications for Minority Employment

Viewing personnel selection and job placement as an open system of ongoing personnel decisions yields several implications relevant to the employment of members of minority groups. These implications bear on issues of (1) differentiation versus unfair discrimination, (2) individualizing the personnel decision process, (3) differential utility in relation to accuracy and error in personnel decisions, (4) suggestions for validating personnel decision processes; and (5) interpreting studies showing different validities for minority and nonminority groups. Some of what follows in this chapter is drawn from the American Psychological Association's Task Force Statement on Job Testing and the Disadvantaged which I edited (Dunnette, 1969), but it contains mostly extensions of that statement.

Diagnosis and Differentiation Versus Unfair Discrimination

Since decisions about selection, training, job placement, promotion, transfer, and job redesign all are encompassed by our broadly conceived system of selection and placement, it should be clear that diagnosis of individual capabilities (differentiation among people) is *central* to its effective administration.

I shall never cease to be amazed by those persons who, in the name of equal opportunity, advocate undifferentiated treatment of all persons—men and women, black and white, old and young—with little or no regard apparently for the greater social good to be served by treating people as individuals rather than as undifferentiated and undistinguishable members of the human race. Those who argue in such a vein confuse valid and useful diagnosis and differentiation with practices of unfair discrimination.

Let me be explicit in seeking to distinguish between the two terms. *Differentiation* involves identifying by individual appraisal methods those persons who possess attributes well suited for certain job situations or for certain specialized training programs. This is the kind of information necessary for planning and organizing other personnel decisions and actions. Such decisions cannot be made in an informed way by discarding differentiating procedures. Without individual diagnosis, many job seekers would undergo a series of employment experiences ending in failure, demoralization, and economic insecurity.

My use of the term *unfair discrimination* can best be understood in relation to the different types of error associated with inaccuracy in personnel decisions. Traditionally, of course, employers have been mostly concerned with minimizing *select-errors*, those erroneous personnel decisions wherein persons selected and placed on a job subsequently fail on that job. Employers have been much less concerned about *reject-errors*, those erroneous personnel decisions wherein persons rejected from a job could, if placed on the job, have been successful. Essentially, *unfair discrimination against a minority group occurs when a firm's personnel decisions yield higher proportions of reject-errors for members of the minority group than for members of the nonminority group.* If higher proportions of potentially successful minority persons than of potentially successful nonminority persons are denied job opportunities, the personnel decision systems leading to the unequal reject-error rates may be said to be discriminating unfairly against the minority group.

In the context of our previous comments, this is a rather stringent definition, for it virtually demands that, over time, employers should give fuller attention to avoiding reject-errors. Their stance needs, therefore, to move away from pure selection strategies and toward vocational guidance and other accommodative strategies designed to assure broader opportunities to persons of *all* groups.

Individualizing the Personnel Decision Process

I am suggesting an approach to personnel decisions which has, as its major aim, a system to assure that decisions about each candidate will be based on the best information available. This means that the thrust of personnel decisions should be toward individualized prediction strategies in which *each* candidate's particular merits and shortcomings are examined in relation to their meaning or interpretability for *all* possible personnel actions—not only selection, but all the rest as well. I have argued elsewhere that decisions about people, jobs, and their interactions are among the most important made by industry, and they deserve to be individualized just as assuredly as those decisions involving the choice of plant sites, buying equipment, or company mergers.

The approach is oriented toward identifying particular subgroups of persons, jobs, and predictors for whom different personnel decision rules may apply. An array of prediction equations and rationally derived decision rules may be developed so that decisions for any given candidate will be based upon information shown to be optimal *for him* at each stage of the personnel decision process. Figure 2–1 is a hypothetical flow chart showing an individualized sequential selection process that might be used for job applicants differing in educational levels and cultural backgrounds. By noting the various decision rules shown in Figure 2–1, the reader may infer the nature of evidence required

FIGURE 2–1.   *Flow Chart Showing Hypothetical Program Emphasizing Individualized Personnel Decision Strategy*

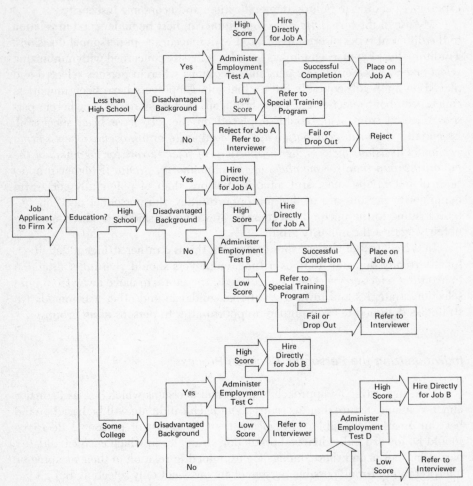

for developing such a flow chart. Listed below are the hypothetical research results or judgments lying behind the choice points and decision rules depicted in the diagram.

- Applicants with high school education or less are considered for Job A; applicants with some college training are considered for Job B.
- An advantaged person with less than high school education is not qualified for Job A, but an interviewer may discover other experiences or skills qualifying him for other jobs in the firm.
- A disadvantaged person with less than high school education may still have aptitude for doing Job A. He is given employment Test A which is appropriate to his background and relevant to behavior requirements in that job; if he scores well, he is hired.
- A disadvantaged person with a high school education is automatically qualified for Job A and is hired directly.
- An advantaged person with high school education may still lack aptitude necessary for doing job A. He is given Test B which is appropriate to his background and relevant to behavioral requirements in that job; if he scores well, he is hired.
- A special training program (or perhaps a probationary period) is available for Job A for low-scoring disadvantaged persons (Test A) and low-scoring advantaged persons (Test B). Disadvantaged persons failing this program are rejected from further consideration, but advantaged persons (who have high school training) are referred to an interviewer who may discover skills relevant to other jobs in the firm.
- Disadvantaged and advantaged persons with college training are given different employment tests (C and D) because they have been separately validated for predicting behavior of disadvantaged and advantaged on Job B; high scorers are hired directly; low scorers are referred to an interviewer for other job possibilities in the firm.

A first impression about these decision rules might reasonably be that they are impractical and that such an idealized flow diagram could never be developed in actuality. In fact, it is idealized. I have made no attempt here to represent the *status quo*. Instead, I seek to make suggestions of what we may hope to accomplish in the future. In that sense, the sequences and linkages of Figure 2–1 represent what I believe firms should strive for as an idealized end result of a series of investigations of the distinguishing patterns of predictor–job-behavior outcomes for persons differing in such factors as education, sex, race, degree of cultural advantage, etc.

In fact, this hypothetical diagram *does* indeed portray rather accurately the present chaotic state of personnel decisions in many firms. Most firms today already use elaborate sequences in their personnel procedures—interviews, reference checking, more interviews, testing, and multiple assessment—closely approximating my diagram in complexity. Certainly, no forthright personnel man would claim that he would not approach his interviewing of a male applicant for the job of company nurse quite differently from that of a female applicant. And it is certain too that black applicants are dealt with quite differently from white applicants. This is as it should be; my contention is merely that such individualized attention should be based on explicit rational or empirical information rather than upon hunch, tradition, or fiat. Most personnel people certainly should prefer basing such decision rules on considered judgment, research evidence, and the fruits of experience. I am hopeful, at the very least, that personnel decision makers will be convinced of the wisdom of developing individualized approaches for dealing with people and that they may be stimulated thereby to develop decision rules necessary for portraying their procedures in the way shown in my diagram. As a starter, they should begin keeping records of exactly how applicants differing in race, sex, education, age, etc. are dealt with. What jobs are they referred to? What interviewers do they see? At what points are hire–reject decisions made and by whom? What tests are administered? What possibilities for training or job redesign are considered? Such an audit, simple as it sounds, would reveal for most firms a rather amazing array of differing practices from time to time and from person to person. The next step would be to determine the basis for these differences, identifying those that make good sense, are rationally defensible and should perhaps be formalized, and identifying others which may *not* be supported either on the basis of good sense or on empirical evidence and which should, therefore, be dispensed with. The audit should then be followed by a series of careful studies designed to discover optimal personnel procedures yielding the most accurate decision patterns to be used with persons differing in age, race, education, cultural background, sex, etc. The net result of all this will, of course, be an individualized system of decision rules empirically and/or formally derived and made explicit as shown in Figure 2–1.

It is noteworthy in this context that the Civil Service Commission has adopted flexible strategies in handling hiring, promotion, and job transfer decisions. According to Maslow (1969), after determining critical elements in a job, they

> . . . make use of all relevant data—test scores, reference checks, experience and training records, and interview protocols—to reach a judgment as to where [an applicant] falls on [each element]. After he is evaluated on each element in turn, we make a final "whole man" appraisal as to his potential or achieved ability for that job. . . . Tests are only one of several alternate sources of evidence about an element. For the inexperienced, an aptitude test score might be relevant; for the experienced, a record of his actual job proficiency would be most meaningful, regardless of test score. So we have great flexibility in the range of information used to reach judgments about the applicant. What we are really after is a reliable judgment about his abilities, regardless of how he developed them" (Maslow, 1969, p. 137).

This general approach is now applied to the staffing of over eight hundred thousand trades and industrial jobs across the nation—impressive testimony, I believe, to the possibility of developing and implementing rationally explicit individualized decision strategies.

DIFFERENTIAL UTILITY, ACCURACY, AND ERROR

A major aim over the years in selection research has been to maximize the so-called *validity* of personnel decisions. Unfortunately, most psychologists and personnel decision makers have probably smiled in self-satisfaction and apparently felt a sense of completion as soon as they have computed a correlation coefficient between some test and some measure of job performance. In fact, a correlation coefficient, though useful as a starting point, yields only sketchy information about the actual usefulness of any procedure for making accurate personnel decisions.

It was not until Cronbach and Gleser (1965) published their classic book *Psychological Tests and Personnel Decisions* that any widespread recognition was given to the essential inadequacy of the so-called validity coefficient as a single index for designating the relative usefulness of a personnel decision procedure. Their concept, *utility*, takes far better account of the relative "goodness" of any personnel procedure in terms of the relative importance of decisions and decision errors made when using it. Utility implies a concern for costs—costs related to setting up and implementing personnel decision procedures *and* costs associated with errors in the decisions made. Estimating costs includes far more than merely tabulating dollar values. Estimates are both objective (such as travel expenses, salaries, and advertising and recruiting costs) and subjective (such as the effects of undesirable job behaviors, possible losses in competitive advantage, and the psychological and attitudinal deficits accompanying job failures and discharges). The concept of utility is extremely relevant to minority group employment, because it directs us to enumerate various possible consequences of personnel decisions and to give careful thought to the many costs associated with different outcomes. Let me clarify this statement with a hypothetical example.

Consider the hypothetical information given in Table 2-1. That table shows the relative probability of blacks and whites achieving satisfactory job performance in an auto assembly plant according to their level on an "employability index." [1] Note that the correlations between the employability index and job performance is relatively high for *both* blacks and whites (.66 for blacks and .45 for whites). Thus, by traditional standards, we would conclude that the procedures composing the employability index were "valid" for predicting job performance. If we, however, use these data to estimate relative

---

[1] The "employability index" can be imagined to be a test of some sort, an interview rating, an estimate of cultural disadvantage, or whatever.

TABLE 2-1   *Hypothetical Probabilities of Satisfactory Job Performance for Blacks and Whites at Various Levels on an "Employability Index" and Proportions of Blacks and Whites at Each Level*

		PROPORTION AT EACH LEVEL		PROBABILITY OF SATISFACTORY PERFORMANCE	
		Blacks	Whites	Blacks	Whites
Employability Index	1	.275	.075	.09	.00
	2	.350	.150	.14	.17
	3	.200	.225	.50	.55
	4	.150	.325	.67	.62
	5	.025	.225	1.00	.67

Proportion successful across all levels — .300   .500

$$r_{Black} = .66 \qquad r_{White} = .45$$

costs of actually employing persons for the job, a somewhat different picture emerges.

Consider, for example, that the plant desires to hire a total of 4000 employees who will be able to perform their jobs satisfactorily. To simplify computations, we shall assume that equal numbers of blacks and whites are recruited and there is *no* turnover.[2] Here are rough estimates of probable costs involved:

(1) Recruiting and screening costs: $100 per applicant.
(2) Cost of training a satisfactory employee: $300 per employee. (This assumes that employees are simply oriented on the job and that satisfactory employees reach full production in two weeks.)
(3) Remedial training cost for an unsatisfactory employee: $1,800. (This assumes the cost of $300 for the initial two weeks plus $150 per week for a ten-week remedial training period when it is determined that the two-week orientation is insufficient.)
(4) Societal costs for welfare payments to unemployed individuals: $900. (This assumes that persons with an index of 2 or 1 will not be employed anywhere and that they will receive welfare payments for twelve weeks at $75 per week. This, of course, is a modest cost estimate because welfare payments are more likely to go on endlessly. I chose twelve weeks simply as a means of equating the time dimension with the proposed length of company training time.)
(5) Societal costs related to riots by black unemployed: $7,500 per rioter. (This obviously is extremely difficult to predict or to estimate. It is included primarily to make the point that a complete analysis of the utility of personnel decisions should take account of society's cost burden as well as that borne

---

[2] Admittedly, the assumption of *no* turnover is unrealistic, being approximated probably only by such organizations as the armed forces. Even so, the example is useful in portraying the concept of utility and the computations are considerably simplified by making the assumption.

exclusively by a firm. It is computed by speculating that the total cost of recent Detroit riots was 75 million dollars and that 10,000 blacks, constituting about 1 percent of the adult male black population, were involved.)

The above estimates, crude though they are, yield the information shown in Table 2-2 for employing persons according to various hiring scores on the employability index.[3] The results are particularly interesting, for they highlight *precisely* the moral dilemma faced by most employers today. In this hypothetical case, the direct cost to the employer is at least somewhat over a thousand dollars per satisfactory employee, if applicants with employability index values of 2 and 1 are rejected. The result of this action would be to reject 62½ percent of black applicants while rejecting only 22½ percent of white applicants. In contrast, if *total* cost is considered, it is apparent that the least costly approach is to hire persons without regard to their employability index. In such an instance, applicants would be hired on a first-come, first-serve basis, or perhaps according to some random procedure. This outcome is particularly interesting in view of the very substantial validities shown for both blacks and whites between employability index values and achievement of satisfactory job performance. It is an example of how validity tells only part of the story. Taking utility into account gives a better view of what actually happens when a procedure is used. Of course, in this example, we have assumed that effective accommodative strategies of remedial training are available. If this were not the case, the results might be quite different.[4] Nonetheless, I doubt that my example is far from reality. Employers today are indeed faced with a difficult choice involving whether to take responsibility for part of society's costs of manpower utilization or to continue to depend upon the public sector to shoulder a major portion of the burden. If they choose the latter course, it would be well for employers to be aware of the economic implications of their decision and to give their blessing to liberal legislation necessary for broadening and overhauling existing public welfare programs.

VALIDATING PERSONNEL DECISION PROCESSES

Validating personnel procedures refers primarily to the process of finding out as much as possible about the behavioral *meaning* to be attached to information available for a person. The major issues relevant to decisions about

---

[3] Societal cost estimates for persons not employed when various cutting scores are used were computed on the basis of a total 4,000 persons rather than on the basis of the total number of applicants screened. Thus, costs are assigned according to the locus of persons (in the firm or not) as a result of the cutting score used.

[4] It should be remembered, however, that the so-called remedial strategy need not necessarily be assumed to be a training program. In fact, within the context of our arguments for adopting individualized approaches, the remedial strategies would differ from person to person based on experience gained in working with them in a kind of "total push" effort to assure satisfactory job outcomes.

TABLE 2–2 Number of Applicants Screened and Related Costs to Company and to Society for Hiring and Training 4,000 Satisfactory Employees According to Various Levels on the "Employability Index"

Hiring Score on Employability Index	Number of Applicants Necessary	Recruiting and Screening Costs	Training Satisfactory	Training Remedial	Welfare Costs	Riot Costs	Total Cost (Company and Societal) for 4,000 Satisfactory Employees	Direct Cost to Company for 4,000 Satisfactory Employees
5	32,000	$3,200,000	$840,000	$2,160,000	$1,350,000	$146,250	$7,696,250	$6,200,000
4	11,100	$1,110,000	$785,000	$2,480,000	$1,350,000	$124,000	$5,849,000	$4,375,000
3	6,950	$ 695,000	$730,000	$2,800,000	$1,350,000	$ 93,600	$5,688,600	$4,225,000
2	4,850	$ 485,000	$565,000	$3,810,000	$ 810,000	$ 41,200	$5,711,200	$4,860,000
1	4,000	$ 400,000	$480,000	$4,320,000	—	—	$5,200,000	$5,200,000

minority group members are: First, what special problems are involved in conducting useful validity studies? Second, what methodological steps are likely to yield the most useful results in such validation investigations?

Measures of job success are difficult to derive. Behavior requirements differ from time to time; and, as we have seen, an individual's job performance may be affected by social and situational factors as well as by actual functional job requirements. Even if behaviors necessary for getting the job done properly are identified and agreed upon, it is especially difficult to operationalize these definitions to form acceptable measures or criteria of job success. The problem is especially acute when supervisory ratings are relied upon as estimates of a subordinate's effectiveness, and this is compounded in situations where minority or nonminority members are called upon to rate the job performance of members of the other group. Recent studies (Kirkpatrick, et al., 1967; Flaugher, et al., 1969) have confirmed the occurrence of biasing elements when employees' job performances are rated by racially different supervisors.

Because of these considerations, the most appropriate criterion for evaluating the usefulness of personnel procedures may be some *direct* measure of the degree of job skill developed by an employee after an appropriate time on the job; in other words, a job sample measure or measure of task proficiency or job knowledge. Such measures were used as criteria in what perhaps are the two best industrial validation studies done so far on employees belonging to minority and nonminority groups (Campbell, et al., 1969; Grant and Bray, 1970).

The study by Campbell, Pike, and Flaugher investigated the correlations between eight aptitude tests and a job knowledge test for 168 black and 297 white medical technicians working in thirty-six Veterans Administration hospitals located throughout the country. Table 2-3 summarizes their results.

TABLE 2–3 *Concurrent Validity Coefficients for Eight Aptitude Tests Against a Job Knowledge Criterion for Black and White Medical Technicians*

| | VALIDITY COEFFICIENTS | |
Test	Blacks (N = 168)	Whites (N = 297)
Subtraction and Multiplication	.34	.23
Vocabulary	.32	.27
Hidden Figures	.15	.14
Necessary Arithmetic	.46	.34
Number Comparison	.23	.14
Gestalt Completion	.25	.17
Picture Number	.21	.16
Paper Folding	.22	.21

SOURCE: Campbell, Pike, and Flaugher, 1969.

Grant and Bray investigated the predictive validity of five aptitude tests against performance in a standardized training program (Learning Assessment Program) for 211 minority and 219 nonminority telephone company employees hired in craft occupations. Their results are summarized in Table 2–4. Rather than comment on their results here, they are used to establish probability estimates in Tables 2-5 and 2-6 later in the chapter.

TABLE 2–4   *Predictive Validity Coefficients Between Aptitude Tests and Level Successfully Completed in the Learning Assessment Program*

| | VALIDITY COEFFICIENTS | |
Test	Minority (N = 211)	Nonminority (N = 219)
School and College Ability Test		
Total Score	.41	.36
Quantitative Score	.41	.37
Verbal Score	.32	.24
Bennett Mech. Comp. Test	.31	.32
Bell System Qualification Test	.38	.38
DAT Abstract Reasoning Test	.38	.50
Crawford Dexterity Test		
Part I	.25	.19
Part II	.16	.17

SOURCE: Grant and Bray, 1970.

In my opinion, the best approach for establishing the relative validities of each of the elements of the total personnel decisions system is through synthetic validation. The procedure involves three steps: (1) analysis of job elements believed to be required for effective performance, including not only those involving functional skills but also those involving adaptive skills, (2) selection of personnel procedures or instruments—tests, interviewing, biographical information, reference checking, experience or proficiency information, or whatever are believed to be indicators of the key elements; and (3) combination of the personnel procedures into a systematic decision strategy.

This approach is especially well-fitted to what I have been arguing for, because it provides a series of explicit steps or guidelines for developing the type of individualized decision system shown in Figure 2-1. Maslow (1969) outlines the advantages inherent in the strategy as follows:

· The focus is on observable abilities and permits far more accurate description of jobs to applicants.
· The clear definition of job elements unifies aspects of the personnel decision process which usually are quite disparate.
· *All* of an applicant's attributes are given attention in a global sense; he is not automatically "locked out" by such factors as educational requirements, cutting scores, training requirements, or delinquency records.
· Training needs may be more clearly specified and goals set for meeting them.
· The use of elements common to many jobs facilitates grouping jobs into meaningful families, thereby aiding processes of job transfer, job redesign, and the development of career ladders.
· A base is laid for appraising the job effectiveness of employees in terms of critical abilities and proficiencies.

These advantages all are important, but the most significant one, I believe, is that the process, in effect, forces a rational analysis of each personnel decision and a systematic accumulation of records relevant to personnel decisions. Such information, gathered over a span of time, provides the basis for validating the total decision-making system rather than merely subunits of it.

INTERPRETING DIFFERENTIAL VALIDITY PATTERNS

More and more research evidence is being gathered showing black–white differences in test scores, job performance measures, and test validities. Most notable are results reported by Campbell, Pike, and Flaugher (1969); Grant and Bray (1970); Futransky and Wagner (1968); Tenopyr (1968); Bentz (1969); Kirkpatrick, Ewen, Barrett, and Katzell (1968); and Wool and Flyer (1969). Surprisingly, instead of adding clarity to discussions of issues involved in testing and minority group employment, these studies have seemed often to add confusion. I believe this is because most investigators have been content to report merely validity coefficients or to draw stylized scatter diagrams (the familiar overlapping ovals) to portray graphically the differential patterns shown by minority and nonminority members. They have not usually taken the crucial step of processing the information to the point where it can be interpreted directly for making personnel decisions. Thus, the investigator's mind seems often to have been boggled by a plethora of mean differences, variability differences and validity differences, and he has put his data aside without ever figuring out what his results mean in the context of individualizing a personnel decision system.

The theme I have been developing throughout this chapter has emphasized differential treatment of minority and nonminority group members when it is believed the accuracy of decisions may be enhanced by so doing. Moreover, my definition of unfair discrimination emphasizes a decision model for interpreting the relative utility of personnel decisions. These arguments suggest, then, that results of validity studies should be presented in terms of probabilities of job success related to different test-score levels, so that differences, if any, in the on-the-job meaning of a given test score for blacks and whites may be clarified and used in the decision process.

To this end, I have converted data provided by Campbell et al. and Grant and Bray to such probability charts. The original data and the probability data are shown in Tables 2-5 and 2-6 for the Campbell and Grant and Bray studies respectively.

The data in Table 2-5 are particularly interesting, for they show vividly how the probability portrayal takes account not only of differences in the two validities, but also of differences in both test and criterion means and differences in both test and criterion variances. The expectancy charts provide a single, easy to understand base for interpreting various predictor scores in

TABLE 2–5   *Means, Standard Deviations, Validities, and Probability Charts for Black and White Medical Technicians (Necessary Arithmetic Test versus Job Knowledge)*

	BLACKS (N = 168)			WHITES (N = 297)		
	Mean	SD	r_{tc}	Mean	SD	r_{tc}
Necessary Arithmetic Test (t)	10.4	3.7	.46	14.0	4.8	.34
Job Knowledge (c)	31.4	10.4		35.7	9.4	

		ESTIMATED PROPORTION IN TEST INTERVAL		MEAN JOB KNOWLEDGE SCORE		PROBABILITY OF BEING IN UPPER HALF ON JOB KNOWLEDGE	
		Black	White	Black	White	Black	White
Score	0–3	.05	.01	21.2	29.4	.07	.31
Interval	4–7	.20	.08	25.0	31.3	.15	.38
on	8–11	.35	.22	30.0	33.1	.32	.45
Necessary	12–15	.29	.31	35.0	35.0	.54	.53
Arith-	16–19	.09	.24	40.5	36.9	.76	.61
metic	20–23	.02	.11	45.5	38.8	.90	.69
Test	23 and above	0	.03	—	40.6	>.90	.75

TABLE 2–6   *Means, Standard Deviations, Validities, and Probability Charts for Minority and Nonminority Telephone Employees*[a]

	MINORITY (N = 211)			NONMINORITY (N = 219)		
	Mean	SD	r_{tc}	Mean	SD	r_{tc}
Sum of SCAT and DAT (t)	32.2	15.9	.48	32.7	15.0	.46
Level Completed (c)	4.1	1.8		4.6	1.8	

		ESTIMATED PROPORTION IN INTERVAL		MEAN LEVEL COMPLETED		PROBABILITY OF COMPLETING LEVEL 4	
		Minority	Non-Minority	Minority	Non-minority	Minority	Non-minority
Score interval	281–295	.07	.03	2.13	2.51	.12	.18
Sum of SCAT	296–310	.19	.14	2.98	3.31	.26	.33
and DAT	311–325	.31	.30	3.83	4.16	.46	.54
Scores	326–340	.28	.32	4.63	4.95	.65	.73
	341–355	.12	.16	5.53	5.76	.83	.86
	356–370	.03	.05	6.38	6.56	.93	.95

[a] Sum of SCAT and DAT Scores Versus Level Completed in Learning Assessent Program.

terms of expected levels of job knowledge. Thus, a black applicant scoring in the 4–7 range on the arithmetic test has only a meager chance (.15 or about 1 in 7) of being in the top half of an employee group on job knowledge, whereas a white scoring in the same range has a .38 chance (or more than 1 in 3) of being in the top half. In contrast, a black scoring in the 16–19 range is *more* likely than a white in that range to end up in the top half on job knowledge.

The data from the AT&T study by Grant and Bray in Table 2-6 illustrate very nicely the situation in which only minor differences in validities, means, and variances occur between groups of minority and nonminority employees. As a result, the the probability charts show essentially equivalent probabilities for various test-score ranges, regardless of the race of the applicant.

I believe probability charts should be developed to summarize and clarify validity studies whenever they are performed. Such charts should then be used by personnel people along with *all* other information available to aid in developing fully informed and individualized judgments about *each* candidate for whom a personnel decision is to be made.

A FINAL COMMENT

I have argued in this chapter in favor of basing decisions about persons, jobs, and their interactions on information about the relative utility of different personnel practices. To do this demands more knowledge about current industrial and government practices in areas related to selection and job placement; and, most importantly, broader recognition and more careful estimation of costs likely to be incurred by decision errors of *both* the select and reject type. As this knowledge is gathered, an automatic consequence will be the discovery and implementation of alternative strategies which will be less costly to firms, individuals, society, and, hopefully, *all* considered together. The desired end result is that each employer will be able to specify quite exactly the nature and basis of his firm's decisions about people, jobs, and their interactions. And, this, in turn will serve as a means of demonstrating that his strategies give full opportunity to the optimal ultilization of human resources available to him.

REFERENCES

Bentz, V. J. *A review of Sears psychological testing policy, research and practices.* Psychological Research and Services Section, Sears, Roebuck Co., 1969.

Campbell, J. T., Pike, L. W., and Flaugher, R. L. *A regression analysis of potential test bias: predicting job knowledge scores from an aptitude battery.* PR-69-6. Princeton, N.J.: Educational Testing Service, 1969.

Dunnette, M. D. (ed.). Job testing and the disadvantaged: APA task force statement on employment testing of minority groups. *American Psychologist,* 1969, *24,* 637–650.

Fine, S. A. *Nature of skill: implications for education and training.* Washington, D.C.:

Proceedings, 75th Annual Convention, American Psychological Association, 1967, 365–366.

Flaugher, R. L., Campbell, J. T., and Pike, L. W. *Ethnic group membership as a moderator of supervisor's rating*. PR-69-5. Princeton, N.J.: Educational Testing Service, 1969.

Futransky, D. L., and Wagner, D. *On the job follow-up of postal clerks hired in San Francisco without employment tests*. Washington, D.C.: U.S. Civil Service Commission, 1968.

Grant, D. L., and Bray, D. W. Validation of employment tests for telephone company installation and repair operations. *Journal of Applied Psychology*, 1970, 54, 7–15.

Kirkpatrick, J. J., Ewen, R. B., Barrett, R. S., and Katzell, R. A. *Testing and fair employment*. New York: New York University Press, 1968.

Maslow, A. P. Issues and strategies in employment of the disadvantaged. In *Proceedings of the 1968 Invitational Conference on Testing Problems*. Princeton, N.J.: Educational Testing Service, 1969, 123–141.

Tenopyr, M. L. *Personnel testing and fair employment practices*. Paper presented at meeting of Western Psychological Association, San Diego, 1968.

Wool, H. and Flyer, E. S. Project 100,000. In P. B. Doeringer (ed.), *Programs to employ the disadvantaged*. Englewood Cliffs, N.J.: Prentice-Hall, 1969, 207–244.

CHAPTER THREE

Career Preference, Choice, and Attainment for Members of Minority Groups

Avner M. Porat and Edward C. Ryterband

INTRODUCTION BY THE EDITORS

The fact that employment can have a career development dimension is often neglected by administrators. In addition to basic principles of recruitment, selection, training, and job placement, career development *requires a longer-term perspective and investment of the organization's resources in seemingly remote programs, such as developing elementary and vocational schools. The notion of career development is particularly relevant to minority group members. In order to recruit an employable work force, the organization must realize that minority group employment requires both the provision of entry level jobs and a contribution to an early environment which assures that minority members receive adequate preparation, and therefore, opportunity in all levels of the employment hierarchy. At present, there is substantial evidence showing that most blacks occupy low-level jobs, which are usually both unskilled and not developmental in nature. This chapter by Porat and Ryterband provides a comprehensive review of relevant literature and documents the need for organizational executives to be concerned about career development as well as providing jobs.*

Porat and Ryterband discount the belief voiced by many administrators

that blacks have low levels of aspiration, which thereby inhibit them from becoming contributing members of organizations. The authors argue that career
choice is best viewed as a process which involves occupational preferences,
occupational choices, and occupational attainments. Within this perspective,
suggestions are offered regarding realistic career development programs for
minority peoples. Firm evidence shows that occupational preferences of black
high school and college students do not differ significantly from their white
counterparts. In addition, black college students are seeking work opportunities
to be original and creative, and they are choosing to work with people and
ideas rather than things. It is interesting to note that occupational preferences
of black college freshmen remain relatively stable throughout their college
career, as compared to the changing preferences of many white college students.

In dramatic contrast, the occupation choices of black and white college
students are quite different. These differences probably reflect the black college students' perceptions of greater limitations in the occupational opportunities open to their racial group. Blacks perceive less opportunity to achieve
their preferences. For example, black participants in management training
programs see less likelihood of attaining managerial positions than their white
counterparts. The validity of this perception is shown in a recent study of 100
of America's largest corporations: only 2.6 percent of their headquarters staffs
are black.

There is other evidence which shows that where increments in the percentage of black employees have been made in large companies, the gains are
more attributable to the absence of whites who are willing to fill these positions
than to a sincere attempt to open meaningful positions. Blacks typically achieve
only token integration. They often sense window dressing at managerial levels.
Furthermore, other data show that the majority of executives do not believe
that companies have any responsibility to hire or train blacks. A smaller percentage believe that companies have the responsibility to educate or motivate
blacks. It is interesting to note that both feelings were particularly strong at
lower levels of management and at the skilled, blue-collar level—persons to
whom most newcomers in the organization are first exposed and with whom
the competition for advancement is most intensely felt. These findings explain
other recent survey data showing only a handful of black professional managers
would ever consider job opportunities in large corporations—over 80 percent
of the group saw their future career opportunities in government jobs or small
business enterprises. Another survey reveals that blacks in large white corporate
structures fear they are more likely than whites to lose their jobs under conditions of economic pressure. In sum, there are reasons for the relatively large
discrepancies in the occupational choices of black and white college students
—i.e., there are greater career restrictions and more limited opportunities for
black advancement.

Recent research confirms earlier findings that blacks do not expect their
occupational aspirations to be realized in contemporary American society. In
the past, the frustration with unequal opportunities probably resulted in alienation from the larger culture, depression, and low self-esteem. Today, it is

significant to note that self-derogation is currently being replaced by growing and diffuse antiwhite sentiment, mistrust of white educational and occupational institutions, and a significant tendency toward separatism. Therefore, in order to expand the availability of minority peoples in the labor force, organizations must take concrete steps to ensure that real opportunities for advancement are in fact present in their organizations and to communicate this clearly to the public. The authors recommend black college recruiters and black fellowships to encourage black students to explore industrial occupations, such as engineering and management or other occupations (which they in fact prefer), which were previously seen as unattainable by blacks.

Although most studies of intelligence and other factors affecting career choice do not clearly distinguish racial from nonracial variables, i.e., racial differences are confounded with social class differences, there is some evidence which suggests that the differences we find are more bound to socioeconomic and environmental factors than to ability differences. However, the low self-esteem and self-rejection, noted in this and other chapters, seem to introduce a strain into black–white relations which results in a tendency for blacks to avoid interracially competitive situations. Furthermore, the recent moves toward separatism may belie an attempt to show the white community that blacks are as capable and ambitious as whites. At the same time, separateness ensures greater probability of success experiences and thereby greater enhancement of self-esteem, while avoiding close and personal and open competition with whites. This avoidance of entering into competition with whites may also account for the reluctance of blacks to pursue higher education or to make occupational choices which require open competition with whites. Of central importance to the business community are recent studies which indicate a trend for business-oriented freshmen to be among the most likely group of black freshmen to change majors before graduation (nearly 50 percent reject business majors before graduation). Blacks show a greater tendency to attribute their outcomes more to luck, fate, or other conditions which are external to their own efforts. One important implication of these findings is that encouraging career development for blacks through higher education alone seems to be doomed to failure. More important is the need to improve blacks' perceptions about themselves, their perceived ability, and the probability for success from their own efforts.

The authors also unfold a number of environmental factors which operate as constraints against career development and advancement among blacks. Primary among these factors is racial isolation and poverty, which characterize many black communities. Limitations in educational opportunities and organizational practices which discriminate against minority group members are also major environmental factors which inhibit the progress of blacks. For example, today's economy prefers people with a high degree of education, sophisticated training, and specialized skills. The lack of financial resources and ineffective communication are identified as primary sources of the gap between the needs for professional education of minorities and actual opportunities in educational institutions. There is need for new recruitment techniques, approaches to teach-

ing, counseling and evaluation procedures, which may be equally needed by whites. These needs cannot be met by efforts of colleges alone. Two examples of marshaled efforts, with industrial, financial, and moral support, are the Consortium for the Negro MBA, which is composed of five universities, and the Council for Opportunity in Graduate Management Education, which is composed of nine universities.

Last, the authors conclude with a prediction of greater industrial separatism, e.g., the development of large black corporations. In lieu of living and working with white organizational discrimination, the major opportunities for blacks may be the development of solid economic and occupational bases in black corporations. This would substantially reduce the black potential in the labor market—a reduction which threatens the survival of modern organizations.

Urban riots and other militant postures among civil rights activists in the late 1960s have changed the emphasis of the civil rights movement. The base of issues has broadened beyond the original question of integrating public facilities and ending de jure segregation in Southern public schools. All over the U.S. people are now being forced to consider a deepening sense of identity among blacks and other minority groups and their growing skepticism concerning the "token" reforms represented by earlier civil rights efforts. The black–white issue has, in the face of growing separatist strains, become part of an effort to fight poverty and better utilize the human resources of all the country's underprivileged groups. One result has been expansion in emphasis from social integration to economic change. Increased attention has been focused on employment and occupational development of the poor, especially members of minority groups. The importance of employment was emphasized in 1966 by the late Senator Robert Kennedy:

> Employment is the only true long run solution (to the racial problems): only if Negroes achieve full and equal employment will they be able to support themselves and their families, become active citizens and not passive objects of our action, become contributing members and not recipients of our charity . . . without employment, without basic economic security and self-sufficiency, any other help we provide will be only temporary in effect (Foley, 1968, pp. 48–9).

STATEMENT OF THE PROBLEM

The problem is not just for securing any type of employment for members of minority groups, but assuring in our generation they will receive adequate opportunity for representation at all levels of the employment hierarchy.

Developing careers rather than merely finding entry jobs is a goal whose attainment is not easily foreseen. Career development means a long-term organizationally sponsored and directed program aimed at developing an individual's full range of skills and experiences. In addition to basic selection and training for an entry job, it envisions transfers and promotions with an eye to expanded capabilities and responsibilities (see Dunnette's discussion, Chapter 2). Such career-development orientation for members of minority groups is still all too rare, and its absence is most easily seen among blacks. When compared with the white population, a high proportion of employed blacks occupy lower-level jobs, as is revealed in Table 3-1. Although there has been some improvement

TABLE 3–1   *Nonwhite as a Percentage of All Workers in Selected Occupations:*
The Changing Job Picture (1960–1969)

	1960	1969
Professional and Technical	4	7
Managers, Officials and Proprietors	2	3
Clerical	5	8
Sales	3	4
Skilled Workers	5	7
Semiskilled Workers	12	14
Unskilled Workers	27	24
Private Household Workers	46	44
Other Service Workers	20	19
Farmers and Farm Workers	16	11
Of All Workers Employed in 1969	—	11

SOURCE: Based on an original chart [Silberman, p. 76] appearing in *Fortune* Magazine, July 1970; Graphic Presentation Services.

since 1960, the changes which have occurred do not meet the needs for two main reasons. First, migration of blacks into industrial centers has increased at a time when the need for unskilled workers is dwindling. This has increased the economic gap between different income levels (Conference Board, 1966). Second, blacks have expressed more active and often militant desires and demands to develop a secure economic base through full proportional representation at all levels of the occupational ladder (America, 1969).

Behavioral science can contribute to the career development of minority groups on various levels. Career development can be viewed as a process in which changes are required at all phases. Changes should be brought about as a consequence of research findings. Data need to be accumulated in three areas. First, the behavioral scientist can explore the personal characteristics of members of minority groups as they affect their choice of occupation and their performance in post-school careers. Second, he can examine the "real" and "perceived" characteristics of the environment that allow or prevent a member of a minority group from achieving equality in career-development opportunities. Third, behavioral scientists can examine the interaction of environmental and personal constraints on the career-choice process of minority group members. Findings are available in many of these areas and are presented in this chapter. Our discussion concentrates on minority group members who have or should be able to obtain the skills for organizational careers at all levels, primarily managerial and professional job categories. Based on those findings there is a need for new directions and action plans which are discussed in the final section.

PERSONAL VARIABLES AFFECTING CAREER DEVELOPMENT

The Career-Choice Model

From an individual's point of view, career choice can be seen as a process involving occupational preferences, choices, and attainments. That process begins with information about occupations and with attractions to or preferences for certain occupations, leading to an occupational choice. The choice is conditioned by the expected availabilities of the preferred occupation to the individual. Finally, the choice process results in the attainment of a particular occupation (Vroom, 1964). An individual's occupational preference, the occupation he tries to attain, and the occupation he actually attains are not necessarily the same and have to be treated separately.

OCCUPATIONAL PREFERENCES. Occupational preferences are assumptions that people make concerning organizational and occupational images, stereotypes, and expectations of the positive outcomes that are likely to be provided by job situations (Dunnette, 1968). The preference will be toward the occupation that is attractive and has a high value for an individual. Stating a preference does not demand that a person take action to realize his preference or know a substantial amount about the content of his preferred occupation. Often preferences are a consequence of insufficient information about many different jobs and the inability of the person to judge whether he would like all that his choice actually involves. For example, Norman and Bessemer (1968) report that students' preferences toward familiar and professional jobs have been reduced when descriptions outlining the actual content of the jobs rather than just the title were provided.

OCCUPATIONAL CHOICE. In contrast, occupational choice requires some action, some striving to attain. A chosen occupation is the one which not only is attractive but for which there is a high perceived probability of its being attained by the individual. The choice might be different from the preference. An individual may choose an occupation other than the one he most prefers because of actual or perceived internal limitations. He may prefer a particular occupation but lack the self-esteem necessary for him to seek fulfillment of his preferences. He thus may be equal to the actual demands of the occupation he prefers but lack the vision or confidence to believe enough in his abilities to act (Korman, 1969). Career choices are affected also by limitations imposed by external conditions, such as economic, ethnic background, education, and environmental constraints. The authors' discussions revealed that black participants in an Executive Development Program attributed their previous careers as teachers, social workers, or policemen to forced choices because of perceived lack of opportunities in management careers.

OCCUPATIONAL ATTAINMENT. Attainment in an occupation is a result of two sets of choices: one by the individual, the other by the organization or by professionals in the community in which he will work. The differences between a person's choices and final occupational attainments may reflect internal problems, e.g., an individual's maturity or ability to foresee the necessary requirements for attaining an occupation (Nugent, 1968). Or the problem may reside outside the individual. An individual may choose but not attain an occupation because he is not "confirmed" by that occupation as eligible or because once on the job his expectations in actual work experience are initially disconfirmed and he leaves.

In order to understand the career-choice process for members of minority groups, we have examined the careers they prefer, aspire to, and actually attain. At each stage we have sought out those variables which affect the choice process of minority group members. We review both personal and environmental variables. In so doing we hope to discover where minority and nonminority individuals are similar and different in their career development and why. This knowledge could hopefully be used to construct realistic career-development programs for minority peoples.

Career Preferences and Choices for Minority Groups

CAREER PREFERENCES. To date most of the published research data gathered on career preferences of minority group members pertain primarily to blacks. Those data, while not in abundant supply, shed light primarily on the career aspirations and expectations from the elementary school through college level. Studies in the early 1960s indicated that blacks looking ahead to advanced study traditionally preferred professional programs such as medicine and law rather than programs in the humanities or applied and basic sciences (Glenn, 1964). A survey reported by Littig (1967) indicated that 90 percent of the subjects, male black college freshmen, aspired to professional occupations as classified according to the U.S. Bureau Directory of Occupational Titles.

A replication of the above study a year later indicated that some preferences were changing. Respondents continued to aspire to traditionally "open" professions such as physicians, teachers, lawyers, ministers; however, there has been an increase in the proportion aspiring to more traditionally "closed" professions such as physicists, airline pilots, judges, and engineers. In particular it was the black with high achievement motivation that, in the 1967 survey, started to aspire to some traditionally closed occupations (Littig, 1968). In comparison, white male college students gave a similarly high preference ranking to professions such as physician and lawyer. However, white students also ranked highly professions such as school superintendent and banker, which were noteworthy in their absence among the more preferred careers cited by the black college students in the 1960 and 1967 samples. While differences between blacks' and whites' occupational preferences still exist, they are becoming less distinct. The preferences of both groups are changing. For example in 1964-65 28 percent of black freshmen at predominantly black colleges preferred elementary or secondary education as a career. Only four years later at the same type of institution, the preference decreased to 23 percent. Changes also occurred for whites. In the decade between 1957 and 1967, preferences for careers in the social sciences increased while preferences for careers in the physical sciences decreased (Freedman, 1967). On the surface, therefore, black and white preferences seem to be merging. However, these data say nothing about the values underlying these preferences.

The occupational preferences for any given individual reflect underlying personal values. These values in turn are reflected in the job characteristics considered important in careers aspired to. For many black college students, altruism or the opportunity to be helpful to others and to be of use to society, used to and still does rank as a very important characteristic in career preference, one which is more important to blacks than whites (Fichter, 1966; Bayer and Boruch, 1969). Other important values for black college students are opportunities to be original and creative, to work with people rather than things, and living and working with ideas (Fichter, 1966). Less frequently mentioned as important characteristics for black college students are opportunities to exercise leadership, to make a lot of money, and to be free from supervision, all values which are also very important to comparable white students. These same white students also mentioned as very important opportunities to have cogenial co-workers, and to have a job which will give a feeling of accomplishment (Dunnette, 1968).

Data on members of other minority groups, such as Mexican-Americans, Puerto Ricans, and American Indians are more scanty than those on blacks. There is some likelihood, however, that the career preferences of other minority group members would be the same as or at least close to those for blacks. Traditionally, blacks seem to have aspired to high-status, open occupations. These were occupations that also required little interaction and competition with whites. More recently (Bayer and Boruch, 1969) their aspirations seem to have broadened. This pattern has been historically noted in other minority groups and thus may apply to today's emergent Mexican-American, Puerto Rican, and Indian minorities. American Jews, in the earlier decades of this century when their acceptability was more in question, preferred occupations as professionals and educators, that provided similar autonomy (*Fortune*, January, 1969). With added security and integration they have broadened their preferences. Thus we suspect similar patterns will be evidenced for other minorities such as the Puerto Rican and Mexican-American which are just now emerging in their efforts for equal opportunity. An early phase of ethnic progress seems to place high value on autonomy in career choices. The importance of such autonomy will decrease as acceptance of the minority increases.

CAREER AND OCCUPATIONAL CHOICES. Normally the response of a college freshman to questions about his career aspirations should be treated as an expression of career preference rather than actual choice. The student has yet to extend any career-relevant efforts in the form of course choices. By the time a college student becomes a senior he has exercised such course-related options and thus asking him the same question about careers to which he aspires would reflect more an occupational choice than a preference. A unique feature of such early preferences for college blacks, however, is that they are more fixed; they change less as the student advances. This unique stability for black college students' preferences (and later choices) seems to reflect the perceived limited and few opportunities open to their racial group. A survey (Fichter, 1966) of 3,000 black college students indicated that 80 percent of them had considered their chosen career by the time they were freshmen in college and that fully 50 percent of them had actually decided on a given career by the beginning of their freshman year. A more extensive 1968 survey provided supporting results. Twice as many white freshmen as black were undecided about career preferences and major field of study (Bayer and Boruch, 1969).

Furthermore, the percentage of black college students choosing a given occupational field remains more stable over their college experience (Fichter, 1966). Table 3-2 shows the distribution of career choices of male and female black respondents as freshmen and as seniors in college. It can be seen from the table that in no case did the percentage of people choosing a particular career as freshmen change by more than 6 percent from the freshman to their

TABLE 3–2   *Career Choices of Blacks Classified by Year in College and Sex*

CAREER FIELDS	CHOICE			
	BLACK MEN		BLACK WOMEN	
	Freshman	Senior	Freshman	Senior
N	1,122	1,148	1,993	2,051
Social Work	2%	5%	5%	10%
Physical Sciences, Engineering	21	17	4	3
Medicine, Health and Biological Sciences	22	17	18	12
Business Fields	7	12	7	6
Elementary and Secondary Education	3	4	17	23
Other Education Fields	25	27	32	32
Social Sciences, Humanities and Law	20	18	17	14

SOURCE: J. H. Fichter (1966), in *The Journal of Negro Education.*

senior years. This unusually high commitment of blacks to a career before obtaining a broad experience indicates a reasoning that where there are few opportunities open to people, there is less cause for them to explore alternative possibilities, which results in an earlier choice (Fichter, 1966).

Noteworthy in Table 3-2 is the fact that the highest percentage of both men and women black students chose teaching professions, especially in "other education fields," which included the teaching of physical education, music, art, agriculture, business trade, industrial arts, and administration (Fichter, 1966). In still another survey of 4,000 black college students from 50 predominantly black colleges, over half of the students surveyed planned on teaching careers (Jaffe, Adams and Meyers, 1966). A study reported by Bayer and Boruch (1969), of predominantly white colleges and universities, shows that 23 percent of the black freshmen attending the colleges planned on these same teaching careers, while at predominantly white universities 11 percent of black freshmen planned on teaching careers. The comparable figures for whites were lower, 19 percent at colleges and only 5 percent at universities. So, while preference for teaching is less pronounced in the predominantly white institutions, the black student still leans more heavily toward teaching, and is probably more likely to continue in that field through graduation.

The limited available data comparing whites' and blacks' career choices suggest a growing overlap in early preferences, but a greater stability from freshman to senior years among blacks. Samples of white and black freshmen indicate whites are more uncertain in their preferences and more likely to change during college. If the projections are true blacks and whites should reveal more divergent career choices as seniors than their freshman preferences indicate. It is apparent that a divergence in college is taking place, since the occupational attainments of blacks are different, as indicated by their lack of integration into higher level occupations. For example, a study of 100 of America's largest corporations showed that in 1966 Blacks constituted only 2.6 percent of their headquarters staffs. Further, a 1968 report·on 4,249 New York City businesses indicated that 43 percent had no blacks and 46 percent had no Puerto Ricans in any white-collar jobs despite the large populations of blacks and Puerto Ricans in the city (Haynes, 1968). Additional data comparing choices for all racial groups would seem essential. Further, reasons for the differences must be uncovered if realistic actions are to be planned. For example, choices of blacks are divergent. The abundant data comparing blacks and whites on a variety of psychological variables can be a useful source of information to explain why. It is to those variables that we now turn our attention.

INTELLIGENCE AND NONCOGNITIVE VARIABLES IN THE CAREER-CHOICE MODEL. The above discussion has suggested that blacks and possibly members of other minority groups have somewhat distinct patterns of career choices and attainments. Few, if any, comprehensive studies have been conducted to extract personal variables that may underlie these distinctions. Typically comparative studies of one or more variables have been conducted to see if there are significant differences between minority and nonminority group members on those variables alone. These differences have not been related to some measure of career preferences, choices, or attainments. Therefore, these comparative studies are weak in providing applied sources of information. The bulk of these studies do not clearly define the racial, ethnic, or other considerations that distinguish minority from nonminority group members. There often is a confusion of economic and ethnic variables due to the fact that most members of ethnic minorities studied, such as the Puerto Ricans, Mexican-Americans, or blacks, have also been of lower socioeconomic status. Still, some of these studies examined variables that should be relevant to understanding the career-choice process.

A widely studied concept that has direct relevance to the career-choice model is intelligence, since a model of unique career development for minority group members might be due to deficiencies in what has been referred to as basic intelligence. A number of studies have compared black and white intelligence and have been reviewed elsewhere (Dreger and Miller, 1968). While the results are equivocal, early publications (Bruce, 1940; McGurk, 1951; and Tanser, 1939) provided support to the finding of significant IQ differences between blacks and whites. More recently Jensen (1969) offers several lines of evidence to support this contention. Still, it will be premature to relate these apparent differences to the frustrating career attainments of blacks.

There are caste and attitudinal differences which, apart from equating education and family income, provide performance-debilitating test-taking sets in subjects from minority groups (Dreger and Miller, 1968; Katz, 1964). The inferior environments of children from minority groups seem to have a cumulative effect. Klineberg (1963) and Lee (1951) have shown that blacks migrating to Northern cities such as New York show increases in IQ as a function of tenure in those cities' school systems.

It is, thus, our interpretation of the above findings that the differences are more a product of the socioeconomic environment than of heredity. When black students were given adequate preparation and a chance to escape the socioeconomic binds, no significant difference was found between them and white students (Hunt and Hardt, 1969).

In using ability variables to explain differences in career attainments for members of minority groups and nonminority groups, one should remember that the question of the magnitude of influences of heredity and environment is still wide open. Two points stand out; for one, socioeconomic environment can make a difference in upgrading performance. Second, there seems to be sufficient indication that enough overlap in basic intelligence exists between blacks and whites to allow us to see both groups as an equally viable pool of candidates for a variety of careers.

When investigated in comparative studies, a wealth of noncognitive variables have been found to differ more than intelligence between races and are directly related to performance measures. These variables focus on the aspirations, expectations, and achievement motivations of minority group members and on their self-concepts. Here we hope to identify specific variables that can account for the unique occupational perspectives of minority group members.

ASPIRATIONS, EXPECTATIONS, AND ACHIEVEMENT MOTIVATIONS OF MINORITY GROUP MEMBERS.   One likely source of enhancing our understanding of minority group members' career choices lies in the further examination of their aspirations and expectations about upward mobility in American society (Frazier, 1962). In addition, it has been found that they attach great importance to education as a means of enhancing their status in society (Reiss and Rhodes, 1959). However, the black's aspiration as compared with his expectations differs from the white's in a very critical way. The black student, though with a level of aspiration equal to or even greater than comparable white college students, does not expect his aspirations to be realized in American society as it exists today (Bowerman and Campbell, 1965). The racial difference increases further if we separate urban blacks from rural ones and look at the aspiration–expectation gap of the urban black (Kuvlesky and Ohlendorf, 1968).

The 1966 survey by Fichter revealed that half of those students expected that it will be twenty years or more before blacks will have truly equal job opportunities in the United States as a whole. Somewhat more optimistically, only 25 percent of these students feel that it will take as much as twenty years for equal job opportunities to exist in the larger Northern cities. In contrast 75 percent or more of the same students expected it will take twenty years or more for equal job opportunities to exist in the Southern states. Nonetheless, of the 3,000 college seniors surveyed almost 90 percent planned further study beyond the college level, recognizing postgraduate study as a necessary qualification for future career development, occupational success, and mobility. A more comprehensive survey in 1968 indicated that 55 percent of the 12,000 black freshmen, compared with 42 percent of the 230,000 white freshmen sampled, planned to work toward a graduate degree (Bayer and Boruch, 1969). Though their expectations are for graduate study, a disappointed note is entered in their opinions concerning the real opportunities they perceive to get postgraduate training in various fields. Surveying twelve major fields including social work, engineering, medicine, business fields, and law, it was noted that 28 to 55 percent of the students in the 1966 study felt that opportunities to get postgraduate training for blacks are less than those for whites (Fichter, 1966).

These perceptions of reduced opportunities for proper training in the light of a known and high-level aspiration to higher socioeconomic status must have severe and frustrating consequences for members of minority groups. We would postulate that their frustration, when independent of white protest movements, would lead only to isolated direct aggression toward educational and occupational institutions that are experienced to be at fault. Direct aggression is less likely because these institutions are large and have power to withstand such reactions. Further these institutions are many in number and symbolize a strong, enforced cultural norm which indicates a pervasively lower social and legal status learned by the black at a very young age (Ausubel and Ausubel, 1963). Finally, these organizations show equivocal evidence of their intent to change their conservative attitude. Until basic attitudinal changes become obvious, recruitment of minority people is difficult and their tenure chancy. Using black recruiters only answers part of the problem. It may get some, but keeping blacks in a state of suspicion still remains an open issue.

The results of these frustrations then are probably more likely to be turned inward into an unresolved acceptance of the futilities involved (Proctor, 1970), an alienation from the larger culture (Vontress, 1970), and most depressing, an all-too-frequent distaste for self. However, this self-hatred, as it has been called, seems to be on the wane (Banks, 1970) and is being replaced by a growing and diffuse antiwhite sentiment. Still, if any aggressions arise from the disparity between aspirations and expectations, it is likely most will still be blunted and displaced. This displacement is likely to move the black toward a separatism, discussed in later sections, which is better understood once we have examined his self-concept variables.

While the "system" is faulty, to change it requires a revolutionary organized movement fighting from within, and few blacks or whites are revolutionaries in a violence-oriented sense of the word. Even where adamant self-acclamation is evident in as in "Black is Beautiful" rhetoric and in black-studies programs (which have limited career relevance), the seemingly chauvinistic language, dress, and behavior (though possibly long overdue) can be seen as a reaction against "oppression," not as positive self-esteem.

At best, to date, the data on achievement motivation of black students are unclear (Epps, 1969). Therefore, we can't support the argument that discriminating experiences as perceived by members of minority groups develop a blunted or lower need for achievement. We can only assume that when compared with whites, they alter self-concepts in some areas in harmful ways (Katz, 1967). It seems likely, however, that needs don't change that easily, just expectations, so that blacks still have the same needs as whites—that is, to involve themselves in efforts required for a high level of educational or occupational achievement. Blacks are entering college and aspiring to post-baccalaureate degrees in greater numbers. Still, self-concepts should be affected by their doubts about their society's willingness to allow them into the careers they aspire to.

Attitudes Toward Career Attainment

SELF-CONCEPT OF MINORITY GROUP MEMBERS. A disproportionately large percentage of minority group members come from socially disadvantaged environments. These environments include low economic status, low social status, low educational achievement, under-employment or no employment, limited participation in community organizations, and limited favorable potential for upward mobility (Gordon, 1967). As a result of these discriminatory or impoverished environments, minority group youngsters see themselves as members of an outgroup, rejected and segregated from the total society. For the teen-ager, this social–racial awareness of his alleged inferiority creates internal doubts and conflicts of self-rejection versus the need for self-acceptance and self-esteem (Wells, 1969). These contradictory attitudes towards himself are further extended toward others and may result in a mistrust of occupational institutions and their willingness to provide meaningful career opportunities.

An attitude of limited ability and rejection by the white establishment should not be confused with a self-image of passivity, withdrawal, and low competence. Among blacks this reflects primarily on interaction with the white world rather than the black's interaction with other blacks (Cohen, 1968). From this generally lower self-concept held by members of minority groups when relating to the white world, a mixture of reverent admiration for the white individual's prestige and power and hatred for the legacy of discrimination seems to be a common outcome (Banks, 1970).

Several studies point out the strain introduced into the performance of blacks in competitive interracial situations. Experiments with black male college students have shown that in work teams composed of blacks and whites of the same IQ, blacks are apt to be (1) passively compliant, (2) rate their own performance as inferior, and (3) express less satisfaction with team experience. These results are seen to be due to a high amount of social threat and/or failure threat perceived by blacks (Katz, 1964). The social-threat and failure-threat variables seem to underlie a reluctance to be in competitive situations of an ego-involving nature. When a task was changed from low to high social threat and failure threat, the white setting became even less favorable than when the black subjects were performing with black peers (Katz and Greenbaum, 1963). Further, the perceived probability of success for blacks was higher when tasks were described as perceptual–motor and less when the task was defined intellectually and related more to basic competencies (Katz, Roberts and Robinson, 1964). Finally, anticipated intellectual comparison with black peers was found to produce a higher level of verbal performance in blacks than when the anticipated comparison was with whites. Even when the subjects were black physicians, lawyers, etc., who have attained professional careers, there was a lower level of enthusiasm toward open competition within the professions than there was among white professionals (Howard, 1966).

One result of the low-level desire for open competition might be the move toward separation which has gained strong momentum in the black community in recent years. On the surface the purpose is to show the white community that blacks are as capable, competitive, and ambitious as whites, but at the same time, bypass the need to compete openly with the white establishment (America, 1969). Another underlying purpose may be to show the black himself that he is capable, i.e., to ensure more success experiences. The reluctance to involve themselves in competitive situations with whites can reflect itself on the minority group member in a number of ways. For one, it can result in reluctance to pursue higher education levels that will expose them to competition with whites. This is evident in many low-income neighborhoods where preference and admiration is not directed toward those position holders who are recognized by the white community, such as civil rights leaders, but rather toward those who made "Easy Street" through local rackets (Foley, 1968) or more recently those who become visible in movements emphasizing Black identity.

Even when education is pursued it can result in occupational choices that reflect a desire to avoid competition with nonminority individuals. Fichter (1966) found 77 percent of black men anticipated career activities and jobs where they could succeed within their own racial group, such as teaching and professional service. In contrast only 18 percent expressed anticipation for careers in jobs requiring competition with whites, such as administration and management. Similar profiles were obtained for the women surveyed. Ninety percent of black women anticipated careers and jobs where competing with whites is negligible, and only 7 percent anticipated careers where competing with whites would be a substantial factor. Other surveys based on the 1960 census support this tendency to avoid competition (Back and Simpson, 1964). More recent surveys indicate more black freshmen are aspiring to business careers. But these are freshmen, and their choice status as seniors is still unknown (Bayer and Boruch, 1969). Fichter's (1966) study indicated that business-oriented freshmen were among the most likely groups of blacks to change majors (nearly 50 percent did not pursue it through to graduation).

Fate Control as a Part of the Self-Concept of Minority Group Members. Fate control is an important aspect of the self-concept of minority group members that would seem related to low levels of occupational expectation and attainments. In the early 1960s, studies have shown that minority group members typically saw themselves as less potent determiners of their own fate and success (Battle and Rotter, 1963). They seemed to rely more on luck, fate, or any other set of conditions outside of their own efforts to explain what happens in their lives. Furthermore, it has been found that Southern college blacks were most high in deference and least high in dominance and autonomy as measured by the Edwards Personal Preference Schedule (Brazziel, 1964).

Low fate control concerning career aspirations could probably be used to explain, at least partially, high school dropout rates of minority group members, and as a result their inability at a later stage to attain more economically promising and rewarding careers. The acceptance of low fate control does result in less negative feelings of the black dropout toward the school itself than is the case among white dropouts (Anderson and Tollman, 1968). The black does not blame the school; it is only a symptom. Leaving helps him to forget the symptom. Among those blacks who do remain in school, the attitude is different. In one study of freshmen, the black students were more likely than whites to feel that their high school preparation would hinder their performance and that they were less well-prepared academically than was the average white student (Hedegard and Brown, 1969). These perceptions are probably realistic, since ghetto and Southern schools, from which most blacks come, are known for their overcrowding and poor curricula.

In the face of these realities, encouraging career development for blacks through higher education alone will be more difficult to achieve. A key to these efforts will be to focus on improving perceptions of blacks about themselves. The importance of self-perceived ability and fate control as career attainment predictors has become evident in two recent studies. The first by Epps (1969a) has identified self-perceived ability as one of two variables that have considerable value as nonability predictors of academic achievement among black students. In the second, a team headed by Gurin pointed out that a black student who perceives a lack of fate control due to environmental barriers may be more highly motivated to break these barriers than would be the one who denies the existence of racial discrimination or attributes difficulties to his lack of success (Gurin et al., 1969).

In addition to the need to focus on personality factors, attention will also have to focus on changing the environmental realities that give birth to these self-derogating perceptions. It is to those environmental features that we now turn our attention.

ENVIRONMENTAL CONSTRAINTS AFFECTING CAREER DEVELOPMENT

In an analysis of the environmental constraints on career development the prime focus falls on opportunities and constraints in the urban setting. The trend of most minority group members is to move from the country to the city. While in 1910 only 29 percent of the blacks in the U.S. lived in urban areas, the percentage has increased to 65 in 1960 and is expected to reach over 75 in 1970 (Kennedy, 1967). Similar migration patterns are evidenced among other minorities such as Puerto Ricans, Indians, etc. Of those moving to urban areas, over 80 percent end up in the central city, from which a white exodus has been in rapid progress for over two decades.

The center city combines racial isolation and poverty conditions with constrained opportunity for career advancement. For the majority of minority group members little has changed since President John F. Kennedy in 1963 described the opportunities for blacks:

The Negro baby born in America today, regardless of the section of the nation in which he is born, has about one half as much chance of completing a high school as a white baby born in the same place on the same day, one third as much chance of completing college, three times as much chance of becoming unemployed, about one seventh as much chance of earning $10,000 a year, a life expectance which is 7 years shorter, and the prospects of earning only half as much (Kennedy, 1967).

The prime reason for these differences is that the minority group member is usually unable to obtain the career opportunities that are open to white Americans. In the previous sections we explored the personal variables that influence preference and choice. In this section the impact of environmental constraints on job attainment are reviewed. The two major environmental factors considered are the educational opportunities and the organizational practices the minority group member experiences in preparing for or entering into a career.

Educational Opportunities for Career Development and Compensatory Education

In recent years considerable discussion and writings have called attention to the importance of providing educational opportunities to the under-privileged, primarily members of minority groups. For the most part the programs that emerged were directed toward two population groups. The main thrust was directed toward education for the very young through programs such as Headstart and the integration of public school systems. A more limited effort was directed toward the unskilled or semiskilled youngster or adult, providing them with technical training through such programs as Job Corps, Neighborhood Youth Corps, Concentrated Employment Programs, Work Incentive Programs, and the Manpower Training and Development Act. The area where little measurable progress has been recorded to date is that of educational opportunity and career development for higher-level occupations which require technical or administrative skills. This area is most significant today because in the past the uneducated could have found positions that required only manual skills and relatively little training. Today's economy, however, prefers people with sophisticated training, a high degree of education, and specialized skills.

There are several reasons for the gap between the needs for such professional education of minorities and the actual achievement of our educational institutions. The more frequent ones are their lack of financial resources, experience, and effective communications with minority groups, as well as the pressing day-to-day problems in other areas—primarily those of campus unrest. Moreover the requirements of the educational programs for members of minority groups are such that new recruitment techniques, approaches to teaching, and counseling and evaluation procedures are desperately required, and because of united resources and experience, these innovations can't in most cases be handled effectively by a single college or university. Therefore, where several schools marshal, their efforts have a better chance to survive. Examples of such programs are the Consortium for the Negro MBA, in which five universities participate, and the Council for Opportunity in Graduate Management Education, in which nine schools of management patricipate.

Progress has been made in overcoming the first hurdle for providing educational opportunity to members of minority groups, that of open or even preferred admittance for minority group members. It started with court decisions to desegregate education in the mid-1950s and increased with schools devoting special attention to locate and attract the disadvantaged (Clement, 1966). Some schools, such as Rutgers University or City University in New York, have proceeded to remove all entry barriers to members of minority groups. In these schools, however, other problems emerged, more than just allocating openings to blacks and other minorities. It was quickly realized that the cultural gap between the new students and the rest of the academic body had to be given special attention. Members of minority groups are not flooding the classrooms of the integrated colleges and universities. Of 7 million American college students in 1969, only 400,000 (6 percent) were blacks and of those, 65 percent were in predominantly black colleges, where there is a 2 to 1 ratio of women to men, or in two-year colleges (23 percent) (Bayer and Boruch, 1969). This large proportion of women, the reverse of the ratios existing among white students, is disturbing, as women typically are disfavored in many higher-level professions.

Even more serious is the evidence that predominantly black colleges do not offer the opportunity for career attainment available to graduates of white or integrated colleges (Coleman et al., 1966; Jencks and Riesman, 1967). So not only are blacks and other minorities underrepresented in the college population, the majority attend colleges which have not been seen as very viable for preparation for careers leading to postgraduate training or organizational careers. Considering just such inadequate preparation (and that is not the only problem), it is not surprising that a black college graduate's lifetime income is less than that of a white man with an eighth-grade education (Young, 1967), and that over the last few decades blacks and other minorities have been losing occupational ground proportionately to the white majority (Hare, 1965).

Since few blacks possess the necessary qualifications to rise in their professions under present-day conditions, and since the qualifications for such advancement are constantly rising, the question arises as to how they can possibly prepare themselves to advance. One obvious approach is an increase in compensatory education at the college and professional level which will aim at improved teaching methods and educational goals that are inspirational and not of the caretaker type. Such an effort will require, in addition to the recruitment effort discussed earlier, an assurance of organized support on three levels—financial, educational, and cultural—which can be provided by a mixture of government and business efforts.

Numerous studies have provided evidence that in the long run only integrated compensatory education will assure adequate preparation for entry into the mainstream of American society (McPartland, 1969; Katz, 1967). The integration cannot be just on the institutional level but has to be at the class or course level. In those schools where integration took place at the class level, both occupational aspirations and achievement scores of black students increased significantly relative to those of blacks from unintegrated schools or schools where individual classes were not integrated (Curtis, 1968). It has also been shown that academic aspirations of blacks in integrated classes increase faster than those of whites in the same school (McWhirt, 1967). At the same time, token integration might not be sufficient, as it might lead to an increased sense of low fate control on the part of the minority group member (Katz, 1969) and an increase in the short-term prejudice and hostility between the majority and the minority members (Eisenman, 1965).

Despite the need for classroom and campus integration, there has been in the last two years a movement among minority group members, especially blacks, for separatism on the campus and in professional training programs. This is often a reaction to the feeling that the minority group member is being put on display (Rose, 1966); that the programs provided by the schools are only tokenism rather than real commitment (Gordon and Wilkerson, 1966); and that the programs fail to provide the practical orientation that the black student has expected (Hedegard and Brown, 1969). In other words, blacks have not been convinced that many of the compensatory educational programs offered will provide them the access and opportunity for attaining their career choices. It is justified by historic experience, which accustomed blacks to view every white action as a means for further exploitation. This is accompanied by frustration developing due to the slow progress of many career-oriented educational programs and by the experiences of minority group members who try to enter the world of "the establishment" or "the white man."

Organizational, Professional, and Social Constraints on Career Attainment

Even if adequate educational opportunity is provided, the question remains whether a member of a minority group will be able to pursue his chosen career without discrimination. The possible difficulty of career attainment, even after the education has been provided, lies often with the need to break into organizations and professions where minority groups are not represented in adequate proportions. In 1967, the Federal Equal Opportunity Commission reported that of 4,249 New York businesses surveyed, 43 percent had no black white-collar employees and that 46 percent had no Puerto Rican white-collar workers (Haynes, 1968). The study further revealed that in 1966, blacks made up only 2.6 percent of the headquarters staffs of these same companies compared with a city-wide average of 5.2 percent blacks in white-collar job categories. Members of minority groups (the data especially pertain to blacks) were also underrepresented in higher-status professions outside of business firms. For example, only 1 percent of the engineering students surveyed in 1963 were black. These black engineers, further, typically avoided sales or production occupations. Rather they tended to concentrate in research and development.

Blacks are also underrepresented as lawyers (1 percent), accountants and auditors (.8 percent), physicians and surgeons (2 percent), clergymen (3 percent), musicians and music teachers (4.8 percent), dentists (7 percent) and teachers (7.8 percent). In the field of teaching, blacks come closest to being proportionally represented. Only in social welfare and recreation were blacks represented (10.7 percent) in proportion to their numbers in the population (Bond, 1966). Finally, black psychologists are also underrepresented. Of the more than 25,000 psychologists listed in the American Psychological Association in 1968, only 398 were black. Of these about 5 percent held academic jobs, and of those 200 only 46 were given appointments in predominantly white colleges (Wispe et al., 1969). In recent years there has been some improvement in blacks penetrating the higher-paid jobs as the rate of employment of blacks between 1960 and 1969 increased at a somewhat faster rate than employment of whites (Silberman, 1970). But since they started from a much lower basis the gains they made during the 1960s left them far short of equality.

This lack of representation of minority group members in the high-level professions and organizational positions often prevents the potential candidate from even trying to gain a position. Gordon (1967) has pointed out that one does draw on a familiar reference group for moral support and for help in persisting in a given direction. For that reason alone it can be expected that the increase in the proportional representation will be slow and painful. In this respect business and professional organizations have not convinced the minorities that their efforts are sincere. It has been claimed by members of minority groups that where gains have been made in increasing the percentage of nonwhite employees in large companies, this is more due to the lack of whites willing and able to fill these positions (Silberman, 1970).

On the other hand the minority group member who has joined a white corporation and has the qualifications to advance is impatient and often interprets traditional advancement practices as discrimination. He is torn between the pressure of the extreme sectors of his racial group for separatism and the promises of the establishment that are slow to materialize. When he interacts with members of the white establishment a cloud of suspicion and oversensitivity affects the behavior of both parties and strains the relationship. Many members of minority groups believe that business organizations are aiming only at token integration at higher levels in the organization and suspect "window-dressing" appointments at many managerial levels.

A study by Goeke and Weymor (1969) has shown that a majority of people already within the organizational world do not believe that companies have the responsibility to hire and train blacks. Of those questioned an even smaller percentage believe that companies have the responsibility to educate and motivate blacks. Both feelings were particularly strong at the levels of lower management and skilled blue-collar workers, to whom many newcomers in the organization are first exposed and with whom the competition for advancement is most intensely felt. Although the above study shows some increase in willingness to train and accept minority group members between 1967 and 1969, many blacks still perceived it as "words rather than commitment to action." In a recent discussion one of the authors had with forty high-ranking black and Spanish-speaking managers ($12,000–$25,000 annual salary) of a major antipoverty program in the Midwest, only a handful said they would consider job opportunities in large corporations. Over 80 percent of the group, which did not include militants, saw their future career opportunities in government jobs or small enterprises.

With those perceived and actual conditions of limited opportunity within the white establishment, many members of minority groups are reluctant to invest in career development which will lead to integration within the white corporate structure. The view of limited opportunity is often accompanied by the feeling of lack of job security in the white establishment, where the newcomer fears he is more apt to lose his job or face strong opposition from white co-workers when an economic squeeze hits the organization (Hoyle, 1969).

This limited opportunity is accompanied by increased sensitivity of minority group members to their ethnic group and to the needs of the poorer members of the community (Holsendolph, 1969). The result is an increased demand by many blacks for the development of black power, not just as a political force, but as an economic and social force (America, 1969). Such a power structure, which is discussed on page 89, will provide members of minority groups with their own avenues for career development and advancement.

MEASUREMENT ISSUES

So far we have noted some of the currently obvious personal and environmental constraints that earmark the unique character of the career-development process of minorities. Improvement of the existing situation will depend both on a more sophisticated assessment of salient dimensions of the underprivileged that affect their career choices and on seeking more effective understanding of the society and institutions that provide (or don't provide) for the actualizing of those choices. The former of these two issues is the focus of this section, while discussion of the societal and institutional issues is left for the concluding section.

Why worry, especially about methods of assessing the disadvantaged? First, because assessments will provide a better understanding of personal makeup as it affects career aspirations and achievements. Second, such understanding needs to be applied to more effective selection, classification, diagnosis of training needs, and performance evaluation of the underprivileged in both their preparatory education and their actual career experiences. Many of the measurement problems are only briefly mentioned here. Abilities measurement for minority group members is complicated by the fact that test norms often do not include them, and in fact test-taking know-how is not a typical experience of the underprivileged. Further, many noncognitive variables act as influential moderators of expressed abilities. Third, empirical work of an experimental nature has thus far been deficient in amount and insensitive to the use of "true" (Campbell, 1957) experimental designs and the impact of the experiment and the experimenter as a social stimulus on the behavior of the underprivileged (Rosenthal, 1963; Katz et al., 1964).

Ability Measurement

Ability tests and the comparison of white and black abilities have been a controversy of long standing that we have already said has been fueled by indecision resulting from a confounding of class and ethnic variables. In addition the race of the examiner and the instruction he provides alter the performance of members of minority groups on those tasks, since they represent confounding demand characteristics apart from the intrinsic content of the task. In comparative studies of intelligence, the functional value (to blacks and whites) of the concepts being investigated and their definitions are quite unclear (Dreger and Miller, 1968).

Beyond the administration of such tests is the question of interpretation. A task force of the Society for the Psychological Study of Social Issues noted in 1964 that the users of tests must acquire special competence in interpreting test scores of minority group individuals for three reasons. First, reliability of minority test scores is lower because of the minority group member's special sensitivity to test-related behavior alluded to above. Second, the performance against which tests are validated reflect other variables besides abilities (e.g., school grades). Third, the valid interpretation of such test scores (done mostly by whites) requires an understanding of the social and cultural background of the test taker (Fishman, 1964).

Noncognitive Variables

Previously we observed that certain noncognitive variables moderate the relationship between abilities and performance of the disadvantaged (e.g., low fate control and high fear of failure decrease performance of adequately endowed blacks in biracial work teams), as well as the career choices of the disadvantaged (e.g., low self-esteem leads to less striving to fulfill occupational preferences). The problem with many of these measures is in part the same as described above for ability tests, only more so. Reliability and predictive utility are typically lower and interpretation more difficult. Further, self-concept, achievement, etc., are usually measured by self-reports which are firmly entrenched in middle-class, white, academic language which is foreign to the subcultures of the disadvantaged.

A further problem with such variables is their nonobvious nature. A whole gamut of dimensions has been studied in the last ten years in attempts to depict the psychological consequences of living as a minority group member in the United States. Low self-esteem, low fate control, perceptions of persecution and rejection, and an aversion to competition with members of the more affluent white majority have all been examined. Still others are possible but again not obvious. Biographical data have mostly been used to differentiate between the disadvantaged and others. But within the "black," "nonwhite," or even "disadvantaged" are many possible clusters of people with different career-relevant behaviors (e.g., high or low adaptability) that could be tied to characteristic family histories and early educational experiences.

In the future, career-development research should take into account the minority group individual's experience and perspective. In pursuing the vision of wanting more integrated career development based on better understanding of the career choices of the black, the white researcher has usually defined the acceptable goal (integration), the acceptable domain (scientific research), and the acceptable variables (achievement motivation). By disallowing participation in defining goals and defining and conducting research by already "measurement-weary" blacks, we create a situation which is to say the least undesirable. Perhaps we should be less afraid that our goals and their achievement are to be compromised by such participation and see that no real knowledge or its implementation is to be accrued if it is not forthcoming from minority group individuals who have more say and thus faith in the scientific process.

SUMMARY AND IMPLICATIONS

The implications of the composite of personal variables and environmental constraints on the career development of members of minority groups are related both to the historic factors of discrimination and the contemporary influences of American culture and economy. As indicated earlier in discussing career development, we are talking of the preference–choice–attainment process. Noteworthy properties of that process for minority groups include the fact that their preferences are similar to those of whites, but choices are made earlier and are more restricted, and minority group attainments are more limited. In the search for policy-making suggestions for career development, it is safe, although disconcerting, to assume that because of environmental constraints and personal motives, blacks and other minorities will continue to live in segregated communities. The main opportunity for members of those communities lies with the development of a solid economic and occupational base within their own racial or ethnic group, and in their own communities or in areas immediately adjacent to them, i.e., organizations seen by minorities. To develop such an occupational base, minority group members have to be supported by new funding opportunities such as massive Federal guarantees and financial incentives aimed at providing leverage, reducing risk, and thereby allowing financial avenues around debilitating ghetto credit merchants. In addition, such an economic base depends on trained individuals who are encouraged to enter those occupational categories where they are underrepresented with the purpose of developing and staffing the occupations needed within their own community. With their own occupational power base established, integration with white organizations on a base of respected power and skills can be sought and achieved. The efforts to develop such an economic and occupational base can capitalize on the spirits of pride developing within the various minority groups, if they are being directed toward competitive coexistence with the white majority rather than destructive separatism. For example, it might behoove minority groups to develop organizations run by them but gaining more revenue outside the ghetto or running black subsidiaries in black neighborhoods. The first would mean more difficulty getting money to start but large growth potential. The second strategy would bring jobs to and keep money in the ghetto. The additional data supplied by research efforts suggested earlier can be utilized in developing new career opportunities along the above lines. But it requires more than just additional data to expand long-term career-development opportunities. It requires the development of new educational approaches that put the emphasis on community self-sufficiency in all occupations necessary without the immediate worries of white competition. It also requires new methods of venture financing, utilizing funds now available only to established organizations. The financing and counseling has to be provided by the majority power structure without the threat of ownership and control by that majority. This approach utilizes many of the principles previously employed in foreign aid programs in Europe immediately after World War II, and more recently in the development programs operated by the UN in developing countries. In developing economically sound communities, the emphasis should be put on gradual withdrawal of the professional job holders who are not members of the community and their replacement by local career people. This requires a predetermined and announced timetable for developing local career talent and their taking over responsibility and authority. A program in this direction should make it possible to expand the occupational base of minority group members and reduce the present gaps between career preference, choice, and attainment.

REFERENCES

America, R. F., Jr. What do you people want? *Harvard Business Review,* March, 1969.
Anderson, J. A., and Tollman, J. C. Attitudes of dropouts toward school. *Psychological Reports,* 1968, 23, 1142.
Astin, A. W., and Nichols, R. C. Life goals and vocational choice. *Journal of Applied Psychology,* 1964, 48, 50–58.

Ausubel, D. P., and Ausubel, P. Ego development among segregated Negro children. In A. H. Pasoore (ed.), *Education in depressed areas.* N.Y. Bureau of Publications, Teachers College, Columbia University, 1963, 109–141.

Back, K., and Simpson, I. H. The dilemma of the Negro professional. *Journal of Social Issues,* 1964, *20,* 60–70.

Banks, W. M. The changing attitudes of black students. *Personnel and Guidance Journal,* 1970, *48* (9), 713–720.

Battle, E., and Rotter, J. B. Children's feeling of personal control as related to social class and ethnic group. *Journal of Personality,* 1963, *31,* 482–490.

Bayer, A. E., and Boruch, R. F. *The Black student in American colleges.* American Council on Education Research Reports, Washington, D.C., 1969, *4* (2).

Bond, H. M. The Negro scholar and professional in America. *The American Negro Reference Book.* Englewood Cliffs, N.J.: Prentice-Hall, 1966, pp. 548–589.

Bowerman, C. E., and Campbell, E. Q. Aspirations of southern youth: A look at racial comparisons. *Trans-Action,* 1965, *2,* 24.

Brazziel, W. Correlates of southern Negro personality. *Journal of Social Issues,* 1964, *20,* 346–353.

Bruce, M. Factors affecting intelligence test performance of whites and Negroes in the rural south. *Archives of Psychology,* New York, 1940.

Campbell, D. T. Factors relevant to the validity of experiments in social settings. *Psychological Bulletin,* 1957, *54,* 297–312.

Clement, R. E. The historical development of higher education for Negro America. *Journal of Negro Education,* 1966, *35,* 299–305.

Cohen, B. P. Black separation is not the answer. *Stanford Today,* 1968, 8–13.

Coleman, J. S., et al. *Equality of educational opportunity.* Washington, D.C.: Office of Education, 1966.

The Conference Board. *Company experience with Negro Employment,* Studies in Personnel Policy, No. 201, National Industrial Conference Board, Inc., New York, 1966.

Curtis, B. W. *The effects of segregation on the vocational aspirations of Negro students.* Unpublished dissertation, University of Maine, 1968.

Dreger, R. M., and Miller, K. S. Comparative psychological studies of Negroes and Whites in the United States: 1959–1965. *Psychological Bulletin Monograph Supplement,* 1968, 70.

Dunnette, M. D. *The psychology of career choice.* Unpublished manuscript, University of Minnesota, 1968.

Eisenman, R. Reducing prejudice by Negro–White contacts. *Journal of Negro Education,* 1965, *34,* (4), 461–462.

Epps, E. G. Negro academic motivation and performance: An overview. *Journal of Social Issues,* 1969, *XXV* (3), 5–12.

Fichter, J. H. Career preparation and expectations of Negro college seniors. *Journal of Negro Education,* 1966, *35,* 322–335.

Fishman, J. Guidelines for testing minority group children. *Journal of Social Issues,* 1964, *20* (2), 129–145.

Frazier, E. F. *Black bourgeoisie.* New York: Collier, 1962.

Freedman, M. B. *The student and campus climates for learning.* New Dimensions in Higher Education, No. 18, U.S. Department of Health, Education and Welfare, 1967.

Foley, E. P. *The achieving ghetto.* Washington, D.C.: The National Press, Inc., 1968.

Fortune. A special issue on American youth. January, 1969, 66–148.

Glenn, N. D. The relative size of the Negro population and Negro occupational status. *Social Forces,* 1964, *43,* 42–49.

Goeke, J. R., and Weymor, C. S. Barriers to hiring the blacks. *Harvard Business Review,* 1969, 144–152.

Gordon, E. W. *The higher education of the disadvantaged.* New Dimensions in Higher Education, U.S. Department of Health, Education and Welfare, 1967.

Gordon, E. W., and Wilkerson, D. A. *Compensatory education for the disadvantaged: Programs and practices, preschool through college.* New York College Entrance Examination Board, 1966, pp. 122–155.

Gurin, P., Gurin, G., Lao, R. C., and Beattie, M. Internal–external control in the motivational dynamics of Negro youth. *Journal of Social Issues,* 1969, XXV (3), 29–54.

Hare, N. Recent trends in the organizational mobility of Negroes 1930–1960. *Social Forces,* 1965, *44* (2), 166–173.

Haynes, J., Jr. Equal job opportunity: The credibility gap. *Harvard Business Review,* May–June 1968, 113–120.

Hedegard, J. M., and Brown, D. R. Encounters of some negro and white freshmen with a public multi-university. *Journal of Social Issues,* 1969, XXV (3), 131–144.

Holsendolph, E. Middle class blacks are moving off the middle. *Fortune,* December 1969, 90–95.

Howard, D. H. An exploratory study of attitudes of Negro professionals toward competition with Whites. *Social Forces,* 1966, *45* (1), 20–27.

Hoyle, K. Job losers, leavers and entrants—a report on the unemployed. *Monthly Labor Review,* April 1969, 24–29.

Hunt, D. E., and Hardt, R. H. The effect of upward bound programs on the attitudes, motivation and academic achievement of Negro students. *Journal of Social Issues,* 1969, XXV (3), 117–130.

Jaffe, A. J., Adams, W., and Meyers, S. G. *Ethnic higher education—Negro colleges in the 1960's.* New York: Research Report, Columbia University, 1966.

Jencks, C., and Riesman, D. The American Negro college. *Harvard Educational Review,* 1967, 37, 3–60.

Jensen, A. R. How much can we boost I.Q. and scholastic achievement? *Harvard Educational Review,* 1969, 1–123.

Katz, I. A critique of personality approaches to Negro performance with research suggestions. *Journal of Social Issues,* 1969, XXV (3), 13–28.

Katz, I. Review of evidence relating to effects of desegregation on the intellectual performance of Negroes. *American Psychologist,* 1964, *19,* 381–399.

Katz, I., and Greenbaum, C. Effects of anxiety, threat and racial environment on task performance of Negro college students. *Journal of Abnormal and Social Psychology,* 1963, *66,* 562–567.

Katz, I., Roberts, S. O., and Robinson, J. M. Effects of task difficulty, race of administrator, and instructions on digit-symbol performance of Negroes. *Journal of Personality and Social Psychology,* 1965, 2, 53–59.

Katz, I. The socialization of academic motivation in minority group children. In D. Levine (ed.), *Nebraska symposium on motivation, 1967.* Lincoln, Neb.: University of Nebraska Press, 1967, pp. 133–191.

Katz, J. M. *The educational Shibboleth: Equality of opportunity in a democratic institution, the public junior college.* Unpublished dissertation, University of California, 1967.

Kennedy, R. F. Policies to combat Negro poverty. In B. J. Berry and J. Meltzer, *Goals for urban America.* Englewood Cliffs, N.J.: Prentice-Hall, 1967.

Klineberg, O. Negro–white differences in intelligence test performance. A new look at an old problem. *American Psychologist,* 1963, *18,* 198–203.

Korman, A. K. Self-esteem as a moderator in vocational choice: Replications and extensions. *Journal of Applied Psychology,* 1969, 53, 188–192.

Kuvlesky, W. P., and Ohlendorf, G. W. A rural–urban comparison of the occupational status orientation of Negro boys. *Rural Sociology,* 1963, *33,* 141–152.

Lee, E. S. Negro intelligence and selective migration: A Philadelphia test of Klineberg's hypothesis. *American Social Review,* 1951, *61,* 227–233.

Licherson, S., and Fugnett, G. V. Negro–white occupational differences in the absence of discrimination. *American Journal of Sociology*, 1967, *73* (2), 188–200.

Littig, L. W. *A pilot study of personality factors related to occupational aspirations of Negro college students*. Final report on Vocational and Technical Education Contract Number 06-6-85-003, Howard University, 1967.

Littig, L. W. Negro personality correlates of aspiration to traditionally open and closed occupations. *Journal of Negro Education*, 1968, *37* (1), 31–36.

McGurk, F. C. J. *Comparisons of the performance of Negro and white high school seniors on cultural and noncultural test questions*. Washington, D.C.: Catholic University Press, 1951.

McPartland, J. The relative influence of school and of class desegregation on the academic achievement of ninth grade Negro students. *Journal of Social Issues*, 1969, *XXV* (3), 93–102.

McWhirt, R. A. *The effects of desegregation on prejudice, academic aspirations, and the self-concept of tenth grade students*. Unpublished dissertation, University of California, 1967.

Norman, R. D., and Bessemer, D. W. Job preferences and preference shifts as a function of job information, familiarity and prestige level. *Journal of Applied Psychology*, 1968, *52*, 280–285.

Nugent, F. A. Relationship of Kuder preference record verification scores to adjustment: Implications for vocational development theory. *Journal of Applied Psychology*, 1968, *52*, 429–431.

Proctor, S. A. Reversing the spiral toward futility. *Personnel and Guidance Journal*. 1970, *48* (9), 707–712.

Reiss, A. J., Jr., and Rhodes, A. L. Are educational norms and goals of conforming, truant and delinquent adolescents influenced by group position in American society? *Journal of Negro Education*, 1959, *28*, 252–267.

Rose, A. M. Graduate training for the "culturally deprived." *Sociology of Education*, 1966, *39*, 201–208.

Rosenthal, R. On the social psychology of the psychological experiment. The experimenter's hypothesis as an unintended determinant of experimental results. *American Scientist*, 1963, 268–283.

CHAPTER FOUR

Behavior Change: Strategies for Human Development Among Disadvantaged Minorities

Lowell W. Hellervik

INTRODUCTION BY THE EDITORS

Once individuals have been recruited and selected for the organization, the next important step is to help them translate their abilities into skills which contribute to the organization's goals. Thus, a set of procedures (e.g., training and development) is required to enable newly hired individuals to develop their skills in ways which are most effective for the particular organization. When applied to minority workers, the organization must learn to provide training which is relevant both to the needs of the worker and to his or her willingness to make meaningful contributions to the organization's objectives. Hellervik notes how "behavior change" is necessary for both the individuals and the organizations. This chapter suggests several innovative methods of behavior change, which, if adopted, would have beneficial impacts upon both disadvantaged individuals and on the organization.

The chapter begins with a brief review of training practices and research on current programs to integrate minority members. In general, training of the disadvantaged falls into the three categories of basic remedial education, skill training, and attitude development. Remedial training is of the traditional classroom type. Skill training is of the "vestibule" type, which is relatively successful in imparting the skills required to do the job. Most attempts to develop job-relevant attitudes have met with little success. Counseling programs are frequently designed to provide the employee with someone to rely upon for employment or personal problems. Counselors have also functioned as organizational ombudsmen—an advocate of the employee or a go-between to reduce organizational constraints. Buddy systems are similar programs usually involving a person who works in the same area.

Available training literature reveals that traditional hard-core training programs fail to cope with the needs and to develop the potential capabilities of disadvantaged workers. Instead of developing more relevant methodologies to work with disadvantaged clients, it appears these programs do little more than simply provide a man with a job. Often they neglect the worker's skill deficiencies, overlook inappropriate work attitudes, and fail to recognize competing forces which result in job termination and organizational disruption. For example, given the available evidence showing the negative influences of minority self attitudes, it is surprising that so few of the programs contain elements which provide the worker with success experiences prior to his beginning a new job.

Most studies show that with some training the disadvantaged worker is generally capable of performing the specific tasks which are required by the job. However, more basic problems are ignored by traditional training programs. For example, there can be important differences in work-related expectations about attendance, tardiness, and other organizational mores. Recent research demonstrates that minority workers do know what is appropriate work behavior, i.e., minority workers do know what is expected of them. Yet, in spite of expressed intentions to maintain standard work habits, minority workers are often prone to be late or miss work or to drop out of training programs. Hellervik proposes that the organization can benefit by finding other methods of helping disadvantaged workers to control and direct their own behavior to accomplish ends which they seek and value. More recently, a substantial number of managers have learned the value of training programs which capitalize on the latent skills of the disadvantaged worker and, at the same time, help him develop work habits which allow him to develop his skills on the job. The remainder of the chapter focuses upon a few innovative approaches to accomplish these ends.

Hellervik's review of the field of behavior modification is an application of B. F. Skinner's operant conditioning principles, which until lately have been ignored in the industrial world. The goal of operant conditioning is the control or shaping of behavior. The basic tenet of the approach holds that a person's behavior is largely governed by the anticipated or experienced consequences of his behavior. Behavior is changed or shaped by rewarding successive approximations of the behavior which is desired. It is important to note that rewards are obtained before perfect work habits are established, e.g., before the worker shows that he can come to work on time every day. In contrast, traditional programs do not offer the reward until the desired work habits are firmly established. Unfortunately, termination of employment usually occurs prior to the perfection of desired work habits. The techniques of behavior modification require careful charting of the behavior and setting of goals by means of conferences between the supervisor and worker. Such programs provide concrete methods of dealing with problems which were previously a source of failure and frustration to supervisors of disadvantaged workers.

Hellervik discusses a variety of possible rewards and some problems which may arise. Money, praise, and tokens are proposed as rewards. If tokens are used, they must be immediately and conveniently exchangeable for a large variety of rewards that may be chosen by the recipient—thus providing the advantage of an individualized incentive plan. Management and employee committees can determine attractive rewards.

There are several advantages to this approach. The use of behavior-change models helps the disadvantaged worker to begin the job faster. New behaviors are also more easily transferred to the job situation. The programs also are more acceptable and involving for front-line supervisors, because they reduce feelings of helplessness and impotence. Hellervik suggests a modification of the buddy system using film clips and videotaped presentations of a co-worker being rewarded for doing what is desired of him. Hellervik hypothesizes that the technique will prove effective to the extent that there are racial and socioeconomic similarities in the observer and the worker in the film. Research is also reviewed which demonstrates the usefulness of lay counselors who are similar to the worker in race and socioeconomic status to augment the above programs.

Last, Hellervik recommends the use of a psychologist as a consultant to aid in the design, implementation, and follow-up of such training programs.

Effective organizational functioning demands members who have skills and abilities that *can* contribute toward the accomplishment of the organization's goals. Further, they must be *willing* to contribute those skills and abilities. Almost always, however, a process of learning is required that enables individuals to contribute their skills in the most effective way for a particular organization. Individuals must learn specific tasks and roles to promote a smoothly functioning, well-integrated, and efficient organization. The organization, too, must learn how to respond to the many needs of its individual members to facilitate the willingness of those members to contribute to organizational objectives.

Effective organizational functioning, then, requires the establishment of a balance, or equilibrium, between individual employees and the formal organization (Bennis, 1966). Each contributes something to the other and, in turn, receives something in exchange for what was contributed. If our society were static, the "fairness" of the exchange might have been discovered long ago, establishing a more nearly permanent equilibrium. However, we live in a dynamic society where change is a fundamental fact of life. The change with which we are confronted as a society has contributed toward disequilibrium within many of our organizations.

A state of equilibrium between many individuals and organizations has been severely disrupted by the development of a large body of relatively un-skilled persons in urban centers. Such persons often lack the skills necessary to contribute to organizations. Conversely, the contributions of organizations to such individuals have often not been sufficient to integrate them effectively into the organization. To move toward restoration of equilibrium, innovative methods must be attempted that will successfully "train" these disadvantaged individuals in skills needed to contribute toward organizational goals. Equally innovative methods must "train" organizations to contribute more effectively toward the needs of the disadvantaged.

Behavior change, then, is necessary for both individuals and organizations if we are to move toward equilibrium. This chapter is designed to suggest several methods of behavior change which would, if implemented by organizational administrators, have impact on both disadvantaged individuals and on their organizations.

THE PROBLEM

As business became responsive to urban problems in the 1960s, it became clear that one of the major contributions business could make toward the solution of these problems was to hire disadvantaged minority persons. The provision of jobs for disadvantaged minorities in urban areas seemed likely to be a more potent force for social welfare than programs to improve housing, medical care, education, transportation, or welfare. Patterns of overt and covert discrimination, inadequate education, and lack of industrial experience had previously prevented such people from qualifying for employment. To hire the disadvantaged, then, meant relaxing the organization's "normal" standards.

Initial "hard-core" hiring programs, however, were often not particularly successful. Organizations found that it was not enough simply to provide a man with a job. An interlocking network of skill deficiencies, inappropriate attitudes, and competing inducements often contributed toward their voluntary or involuntary termination of work or toward behavior that was somehow disruptive to the organization.

Simultaneously, however, increasing numbers of management people were coming to agree that companies *do* have a responsibility to hire and train minorities (Goeke and Weymar, 1969). This increasing commitment, then, counterbalanced some of the initial discouragements and cynicism resulting when the outcomes of early hiring programs were less favorable than expected. Felt social concern, a desire to keep compliance officers from the door, and reimbursement through governmental agencies for training the disadvantaged, combined to yield a plethora of programs designed to adapt the organization to the disadvantaged and to change the behavior of the disadvantaged.

For organizations, then, the employment of such minority groups typically involves adaptations of standard operating procedures to enable the organization to capitalize fully on the latent abilities of these new employees. The adaptations themselves infer that organizations are changing as they attempt to cope with the problems inherent in the new labor force. Perhaps even greater emphasis, however, has been placed on changing the behavior of members of the disadvantaged minorities—to help them acquire the skills and behaviors that will enable them to be contributing members of the organization.

Survey of Training Practices

A survey of existing practices serves as a focus for discussion of both needs of the disadvantaged minority person (as determined by the training programs) and needs of the organization to deal more effectively with him. Most training efforts to date have fallen into three areas for the individual disadvantaged: (1) basic, remedial education; (2) skill training; (3) attitude development.

Remedial education has typically been designed to upgrade basic skills in reading, arithmetic, and any other area specifically called for in the intended job. A certain variation in these attempts is apparent. Some have tried for reading and/or arithmetic improvement in two weeks, while others have carried on for a year or more. Some programs have been conducted "in-house"; others have used community schools and other agencies. Some have used programmed learning technology; others have concentrated on more traditional approaches. Almost all, however, have tied themselves to "teaching" rather than "student learning" by setting time limits on courses that all disadvantaged must pursue. Thus, instead of concerning themselves with developing creative methodologies that would result in behavior change (learning) on the part of students, trainers have tended instead simply to cover material they felt the students should know.

In terms of skill training the variation in programs is more easily connected with the particular skill being taught. Typically a "vestibule" training paradigm has been used, where the trainee is given instruction and guided experience at the tasks he will be required to perform on the job. This training has occurred in technical schools or in annexes near the area where the individuals will ultimately be working. Since most jobs offered have been entry-level positions, the task requirements have usually been relatively limited and have not required extensive training periods. Still, according to Johnson (1969) instructors in such training programs report that it may take two or three times longer than normal to cover material with the hard-core. His most important rule for success is to "be specific," to stay away from abstractions. The results of most programs, however, have indicated that the disadvantaged *can* do the work when placed on the job. Representative of these findings is Hellervik's (1969), where only 2 percent of all terminations occurred because of lack of ability to do the work. Apparently the training programs are "doing the job" in this domain, though very few studies have used control groups placed on the job without skills training. Successful performance of trainees, then, can't necessarily be attributed to training.

It is the third area—"attitude development"—that has been most troublesome, least understood, and most frustrating. These programs (Doeringer, 1969) have proceeded under the assumption that almost all recruits have been part of a subculture where steady employment has not been the usual pattern. There-fore, they are presumably unaware of the expectations of employers and do not know what specific job behaviors and attitudes are required. While this author questions that point of view, let us for the moment accept it. Programs directed toward attitude change or toward job behavior change have been quite diverse and too often lacking in clearly specified objectives. One large Eastern manu-facturer, for example, aimed its training at teaching job skills as well as "social-ization and citizenship abilities." This course, then, included such subjects as the black man's contribution to American history. Other programs have included more extensive discussion of problems relating to all minority groups, in the hope that the example of other minorities successfully coping with their status would better enable blacks to do so.

Some companies have used group methods in attempting to assimilate the disadvantaged. Specific techniques have varied from simply group orientations to the company and plant, to quasi-encounter groups. Johnson (1969) reports, "It is clear that the trainees in general do not enjoy sensitivity training. . . . They go along with the sensitivity sessions, and may pretend to see the light in vary-ing degrees, but it is doubtful that such training is achieving much of the desired effect among the hard-core." Most group sessions, however, have dealt with the demands of the work situation. Discussions, then, revolved around such issues as absenteeism, discipline, tardiness, job responsibility, and the psychological aspects of working in a particular setting. In the latter case, role-playing tech-niques have been used to desensitize the disadvantaged to the demands of foremen or supervisors by explaining, then playing out, the dynamics of a typical work situation.

Organizations have not placed the onus for change entirely on the indi-vidual. Most organizations have undertaken programs to help themselves adapt to the disadvantaged. Perhaps the most common approach has been an "aware-ness" program of some sort ("Awareness Training," 1968). Implicit in this strategy has been the belief that greater insight into the nature of disadvantaged persons would develop improved skill in dealing with them. In many instances such programs have stressed the socioeconomic factors responsible for molding the disadvantaged person's make-up. To build respect for the particular minority group, its heritage and contributions to our society have been explained.

Often, some form of "perception" training is a part of such programs. The confusion, bewilderment, and uncertainty of the disadvantaged as they enter employment may be pointed out by group exercises, discussions, or mechanical means as multifaceted glasses. Again, the objective is to increase understanding and insight into the "life space" of the disadvantaged which presumably results in greater flexibility in the organization's willingness and capability for adapting to previously unemployable persons.

Aside from "insight" strategies and mechanical support (such as reimburs-ing work-group leaders for the period of time judged reasonable for a man to become fully productive), coping strategies seem relatively weak and haphazard. Even mechanical support is often not sufficient to alleviate pressure on the first-line supervisor, the major point of contact between the organization and the unemployable. The training manager, the supervisor's supervisor, and the organization in general seem unable to answer the conscientious supervisor's plea for help in dealing with specific persons who are not "with the program." Further, the awareness sessions themselves often had unexpected side effects. In their eagerness to do their part, some supervisors may have shown too much empathy (Johnson, 1969). Once they understood the background of the trainee, some supervisors relaxed performance standards too much. In turn, this led to fear of establishing double standards. Training programs, then, sometimes resulted in greater organizational flexibility but the specific outcomes were relatively uncontrolled, and virtually no help was available to supervisors who needed help on specific problem cases.

Many organizations have focused on a "counseling" program as a means of assisting the man with problems that cut across training programs, job situations, and personal difficulties (Johnson, 1969). In these programs, each new employee has been assigned a counselor who has been designated as the person the employee should turn to whenever he had a problem in the organization or in his personal life. Most counselors have been selected on the basis of their ability to understand the employee's problems and identify with him; if that person was of the same minority group as the employee, so much the better. However, a quality of empathy has been paramount in the selection of counselors. Very few counselors have been selected on the basis of professional counseling qualifications; instead, they have been chosen from within the company, usually at a supervisory or management level. It is not surprising, then, that the counselor's role has typically been nonpsychologically oriented. Examples of problems counselors have dealt with are ensuring that employees have alarm clocks, know the bus routes, and understand time-clock procedures.

At a somewhat more complex level, they have functioned as organizational ombudsmen. In this role, they have functioned as the individual's advocate, helping him achieve his goals where they might otherwise have been ignored or blocked by organizational constraints. On the other hand, they have also served as interpreters of organizational policies, practices, and procedures to the hard-core. In addition, such counselors have given employees guidance in personal affairs such as the use of credit, handling of garnishments, and dealing with legal problems. Regrettably, virtually no data are available on the effectiveness of different counselors, different counseling styles, or counselor–client interaction. In almost all cases the counselor has been from the same minority group as the new employee.

A "buddy system" is a widely used strategy for facilitating assimilation into the organization. The new employee is assigned to a "buddy," usually an experienced worker in the same area. In some respects this approach is similar to a counseling program. However, the "buddy" is better able to show the new employee "the ropes" of working in that area day by day. He can have lunch with him, help him perform his task, show him to the rest rooms, and otherwise help him feel comfortable in his new work environment.

This overview of present training practices has been general and brief. No attempt has been made to describe specific programs, and only the general trends in training have been explicated. For the reader interested in more detail, Doeringer's (1969) book provides an excellent beginning.

Training Needs

Although much has been said about blacks low self-esteem and confused self-identity (see "Cultural and Personality Factors in Minority Group Behavior," this volume), very little effort has been made in training programs to date to approach this problem directly. Instead, the emphasis has been on preparing blacks to do a job that will provide them with a success experience. This seems to make good sense. Success experiences can probably do far more than therapy to enhance one's self-esteem. The major need, then, is to ensure that success experiences *do,* indeed, occur (for *both* the disadvantaged *and* the organization) rather than shifting the thrust of training toward a direct therapeutic assault on low self-esteem. Further, recent evidence suggests that low self-esteem is not uniformly possessed by the disadvantaged (Hellervik, 1969). That is, many disadvantaged do not suffer from a chronic lack of self-esteem.

Most studies have shown the disadvantaged to be capable of performing the tasks involved with their job. The more basic problems, then, are associated with their tendency to violate organizational expectations in the realm of attendance, tardiness, and organizational mores. Some have postulated that the disadvantaged don't know what is expected of them. That is, they do not understand that their employers expect them to come to work consistently, to be on time, and to exhibit "appropriate" work behavior. However, attitude questionnaire results do not seem to substantiate this hypothesis (Kirchner and Lucas, 1969). If anything, in fact, poorer performers and more greatly disadvantaged persons may be more likely than others to express "establishment" attitudes about the importance of "correct" work behavior (Hellervik, 1969). Despite appropriateness of the attitudes and the intentions they express, they are often prone to miss work, drop out of training programs or employment, and generally behave in ways opposed to their stated attitudes. Apparently, then, the problem is one of controlling and directing their own behavior to accomplish the ends that they themselves say they seek and value.

Despite the vigor with which many organizations have thrown themselves into training the hard-core, and the generally encouraging results made public, there are signs that the training programs have not been as successful as executives had originally hoped. The published data and press releases may not accurately represent management's perceptions of the success or failure of training programs for the disadvantaged. Cohn (1970), a management consultant in urban affairs programs, recently completed a survey suggesting that businesses' willingness to support such programs is waning, and that current activities are under close scrutiny. He listed four reasons for the decline:

1. Public and governmental pressures to develop such programs have diminished.
2. Urban programs have proved more costly than anticipated.
3. Such programs require more skills than many companies realized at the start.
4. Some programs have affected the internal life of large companies in unexpected—and often unwelcome—ways.

Cohn goes on to say, "A dozen or so companies have pulled out of urban affairs completely; others are saying that they cannot handle training the hard-core, that perhaps it takes professionals with skills business doesn't have."

This survey suggests that organizational decision makers question whether the urban affairs programs are "worth their salt," despite their publicity-oriented press clippings. Present cost cutting in training budgets certainly contributes, but decision makers at the top have probably tended to be more "committed" to the programs than "convinced" that the programs were accomplishing their objectives. If executives had better evidence of success, the costs would undoubtedly not seem so great. If this is true, it is incumbent upon behavioral scientists to find more effective and/or less expensive means of training the disadvantaged.

Some might argue that attempts to change individuals are less important than changing the behavior of the organization. Regardless of the merits of that argument, it seems clear that—from a practical point of view—the larger degree of adaptation will have to occur in those disadvantaged who are under consideration for organizational membership. Practically speaking, they will have to learn to "live by the rules" of the majority to some extent. However, the organization's attempts to facilitate behavior change in the disadvantaged actually means that the organization is adapting itself as well (though perhaps it could do more). The process of accommodation between organization and individual is greatly furthered by the organization's efforts to facilitate behavior change in the individual.

In integrating organizations, the most attention to date has been given to the disadvantaged hard-core. Increasingly, efforts at upgrading employees are being made, and educated minorities are being hired to hold professional, technical, and managerial positions. Integrating talented minorities into the organization spotlights problems worthy of discussion, also. However, the difficulties organizations have encountered in dealing effectively with the hard-core suggest the need to devote the major portion of this chapter to that problem.

Because of the critical importance of developing and maintaining appropriate work habits such as attendance and punctuality, and of developing and maintaining a measure of self-discipline—accepting supervisory direction, obeying work rules, etc.—the largest portion of the remainder of the chapter will be directed toward discussing those aspects of behavior change, particularly in the hard-core. (Notice, too, the emphasis here is on behavior rather than attitudes.)

Although job-skill acquisition is also important and undoubtedly feeds into the acquisition of appropriate work habits, such skill attainments, at best, are a necessary but not sufficient condition for "correct" work behavior. The same is true of basic education. Except in cases where remedial training is necessary to perform a specific task (such as observing safety signs), basic education is largely related to the individual's longer-range promotability. Too often, however, a man's basic work record interferes with his potential for promotion long before the question of his general ability to learn higher-level jobs comes up. Thus, the most critical and most vexing problem for behavioral scientists is to ensure success experiences by improved work habits and behavior.

The question, then, is "How?" How does an organizational management team go about fulfilling a social obligation that it feels with an increasing sense of urgency (according to surveys quoted earlier) and presumed frustration over cost-benefit factors? What strategies might be pursued to adapt effectively to minority problems without seriously jeopardizing competitiveness in the marketplace? What behavior-change methods are most efficient? How might they be applied? These are the kinds of questions that will be dealt with in the remainder of the chapter.

STRATEGIES FOR IMPROVED BEHAVIOR-CHANGE EFFORTS

The field of behavior modification seems to hold considerable promise for contributing to the solution of adaptation problems. B. F. Skinner's laboratory work on operant conditioning principles provided the impetus for behavioral scientists to begin applying these principles to problems of behavior change. The industrial world has largely ignored the remarkable work being done in this area. This isn't surprising, however. Even in the fields of counseling and psychotherapy, where the application of learning theory did have specifiable implications, these implications were largely ignored. By 1966, however, C. H. Patterson was able to say that behavior modifiers were taking on the characteristics of a new "school" of counseling and psychotherapy, having even begun publication of their own journal. It is now time for business organizations to begin the systematic investigation of how operant techniques can be applied in their settings.

Operant methodologies stress the importance of carefully observing the relationship between what a person does in a particular circumstance and what happens to him immediately following his act in that circumstance. Fundamentally, operant conditioning principles center around these facts: (1) behaviors (or actions) that lead to reward or the removal of pain or discomfort are strengthened—made more likely to occur again in similar circumstances in the future; (2) behaviors that lead to pain, discomfort, or loss of rewards are weakened—made less likely to occur again in the future. Essentially a person's behavior is influenced by its consequences.

Operant methodology facilitates precision in a number of ways. Since one of these ways is the intensive study of individual subjects, its general approach to studying behavior can potentially yield an answer to the oft-asked supervisory question, "What can be done about Jones?" With close observation and firm experimental control the subject tends to behave quite predictably from observation to observation. The recording of this behavior provides a stable "baseline" condition which serves as an anchoring point for the detection of behavior change when the treatment variable is presented. This approach eliminates one of the most difficult and damaging aspects of traditional psychological studies, that of intersubject variability, which enervates the power of a statistical study to make predictions about a specific individual (Honig, 1966).

Much of the initial thrust of behavior modifiers was directed toward challenging therapists who espoused a medical model of maladaptiveness. According to such therapists, "mental illness" is a viable concept, with illnesses attributable to dysfunctioning of elaborate, abstract psychodynamic constructs (such as the ego, aggression, hostility, etc.). Such constructs were developed as abstractions based on specific behaviors, because the constructs were assumed to have greater power for explaining and predicting behavior. According to Bandura (1969), however, "The preoccupation with internal psychic agents— energized traits—has been largely responsible for the limited progress in development of empirically sound principles of human behavior."

Critics of the medical model have been especially reproving with regard to the circularity of that model. Abstract "disease" entities are inferred from samples of behavior. However, these psychic abstractions are not only given existence and substance independent of the "symptomatic" behavior from which they were inferred. The abstractions are then used as an *explanation* of the basic behavioral referents observed, and a basic psychopathology is presumed to underlie the behavior. In behavior modification terms, however, the symptoms *are* the "illllness." The symptoms of maladaptive behavior are the loci of treatment, rather than simply being representative of some unconscious conflict or complex that must be worked through and resolved. In much the same way, behavioral modifiers would be more concerned about a disadvantaged person's present behavior pattern (symptoms) than the origins of the behavior. Behavior that departs widely from social norms or is harmful to the individual is simply a result of inadequate reinforcement history and should be viewed as learned behavior. Therefore, behavior modifiers work on specific behavior where relearning is needed—"symptoms"—rather than concerning themselves with the "dynamics" of a case.

Application of learning-theory principles to the change of human behavior has made great progress in the past several years. A variety of techniques is now available for treating problems of considerable diversity—desensitization, counterconditioning, conditioned aversion, vicarious conditioning, etc. Many hospitals have established wards where learning principles are rigorously enforced in treatment. "Token" economies have been established in many hospitals which require patients to "earn" their rewards or reinforcers (whatever they may be) by behaving appropriately. Instead of nurses dressing patients, the patients are required to dress themselves and earn tokens that can be exchanged for cigarettes, candy, and other valued commodities at the ward "store." Some hospitals attach devices to water fountains, candy machines, etc. To require tokens for even the basics, such as a drink of water, provides considerable reinforcement power for the staff through the tokens.

Increasingly, application of these techniques is being extended beyond the medical setting into more normal realms of behavior. Counseling psychologists have used such techniques in school settings to shape vocational information-seeking behavior (Krumboltz and Thoresen, 1964) as well as increased ability to make decisions (Ryan and Krumboltz, 1964). Educators are applying its principles in the classroom (Neisworth, Deno, and Jenkins, 1969). Very little has apparently been done, however, to utilize such procedures in industrial settings, despite the potential that seems to exist for changing behavior through their use.

Principles of Behavior Modification

The basic process involved in operant conditioning is that of shaping the desired behavior. Shaping is accomplished through the principles of reinforcing successive approximations to the goal, thereby eventually bringing about the desired behavior. This infers that the acquisition of the desired response class is a gradual process beginning with the reinforcement of even minimal evidence of behavior in that response class. As reinforcements are administered, however, the criteria for reinforcement are successively increased until the response class is firmly established in the subject's behavioral repertoire. This procedure is quite distinct from early experiments where reinforcement was made available only after successful *completion* of a goal-oriented task, such as in Thorndike's puzzle boxes.

The latter procedure is the one typically employed in organizational settings. An employee is not considered a "steady" employee (and therefore is not eligible for reinforcement) until he has clearly demonstrated his capability for being at work on time, every day. In essence, then, no reinforcement is presented until the goal—"perfect" work habits—is attained. In the case of the disadvantaged employee, however, he has typically not held a permanent job, and he is not accustomed to being at a certain place at a specified time. His initial attempts to get to work on time every day, then, should probably be considered as approximations to the eventual goal. Following the shaping strategy, the behavior requirements should be somewhat stiffer each week in order for the individual to receive reinforcements. Many supervisors, in their desire to help solve urban problems and to carry out company policy have—especially at the urging of counselors—been willing to overlook some instances of inappropriate work behavior. However, without the systematic approach to behavior provided by operant methodology, their efforts have had only haphazard success. This, too, accounts for much of the ambiguity, uncertainty, general confusion, and anxiety evident in supervisors who rightly want to know "What am I supposed to do with these guys?" This approach, however, argues strongly for adopting an individual methodology. It means careful recording and charting of individual behavior over time to know as accurately as possible where the individual is in the shaping procedure.

There is nothing in this procedure that is occult or mystical. Debates continue to rage on over the question of whether or not subjects of operant methodology are or need to be "aware" of the reinforcement contingencies involved with the procedure. Most behavior modifiers, however, see the issue of awareness as interesting but irrelevant and simply as the remains of the medical model. The important dimensions are the observable behavior—consequence linkages in a given situation without regard to whether or not the individual is "aware" of what happens. Carrying this argument one step further, then, it may be entirely appropriate for the dispenser of reinforcement—in this case the supervisor or counselor—to sit down in a goal-planning session with the individual and set goals for each succeeding week, month, and year. His awareness of the "standard" required to receive reinforcement will usually help speed his responses in that direction.

One side problem or benefit to this approach is the necessity that the supervisor speak in specific behavioral terms. It isn't enough for him to say, "You've got to shape up, man!" He must be specific about the behavioral referents that have led him to his abstract inferences about the individual being "hostile," "lazy," or "indifferent." Then, he must skillfully select the behaviors judged least painfully changed by the individual and begin the elimination of that behavior, while rewording initial attempts at the desired behavioral response class. Failure to receive any reinforcement in early attempts to meet the behavioral expectations could easily impel the individual "back to the streets." The process, then, requires analytical thought and a considerable level of sensitivity to the timing, quantity, and type of reinforcers offered by the supervisor.

In striving to instil a "good attitude" in a newly hired employee, this strategy would first call for identifying those behaviors that cause the supervisor to think the employee has a "good," "indifferent," or "bad" attitude. For purposes of simplicity, let us assume that two behavioral incidents are in evidence that suggest the employee has a "bad attitude." First, she comes late to work, and second, she consistently tarries too long on her coffee break. During a goal-setting session with a nonaccusatory psychological climate, the supervisor should discuss the problem with the employee to be certain there are no obvious problems involved such as lack of an alarm clock. Given that no such problems exist, the supervisor should determine which of the two problems is easier to correct and concentrate on that problem until it is solved. In our example, the supervisor may diagnose the "late from coffee break" behavior as being easier to change (though he may discuss both problems with her). Together, the supervisor and employee should develop charts to record each day's behavior pattern—one might be maintained by each of them. At this point, the supervisor must be especially alert to the employee's "on-time" behavior and reward it appropriately, until the behavior is firmly part of the employee's work habits. At that point, a similar plan should be pursued with the remaining behavior problem.

Reinforcers

One of the most difficult questions, strangely enough, would seem to be the question of the reinforcer. What is rewarding to the newly hired disadvantaged employee? Even more difficult, what reinforcers are available within the organization that are more attractive than what he might have available on the streets? Such competing inducements (drinking wine, gambling, doing nothing, chasing girls, etc.—all financed by "hustling" of some kind) are probably one of the major reasons for high termination rates among the "hard-core" disadvantaged. Other, *less* "hard-core" disadvantaged would not look at such inducements as "competing" with conventional family life and responsibility. Thus, reinforcers must be found that will generalize to most people and most situations if they are to be practical for organizations to implement.

In the search for generalized reinforcers, money certainly has to be high on the list. However, many hard-core are able to make more money on a "game" or hustling activity than on the job. Also, union contracts and rigid organizational pay practices tend to interfere with money's potential as a reinforcer. In fact, reinforcement given in the form of pay on a fixed schedule, e.g., every Friday (or whichever day or week is applicable) is self-defeating, as any foreman intuitively knows. Attendance on the day of pay is very high, but the following two days attendance typically drops sharply, improving again until the next pay day. This routine agrees fairly well with laboratory findings on fixed-interval reinforcement schedules. More flexibility in organizational dispensation of money as a reinforcer for shaping appropriate work behavior seems necessary. Various schedules of reinforcement can be tried, but it would certainly seem that either varying the time interval between payment or varying the amounts of payment would lend considerable power compared to present practices.

Praise as a generalized reinforcer is important, too, but it is fraught with difficulty. The initial suspicion and distrust with which minority people enter the work force cause verbal recognition to be rejected. Also, the source of praise is crucially important. If the person's peer group rejects him because he was praised by a nonvalued supervisor, the praise was probably worse than nothing. Other generalized reinforcers, such as fringe benefits, status, friendship, completion of activity, achievement, energy expenditure, skill acquisition, and personal growth have their limitations, too. What is needed, then, is a careful analysis of the available organizational reinforcers and their potential reinforcement power for each individual.

One solution to this problem of individual differences in preferences has been the development of a medium of exchange—a token—used throughout a given group. This in turn alleviates concern about reinforcer satiation, since the tokens can be exchanged for a wide variety of reinforcing privileges and commodities. A token refers to any unit of exchange with which the individual may purchase available rewards. Tokens function like money in that their value is determined by their purchasing power, and the choice of purchase is determined by the purchaser. In a "token economy" the tokens become the "reinforcement" or immediate consequence of a performance.

Tokens must be immediately and conveniently exchangeable for the available rewards. These rewards could be determined by employee committees working in conjunction with management. The immediate rewards available through such a system could easily have positive effects on the individual's future performance by increasing his expectancy of success.

Further, the frequent dispensing of tokens (rewards) should have definite impact in the realm of social-exchange theory. Thibaut and Kelley (1959) and others have shown that one who provides positive outcomes tends to be valued and liked and that greater positive rewards tend to be given to those one likes. If the granting of tokens can break the cycle of mistrust and dislike, then, it is conceivable that a healthier, more constructive "exchange" between the individual and the organization could be initiated that would yield successively more favorable outcomes for each. Involving the disadvantaged in determining which rewards should "back up" the tokens should have further impact in developing a notion of fair exchange between them and the organization.

The use of token economies in schools and hospitals is no longer rare. The possibility of establishing token economies within business organizations is intriguing but relatively untried. Since a token economy is modeled after life *outside* hospitals, it is ironic that the major impetus for its use has come from *within* hospitals rather than from within "outside" organizations. Again, of course, one of the problems is that of dealing with organizational strictures and the potential charges of "unfairness" in dispensing such reinforcers to the disadvantaged only. It might ultimately be possible to allocate resources to "back up" the tokens for *all* employees. For example, tokens can be used to buy privileges as well as commodities. Thus, as a solution to the absentee problem, organizations might grant days off as a privilege to be purchased with tokens. The manageability of scheduled time-off under such circumstances should be a great improvement over present conditions of high, unpredictable absenteeism, and the attractiveness of this privilege should prove to be a significant incentive to employees. Another possibility, more easily implemented, might be the establishment of a token economy among the employees in pre-employment training. This would suggest a base rate of pay, with tokens (backed by significant added money) to be earned for successive approximations to desired work behavior.

Training periods, too, should place emphasis on specific work habit objectives, rather than simply holding men in training for four weeks and, if they then can perform the tasks, put them on the job. Individualized development strategies should be employed now, before businesses' training efforts get locked into the "time-on-program" pattern that educational institutions have historically been in. This suggests an indefinite probationary period with the trainee moving to the job *only* when he has reached all task *and* behavior objectives.

An approach similar to Neisworth, Deno, and Jenkins's (1969) contingency classroom management deserves application to the business setting. Their handbook explains in layman's terms how learning theory can be applied to controlling both individual and group classroom behavior. Drawing from the work of Lindsley and Homme they explain their approach in terms of "consequences" of behavior (thereby nicely avoiding getting tangled up with the semantics of positive reinforcement, punishment, and other technical terms). They then outline a basic procedure to be followed in "motivating" and directing the behavior of students.

This basic procedure includes four steps. *First,* a behavior change "target" is selected. A target is, of course, a precise way of stating objectives (for example, coming to work regularly). The target objective, however, must satisfy two criteria: countability (requiring an observable unit of behavior) and directionality (the desired direction of change). The *second* step is to change the consequences of the behavior. A "strengthening" consequence increases the frequency of the behavior, and a "weakening" consequence decreases the frequency of the behavior. However, the effects of a consequence can be ascertained only by careful observation of those effects on the behavior. A consequence (or reinforcer) selected for use prior to attempts to change the behavior can only be said to have "probable" effects. Also, the consequences must be given immediately and with consistency. The *third* procedural step is to keep accurate records of attempts to change behavior. This enables the behavior changer to determine the current status of the particular behavior and enables him to know whether he is succeeding in his attempts to change it. The *fourth* step is to shape the behavior through successive approximations.

The simplicity, brevity, and power of this approach are great. More than any other method of behavior change, this should hold appeal for front-line supervisors. The method calls for the active participation of the supervisor and removes the feeling of impotence and helplessness that overwhelms many in dealing with the disadvantaged minority person.

Durability of Behavior Change

One of the often-raised questions concerning the methodology of behavior modification is, "Will the behavior that has been modified under the influence of artificial contingency management persist when those contingencies are removed?" Obviously, such artificial reinforcements cannot often be maintained forever, and unless the response patterns endure long after the specially created contingencies have been discontinued, then the utility of behavior modification procedures is greatly weakened. Fortunately, there are ways in which the behavior modifier can ensure that existing behavior is not readily extinguished. One method of accomplishing this end is to change gradually from a continuous reinforcement schedule (rewarding *every* desired behavior) to increasingly variable amounts and timing of rewards, so that the reward consequences occur only periodically. Laboratory studies have shown that intermittently reinforced behavior persists long, long after the last reward was offered. Staats and Butterfield (1965) have also shown that the same end can be accomplished by reducing the amount of reward following the desired behavior or by increasing the amount of behavior required per reinforcement.

A second and probably most powerful means of ensuring durability of behavior change is to "develop and sustain behavioral repertoires to the point where the individual makes successful contact with existing sources of positive reinforcement" (Bandura, 1969). This principle assumes that there are many sources of *potential* rewards available in an individual's environment that are inaccessible to him because of his deficiencies in various social or job skills. The acquisition of these skills above a threshold level through an artificial program of contingency management would thus make those reinforcements available to the individual. Those reinforcements, in turn, would support the behavior initially established through the more artificial means. A number of individual case studies (Allen et al., 1964) have shown that the source of reinforcement can be changed by improving the social skills of the subject. Allen shifted the source of reinforcement for an extremely withdrawn girl from the adult behavior-changer to her peer group. That is, her teacher's attentiveness to her was made contingent upon her engaging in play with other children. Eventually, the girl became more socially skilled, deriving increasing enjoyment from the play itself, and the adult reinforcement was no longer necessary.

In the same way, the tokens or other "artificial" rewards might be required initially to help shape a newly hired employee's work habits. However, once the employee is deriving enjoyment from the work itself, his co-workers, his paycheck, or other sources of reward on the job, the "artificial" reinforcement may no longer be necessary.

A third means of maintaining the acquired behavior is by changing the reinforcer itself. This is especially applicable to the disadvantaged. For example, to acquire complex behaviors or to strive for achievement, most people must be capable of deferring gratification for a considerable period of time. Meanwhile, they must engage in rather strenuous and disciplined work or study activities. Since minority persons have typically not been reinforced for such behaviors, these behaviors have not been learned or they have been "unlearned." Exhortations and various pressures to change or to delay gratification are probably not as effective as applying an arbitrary reinforcement contingency to *develop* skills of gratification delay. Once these abilities to delay gratification are developed, they will actually accomplish more on the job which, in turn, will produce natural reinforcing consequences in the form of achievements. Many forms of behavior, such as communicative facility and manipulatory skills, which permit an individual to have better control over his environment, persist in the absence of much social reinforcement because of their self-reinforcing qualities.

The highest level of durability and stability of behavior is achieved when that behavior generates self-evaluative and self-reinforcing consequences. This is especially true in the case of older children and adults. Unfortunately, many disadvantaged persons do not typically set themselves standards of behavior and then self-administer rewarding or punishing consequences related to their performance against those standards. The evaluation of one's own performances that fall short of, match, or exceed a reference group, results largely from past differential reinforcements in comparison with others. Differential achievements, then, are eventually abstracted and applied to new endeavors on a self-reinforcing basis. That is, the individual has developed "standards" for himself and doesn't feel good (doesn't reinforce himself) about what he does unless he meets or exceeds those standards. At this point accomplishments are likely to elicit self-reinforcing responses irrespective of the specific performances being compared. Self-monitored reinforcement, then, can do an excellent job of maintaining behavior and, in fact, in many cases will "override" external reinforcers. In a study by Bandura and Perloff (1967), children in a "self-monitored" experimental group imposed upon themselves the most highly unfavorable schedules of reinforcement and, therefore, worked harder than control groups reinforced externally.

It would seem critically important, then, to develop self-reinforcement systems in the disadvantaged that make self-reward contingent upon appropriate work behavior and accomplishments. The charting of one's own clerical output would be a good way of developing this skill. The work of McClelland (1969) and his associates is directly relevant here. A training program based on the need for achievement research trains disadvantaged persons in thinking easily and spontaneously about: doing better, the obstacles to doing better, the means of overcoming obstacles, and the joys and disappointments of the "achievement game." Privately and in groups, participants discuss their motives and aspirations and the role they want achievement motivation to play in their lives. In self-reinforcement terms they are taught how to set realistic goals for themselves and encouraged to administer self-reinforcements when those goals are accomplished.

Operant conditioning techniques are no longer applicable only to pigeons. They hold out great promise for assisting the hard-core employee learn or acquire behavior appropriate to his job and they are an excellent potential tool for the use of supervisors who want to be able to help.

Modeling

To date, buddies have been used largely as administrative helpers, assisting the organization orient the new employee to the work place. The buddy's full potential as a model has very rarely been capitalized upon, though some lip service may be given to the notion.

The behavior of an observer can be greatly modified as a function of seeing other people's behavior and its consequences for them. Thus, observation of an act with rewarding consequences for the behavior generally enhances the probability of similar behavior by the observer, whereas watching punishing outcomes has an inhibiting effect on behavior. Various investigators (Kanfer, 1965; Rosenbaum and Bruning, 1965; and Bruning, 1965) have shown that this "vicarious reinforcement" is governed by many of the same principles as direct reinforcement, with vicarious reinforcement having been shown to shape changes in behavior of at least the same magnitude as direct reinforcement. The likelihood of a modeling event causing behavior change in an observer will be greatly enhanced under conditions where there is ambiguity about the kind of behavior that is punished or rewarded and where the observer of the model believes that the model's contingencies apply to himself as well.

Observation of models receiving reinforcing outcomes to behavior and the model's reaction to those outcomes (pleasure, pain, etc.) may have a motivational effect on the observer. For example, an observer in a state of food deprivation will be more likely to exhibit imitative behavior than an observer in a state of food satisfaction. In the same way, the intensity or magnitude of the reinforcers will yield differential motivational effects (Bruning, 1965). As is true of direct reinforcement, incentive-produced motivation in an observer greatly affects the speed, intensity, and persistence of the behavior in question. In general, then, a vicarious reinforcement event provides: information concerning the contingencies of reinforcement in a particular setting; displays of incentives possessing activating qualities; and, affective cues from models being reinforced or punished. Fortunately, observers do not need to witness these events "in the flesh." Most studies use films of role models to display the vicarious reinforcement event.

As with direct reinforcement techniques, there is not much evidence that organizations are systematically applying knowledge of the principles of modeling (vicarious reinforcement) in their training efforts. To a certain extent, members of a minority group who have "made it" through the training are often "modeled" to trainees. However, this procedure is more akin to "identification" processes than reinforcement, since it typically deals with the global concept of success, rather than with the more specific behaviors required to move along toward success through successive approximations.

If Bandura's postulations are correct, however, new employees should frequently observe models behaving in a variety of circumstances. A lengthy series of short film clips should be developed dealing with every behavioral situation that trainees need to learn how to handle. For example, a model coping with a foreman who is not understanding and hyperaggressive could well be filmed with several strategies and outcomes provided, both rewarding and punishing in nature. Several vicarious reinforcement events revolving around the same problem should greatly facilitate discriminative learning on how to cope with angry foremen. Models could be filmed showing an employee's chain of behavior in setting the alarm clock, getting up when it rings, getting to the bus on time, and making it to work on time. Another series of modeling film clips could be constructed revolving around the absentee problem. Oftentimes, disadvantaged persons are looked at suspiciously because of their absence and their stated reason for being absent—for example, "My dad's cousin in Podunk Junction got sick and I went to help him out." It would be helpful to assist trainees to discriminate between "legitimate" and "illegitimate" reasons for missing work. Thus, another series of film clips might be made showing positive and negative consequences for a model's behavior in attending or missing work.

Although the research has not yet been conclusive, it seems reasonable to believe that modeling will change an observer's behavior as a function of the comparability of reinforcement contingencies in the eyes of the observer. It is unlikely that a young, black, disadvantaged, urban worker would change behavior in a desired direction by using an older, white, professional model. On the other hand, the greater the similarity between the model and the observer (in the eyes of the observer), the greater the likelihood of behavior change. To facilitate change through a "buddy," then, the buddy must be perceived by the employee as being relatively similar to him in terms of the social sanctions that would be applied in response to specific behavior. Often this will mean the selection of buddies from among men of similar race and similar socioeconomic status, even if another man's empathy or work behavior is somewhat more desirable. To achieve maximum impact a trade-off may need to be struck between a model who would exhibit ideal work behavior and one who would be seen as realistic to a disadvantaged observer.

One large company has begun application of these techniques.[1] Their goal is to change work-related attitudes and behaviors of both the supervisors and the new minority employees. To accomplish this, a sequence of modeling, role playing, and reinforcement in anxiety-producing situations has been arranged so that both the employees and supervisors will be trained simultaneously. The importance of parallel programs for supervisors and for disadvantaged individuals is that supervisors will be better prepared to behave appropriately with new employees, while the new employees will be learning behaviors more consistent with organizational needs.

Supervisors and new employees observe actors in videotapes that are based on scenes that have actually occurred in the company. Instructors discuss with them the benefits that all parties can derive from participation in the sessions. The purpose of the videotape is to increase the behavioral repertory of foremen and new employees rather than to limit response alternatives. Supervisors observe videotapes involving the following themes: foreman helping a worker adjust to a strange environment; foreman exercising patience and understanding with new employees to keep them from quitting when facing frustration; foreman using patience, repetition, and sensitivity to help teach an employee a new job; a foreman staying calm and using tact when facing a personnel problem; a foreman helping a new employee be accepted by other workers.

New employees observe videotapes involving the following themes: asking the foreman for orientation to a strange environment (taking the initiative); staying rather than quitting when faced with a problem; being late or absent a great deal makes it bad for others as well as himself; the foreman can be trusted; taking pride in one's work as a way to advancement.

While this program is still experimental, it is one of the few under way at

---

[1] Paul Johnson, personal communication.

this time that is explicitly based on the principles of modeling and social learning now being discovered. It deserves modeling by other organizations.

"Lay Counseling"

As was described earlier, the organizational counselor has been a central person in the attempts of organizations to reach and assimilate the disadvantaged. Despite the centrality of the counselor's position in many of these projects, there is a dearth of information in the project reports about the qualifications and affiliations of counseling personnel. Some projects have employed professionally trained counselors from formal counselor-training programs. Others have used members of the work force and simply assigned them the title and responsibilities of "counselor" after little or no training. For the most part, however, it seems that the counselors have not engaged in counseling as much as they have functioned as advisors, ensuring that the employees knew what was expected of them and supporting them within the organizations (as ombudsmen) when that was appropriate. The term "counselor," then, has been very loosely used and issues relevant to counselor role within organizations merit further consideration.

Truax and Carkhuff (1967) cite their own research and that of others as converging on three basic facilitative conditions that are prerequisite for effective counseling. These facilitative conditions include "accurate empathy, nonpossessive warmth, and genuineness." [2] However, it is becoming increasingly clear that trained professionals have no corner on the market as far as these qualities are concerned. Studies in community mental-health programs, counseling, and therapy indicate that nonprofessionals ("lay" counselors) are at least as capable of exhibiting those qualities as the trained professional.

Rioch (1963) conducted one of the early lay-therapist programs. The results of the program indicated that specially selected, sophisticated, and educated housewives could learn from long-term psychoanalytic training and be judged as effective as "experts" by independent judges. Harvey (1964) selected persons who had especially successful marital relationships and trained them in two evenings a week for about eighteen months. These lay counselors brought about marital-counseling case outcomes that were slightly better than their professionally trained counterparts.

Of special interest, however, is the work of Truax and Carkhuff (1967). They evaluated the therapeutic functioning of laymen after 100 hours of training, by comparing experienced counselors and psychotherapists with inexperienced counseling students and lay counselors. The results suggested that in this relatively short training period both the students and the lay personnel were brought to function at levels of change facilitation (that is, showed accurate

---

[2] Each of these is roughly defined as follows: "accurate empathy" is the counselor's sensitivity to current feelings *and* his ability to verbalize them for the counselee; "nonpossessive warmth" means accepting the person as he is without conditions; "genuineness" means being oneself, saying what one thinks, being un-defensive.

empathy, warmth, and genuineness) commensurate with those of experienced therapists. Similar studies have been done with "lay" group counseling and with individual counseling in different settings. Overall, Truax and Carkhuff conclude that the available evidence suggests positive benefit for relatively brief training periods with inexperienced "lay counselors."

Because of the success of these efforts, growing interest has been evident in using nonprofessionals for counseling purposes. These persons are known as "lay therapists," "indigenous nonprofessionals," "lay counselors," "paraprofessionals," etc. Reiff and Riessman (1965) suggest that the human-service professions must reach out toward potential users of their service more effectively than they have done in the past. They suggest that this change can best be effected by using the "indigenous nonprofessional." This person's role is to complement the professional, not only by merely taking over lesser administrative tasks but also by actually working in what have heretofore been "forbidden" realms of counseling and therapy. The shortages of professional people to perform these functions, of course, add a measure of urgency to the need for such persons. Reiff and Riessman state "only a crash program on a large enough scale to be called a 'movement' to recruit, train and employ indigenous nonprofessionals in new capacities can meet the problems of manpower utilization and need."

In addition to simply easing professional manpower requirements, an added value of the use of nonprofessionals is their capability for acting as a bridge between the middle-class-oriented professional and the employee from the lower socioeconomic groups. The ability to establish communication across socioeconomic lines is rooted in their background, and thus is based on things they have done rather than what they have been taught in school. Typically, the lay counselor is poor, is from the neighborhood, and is from the same minority group as the employee. These attibutes make him more acceptable to the employee and ward off the suspicion, distrust, or obsequiousness which sometimes characterize the attitude of the disadvantaged toward professionals. In essence, then, the lay counselor is a "significant other" to the employee. The "style" of the lay counselor is probably related to his effectiveness, since he tends to view another person's behavior in terms of focus on external behavior rather than internal dynamics of the case: he tends to call for action and is less accepting of delay and "talk therapy."

In summary, researchers such as Truax and Carkhuff believe that nonprofessional trainees can learn to implement accurate empathic understanding, warmth, and genuineness, the qualities which in turn allow for behavior change in people. Lay counselors learn these behaviors in "much the same way that people learn to drive a car or play bridge. It may be more demanding, much more complicated, and involve more of himself, but the process of learning is similar" (Truax and Carkhuff, 1965).

What does a training program for lay counselors include? Truax and Carkhuff argue strongly for an approach combining didactic and experiential techniques. In the didactic (pedagogic or intellectual) approach, the emphasis is upon the direct structuring of the learning experience. This means shaping the thinking and building skills of the trainee in whatever direction the trainer believes is appropriate. Lecture-discussions involving an approach to counseling within the context of an organization, would probably "kick off" such a training program. A philosophical or theoretical base for the counselor's actions would likely be part of such sessions. Behavior modification theory could also be taught. Heaviest emphasis by far, however, would be placed on practical counseling experience. Counseling sessions would be video- and audiotaped for playback and extensive critique by fellow trainees and staff.

The second approach to training such lay counselors is relationship oriented or experientially based. Various types of group experiences (such as "sensitivity" training) for the trainees and individual counseling for each of the trainees provide a foundation of direct growth experiences in a non-threatening atmosphere. In turn, the security of the psychological atmosphere permits the trainee to try new approaches and gradually evolve into the most effective counselor he can be. Presumably, the experiential phase of training also builds a quality of warmth, honesty, and openness that makes the attainment of those behavior goals easier during the didactic aspects of training.

According to Truax and Carkhuff, "traditionally, these approaches (didactic versus experiential) have operated to the exclusion of one another." However, there is no logical reason why they must. In fact, most evidence suggests that learning best occurs when teachers actively shape trainee behavior within the context of a free and open psychological climate. In the short space of two weeks (with some overtime), Truax and Carkhuff have shown they can train laymen to be effective counselors. Just in relieving new counselors' anxieties the expenditures of time and money would be worth it. But if these facilitative qualities of empathy, warmth, and genuineness can be shaped in prospective counselors, why not? Hellervik (1969) has shown that industrial counselors rated high on those dimensions have greater retention rates than those counselors rated low. It appears, then, that there is a "bottom line" payoff (in the form of lower recruiting costs) involved that urges broader application of such training techniques.

IMPLICATIONS

We have explored three major areas where increasing behavioral science knowledge can contribute toward behavior change in disadvantaged minorities. Certainly there is no disagreement with Nadler's (1970) argument for a "support systems" approach to helping the hard-core adjust to work. It is imperative to contruct the five main elements he lists: organizational involvement, pre-training preparation, training support, job linkage, and follow-up procedures. The problem arises at the "nitty-gritty" level, i.e., how does one provide "pretraining preparation" that will ensure a truly "prepared" employee?

Toward this end, it seems imperative that a behavioral scientist—either a learning psychologist with a soft head or a counseling psychologist with a hard head—be given decision-making responsibility for the construction of training programs. He must work in concert with the project administrator to ensure that the ultimate design of learning experiences is in accord with behavioral science principles, with special emphasis on such concepts as behavior modification, modeling, and lay counseling. Once the program is under way, he must be the resource person available to lay counselors, supervisors, or managers who need help with specific adaptive problems. (Note: It isn't enough to draw up a well-designed program, only to leave it totally in the hands of persons uninformed in the behavioral sciences.)

This organizational counselor must have available a variety of possible interventions of learning treatments to be made available to both individuals and organizational units. These treatments should be aimed at modifying in a constructive way the interaction between the employee and his physical, social, and psychological environment. These interventions may be "direct," such as in the counseling relationship, where the lay counselors work directly with the employee to effect the desired behavior change. In turn, this relationship could lead to other individual treatments such as counterconditioning, desensitization, etc. On the other hand, the intervention may be "indirect," where the treatment of choice may be to work through consulting relationships with "significant others" within the employee's environment (supervisors, peers, etc.). Often this will mean the removal of organizational constraints preventing the full growth of individuals. This behavioral scientist, then, should be a designer and programmer of learning experiences optimally designed to allow for the maximum growth of each individual.

The programs that have been launched within organizations to help the disadvantaged minorities overcome their educational and environmental handicaps have been innovative and have served a useful purpose. However, it is now time to apply *systematically* the findings of the behavioral sciences to these training programs. If not, the signs of business disenchantment over its capability for coping with urban problems may continue to increase. The plight of the cities and our disadvantaged minorities deserves a fully intensive effort rather than a mere collection of programs. Only such an effort will avoid wasting the human resources available, thereby unlocking men's potential abilities and allowing each individual to develop his to the fullest.

REFERENCES

Allen, K. E., Hart, B., Buell, J. S., Harris, F. R., and Wolf, M. M. Effects of social reinforcement on isolate behavior of a nursery school child. *Child Development*, 1964, 35, 511–518.

"Awareness Training." *Industrial Relations News*, Industrial Relations Counselors, Inc., New York, 1968.

Bandura, A. *Principles of behavior modification*. New York: Holt, 1969.

Bandura, A., and Perloff, B. The efficacy of self-monitoring reinforcement systems. *Journal of Personality and Social Psychology,* 1967, 7, 111–116.

Bennis, W. G. Organizational developments and the fate of bureaucracy. *Industrial Management Review,* 1966, 7, 41–56.

Bruning, J. L. Direct and vicarious effects of a shift in magnitude of reward on performance. *Journal of Personality and Social Psychology,* 1965, 2, 278–282.

Cohn, J. Is business pulling out of the ghetto? *Business Week,* 1970, 2114, 23.

Doeringer, P. B. (ed.) *Programs to employ the disadvantaged.* Englewood Cliffs, N.J.: Prentice-Hall, 1969.

Goeke, J. R., and Weymar, C. S. Barriers to hiring the blacks. *Harvard Business Review,* 1969, 47, 144–152.

Harvey, L. V. The use of nonprofessional auxiliary counselors in staffing a counseling service. *Journal of Counseling Psychology,* 1964, 11, 348–357.

Hellervik, L. W. Project 250. Unpublished manuscript, Personnel Decisions, Inc., Minneapolis, Minnesota, 1969.

Honig, W. K. *Operant behavior: Areas of research and application.* New York: Appleton-Century-Crofts, 1966.

Johnson, L. A. *Employing the hard-core unemployed.* American Management Association, Inc., 1969.

Johnson, P. Personal communication.

Kanfer, F. H. Vicarious human reinforcement: A glimpse into the black box. In L. Krasner & L. P. Ullman (eds.), *Research in behavior modification.* New York: Holt, 1965, pp. 244–267.

Kirchner, W., and Lucas, J. A. Secrets and speculation about work attitudes and job performance of hard-core unemployed. Unpublished manuscript, Minn. Mining & Mfg. Co., Minneapolis, Minnesota, 1969.

Krumboltz, J. D., and Thoreson, C. E. The effect of behavioral counseling in group and individual settings on information seeking behavior. *Journal of Counseling Psychology,* 1964, 11, 324–333.

McClelland. D. Black capitalism: Making it work. *Think,* 1969, 35, 6–11.

Nadler, L. Helping the hard-core adjust to the world of work. *Harvard Business Review,* 1970, 48, 117–126.

Neisworth, J. T., Deno, S. L., and Jenkins, J. R. *Student motivation and classroom management.* Newark: Behavior Technics, 1969.

Patterson, C. H. Counseling. In P. R. Farnsworth (ed.), *Annual review of psychology.* Palo Alto, Calif.: Annual Reviews, Inc., 1966, pp. 79–110.

Reiff, R., and Riessman, F. *The indigenous nonprofessional.* New York: Community Mental Health Journals, 1965.

Rioch, M. J., et al. NIMH study in training mental health counselors. *American Journal of Orthopsychiatry,* 1963, 33, 678–689.

Rosenbaum, M. E., and Bruning, J. L. Direct and vicarious effects of variations in percentage of reinforcement on performance. *Child Development,* 1966, 37, 959–966.

Ryan, T. A., and Krumboltz, J. D. Effect of planned reinforcement counseling on client decision-making behavior. *Journal of Counseling Psychology,* 1964, 11, 315–323.

Staats, A. W., and Butterfield, W. H. Treatment of reading in a culturally deprived juvenile delinquent: An application of reinforcement principles. *Child Development,* 1965, 36, 925–942.

Thibaut, J. W., and Kelley, H. H. *The social psychology of groups.* New York: Wiley, 1959.

Truax, C. B., and Carkhuff, R. R. *Toward effective counseling and psychotherapy: Training and practice.* Chicago: Aldine Press, 1967.

CHAPTER FIVE

Cultural and Personality Factors in Minority Group Behavior: A Critical Review

Irwin Katz

INTRODUCTION BY THE EDITORS

Many of us believe that the behavior of minority group members and the poor is determined by a common core of cultural norms and personality traits which make it difficult for the disadvantaged to take advantage of any expansion in educational or occupational opportunities. Unfortunately, the attribution of debilitating cultural norms and personality traits to minority and poverty groups has often led executives to formulate inappropriate goals and strategies for the consignment of organizational resources to minority and poverty groups. For example, many current industrial programs for the disadvantaged place undue emphasis on producing psychological change in people, rather than teaching concrete and relevant job skills, which expand and improve job openings and which provide realistic opportunities for advancement within the company. These cultural norms and personality traits which are alleged to be distinctive among blacks are also alleged to affect achievement in modern industrial society. Katz raises powerful questions and considerable evidence which calls into question the notion of distinctive cultural norms and personality traits.

Advocates of the distinctive subculture position propose that differences

127

between mainstream and ghetto behavior can be attributed to cultural deprivations, norms, values, and beliefs, which are unique to the lowest social-class environments. For example, there is some research on slum subcultures which shows a disproportionate concentration of females as heads of households. This supposedly contributes to negative self-identity, a lack of preparation of youth for stable employment, and a minimum of organization within the family and community, etc. However, before deciding such characteristics of slum culture constitute immutable impediments to effective industrial integration, it is important to examine the validity of these conclusions. Katz's careful review of this research raises serious questions about the actual accuracy as well as the generalizability of these findings. He identifies serious methodological flaws in these studies, such as small sample sizes (e.g., one family as a sample), nonrepresentativeness of the sampling (e.g., cultures other than American), absence of appropriate nondisadvantaged comparison groups, and so forth. In addition to identifying needed research, Katz marshals considerable evidence suggesting the need for less emphasis upon distinctive culture explanations.

Instead of differences in cultural values, Katz concludes that ghetto behavior represents a pragmatic adjustment to chronic unemployment and relatively constant barriers against entry into the labor market, such as lack of job-relevant education or skills, constraints against admission into labor unions, etc. That is to say, the ghetto black's apparent indifference to employment is not rooted in culture-bound values which reject the work ethic, but is more a reflection of situational factors which promote styles of behavior that are required for survival in the ghetto subculture. Poverty is not a preferred way of life. Katz reviews research which shows that the ghetto child learns by observing his unemployed father and other restrictive occupational models of unskilled or menial service jobs. Such models do not emphasize either the dignity of the worker or the methods and rewards of hard work and self-improvement. Without models of adults and friends who are successfully employed in factories or offices, the common experience of rejection and discrimination leads to a set of strategies and solutions for survival which frequently do not match the "ideal" of regular employment. There are some important implications of this explanation of ghetto unemployment for organizations that attempt to take advantage of the richness of labor resources which reside in ghetto areas. For example, the group-sanctioned adaptions to chronic unemployment, including distrust of "the system" and castigation of routine work, make it difficult for individuals to reject peer pressure and take advantage of new opportunities. However, it is important to note that research evidence demonstrates that disadvantaged minority members do privately aspire to the same employment advantages as whites in the dominant culture. Thus their attitudes of cynicism and mistrust of the industrial world never fully acquire the influential character of actual cultural norms. It therefore seems highly likely that peer pressures could be overcome if an organization were to introduce a conspicuous, large-scale employment program including a large number of well-paying and attractive jobs. A program is most likely to succeed when the training and job character-

istics match the requirements discussed throughout this chapter and the other chapters in this volume.

The composite profile emerging from an uncritical *review of existing research reveals a "personality deficit" stereotype of blacks which includes low self-esteem, chronic and diffuse hostility and distrust, anxiety and hostile rejection of one's own race, identification with the white majority, lower self-expectancy, seeing the factors that control the gratifications one receives as lying outside one's own control, and shorter delay of gratification, etc. A number of these distinctive personality traits which are alleged to affect adversely black achievement are examined by Katz in relation to four questions: (1) Does research show personality differences between individuals from poor versus affluent backgrounds? (2) If there are such differences, do they influence differences in achievement? (3) If there are such differences, are they attributable to early family experiences? (4) If there are such differences, how can they be changed? While there seems to be wide acceptance of the personality deficit notion in the poverty literature, Katz's insightful review reveals only weak and equivocal support. For example, willingness to postpone reward is more strongly influenced by success and failure experiences on the job, which affect a worker's confidence in his ability to perform the task well enough to obtain the reward, and the degree of his trust in the person who controls the rewards.*

When social-class differences are controlled, research shows there are only very small differences in aspirations of black and white children. The differences occur in their expectations about achieving goals. Lower-class blacks, probably realistically, expect to attain lower goals. Of particular importance to organizations, there is also research evidence which suggests that these personality characteristics can be modified by changes in situational factors—particularly with success experiences. In sum, while there is ample evidence that minority group employees with spotty or nonexistent job histories and inadequate education have special problems of anxiety, low self-confidence, and undeveloped work habits, it seems even in the case of this marginal group, culture and personality traits are less important in job adjustment than objective features both on and off the job. For example, more recent research shows that the major cause of job termination by hard-core recruits appears to be the poor quality of working conditions in the entry positions where they were assigned.

In exchange for a reliable and badly needed work force, an organization can invest in improving living conditions and educational opportunities of minorities and design training programs which provide skills required to achieve fair and equal pay for success on meaningful jobs.

A recurrent theme in the literature on minority groups and poverty is that the cultural forms and personality traits of the poor make it difficult for them to respond to expanding economic opportunities. This point of view has been advanced by many social scientists (e.g., McClelland, 1961; Glazer and Moynihan, 1963; Oscar Lewis, 1965; Frazier, 1966; and Coleman, 1969) and has had a strong influence on the formulation of goals and strategies in federally sponsored manpower program. In a survey of thirty-five Labor Department projects for disadvantaged youths, Gordon[1] found that their most important general feature was a tendency to locate the problem of youth unemployment in the unemployed youths themselves. The programs concentrated on producing psychological change in the youths rather than on teaching them concrete job skills and creating more and better job openings.

Yet the amount of systematic evidence that can be marshaled in support of culture and personality explanations of poverty is small indeed. All too often, as Valentine (1968), Hannerz (1969), Billingsley (1968), and others have noted, interpretations of ghetto life in terms of social and personal disorganization have involved an application of dubious theoretical assumptions to inappropriate descriptive data. Thus Valentine (1968) has called attention to the common tendency among writers on the poor to confuse demographic statistics (e.g., incidence of female-headed households) with cultural patterns, instead of trying to discover by independent investigation the patterns that underlie such data. He observed that the logical leap from social statistics, which are deviant in terms of middle-class norms, to a model of lower-class disorder and instability, effectively eliminates consideration of possible cultural forms (such as consensual union, as opposed to legal marriage) that might have their own order and functions.

The present essay will discuss this and other issues in the study of minority group behavior, and implications for the integration of organizations. The focus will be mainly—but not exclusively—upon studies of blacks, the largest disadvantaged ethnic minority in America, and the one that has been most frequently investigated.

At the outset it should be recognized that there is a fair amount of overlap in the meaning of the terms "culture" and "personality"; both refer to values, beliefs, standards of conduct, and the like. One basis for differentiation is the kind of data-gathering techniques employed in connection with each term. Culture refers to phenomena that are studied most satisfactorily through the ethnographic methods of the anthropologist, typically consisting of direct observation of community life combined with intensive interviewing of selected informants. Personality, on the other hand, denotes individual difference variables that are investigated most directly by means of psychometric testing of samples representing defined population groups or subgroups. Use of these reasonably independent measurement operations helps one to avoid the pitfall of circular reasoning when examining culture–personality relationships.

Substantively, culture refers to social sharing—to the group processes whereby ideas and values and behavioral forms get transmitted from generation to generation, and then maintained through the exercise of social influence (Hannerz, 1969). Culture represents an adaptation of a particular people to the external conditions of life, embodying traditional beliefs, interpretations, and

[1] J. E. Gordon's material is presented in an undated mimeographed report at the University of Michigan: *Testing, counseling, and supportive services for disadvantaged youth.*

rules of conduct that often tend to endure even in the face of changing objective circumstances. In contrast, personality deals primarily with the psychology and behavioral tendencies of the individual—conceived as relatively distinctive attributes. Their description per se need have no implications regarding the particular kinds of factors (biological, physical, environmental, or social) that govern their development and persistence. Thus the fact that a given personality trait is frequently observed in an urban ghetto does not in itself suggest cultural causation, since those who possess the trait may simply have been exposed to a common external influence, such as racial discrimination. By the same token, minority culture may have effects on personality, but the specific nature of these personality effects can only be determined through careful psychological study of individuals. This point tends to get ignored by many cultural anthropologists, who like to infer personality characteristics from ethnographic material and then regard their inferences as established facts, rather than as hypotheses to be tested.

To the extent that members of disadvantaged minority groups react to various objective situations and events in a different way from members of the mainstream society, it is desirable to distinguish between those behavior patterns that are determined by minority subculture and those that are personality-based but not necessarily cultural. For example, if inner-city youths often seem disinterested in school work, it is clearly of some importance to know whether their indifference to formal learning is rooted in a lower-class value system that rejects middle-class achievement goals, or a defensive response to early experiences of frustration and failure in the classroom. If pupils' low motivation is a product of the ghetto subculture, the possibilities for changing their behavior without changing the attitudes of parents and other adults in the ghetto community would seem to be highly restricted. But if the problem is one of children's chronic feelings of intellectual inadequacy and anxiety about academic failure, then the appropriate strategy for remediation must be focused on the school environment itself, particularly the attitudes and behavior of teachers.

In the following section some recent research on lower-class life styles is reviewed. The coverage is not exhaustive, but rather concentrates on a small number of studies that have had an important impact upon current thinking about ghetto culture. Following the review, some central methodological and theoretical issues connected with the notion of a distinctive lower-class subculture are examined.

THE CULTURE OF THE DISADVANTAGED

Empirical Studies

Perhaps the best known anthropological studies of lower-class life to appear in recent years are those of Oscar Lewis. Based upon his research on Mexican and Puerto Rican families, Lewis (1959, 1965) introduced the idea of a "culture of poverty" that transcends racial, national, and regional boundaries. The culture of poverty is supposed to flourish among people who came from the lower strata of a rapidly changing society and are already partially alienated from it, a designation that clearly fits many inhabitants of urban slums in the United States.

Lewis's (1965) list of crucial characteristics of the slum subculture runs heavily to items that would constitute impediments to integration into mainstream society. At the local community level he finds "above all a minimum of organization. . . . Most primitive peoples have achieved a higher level of socio-cultural organization than our modern urban slum dwellers" (pp. xlvi-xlvii). The major features of the culture of poverty at the family level are "the absence of childhood as a specially prolonged and protected stage in the life cycle, early initiation into sex, free unions or consensual marriages, a relatively high incidence of the abandonment of wives and children, a trend toward female- or mother-centered families. . . a strong predisposition to authoritarianism. . . verbal emphasis upon family solidarity which is only rarely achieved. . ." (p. xlvii). At the level of the individual

> the major characteristics are a strong feeling of marginality, of helplessness, of dependence and of inferiority . . . a high incidence of maternal deprivation, of orality, of weak ego structure, confusion of sexual identification, a lack of impulse control, a strong present-time orientation with relatively little ability to defer gratification and to plan for the future, a sense of resignation and fatalism, a widespread belief in male superiority, and a high tolerance for psychological pathology of all sorts (p. xlviii).

Lewis believes that the culture of poverty is not lacking in adaptive functions for people who are excluded from most sectors of the mainstream economy. But he sees it as being, on the whole, a relatively thin culture, providing little support or long-range satisfaction for the individual, encouraging mistrust and tending to magnify helplessness and isolation, so that "the poverty of culture is one of the crucial aspects of the culture of poverty" (p. lii). Moreover, he sees little possibility for adaptive change if the material conditions of life were to improve: "It is much more difficult to eliminate the culture of poverty than to eliminate poverty *per se*" (p. li).

It is important to note that Lewis's generalizations about the poor are more in the nature of explanatory hypotheses than of well-supported findings. Most of the field research reported in *La Vida*, the book from which the foregoing quotations were taken, deals with the experiences of a single family in San Juan and New York, a family which is not even presented as a typical Puerto Rican family but rather as representative of one style of life in a Puerto Rican Slum. Lewis acknowledges that the prevalence of this style of life cannot be determined until we have many comparable studies from other slums in Puerto Rico and elsewhere. Indeed, it is Lewis's opinion that there is relatively little of what he calls the culture of poverty in the United States. His "rough guess" is that only 20 percent of the population below the poverty line—between 6 and 10 million people—have characteristics which would justify classifying their way of life as that of a culture of poverty.

Turning to studies done in the United States, various aspects of black lower-class urban life have been vividly described by Drake and Cayton (1962), Clark (1965), Rainwater (1966), Hylan Lewis (1965), Liebow (1967), and others. Rainwater reports on an extensive ethnographic investigation of very low-income families living in a large public housing project in St. Louis. Over half of the families were receiving some sort of public financial assistance. Many of the major features of the poverty life style described by Oscar Lewis for Mexicans and Puerto Ricans were observed in the housing project. Half of all the project families had female heads, who generally ran their households with a minimum of organization. Rainwater writes: "The children quickly learn to fend for themselves, to go to the store. . . to watch after themselves, to amuse themselves, to set their own schedules of sleeping, eating, and going to school. . . . There is not the deep psychological involvement with babies which has been observed with the working-class mother. The babies are cared for on a catch-as-catch-can basis" (pp. 195–196).

Rainwater contends that the family forms, which he believes represent an adaptation to economic pressure and racial discrimination, have a profoundly deleterious effect on the psychosocial development of the children who grew up in them. In black slum culture "growing up involves an ever-increasing appreciation of one's shortcomings, of the impossibility of finding a self-sufficient and gratifying way of living. It is in the family first and most devastatingly that one learns these lessons" (pp. 203–204). Thus the child develops an "inability to embark hopefully on any course of action that might make things better, particularly action which involves cooperating and trusting attitudes toward others" (p. 204).

Contributing further to the development of a negative self-identity, according to Rainwater, is the fact that in lower-class culture human nature is conceived of as essentially bad, destructive, and immoral. Parents are on the alert as the child matures for evidence that he is as bad as everyone else, and the child is constantly exposed to identity labeling as a bad person. Thus as he grows up and experiences the world as essentially frustrating, it is easy for him to conclude that his frustrations are a result of his own deficiencies, moral and otherwise.

Rainwater suggests that the slum world encourages three kinds of "strategies for survival." One is the strategy of the *expressive life style* which entails an effort to make oneself interesting and attractive to others so that one is better able to manipulate their behavior along lines that will provide some immediate gratification. He writes:

Negro slum culture provides many examples of techniques for seduction, of persuading others to give you what you want in situations where you have very little that is tangible to offer in return. In order to get what you want you learn to "work game," a strategy which requires a high development of a certain kind of verbal facility, a sophisticated manipulation of promise and interim reward (pp. 206–207).

When the expressive strategy fails or when it is unavailable, a *violent* strategy may be adopted in which force is used against others. Finally, and increasingly as the individual grows older, there is the *depressive* strategy in which goals and interests are constricted to the bare necessities for physical survival.

These strategies for survival are somewhat similar to Miller's (1965) "focal concerns of lower-class culture," which he believes are shared by about 25 million Americans (a much larger number than Oscar Lewis places in the culture of poverty category). Miller's thesis is that the focal areas or issues about which lower-class people are concerned and anxious constitute a distinctive *patterning* of concerns differing significantly from that of American middle-class culture. Six major areas, arranged in order of importance, are stated in terms of polar opposites: (1) trouble with the law versus law-abiding behavior; (2) toughness and masculinity versus weakness and effeminacy; (3) smartness in manipulating the environment as against gullibility and willingness to work hard; (4) excitement and thrill as opposed to safety and routine; (5) good fortune and luck or their opposites; and (6) autonomy and freedom versus dependency and constraint.

THE WORLD OF THE LOWER-CLASS WORKER.　A few writers have dealt with the social world of the black male as it affects, and is affected by, his job experiences. Drawing on his observations in two Southern communities, Himes (1968) asserts that lower-class black boys are deprived of certain kinds of early socialization for work that normally prepares their white age peers for well-paying employment in later life. Not having daily association with parents, neighbors, and friends who are engaged as modern workers in factories and offices, the lower-class black youth is not exposed to the casual talk and informal interaction that enables his white counterpart to identify with the role of the skilled worker. On the contrary, most lower-class black males are presented with occupational models—unskilled and service workers—irrelevant for the main sectors of the labor market. These black youths do not overhear adults in the "shop talk" that can acquaint them with the daily routine, general atmosphere, and occupational *dramatis personae* of an industrial or business setting. Nor can they acquire the ideology and values of the labor union, which emphasize the dignity of the worker and the desirability of pursuing individual goals through collective action. Further, workers who are restricted to the fringes of the occupational structure are alienated from the mainstream ethos of hard work and self-improvement as the means to advancement. The negative or indifferent attitudes that they often hold toward their menial, dead-end jobs tend to get conveyed to their children, whereas the white child's observations of successful relatives serve to validate for him the value of pursuing the Protestant middle-class ethic. According to Himes, the total effect of these work-related cultural deprivations is a "trained unreadiness for smooth transition from family, school and neighborhood to the social world and technical role of work" (p. 192).

Another investigator, Liebow (1967), has provided a perceptive account of the daily lives of twenty or more chronically unemployed and underemployed "street-corner" men in Washington, D.C. These are men who lack the education and skills requisite for getting and holding attractive, well-paying jobs. To Liebow the single most important fact about the individuals he studied was their deep sense of personal failure at not being able to support themselves and their families at a level above that of bare subsistence. Unable to be "the man of the house" to his wife and children, the marginal worker increasingly turns to the street corner and the company of other men like himself, where a "shadow system of values constructed out of public fictions serves to accommodate such men as he, permitting them to be men once again provided they do not look too closely at one another's credentials" (p. 213). There is a socially shared awareness of the inevitability of defeat with each new venture into the arena of work. Liebow writes that:

> Those who are or have been married know it well. It is the experience of the individual and the group; of their fathers and probably their sons. Convinced of their inadequacies, not only do they not seek out those few better-paying jobs which test their resources, but they actively avoid them, gravitating in a mass to the menial, routine jobs which offer no challenge—and therefore pose no threat—to the already diminished images they have of themselves (p. 54).

Is There a Lower-Class Subculture?

In critically examining the proposition that there exists in the United States a distinctive lower-class subculture there appear to be three main points at issue. First, are published accounts of ghetto life (a few of which have just been briefly reviewed) descriptively accurate and generalizable to known populations? Second, do apparent differences between ghetto and mainstream behavior mainly reflect differences in culture—i.e., in socially transmitted values, beliefs, and norms—or do they reflect the individual's functional adaptations to different sets of situational factors? Third, assuming that distinctive lower-class subcultural patterns do exist, how are they related to mainstream culture? That is, are they opposed to, supportive of, or neutrally related to mainstream culture?

DESCRIPTIVE ACCURACY. Advocates of the poverty subculture approach have sometimes presented "descriptions" of the poor that were actually only contentions based either upon personal impressions or informal observations of very limited scope. Even when careful ethnological research has been done, the representativeness of the samples studied has often been in doubt. For example, Rainwater (1966) reports that half of the housing project families he investigated in St. Louis had female heads, and more than half were on public welfare. But Billingsley (1968) cites Labor Department statistics to the effect that the majority of poor blacks in the United States live in self-supporting nuclear families headed by men. The Federal data show that among families with incomes below $3,000 in 1966, nearly 60 percent were headed by husbands and fathers. Among these with incomes between $3,000 and $5,000, the proportion of male-headed families increased to nearly 75 percent. As income increased further the proportion of male-headed families increased.

Billingsley notes that whereas 41 percent of blacks were living in poverty in 1966, only 14 percent—about one third—were supported by public welfare. He further estimates that not more than 15 to 20 percent of all black families fell into the *nonworking poor* category, made up of families headed by members who were intermittently, if at all, employed, and who had very low levels of education and job skills.

Even large-scale demographic studies, such as the decennial census and the Labor Department surveys, can significantly distort the realities of minority group and lower-class behavior. For example, Taeuber (1969) calls attention to the severe problem of biased undernumeration of urban black males by the census, particularly of males between twenty and thirty-nine years of age. And Killingsworth (1969) shows that the procedures used by the Labor Department in its periodic assessments of national unemployment virtually guarantee that male unemployment in low-income groups will be seriously underestimated. Another common source of error in the gathering and presentation of demographic data on minority groups is the failure to provide appropriate comparisons. In a critical examination of the view that matriarchy is a distinctively black phenomenon, Hyman (1969) shows how empirical support for the notion tends to diminish when black families are compared with white families of similar economic status. Comparing poor urban blacks with urban whites who were also living below the poverty line in 1966, the difference in proportion of female-headed households is a moderate 9 percent. In various high-income strata the race differences are always below 5 percent. Thus, the female-headed family, which appears to be a distinctively black phenomenon when viewed in isolation from white population statistics, becomes much more of a class phenomenon when the appropriate racial comparisons are made.

INTERPRETATION OF BEHAVIORAL DIFFERENCES.   Even at the lowest poverty levels one observes a wide variety of coping behaviors, according to Hylan Lewis (1965). Materials gathered in a field study of poor blacks in Washington, D.C. led Lewis to reject the idea that either the quality of life in most low-income neighborhoods or the child-rearing practices of most low-income families could be interpreted as a product of a distinctive subcultural system. He found little of the kind of uniformity of behavior or common values suggested by this phrase. Rather what he saw was "a broad spectrum of pragmatic adjustments to external and internal stresses and deprivations." Poverty life styles did not appear to represent a preferred or chosen way of life.

Similarly, Valentine (1968) asserts that most lower-class social relationships and group forms may represent situational adaptations with little or no specific subcultural rationale. He believes that the "poverty of culture" attitudes and orientations enumerated by Oscar Lewis—apathy, passivity, unwillingness to defer gratification, distrust of others, spatial and temporal provincialism, and the like—are so strikingly consistent with external constraints as to make it unnecessary to interpret them as reflecting socially transmitted values and beliefs.

Hannerz (1969) agrees with Valentine that an emphasis on situational factors is useful, but he advises against adopting an either–or position on whether behavior is situationally or culturally determined. His reasons are twofold. First, culture does not exist independently of the situation, but is in fact a means of adaptation to objective circumstances. Second, modes of action can be both learned from an older generation and also influenced by external constraints. Given this dual determination of behavior, the problem of distinguishing between cultural and situational factors is necessarily a difficult one.

Hannerz argues for the usefulness of a minimal, or "soft" definition of culturalness in analyses of lower-class life, in which the attempt should be to identify relatively subtle, implicit processes of social sharing, such as learning through role modeling. He contrasts this with the "hard" culture concept which encompasses only strong, well articulated, and readily identifiable norms and values. Since explicit values are usually mainstream-oriented (cf. Proshansky and Newton's [1968] review of relevant research) on achievement values, the "hard" usage leads to the conclusion that there is little, if any, culture which is unique to the ghetto.

But should the prevalence of ghetto-specific forms of behavior, even if transmitted by precept, be taken as sufficient evidence of culturalness? Could not the existence of these forms, in the absence of explicitly formulated value-orientations, be totally dependent upon the common experiencing of pressures from the external system? Hannerz's reply is that behaviors acquire an aura of legitimacy by virtue of being statistically normative. The child who learns by precept from observing the behavior of his unemployed father is also observing other adults behaving similarly. Moreover, the individual who learns by precept is not merely imitating a particular type of behavior, but is learning a technique of adaptation. Adults model solutions of adaptation problems that young people will be able to use when they encounter the relevant situations. Hannerz also notes that behaviors prevalent in a community become embedded in group-shared interpretations, explanations, and understandings of events and experiences. Since there are undoubtedly many different sharing groups among the poor, an important task for future research would seem to be the identification of culturally significant social aggregates and the specification of cognitive and behavioral dispositions that are subject to subcultural influence. In the past, advocates of the culture of poverty viewpoint have been criticized for failing to state precisely what types of behavior are under its control.

An important reason for investigating whether there are subcultural adaptations is that they may operate as barriers to behavior change when external constraints are weakened. For example, to the extent that there exist group-sanctioned adaptations to chronic unemployment that involve distrust of the external system and rejection of routine work and its rewards, peer pressure to conform would make it difficult for individuals to avail themselves of new job opportunities. But Hannerz believes that if there were to occur a "conspicuous large-scale reduction of macrostructural constraints" such group pressures would be weakened. That is, peer pressure against accepting regular employment could not be sustained if attractive jobs were to become widely available. Eventually the monetary rewards and gains in self-esteem to be had through involvement in the world of work would become so evident that old attitudes of cynicism and mistrust about "the system" would have to change.

RELATIONSHIP BETWEEN SUBCULTURE AND OVERALL CULTURE. If it is the case that economically disadvantaged minority groups have distinctive subcultural characteristics then it is also true that the significance of these elements can be understood only when considered in relation to the overall culture. As Rainwater (1970) puts it, "Discussions of lower class culture in isolation from the social, economic and ecological setting to which that culture is an adaptation will generally prove to be misleading (and, with respect to policy, pernicious)" (p. 147). The problem for research is to specify which components are unique and to establish whether the unique components stand in opposition to comparable mainstream traits, or in some other relationship to them.

One attempt to define this interface has been Rodman's concept of the "lower-class value stretch," an adaptive mechanism whereby the lower-class person reconciles a preference for the general values of the society with the realities of his everyday life. According to Rodman, the lower-class person retains these general societal values, but also develops an alternative set of values: "Without abandoning the values placed upon success. . . he stretches the values so that lesser degrees of success also become desirable. Without abandoning the values of marriage and legitimate childbirth he stretches these values so that a non-legal union and legally illegitimate children are also desirable" (p. 277). The result is that the poor tend to have a wider range of values than others within the society, and because of this their commitment to any particular value tends to be weaker.

Rainwater (1970) adds to Rodman's "value stretch" concept the idea that the substitute goals of the lower class never acquire fully normative character. Rather, the rules of lower-class behavior tend to become "pseudo-normative"— lower-class actors pretend to one another that their distinctive standards of conduct have full moral justification, "but careful observation of behavior belies that fact." Liebow's (1967) investigation of the world of street-corner men seems to support Rainwater's view that, in the main, the poor do not escape the normative influence of the dominant culture. Liebow observed in his subjects a deep sense of shame at not being able to play the traditional male role, a feeling they tried to mitigate through the sharing of elaborate fictions. Clark (1965) provides an intriguing and poignant account of how white values sometimes dominate the private fantasies of ghetto youths. He describes the behavior of young men observed at Harlem Youth Opportunities Unlimited (HARYOU):

Many of these marginal, upward-striving teen-agers allowed others to believe that they were college students. One young man told his friends that he was a major in psychology. He had enrolled in the classes of a Negro professor with whom he identified, and he described those lectures in detail to his friends. The fact is that he was a drop-out from high school. Others dressed like college students and went to college campuses where they walked among the students, attempting to feel a part of a life they longed for and could not attain. Some carried attaché cases wherever they went—often literally empty (p. 66).

Hannerz (1969) proposes a useful distinction for viewing the relation between lower-class and mainstream culture. Empirically, he states, subcultural elements may be either qualitatively different from, and opposed to, comparable elements of the general culture, or they may represent additions to general culture. The former type is more likely to block adaptive changes in behavior as external constraints diminish.

All of the foregoing conceptions must be regarded as tentative, pending the accumulation of further evidence. Like virtually all current theories about the life styles of disadvantaged groups, they have yet to be adequately tested by means of systematic ethnographic investigations employing suitable sampling procedures and nondisadvantaged comparison groups.

PERSONALITY CHARACTERISTICS OF THE DISADVANTAGED

Scanning the research literature on minority group personality, Pettigrew (1964a) observes that, "From tattoos . . . to tongue-rolling . . . an incredible variety of psychological studies of the Negro American has been conducted in recent decades . . . yet many of the most basic and important personality questions . . . have not received even tentative answers" (p. 4). He attributes this lack to the narrow framework of previous research, limited mainly to such areas as intelligence testing, and "adjustment" defined in terms of tests standardized on whites, and believes that a more productive trend has been the depth analyses of the black personality by psychotherapists. Part of the problem has been the formidable methodological difficulties connected with devising testing instruments suitable for minority group subjects and with setting up appropriate control groups.

The present discussion deals primarily with hypotheses and research relating to whether blacks possess distinctive personality traits that affect their capacity for achievement in modern industrial society. Much of the relevant research has dealt with academic performance.

Hypotheses About Effects of Early Socialization

Some psychologists, especially those who are psychoanalytically oriented, attribute the relatively low academic achievement of minority group students to a basic failure of the socialization process in the home. According to these authors, early childhood experiences in poverty environments create enduring personality formations that are inimical to effective achievement striving not only in the classroom but, indeed, in virtually all areas of life. Thus Ausubel and Ausubel (1963) stress two features of child rearing which they assume to be typical of low-income black families. One is a harsh authoritarianism of parents, who emphasize punitive forms of control and place considerable social and emotional distance between themselves and their children. The other feature is the early relaxation of close parental supervision, which makes the child precociously independent of adult influence but exposes him to the exaggerated socializing influence of the peer group. These conditions, in combination with the child's growing awareness of the stigma attached to being black in a white-dominated society, are supposed to create a personality marked by feelings of unworthiness, lack of self-controlling mechanisms, and hostile rejection of adult values.

Similarly, Bettelheim (1964) believes "that human personality is shaped in infancy, and that the early characteristics are extremely resistant to change." He claims that in the case of the black child the earliest experiences of life often condition "a life-long distrust of others (including one's teachers and what they teach) and of oneself." Mistrust, shame, and doubt become the dominant characteristics in children from culturally deprived homes or disadvantaged ones. He concludes that the lower-class black child is foredoomed to fail academically before he enters kindergarten or first grade.

The views expressed by the Ausubels and Bettelheim on the personality effects of lower-class family experiences are similar to conclusions reached by Rainwater (1966) from his field observations. Another writer who postulates inadequate socialization in the black home is McClelland (1961). He maintains that because of the woman-centered structure of the black family, and the persistence of child-rearing practices that originated in slavery, blacks as a group are lacking in the *need to achieve* (*n* Ach), a personality characteristic that impels individuals to strive for excellence in whatever tasks they undertake. McClelland takes for granted that strong mother-dependency weakens the development of *n* Ach in sons. Moreover, "Negro slaves . . . developed child-rearing practices calculated to produce obedience and responsibility not *n* Ach, and their descendants, while free, should still show the effects of such training in lower *n* Ach—which in fact is exactly the case . . ." (pp. 376–377).

Family structure is emphasized by Pettigrew (1964b), Bronfenbrenner (1967), Moynihan (U.S. Department of Labor, 1965), and others, who point to the relatively high incidence of father absence in lower-class families as a major cause of academic indifference and failure on the part of children, especially boys. Presumably, father-deprived boys, lacking a masculine role model with which to identify, develop personalities marked by impulsivity, effeminacy, and immature dependency. (However, earlier in the chapter the author cited evidence showing that even among blacks living below the poverty level, the majority of families were headed by husbands and fathers; furthermore, racial differences in the proportion of female-headed households at various income levels tend to be relatively small.)

In evaluating the evidence relating to these "personality deficit" explanations of the low achievement of disadvantaged groups one would want to ask not only (a) whether specific personality differences have been found between individuals from backgrounds of poverty and affluence, but also (b) whether demonstrated personality differences have been related to differences in achievement. If empirical findings indicate that the disadvantaged student does possess traits that are academically detrimental, it should then be asked (c) whether the traits have been shown to the products of early family influences, and (d) whether the traits appear to be relatively unmodifiable, once formed. Measured by these criteria, research findings do not provide strong, unequivocal support for a "personality deficit" viewpoint, despite its wide acceptance in the clinical literature on poverty.

Empirical Studies

SELF-ESTEEM.   Much of the empirical work on black personality has been stimulated by the notion that members of this group still bear a "mark of oppression" that represents the emotional wound of living in a white world of prejudice and discrimination. Thus a frequently studied characteristic of blacks is their inclination toward hostile rejection of their own race and identification with the white majority. This identity conflict has been found repeatedly in both the North and South, with a variety of projective techniques being used to measure the racial evaluations of whites and blacks. (The investigations are reviewed by Proshansky and Newton, 1968.) Derogation of their own race appears in minority children as early as age three, remaining strong until later childhood when it tends to become less apparent (perhaps being still present, but concealed.) Hence the development of the characteristic cannot be attributed to school influences alone. On the other hand, it has not yet been related to social class or family factors. At the present time virtually nothing is definitely known about the effect of racial derogation on school performance.

To the extent that the child believes he belongs to an intellectually inferior group, he might be expected to lack the confidence to strive for success in the classroom. However, most of the students of racial identity have dealt with children's evaluations of their group's moral, social, and physical-appearance characteristics, and not with evaluations of intellectual attributes. Theoretically, there is no compelling reason why attitudes about nonintellectual traits should be closely tied to scholastic motivation. Smith (1968) makes this point in a recent paper on the socialization of personal competence. It is conceivable, however, that a generally negative self-concept could have an adverse effect upon vocational performance, especially in job situations requiring interaction with whites. In an experiment on small biracial work team, Katz and Benjamin (1960) observed that young black adults felt inadequate and oriented compliantly toward white age peers, even in the face of objective evidence of equal mental ability.

Where *academic* self-esteem has been investigated in black and white youth the findings on race differences have been mixed. Wylie and Hutchins (1967) reported that lower-class black children expressed more favorable conceptions of their own academic ability than did lower-class whites; in a study by Gibby and Gabler (1968) black pupils scored higher than white pupils, equated on IQ, in ratings of their own intellectual ability; and Coleman et al. (1966) found levels of academic self-esteem to be highly similar in black and white adolescents.

Another characteristic that is supposed to be associated with the "mark of oppression" is chronic diffuse hostility and distrust. Using projective tests, Hammer (1953) and Mussen (1953) found differences in amount of fantasy aggression expressed by black and white children. Projective data gathered by Karon (1958) suggest that adult and adolescent blacks, particularly in the South, tend toward extreme repression of aggressive impulses. But the specific sources of aggressive impulses in black children, their stability over time, and their possible relationship to academic failure, have not been adequately investigated. It is interesting to note that Sarason and his associates (1960) have concluded from their research on white children that fear and hostility regarding adult authorities are important elements in the development of school anxiety.

ANXIETY. Evidence that black pupils in racially isolated schools have inordinately high levels of anxiety has recently been obtained by Feld and Lewis (1967). These investigators administered the *Test Anxiety Scale for Children* to the entire second-grade population of a large school system in the eastern part of the United States. Blacks were found to have substantially higher anxiety scores than whites not only on the total scale but also on each of four subscales which were derived by means of factor analysis: test anxiety, remote school concern (e.g., "When you are in bed at night, do you sometimes worry about how you are going to do in class the next day?"), poor self-evaluation, and somatic signs of anxiety. Interestingly, a group of black children in racially mixed schools obtained scores about midway between those of the de facto segregated black and white samples. However, the meaning of this comparison is not entirely clear, since the black children in desegregated schools came from homes of relatively high socioeconomic status, a factor found to be associated with low anxiety. Sex differences appeared for white pupils—white boys obtained lower anxiety scores than white girls—but not for blacks.

School anxiety in black boys and girls was strongly related to the mother's educational level when other home factors were controlled, a finding that is consistent with the research of the Sarason group (Sarason et al., 1960; Hill and Sarason, 1966) on white children which reveals that parental influence is a key determinant of school anxiety. In another relevant study, Katz (1967) has analyzed the role of parental behavior and attitudes by means of Baron's Reinforcement History Questionnaire, which inquires of the child about characteristic parental reactions in a variety of situations. Katz found that among Northern black boys (though not among girls) school anxiety and a propensity for devaluation of their own performance (which were interrelated) were each in turn related to the predominance of negative reinforcements from parents—to reports of low parental interest and acceptance and high parental punitiveness. Moreover, these variables—anxiety, self-devaluation, and perceived parental punitiveness—were all related to school achievement. Katz's data extend to black boys one of the main findings of Hill and Sarason—the substantial linkage of school anxiety and academic failure—and shed additional light on the kind of family socialization practices that give rise to school anxiety.

If inadequate social reinforcement in the lower-class black home figures importantly in the development of emotional blocks to learning, it would be desirable to know a great deal more than we do at present about the child-rearing values, attitudes, and behavior of black parents. The most relevant recent studies have involved class comparisons of black mother–child interactions based on direct observations of behavior. Kamii (1965) compared maternal behavior toward four-year-old children of lower-class and upper-middle-class mothers in a Midwestern community. The two groups differed considerably in their socialization practices. Middle-class mothers were observed to gratify children's affectional and security needs, to use rational influence techniques, to encourage and reward children for verbal efforts, and generally to reinforce desirable behavior significantly more often than lower-class mothers. Another investigation in the North (Hess et al., 1965) sampled a wide social spectrum of black families. Four social-class groups of mothers and their four-year-old children were selected. In general, the class differences observed in maternal attitudes and behavior were consistent with those reported by Kamii: upper-middle-class mothers praised the child's achievement efforts more than did other mothers, and were more likely to favor supportiveness as opposed to demanding unquestioned obedience to injunctions and commands.

The observations of Kamii and Hess et al. were consistent with general sociological knowledge: in crowded lower-class homes, where mothers often are away at work during the day and both parents lack intellectual sophistication, the child's early efforts at verbal and cognitive mastery are less likely to be favorably reinforced than in middle-class homes, resulting in lower expectations of reward for intellectual effort. Low expectation of reward in combination with relatively high expectation of punishment for failure to meet adult demands probably lays the groundwork for the later emergence of school anxiety.

Thus school anxiety would seem to qualify as a personality factor that is (a) characteristic of lower-class children, (b) related to academic performance, and (c) an outcome of early experiences in the home. However, there is good reason to believe that conditions in the school can greatly modify this characteristic. In their longitudinal study of white pupils, Hill and Sarason report little relationship between anxiety scores obtained before and after a four-year interval. Moreover changes in anxiety scores were associated with changes in academic attainment. Presumably the changes are in some measure a reflection of different types of experience in the classroom and in the total school culture.

ACHIEVEMENT MOTIVES AND VALUES.   Negroes are often assumed to be lacking the *need for achievement,* as measured through fantasy productions. This need is defined as a personality characteristic that impels individuals to strive for success whenever their performance at a task can be evaluated against a standard of excellence (McClelland, 1953; Atkinson, 1964). A few studies have compared the need for achievement of black and white youths and reported generally higher scores for low-status whites than for blacks (Mussen, 1953; Rosen, 1959; Lott and Lott, 1963; Mingione, 1965). However, there are a good many difficulties with the concept of a global achievement motive as embodied in the fantasy-based measure, which have recently been reviewed by Smith (1968). As Smith puts it:

> There are questions about its generality . . . its openness to influences that contaminate its value as a measure of motivation. The findings in regard to its relationships to achievement-oriented behavior have been ambiguous. . . . Given this less than encouraging record, one suspects that there has been slippage between the theoretical definition of the motive and what has actually been captured in the measurements.

The problem of the generality of the achievement motive is especially relevant to the study of class and cultural differences in academic performance. For example, the lower-class black student's disinterest in classroom learning may be less a matter of his lacking the achievement motive than of its being directed into nonintellectual pursuits. In comparing the behavior of individuals from different social backgrounds, it may be necessary to abandon entirely the concept of a single global achievement motive in favor of a notion of many relatively independent achievement motives that are specific to particular areas of endeavor.

With respect to achievement *values*, an extensive literature on educational and job aspirations and expectations has been ably reviewed by Proshansky and Newton (1968). Studies of black and white children and their parents generally show only small differences when social class is controlled. Comparing classes, aspirations of high- and low-income black adults and children are consistently reported as high—most individuals at both economic levels desire college attendance and professional or white-collar occupations. However, when realistic expectations of achieving the goals are measured, stable class differences appear: these more *functionally relevant* goal levels are lower among low-income students and parents. (Though even statements from poor blacks of what they "realistically" expect to achieve are often unrealistically high, when measured against the objective availability of the stated goals or against actual striving behavior.) Thus it seems that the main difference between the achievement orientations of the poor and the affluent lies not in the choice of goals, but in expectations of attaining them.

Locus of Control.   A predisposition which is strongly associated with scholastic achievement (though the nature of the causal relationship has not been empirically unraveled) is Rotter, Seeman, and Liverant's (1962) *sense of personal control of the environment.* Individuals differ in the extent to which they feel they can extract material and social benefits from the environment through their own efforts. In its broadest meaning, this construct refers to the degree to which people have a sense of efficacy, or power, and accept personal responsibility for what happens to them. It has been applied more specifically to children in intellectual achievement situations by means of a questionnaire which assesses the extent to which favorable reactions from parents, teachers, and peers are believed by the child to depend either upon the quality of his own efforts or upon extraneous factors (such as luck, or the personal bias or whim of the evaluator) (Crandall et al., 1965). The sense of internal control has been found to be stronger in white children and adults than in blacks, and stronger in the middle class than in the working class (Battle and Rotter, 1963; Lefcourt and Ladwig, 1965; Crandall et al., 1965; Coleman et al., 1966).

A person's feelings about whether his own efforts determine his external rewards clearly should affect his expectancy of success, hence his willingness to strive. His level of performance should in turn affect the rate at which the environment dispenses rewards, hence his sense of internal control. Thus Crandall and others (1962) found that white grade-school boys who felt they controlled their reinforcements got high scores on intellectual tests and engaged in much intellectual free-play behavior. Similarly, in their nationwide survey of public-school students, Coleman and his co-workers (1966) found internality related to academic achievement in both whites and blacks.

The Coleman team measured three types of student attitude relevant to academic motivation: interest in school work, self-concept as regards ability, and sense of control of own rewards. For black students, sense of control was clearly the most important attitude, accounting for much more of the differences in verbal achievement than either of the others. Moreover, the relation of blacks' sense of control to achievement was considerably stronger than that of any family-background factor. Finally, comparing races revealed that among older children sense of fate control accounted for about three times as much test variance among blacks as whites (a result which the Coleman Report points out is not attributable to racial differences in variability of fate-control scores).

Since the Coleman findings represent merely empirical correlations, the causal connections between sense of internal control and other variables can only be surmised. Nonetheless, there are strong suggestions in the data regarding the relative importance of home and school determinants. For blacks, sense of control was little influenced by home factors or objective school characteristics, but one factor apparently affected it strongly: as the proportion of white students in school enrollments increased, blacks' sense of internality grew stronger. This suggests that black pupils attending predominantly white schools had a stronger sense of the availability of opportunities for present and future achievement.

From a recent report by Gurin (1968), we learn that measures of internality taken on job trainees (mostly blacks) prior to completion of the training program and again after being out on jobs for a while were both significantly related to job success. But the latter correlation was higher, suggesting a reciprocal relationship between the attitude and achievement.

Thus the findings on internality suggest it may prove to be a personal quality of considerable importance in performance, yet one which is relatively lacking in blacks and lower-class whites. It is not closely related to home background factors; rather it seems to be highly responsive to whether the person is inside or outside of the mainstream "system" (i.e., is attending a segregated or integrated school).

PERSONALITY EFFECTS OF FATHER ABSENCE.   In this overview of research on black personality, reference should be made to father absence, since a number of writers have asserted that father absence in black homes is a major cause of academic failure. While it is a plausible assumption that father absence has some effects on personality development (the evidence, based mainly on studies of white children, has been reviewed by Biller, 1970), the case for its influence on intellectual achievement is far from clear. Biller cites a few studies reporting intellectual deficits in father-absent children; other investigations have found the opposite. Regarding the latter, Whiteman and Deutsch (1968) found no relationship between black children's reading skills and family intactness. Similarly, in the national survey by Coleman et al. (1966) and Wilson's California study (U.S. Commission on Civil Rights, 1967) the presence or absence of a father was not a factor in the scholastic attitudes or achievement of lower-class black or white students. Moreover, Feld and Lewis (1967) found virtually no relationship between family intactness and school anxiety.

EXPECTANCY.   Recently the Gurins (1970) have suggested that the concept of expectancy be used to integrate personality and situational approaches to the problem of low educational and economic attainment among the disadvantaged. The expectancy approach is exemplified by the experiments of Atkinson and his associates (Atkinson and Feather, 1966; Atkinson, 1964), in which subjective probabilities of success at specific tasks are manipulated by imparting to subjects fictitious information about the difficulty of tasks. Quality of performance, persistence, and choice of task goals appear to be influenced by subjects' perceptions of the likelihood of success.

The Gurins believe that the expectancy construct "has obvious implications for the psychologist inclined to approach problems of poverty by focusing on internal dynamics of the poor. It forces him to relate motivational analysis to realistically available rewards and limitations" (p. 85). The expectancy framework also forces those who emphasize reality issues to consider individual factors, some expectancies "are to some extent generalized dispositions that develop, like other personality dispositions, out of an individual's life history of relevant success and failure experiences" (p. 85).

In previous research using feedback, changes in expectancies about future outcomes tended to be limited to the same task as the one on which success or failure feedback was given, and to be of short duration. Hence, an important problem for research would seem to be to discover the objective reinforcement conditions that can produce enduring change upward in generalized expectancies of reward for achievement efforts.

Another important question has to do with the effect of changed expectancies on behavior. Experimental studies reviewed by the Gurins indicate that the effect on future performance of raising a person's expectancy of success is complicated, and as yet poorly understood.

An interesting use of the expectancy construct is to be found in the work of Mischel (1966) and his colleagues on delay of gratification. Initially, Mischel set out to show that socially disadvantaged children (lower-class and father-deprived), as compared with other children, would prefer small but immediate rewards over large rewards that entailed waiting. His original assumption was that the capacity to delay gratification was a stable personality disposition laid down in early family socialization. More recently, however, he has demonstrated that children's readiness to postpone rewards is strongly influenced by the circumstances in which the choice is offered. These include success and failure experiences that affect the child's confidence of performing well enough to attain the delayed reward, and his degree of trust in the experimenter.

IMPLICATIONS FOR INTEGRATING THE ORGANIZATION

Perhaps the single most important conclusion to be drawn about the culture and personality of black Americans is that very few, if any, sweeping generalizations are warranted regarding distinctive traits. Whereas the bulk of previous research on black subculture has dealt with an extremely deprived underclass, the fact is that today a substantial majority of black male adults have stable employment at wages and salaries above the poverty level. Moreover, the decade of the 1960s saw a dramatic shift upward in the average educational level of young blacks. Labor Department statistics show that in 1969, 60 percent of black men twenty-five to twenty-nine years of age had completed four years of high school or some college, as compared with 36 percent in 1960. Although the *quality* of schooling received by blacks is usually inferior to that received by whites, it is nonetheless significant that more and more black youths are availing themselves of existing educational opportunities.

Turning to the problem of providing jobs for the so-called hard-core un-employed—usually defined as men with low educational levels and little or no previous experience of steady employment—one should recognize that this group constitutes a quite small proportion of the total black labor force. Yet even with respect to this special group of marginal workers caution must be exercised in ascribing psychological characteristics that set them off from other workers. Regarding values and goals, for example, Guion and Smith, in their contribution to this volume, mention a job satisfaction survey among "underprivileged workers" in which rankings by blacks and whites of sixteen motivational factors were compared, with a median deviation of only one point being found between the two sets of rankings. Similarly, in an elaborate study of the attitudes of black high-school dropouts enrolled in a job-training program, Bradford (1967) found general acceptance of the mainstream beliefs that work is important and that occupational advancement comes through hard work.

While there is ample evidence that minority group employees with spotty or nonexistent job histories and inadequate education have special problems of anxiety, low self-confidence, and undeveloped work habits, it would seem that even in the case of this marginal group, culture and personality traits are less important factors in job adjustment than objective features of the in-job and off-job situations. Of these, the in-job situation is probably the more critical. For certain types of employment—including the blue-collar jobs typically given to workers in hard-core recruitment programs—it is hardly necessary to know anything about worker characteristics in order to predict high turnover rates. In a study or marginal workers hired by a major manufacturing company, Quinn, Fine, and Levitin (1970) found that personality factors as such had little relationship to termination, although a few individual variables, such as stability of previous employment, marital status, and being the main breadwinner in a household, were predictive of turnover. The major cause of job termination appeared to be the poor quality of working conditions in the entry-level positions to which the hard-core recruits were assigned.

The living conditions of marginal workers also raise barriers to their achievement. Guion and Smith, in their chapter, discuss the deleterious effect that hidden malnutrition and related health problems can have on the deprived worker's motivation and productivity. Some insight into the magnitude of such difficulties is provided in a report by Janger and Schaeffer (1970) on 100 company programs to employ the disadvantaged. These authors describe the unfavorable home conditions of the typical minority group high-school dropout. For example:

> Equitable's counselors found their trainees living in noisy, crowded housing, with one bathroom shared by several families. Merely going to sleep early, or waking up and getting ready for work, were tasks much more difficult for the slum dropout than for his middle-class counterpart . . . . Discussion with the counselor discloses that often dropouts did not eat properly. In winter apartments might not be heated. Pipes frequently froze. While dropouts may not have suffered from incapacitating ailments, physical examinations showed a prevalence of dental ailments and many trainees seemed to lack stamina. Histories of major illness were prevalent. . . . [The] hard-core tend to suffer from a greater prevalence of gastrointestinal upsets and upper respiratory infections commonly associated with anxiety (p. 51).

Social and Psychological Factors

The main individual factors associated with unsatisfactory job performance on the part of minority group workers appear to be distrust of the organizational system and anxiety. Marginal workers tend to doubt that the benefits normally available to white employees—principally job security and promotional opportunities—are equally available to them. Unfortunately, this pessimism and distrust is often well-founded. Consider, for example, the massive layoffs of employees recruited under hard-core job programs that have occurred in the automobile industry during the 1970 recession. Even under more favorable conditions, black workers often have reason to be apprehensive about the system. In a survey of twenty companies which were publicly pledged to a program of action in equal employment opportunity, Ferman and others (1966) found that black blue-collar workers tended to be excluded from informal job experiences that could lead to promotion. Substantially fewer black than white employees reported having the opportunity to become familiar with work other than their own—work involving different skills or greater responsibility—through job trading or job "filling in." The black workers fully recognized the importance for promotion of the white workers' informal social groupings, groupings from which they felt excluded.

Sometimes low self-esteem and fear of failure on the part of the minority person feed into his distrust of the system, resulting in extreme passivity and defensiveness. Thus Ferman found that black industrial workers did not apply for promotions even when they were available. Middle-class blacks brought into high-status jobs are not immune from these feelings. Clark (1965) comments that "they do not generally react with the overt, active hostility prevalent in many members of the 'working class,' but they, too, are often hostile, in ways similar to the larger pattern of white middle-class competitiveness, yet complicated by the persistent problems of racial anxiety, hypersensitivity, and defensiveness" (p. 59).

Policy Recommendations

The recommendations for organizational practices that follow from the preceding are straightforward. In fact, most of what follows is very similar to recommendations appearing elsewhere in this volume. The essential point is that managers must do all in their power to create an atmosphere conducive to the development in minority workers of self-confidence, trust, and the expectancy that their efforts will be fairly and equitably rewarded.

1. Trust in the organization will grow as black workers perceive that promotions are in fact available to minority persons with backgrounds and qualifications similar to their own. This perception will occur when a noticeable and substantial number of black employees have been placed in jobs at all status levels, entailing various degrees of skill and responsibility. The higher-status employees will also serve as role models with whom the new worker can identify; by acting as trainers and supervisors they can provide the supportiveness and acceptance that is needed to allay his anxiety about failing at the job. Finally, having supervisors and peers of his own race will enable the black worker to gratify his need for friendships on the job, a need that is known to be important to blue-collar workers, regardless of their race.

2. As Porter (1970) has noted, reward experiences should be tailored to the

needs of marginal workers, particularly those whose job qualifications are marginal. With regard to the *nature* of rewards, in addition to wages it is likely that recognition and sense of achievement are important. The need for achievement can be gratified by providing work that is neither boring nor too difficult, but rather is moderately challenging, so that adequate performance will be followed by a feeling of accomplishment. Regarding the *scheduling* of rewards, Porter stresses the importance of providing early reward experiences for the marginal worker that will keep him in the work situation and establish an expectancy that his efforts produce desirable payoffs. Porter points out that the scheduling of monetary reward for the new marginal worker may have to be modified considerably from the ordinary reward schedules applicable to other employees. This could mean initially paying the marginal worker part of his wages on a daily basis and part on a weekly basis, with perhaps a bonus at one- or two-week intervals for steady attendance.

3. Organizations concerned about their future manpower needs should do whatever they can to improve community conditions which vitally affect the well-being and productive capabilities of the poor. For example, as more and more industrial plants and businesses become located in suburban areas the urban poor are being excluded from job opportunities because housing is not available to them outside of the inner-city ghettoes. Organizations should find ways to encourage the building of suitable low-cost housing in the suburbs, even if this entails financial investment on their part. Organizations should also involve themselves in public and private efforts to upgrade the quality of education available to economically disadvantaged children and youths at all levels from pre-kindergarten to college and professional school. To a greater extent than in the past, business and industry should provide technical assistance, as well as financial support, for the improvement of school facilities and instructional methods, of both the academic and technological variety. As a final example, organizations should more actively promote the development of needed health and welfare programs at the national, state, and local levels.

REFERENCES

Atkinson, J. W. *An introduction to motivation.* New York: Van Nostrand, 1964.

Atkinson, J. W., and Feather, N. T. *A theory of achievement motivation.* New York: Wiley, 1966.

Ausubel, D. P., and Ausubel, P. Ego development among segregated Negro children. In A. H. Passow (ed.), *Education in depressed areas.* New York: Bureau of Publications, Teachers College, Columbia University, 1963.

Battle, E., and Rotter, J. Children's feelings of personal control as related to social class and ethnic group. *Journal of Personality,* 1963, *31,* 482–490.

Bettelheim, B. Review of B. S. Bloom's *Stability and change in human characteristics. New York Review of Books,* September 10, 1964, *3,* 1–4.

Biller, H. B. Father absence and the personality development of the male child. *Developmental Psychology,* 1970, *2,* 181–201.

Billingsley, A. *Black families in white America.* Englewood Cliffs, N.J.: Prentice–Hall, 1968.

Bradford, D. L. The formation of achievement attitudes among lower class Negro youth. *Dissertation Abstracts,* 1967, *28* (1-A), 293–294.

Bronfenbrenner, U. The psychological cost of quality and equality in education. *Child Development,* 1967, *38,* 909–925.

Clark, K. B. *Dark ghetto.* New York: Harper, 1965.

Coleman, J. S., et al. *Equality of educational opportunity.* U.S. Department of Health, Education and Welfare. Washington, D.C.: U.S. Government Printing Office, 1966.

Coleman, J. S. Race relations and social change. In I. Katz and Patricia Gurin (eds.), *Race and the social sciences.* New York: Basic Books, 1969, pp. 274–341.

Crandall, V. C., Katkovsky, W., and Crandall, V. J. Children's beliefs in their own control of reinforcements in intellectual–academic situations. *Child Development,* 1965, *36,* 91–109.

Crandall, V. J., Katkovsky, W., and Preston, A. Motivation and ability determinants of young children's intellectual achievement behaviors. *Child Development,* 1962, *33,* 643–661.

Drake St. C., and Cayton, H. R. *Black metropolis.* New York: Harper Torchbooks, 1962.

Feld, S., and Lewis, J. The assessment of achievement anxieties in children. Mental Health Study Center, NIMH, 1967, *MS.*

Ferman, L. A. *The Negro and equal employment opportunities: a review of management experiences in twenty companies.* Ann Arbor, Mich.: Institute of Labor and Industrial Relations, University of Michigan, 1966.

Frazier, E. F. *The Negro family in the United States.* Chicago: University of Chicago Press, 1966.

Gibby, R. G., Sr., and Gabler, R. The self-concept of Negro and white children. *Journal of Clinical Psychology,* 168, *23,* 144–148.

Glazer, N., and Moynihan, D. P. *Beyond the melting pot.* Cambridge, Mass.: M.I.T. Press, 1963.

Gurin, G. *Inner-city youth in a job training project.* Ann Arbor, Mich.: Survey Research Center, University of Michigan, 1968 (mimeographed report).

Gurin, G., and Gurin, P. Expectancy theory in the study of poverty. *Journal of Social Issues,* 1970, *26,* No. 2, 83–104.

Hammer, E. F. Frustration-aggression hypothesis extended to socio-racial areas. *Psychiatry Quarterly,* 1953, *27,* 597–607.

Hannerz, U. *Soulside.* New York: Columbia University Press, 1969.

Hess, R. D., Shipman, V., and Jackson, D. Early experience and the socialization of cognitive modes in children. *Child Development,* 1965, *36,* 869–886.

Hill, K. T., and Sarason, S. B. The relation of test anxiety and defensiveness to test and school performance over the elementary school years: A further longitudinal study. *Monograph of the Society for Research in Child Development,* 1966, *31* (Whole No. 2).

Himes, J. S. Some work-related deprivations of lower-class Negro youths. In L. A. Ferman, J. A. Kornbluh, and A. Haber (eds.), *Poverty in America.* Ann Arbor, Mich.: University of Michigan Press, 1965, pp. 384–389.

Hyman, H. H., and Reed, J. S. "Black matriarchy" reconsidered: evidence from secondary analysis of sample surveys. *Public Opinion Quarterly,* 1969, *33,* 346–354.

Janger, A. R., and Schaeffer, R. G. *Managing programs to employ the disadvantaged.* New York: National Industrial Conference Board, 1970.

Kamii, C. K. *Socioeconomic class differences in the preschool socialization practices of Negro mothers.* Unpublished doctoral dissertation, University of Michigan, 1965.

Karon, B. P. *The Negro personality.* New York: Springer, 1958.

Katz, I. The socialization of academic motivation in minority group children. In

D. Levine (ed.), *Nebraska symposium on motivation*. Lincoln, Neb.: University of Nebraska Press, 1967.

Katz, I., Henchy, T., and Allen, H. Effect of race of tester, approval–disapproval and need on learning in Negro boys. *Journal of Personality and Social Psychology,* 1968, *8,* 38–42.

Killingsworth, C. C. Jobs and income for Negroes. In I. Katz and P. Gurin (eds.), *Race and the social sciences.* New York: Basic Books, 1969, pp. 194–273.

Lefcourt, H. M., and Ladwig, G. W. The American Negro: a problem in expectancies. *Journal of Personality and Social Psychology,* 1965, *1,* 377–390.

Lewis, H. Child rearing among low-income families. In L. A. Ferman, J. L. Kornbluh, and A. Haber (eds.), *Poverty in America.* Ann Arbor, Mich.: University of Michigan Press, 1965, pp. 342–352.

Lewis, O. *Five families.* New York: Basic Books, 1959.

Lewis, O. *La vida.* New York: Vintage Books, 1966.

Liebow, E. *Tally's corner.* Boston: Little, Brown, 1967.

Lott, B. E., and Lott, A. J. *Negro and white youth.* New York: Holt, 1963.

McClelland, D. C. *The achieving society.* New York: Van Nostrand, 1961.

McClelland, D. C., Atkinson, J. W., Clark, R. W., and Lowell, E. L. *The achievement motive.* New York: Appleton-Century-Crofts, 1953.

Miller, W. B. Focal concerns of lower-class culture. In L. A. Ferman, J. L. Kornbluh, and A. Haber (eds.), *Poverty in America.* Ann Arbor, Mich.: University of Michigan Press, 1965, pp. 261–269.

Mingione, A. Need for achievement in Negro and white children. *Journal of Consulting Psychology,* 1965, *29,* 108–111.

Mischel, W. Theory and research on the antecedents of self-imposed delay of reward. In B. Maher (ed.), *Progress in experimental personality research,* Vol. 3. New York: Academic Press, 1966.

Mussen, P. H. Differences between the TAT responses of Negro and white boys. *Journal of Consulting Psychology,* 1953, *17,* 373–376.

Pettigrew, T. F. Negro American personality: Why isn't more known? *Journal of Social Issues,* 1964, *20,* 4–23. (a)

Pettigrew, T. F. *A profile of the Negro American.* Princeton: Van Nostrand, 1964. (b)

Porter, L. W. The use of rewards in motivating marginal members of the work force. Washington, D.C.: Performance Research, Inc., 1970 (mimeographed report).

Proshansky, H., and Newton, P. The nature and meaning of Negro self-identity. In M. Deutsch, I. Katz, and A. Jensen (eds.), *Social class, race, and psychological development.* New York: Holt, 1968, pp. 178–218.

Quinn, R. P., Fine, B. D., and Levitin, T. Turnover and training. Ann Arbor, Mich.: Survey Research Center, University of Michigan, 1970 (mimeographed report).

Rainwater, L. Crucible of identity: The Negro lower-class family. *Daedalus,* Winter, 1966, *95,* No. 1, 172–216.

Rainwater, L. The problem of lower class culture. *Journal of Social Issues,* 1970, *26,* No. 2, 133–148.

Rodman, H. The lower-class value stretch. In L. A. Ferman, J. L. Kornbluh, and A. Haber (eds.), *Poverty in America.* Ann Arbor, Mich.: University of Michigan Press, 1965, pp. 270–284.

Rosen, B. C. Race, ethnicity and the achievement syndrome. *American Sociological Review,* 1959, *24,* 417–460.

Rotter, J., Seeman, M., and Liverant, S. Internal vs. external control of reinforcement: A major variable in behavior theory. In N. F. Washburne (ed.), *Decisions, values and groups,* Vol. 2. London: Pergamon Press, 1962.

Sarason, S. B., Davidson, K. S., Lighthall, F. F., Waite, R. R., and Ruebush, B. K. *Anxiety in elementary school children.* New York: Wiley, 1960.

Smith, M. B. Competence and socialization. In J. A. Clausen (ed.), *Socialization and society.* New York: Little, Brown, 1968.

Taeuber, K. E. Negro population and housing: demographic aspects of a social accounting scheme. In I. Katz and P. Gurin (eds.), *Race and the social sciences.* New York: Basic Books, 1969, pp. 145–193.

U.S. Commission on Civil Rights. *Racial isolation in the public schools.* Washington, D.C.: U.S. Government Printing Office, 1967.

U.S. Department of Labor. *The Negro family.* Washington, D.C.: U.S. Government Printing Office, 1965.

Valentine, C. A. *Culture and poverty.* Chicago: University of Chicago Press, 1968.

Whiteman, M., and Deutsch, M. Some effects of social class and race on children's language and intellectual abilities. In M. Deutsch, I. Katz, and A. Jensen (eds.), *Social class, race, and psychological development.* New York: Holt, 1968.

Wylie, R. C., and Hutchins, E. B. Schoolwork-ability estimates and aspirations as a function of socio-economic level, race, and sex. *Psychological Reports,* 1967, *21,* 781–808.

CHAPTER SIX

Motivation

Robert M. Guion and Patricia Cain Smith

INTRODUCTION BY THE EDITORS

The effectiveness of an organization depends upon employee acceptance of at least some of the organization's goals or employee willingness to perform assigned tasks with reasonable efforts and with few absences or little turnover. Effectiveness therefore involves the concept of motivation. *Guion and Smith propose a motivational model which is based upon intentions to achieve a specific task (e.g., production quotas) and more general goals which lead to effective organizational action. This chapter focuses on questions such as how newcomers can be stimulated to specify intentions which are in concert with organizational goals, learn how to set productions goals which yield success experiences, and set intentions to start work on time, etc. An excellent summary of the authors' responses to these questions is presented at the end of the chapter. In the absence of specifically relevent research, policy suggestions are offered throughout the chapter. They are posed as important questions which can be answered best by collaborative efforts of social scientists and organizational administrators.*

Guion and Smith point to the importance of goals which are both explicitly specified and job relevant and which match the needs and skill level of the minority workers, as well as enhancing the efficient functioning of the organization. They stress the need to establish goal-setting habits early in the training of new employees.

Guion and Smith also identify factors which actively stimulate and sustain goal setting and which determine the immediacy and specificity of job-related goals. First, environmental stimulation (or lack of it) is likely to increase (or decrease) goal-setting behavior. For example, pleasant stimulation can be introduced into the work setting via lighting, color, music, cafeteria foods, rest breaks, and so forth. Job enrichment is another way to encourage individual and group goal setting. Sometimes supplementing the workers' diets with a free breakfast or a nutritious supplement is yet another way to improve job performance; poor diets have been shown to have deleterious effects on job performance. Guion and Smith describe a well-controlled, industrial study of the effects of providing vitamin pills to the labor force. It was found that unauthorized absences were reduced and turnover was systematically and cumulatively lower for the employees who took the vitamins.

Both the specificity of goals and the choice of goals are influenced by prior experiences and habits concerning goal setting. Guion and Smith recommend that learning to set organizationally relevant tasks and social goals be an intimate part of any training program, e.g., to begin new work habits as soon as possible. The administrator should be cognizant of the need to help inexperienced workers set goals which are, at first, attainable, and then to provide continuing guidance toward successive increases in the goal levels. The matching of goal setting to the newcomers' level of competence will also increase his acceptability among co-workers. Research has shown that competent newcomers are more accepted than incompetent newcomers—regardless of their race. Intentions to achieve or reject goals are also determined by expectancies about the rewards which will ensue. Of course, the consequences of goal attainment may vary in pleasantness, importance, social acceptability, and various other secondary results. Although each person may come to the organization with a unique past history of work, training in goal setting can establish a common ground for all new employees. Training tasks must be designed so that early and visible completion of tasks can be achieved by all participants in training, regardless of differences in their prior experience. Training supervisors should be both supportive and consistent. There is some research which hints at the value of black supervisors for new black trainees—especially during the training period.

Intentions, goal setting, and expectancies are intimately linked to the question of reward. Stated simply, the employee may ask: "How much effort is this goal worth to me?" Increased effort may be valued, if it brings an increase in pay, or alternatively, not valued if the production brings the reputation of "rate buster" and rejection by co-workers. Guion and Smith draw attention to the notion that the completion of a task in itself can be attractive and rewarding. The first step is to ensure that the task has some point(s) at which the worker recognizes he has completed at least some part of the task. The intervals before these increments should be not so long that the task seems endless, nor so short that the task seems repetitive. Optimal length is an empirical question.

Achievement motivation and fear of failure are identified as potential factors which may affect goal-setting behavior. The authors argue that success ex-

*periences should occur early in the training period. Under conditions of extern-
ally imposed goals or at modest levels of achievement with tangible rewards
obtained immediately on goal attainment, such success experiences become
steps toward more realistic standards and greater self-acceptance.*

*In discussing working conditions, Guion and Smith propose that if "fair"
supervision, praise, pay, and respect from co-workers are factors which affect
goal setting, then their effect would be the same regardless of the ethnic origin
of the workers. More importance, however, is attached to tangible, extrinsic
rewards, such as pay, by workers of lower* socioeconomic classes.

Smooth organizational functioning obviously requires that at least some of the
goals of employees be consonant with those of administrators. It also involves
the capability and the willingness to perform assigned tasks with conflict or
defensiveness among individuals minimized. Reasonable effort should be expended, by both employees and administrators, to reach goals. Absences and
turnover should be comparably low between white and black, inexperienced
and experienced ghetto and middle-class employees. Friction between such
groups should be minimal.

All of these organizational goals involve the concept of motivation.
Managers should be as well able to handle the problems of the "can but won't"
as those of the "can't and will." How should new employees be introduced into
the working situation? What do they bring into the job on the basis of previous
experience in life? What special motivational problems are present when
employees who have accepted the values of an industrial society are mixed
with employees with little or no prior occupational history?

These and many other motivational problems simply have *not* been
investigated, due largely to the desire of administrators to take immediate
action rather than to undertake the tedious process of experimentation and
evaluation to determine which actions will be effective. Our discussion, therefore, will have to center on modern theory, with some tentative recommendations and some suggestions for immediate research.

It is a truism that the motivational problems involved in the integration of
an organization cannot be intelligently discussed without an intelligent idea
of what is meant by motivation. Unfortunately, it is not easy to specify a
generally acceptable set of meanings. One of us once collated various definitions of motivation, enough to fill about five pages. Many of these definitions
bore little resemblance to each other. Only a few of them seemed to have
something to do with movement, the root meaning of the word.

As Appley (1970), Berkowitz (1968), and others on through the alphabet
have pointed out, the concept of motivation is highly unsatisfactory. Perhaps
the difficulty is that too many concepts are too far removed from that root concern with movement. Actual physical movement may provide a starting point
for a discussion of motivational phenomena.

We choose to start from a simple statement about the observation of movement: when it occurs, the observer can perceive and report evidence of the expenditure of effort. This is as true for the movement of machines as for the movement of people. If a train is chugging up a steep hill, an observer can note that the train is "working hard." Human workers moving psychologically or physically, by exhibiting initiative, tension, perseverence, or perspiration, can also be observed to be "working hard." Similarly, at the end of a day, a worker moving slowly and rather aimlessly around his work area can be perceived as coasting, i.e., as expending relatively little effort. In short, when people are moving, doing something, making something happen, or preventing something from happening—that is, when they are motivated—an observer who understands their movements can observe and draw inferences about a concomitant level of effort expenditure. (See Lifson, 1953, p. 10 for a correlation of .46 between rating, by workers and observers, concerning effort required.)

The question, then, of what motivates people becomes a question of what induces them to expend some observable level of effort in making a physical or psychological movement.

A TASK-RELATED VIEW OF MOTIVATION

Our approach follows somewhat that of Ryan (1970) in that it emphasizes an individual's intention to do something or to accomplish something. The nature of an intention is defined by the tasks it sets; examples may include intending to move to some point, to do something to an object, to communicate an idea, or to learn a skill.

Intentional behavior is clearly goal-oriented. A task, it should be noted, may be a goal in itself, such that merely doing the thing (e.g., playing solitaire) may be all that one intends. In contrast, a task may be a means for the achievement of a goal; the goal may be extrinsic, such as receiving money in exchange for the performance of the task, or it may be intrinsic to the task itself, such as achieving a sense of competence and mastery. Thus any given task one intends to carry out may be thought of as having means-character or goal-character, or both, characteristics first identified by Ryan and Smith (1954).

Goal setting occurs even in the most unlikely situations. For example, Wijting (1970) wanted to determine performance level when the task was fully learned. He hired subjects to do the abominable task described by Graen (1969) of rounding numbers from a computer printout and recording them. It is difficult to think of this task as having goal-character. Perversely, however, the subjects persisted in setting ever-higher goals for themselves; at each session they tried to do more than they had done at the previous one.

The task itself may have no intrinsic goal-character, but the intention to improve one's performance has the effect of giving it such a role. In fact, a goal may itself have means-character as the path to be taken for the attainment of yet another goal, as in the case of the housewife who sets herself the task of hurrying through dishes so she can sit down to watch television. An aversive task may have goal-character simply in terms of getting it over with.

In short, people *will* set goals, and these goals may not be those that would superficially seem appropriate from an observer's or "organizational" point of view. Managers as well as employees set goals. It should be *management's* goal to induce the employee to set goals appropriate both to the individual and to the organization. Inappropriate goals might include restriction of output to conform with the custom of one's working group, achieving only the minimum to prevent being discharged, or actual sabotage. Appropriate goals might include exceeding x percent of some standard of productivity, maintaining no more than y percent of errors, being absent no more than z percent of the time, smoothing over an interpersonal conflict at work, or preparing onself for promotion.

It is important to note that goal-setting precedes the expenditure of effort. This does not imply that goals are always specifically set; considerable variation in the specificity of goals may be anticipated from person to person and from situation to situation. The middle-aged man who takes up jogging may, of course, set himself a very specific schedule of improvement in the number of minutes or number of miles defining his endurance; another one may simply intend to do as much jogging as the spirit and flesh, in whatever combination, can endure.

From the example it seems clear that we *do* suggest that the amount of effort expended at a task will be *greater when goals are more explicitly stated.* Moreover, although behavior can be motivated by vague or general intentions to achieve vague or general goals, vagueness inhibits clear definition of the task and leads to little or no demonstrable outcome. (The intention to become the world's most famous concert violinist has little impact until it is broken up into more specific goals such as practicing at least three hours each day.)

This tendency to set goals is one reason we prefer the study of intentional behavior as our approach to the topic of motivation.[1] For psychologists primarily concerned with behavior at work, the focus on intentional behavior is particularly relevant. We suggest that performance of assigned tasks at a job depends on the goals set or accepted, on the specificity of these goals, and, in fact, on whether any goals are intentionally set at all.

Intentional behavior also deserves further attention, particularly if integration of the organization implies bringing into the group people who have rarely held regular employment and who may have no relevant experience in setting or accepting work goals. When dealing with such newcomers, the practical question is: "How can they be stimulated to specify intentions which are in concert with organizational goals?" As examples, how can employees be

---

[1] We are fully aware that unintentional behavior occurs, whether it be habitual behavior or aimless behavior, and that it is a legitimate concern of psychologists engaged in a broad study of motivation.

stimulated to learn how to set production goals, or to set intentions to start to work on time and keep at it until the working day is over, or to intend to accept instruction and supervision? For old-timers, it is an equally practical question to ask, "How do they intend to react to a changed situation?" Established employees may have to learn to set new kinds of goals, such as getting along with newcomers who are in some way "different."

Failure to set goals, or setting inappropriate goals, may have a severely disruptive role in organizational life. Major disruptions are often the consequence of deliberate or intentional acts which are inappropriate—even though disruption itself may not have been the intention. An organization in which one of us has been consulting has provided a relevant anecdote. One woman employee said, with reference to programs of jobs for the usually unemployed, "We've been working here for thirty years and working hard. Now they bring 'them' in and 'they' don't have to do anything." We do not know what this woman intends to do in response to her changed situation, any more than we understand the intentions of the "them" she refers to. We do believe that her behavior—and "theirs"—will ultimately be better understood in terms of intentions than in terms of unconscious resentments. Her hostility, at least, is certainly not unconscious. A person like this woman will probably not intend to be disruptive. However, she will, in effect, be disruptive if she will not continue to set the same work goals she has set in the past.

What factors will influence her goals? We have no immediate answer to this excellent question. But it may help to consider what Brewster Smith (1969)[2] called "intrinsic motivation," referring to behavior in which the outcomes are the result of one's own activity rather than such extrinsic reward or punishment as reflected appraisals of one's qualities and performance from others. Of course, the evaluation of the outcomes of one's own activity is not entirely independent of the reflected evaluations; the opinions and attitudes of others to provide one with a set of standards to apply. To try to state Smith's position in our terms, we may say that setting specific goals—goals that represent challenge—requires confidence that the intentions can, in fact, be carried out successfully and that the success will be sufficiently objective to be observed by others. Conversely, in a situation where one can accurately predict that the outcome of his effort will be failure and that the failure will be accompanied by indifference or disapproval from others, there is little intrinsic reason to set any goal at all.

This is precisely the situation faced by all too many black children, especially boys, in school. Katz (1967) reported the use of a "Reinforcement History Questionnaire" asking children how parents respond to the effort expended by the children and to its success or failure. Black boys with low scholastic achievement, anxiety, and low self-esteem (a frequently recurring

---

[2] White (1959) used a related concept which he calls "effectance motivation." According to White, one major source of motivation is a desire for a "feeling of efficacy."

combination) tended to report low parental interest or acceptance and much parental punishment. What is there, in such a syndrome, to produce any feeling of competence to deal with the academic world so that academically relevant goals may be set?

There is evidence that black youth have a greater tendency than whites to attribute happenings to their environment rather than to the results of their own actions. They have a reduced tendency to attribute events to internal control, and hence less belief in their own ability to modify the situation (Gurin, Gurin, Lao, and Beattie, 1969).

Returning to the indignant woman quoted earlier, in what way can she be said to be competent to control her situation? She may, of course, take great pride in her superior competence in meeting the demands of the job, and she may therefore set increasingly higher personal goals; that is, her motivation may be primarily intrinsic. If, however, her level of superiority is not sufficiently great, or if she gives greater attention to the perceived fact that she and the newcomer receive similar rewards for grossly different levels of effort and performance, her judged recourse may be to set her goals appreciably lower than her past performance.

Our task-related view of motivation begins with the observation that people do, as a matter of course, set goals and that they will, so long as the goals remain unchanged, expend intentionally the effort necessary to work toward the achievement of their goals. Stated more briefly, from their goals they define for themselves the tasks they intend to carry out. Integrating an organization requires the maintenance of those goals that have been necessary for the smooth functioning of the organization all along; it requires in addition that the newly integrated employees accept these organizationally appropriate goals and that older employees set new goals of interpersonal behavior. Integration, therefore, calls for some fairly specific sorts of intentions, about which we are admittedly not very sure. One point, however, seems clear: effort expenditure will be greater and more appropriate from an organizational point of view if goals are clearly specifiable, mutually accepted, and attainable through behavior the individual can carry out with objectively observable levels of success on the task.

FACTORS INFLUENCING GOAL SETTING

Before we can properly concern ourselves with work motivation in an integrated setting, we need to consider more systematically the devices or factors by which goal-setting activity is stimulated and sustained and by which the specificity and immediacy of goals is determined. In doing so, we shall borrow from research stimulated by other points of view, bending it appropriately to fit our concern with intentional behavior.

Activation, Arousal, and Activity Level

It is perhaps desirable to include within the general concept of motivation a base line of overall reactivity related to the individual's predisposition to respond. The notion of a general activity level may provide such a base.

It seems likely on the basis of common sense and everyday observation (but without rigorous proof) that activity level is a relatively stable trait, manifested in a general tendency to be alert, to attend to stimuli, to react and to respond readily, both with changes in physiological states and with changes in overt behavior. This general tendency may well exist as a temperamental factor determining the probability of setting goals, their specificity, and the level of effort required to reach them.

Accepting the idea of a generalized personal activity level, we know very little about its origins. There are probably genetic determinants; there are biochemical correlates that seem to be antecedent (Mueller, Kasl, Brooks, and Cobb, 1970). There are almost certainly emotional affects related to interpersonal relationships.

ENVIRONMENTAL STIMULATION. From whatever base line is provided by such a general characteristic, it seems self-evident that changes in activity level occur from time to time; that is, at some points in time the individual's reactivity is increased because of increases in environmental stimulation. Certainly, lack of such stimulation has drastic effects on the development of children and on the behavior of adults, as in sensory-deprivation studies. This increased reactivity from environmental stimulation, including the human environment, suggests that goal setting may also be related to the more temporary conditions of arousal or activation (Duffy, 1962). One very important and controllable source of activity level, then, is probably environmental stimulation. Planned programs of stimulation should have favorable effects— but only up to a point. Very strong stimulation is aversive and does not facilitate performance or learning or, by implication, goal setting.

NUTRITION. Nutrition has striking effects. Imparato (1969) has surveyed the literature on the relationships of nutrition to behavior. The low level of vitamin, mineral, protein, and often caloric content of American diets has been well documented, even for middle-class whites. Malnutrition has repeatedly been shown to have greater and more lasting effects on children than on adults.

The effects of malnutrition on performance, both on tests and in the working situation, have seldom been evaluated in controlled studies. Although this lack of control is overwhelming, so also is the convergence of evidence of effect. As a consequence of malnutrition, deficits in attention, possibly irreparable, are occurring widely on the European and American continents, as well as in Africa and Asia. In the United States, a particularly undernourished group is the blacks who have migrated north into the large cities, where they lose even the inadequate protection which came from eating the products of the farm.

In one of the few well-controlled industrial experiments on nutrition, Borsook (1945) studied the effects of the introduction of vitamin pills on male industrial workers who were, presumably, selecting vitamin-poor foods. Unauthorized absences declined in the second six months of the study for experimental subjects, while remaining at the initial level for (matched) placebo and control groups. Turnover was systematically and cumulatively lower for the experimental group. In the series of experiments called the Minnesota Starvation Studies, after prolonged semistarvation (intended to match concentration camp diets) decrements were reported in physical strength, psychomotor performance, and emotional control (e.g., Brozek, Guetzkow, Mickelson, and Keys, 1946; Keys, Brozek, Henschel, Mickelson, and Taylor, 1950). These changes may be secondary effects associated with diminished desire to work, but could be interpreted as decreased level of activity as well.

Almost all of these studies suffer from lack of experimental control, and should, theoretically, be replicated. It would, however, be surprising if any experimenter wished to undertake research involving so much danger.

ORGANIZATIONAL IMPLICATIONS.   Level of general activity, whatever the factors determining it, can be hypothesized to be important to motivation in the working situation, as measured by absence, turnover, production, and accidents.

All of this leads to the practical question of what might be effective in increasing level of general activity. Three courses of action seem obvious even though their effectiveness has not as yet been tested empirically.

1. Increase overall pleasant stimulation in the working situation—always with the worker's preferences in view. Lighting, music, cafeteria foods, rest breaks, and other environmental conditions should be varied, whenever plausible, and level of activity measured, in controlled studies. At least one study (Smith and Curnow, 1966) has shown that activity is increased by increasing the loudness of background music (the subjects were not workers but shoppers in supermarkets).

Common sense indicates that stimulation should be pleasant, although there is evidence that any stimulation is more activating than none. One device for determining whether musical stimulation, for example, is pleasant is balloting for a "Hit Parade" for the best records of the week, to be played during the last work period of the week. This permits any sort of music, including "soul music," to find its way toward the top of the list, to give a guideline for what should be played the following week. If there are indeed black–white differences, this procedure allows them to appear. Attention might also be given to the activating (and perhaps differentially activating) effects of bright color and bold design on walls.

2. Encourage goal setting. Combining units into meaningful units may not be sufficient to induce the worker with low activity level to think about the

approach of the end of a task, and to work toward it, but verbal encouragement could help. It is pure conjecture, but it seems likely that working toward a defined goal increases level of activity. Goal setting is one of the most pervasive of all phenomena displayed by men at work, but it may not have developed among the hard-core unemployed due to lack of working experience. Goals should, of course, be readily attainable at first, and increased with experience. If goals cannot be set for the individual, group goals are possible in some situations and seem (on the basis of indirect evidence) to encourage identification with the work group.

If goals that are extremely easy to attain are established, by the individual or the organization, the worker may lose interest in them; that is, they no longer provide a source of genuine stimulation. However, where small units of work that provide no intrinsic motivation can be combined into meaningful and more challenging units, with clearly identifiable ends, apparently dull work can become stimulating. Many job enrichment programs represent an application of this principle.

3. Supplement workers' diets. Since nutrition is likely to be a problem, some way of supplementing the diet seems desirable. Deficits from childhood malnutrition are largely irreversible, but adult lacks can be replenished more easily. A suggestion, which seems linked to the persistent problem of absenteeism and tardiness of the hard core, is that the company provide a free breakfast to all employees. At least one company, the Great Lakes Insurance Company, subsidized breakfasts for disturbed school children in Detroit's inner city, although there has been no report of the results as yet (New Detroit Committee, 1968, pp. 49–50).

Habit

We reject any notion of motivation that ignores the background of the individual. We suggest that the goals an individual sets for himself are determined not only by the stimulus characteristics of his immediate situation but also by the personal characteristics he brings to the situation from his past history. From this, it would not be surprising to discover that people with widely different cultural backgrounds, and therefore with widely different culturally determined habits, would choose different kinds of goals.

The choice of a goal depends upon habits of thinking. Much of the literature on achievement motivation, at least as measured by fantasy, can probably be explained in terms of a habit of choosing competitive goals over internalized or cooperative ones. The choice of highly visible goals (i.e., goals which, when attained, produce widespread notice and approval) as opposed to private, personal goals may also be seen as habitual. Similarly, the choice of vindictive goals may be stimulated by habitual attitudes of vindictiveness, and the goal of containment of minority groups may be stimulated by nothing more sinister than a habitual belief in a stereotype.

The degree of specificity or immediacy of goals may also be seen partly as a function of prior habit. Intuitively, it is attractive to suppose that those who have made a habit of goal setting (e.g., in management by objectives) will find it easier in ordinary circumstances to phrase their goals with greater specificity than could those without such habits or training. The habitual goal setter may express the intention "to improve by a factor of 15 percent within three months," while one for whom goal setting in specific terms is not yet a habit may simply intend to "do better."

Both choice of goals and their specificity are influenced by roles acquired from prior experience and persistently followed, providing a constellation of habits. An example exists in roles derived from family experience. Family structure in the ghetto is not similar to that of Northern whites, but it is very similar to that of the tenant farmers in the rural South. To oversimplify, the structure is matriarchical. The mother is the head of the family, and also the principal laborer. The father is either absent, or not a model for inducing good, and regular, work habits. Men are not expected to support their families, and do not (as we use the term) intend to do so. These role-induced habits generalize; there seem to be indications that, among the hard-core unemployed, women adapt more readily than men to the working situation; that is, they are more likely to accept or develop organizationally appropriate goals.

A parallel situation regarding social goals may exist in organizations or organizational levels that have not historically been integrated. One with a prior habit of avoiding contact with members of minority groups, or even one who has never developed a habit of association, has very little practice in setting organizationally appropriate social goals. The level of prior experience almost certainly influences the degree of specificity; there is surely a discernible difference in goal specificity and in subsequent intentional behavior between one who has a vague goal "to be nice and not cause trouble" and another whose goal is "to get acquainted" with a newcomer through specific acts such as helping him through an orientation period or inviting him to join a car pool.

Whether inexperience is related to work goals or to social goals, what seems to be needed for the inexperienced is training programs intended to establish habits of goal setting. Such training probably needs to be highly in-dividualized, and the techniques of behavior modification which have proven valuable in clinical and community psychology may well be worth applying here. In either field of deficiency, workers need help in establishing simple and attainable goals, successful practice in selecting behavior appropriate to their attainment, and guidance in successive increases in goal levels. And the prin-ciples necessary for the establishment of appropriate goal-setting habits related to productivity are probably not different from those necessary for the establish-ment of goal-setting behavior that will genuinely rather than superficially integrate an organization.

It is important to note, and not just in passing, that training in the setting of work goals is concomitant with training for simple competence. It seems quite clear that the acceptance of minority group members not previously included within an organization will depend at least in part upon the competence with which they do their assigned tasks. A laboratory investigation by Fromkin, Klimoski, and Flanagan (1971) illlustrates the point: groups with feedback indicating success evaluated newcomers on the basis of task competency, not on race. Although evaluations of newcomers in the failure groups were related to race, they were also clearly a function of competence. The implication seems clear; training of inexperienced workers is as necessary for group acceptance as for the more usual concerns of production.

Expectancies

One's personal history partially determines his goals by providing him with cues about the probable outcomes of various options. One's intentions are set, at least in part, in terms of his expectations. Choices between alternative courses of action or between different levels of attainment of goals may vary in anticipated consequences. Specific outcomes may be expected to vary in pleasantness, importance, social acceptability, or secondary results. Specific tasks as means to goals may vary in anticipated interest, difficulty, social acceptability, or risk. Evaluations of outcomes and tasks are not, of course, entirely historical; specific characteristics within a situation may well elicit specific responses, as will feedback at intermediate task points. Personality characteristics, such as available coping mechanisms, authoritarian attitudes, or sense of personal competence or self-esteem, also influence general expectations. Nevertheless, experience is probably the primary determiner of expectancies.

Elements within organizational work settings include authority, channels of communication, physical restrictions on movement or action, informal social structures, or causal social interactions, as well as assigned tasks. Any one of these elements, to some degree, has probably been included also in the personal histories of individuals who enter the organization; each one has had some kind of prior experience with figures of authority, utilizing channels of communication, being in enclosed or otherwise restrictive areas, and so on. There are surely individual differences in details of these experiences; just as surely there are differences associated with cultural backgrounds. The experience of blacks or Mexican-Americans with regard to society's authority figures (e.g., police or teachers) is generally considered to be quite different from that of middle-class whites. For those who speak standard "American," experiences with communication are quite different from the experiences of those who speak "Tex-Mex" or a black dialect.

Such differences in experience include differences in experienced outcomes, and these differences lead to different expectancies with regard to the work situation. One who has experienced authorities as helpful, and who has been able to communicate his problem clearly, will perceive a supervisor as one who will provide help if he has trouble performing his assigned tasks; those whose experience is more negative may expect further trouble if they admit their difficulties to the boss.

It is too glib to suggest merely that supervisors and managers must become sensitive to the differences in expectancies of different groups of employees. It may be more realistic to suggest that training in goal setting, either of work or of interpersonal goals, be organized so that early expectancies within the organization become common across groups. For example, supervisors must from the outset attempt to demonstrate consistently both a nurturant and a structuring response to subordinates. As a further example, early tasks must be organized so that early and visible completion of tasks is probable for all employees, regardless of prior experience. By systematic attempts to create a common set of expectancies for all the various elements of the work situation, the effect of subgroup initial differences in expectancy may be minimized.

Rewards, Values, and Social Comparisons

In a sense, intentional behavior is intrinsically motivating. That is, the individual sets his own goals and then expends the effort needed to demonstrate to himself that he could, or that he almost could, reach his goal. It is a closed system that does not require and may not even permit intrusion from outside.

Many intentions, however, receive their stimulation from external forces. A school system, for example, has its traditional ways of grading; students are likely to set their goals in terms of grade-point averages, honor-roll standards, or simply graduation. Factories offer money, fringe benefits, and, occasionally, promotions in exchange for work, without ever making explicit any relationship between these rewards and the amount or quality of work performed. Workers may set intrinsic goals, or they may set goals in terms of some generally accepted concept of a fair day's work. Husbands and children may carry out household tasks, not to achieve any intrinsic pleasure from doing them, but to win a reward or avoid a punishment tendered by wife or mother. Such extrinsic considerations have been central to many motivational theories.[3]

There is, nevertheless, an intrinsic question of values implicit in any discussion of goal setting. Stated most simply, the question for each individual is, "How much effort is this level of this goal worth?" It is well worth the effort, for example, for Wijting's subjects to round enough numbers for the task to be a challenge rather than a drudgery. It is worth the bakery-truck driver's effort to work a fifty-five- to sixty-hour week to bring in more money. It may not be worth the effort on a piece-rate job to produce twice as much as the man nearby if the extra income signifies increased taxation or a reputation as a "rate buster." Value, in this sense, is simply a matter of placing an evaluative tag

---

[3] We need not bother ourselves very much about the role of reward and punishment, per se, in the setting of intentions. People habituated to thinking about motivation in other terms—need reduction, expectancy theories, incentive theories in general—need do only slight semantic maneuvering to feel comfortable.

on an outcome, the evaluation being expressed in something like units of effort. It is not very different from concepts of valence or attitude direction and intensity.

The setting of goals is inextricably related to one's judgments of right or wrong, or better or worse, as he understands such judgments in the light of his own heritage. His heritage, moreover, is not exactly like that of someone else; once upon a time the small town of Middle America may have been homogenized, but this is certainly no longer true. Prevailing and perhaps relatively uniform values exemplified by the Protestant ethic no longer seem to have been given in stone to all men. This fact poses a serious question to the student of intentional behavior, particularly when confronted with the fact of people intentionally renouncing the values of their forebearers. Brewster Smith has summed it up well:

The old myth had it that man lost his precultural innocence when, biting the fruit of the Tree of Knowledge, he became aware of Good and Evil. In becoming modern, Man has taken a second portentous bite of the same fruit. There are alternative versions of Good and Evil, he discovers to his discomfiture, and it is up to him to choose the commitments he is to live by. From this emerging view that can no longer turn to authoritative interpretations of tradition or divine revelation to resolve questions of value, it makes no sense at all for us to encyst ourselves behind a pass-the-buck notion that we can leave value judgments to some other discipline that specializes in them. There is no discipline that has this mythical competence: the humanist and the theologian speak with no greater authority than we. We are all in it together (Smith, 1969, p. 185).

There is a lesser kind of borrowing from one's social environment that is more easily recognized as psychological; it has been studied in recent years under the heading of "social comparisons." We shall not in this chapter undertake a review of the ideas that have emerged from these studies; we shall restrict our interest to one of the older topics.

One's estimate of his personal competence influences the setting of his goals. That self-estimate depends in large measure on how the individual compares himself with others around him. If others performing the same task perform better or poorer than he, in his perception of reality, then his self-estimate of his own competence is lowered or raised, respectively. One would expect a correlation between self-estimate and goal setting. Such a correlation seems demonstrated in the report by Katz (1967) that low-achieving black boys are, in fact, highly self-critical.

An appropriate organizational prescription may be to attempt to increase job involvement so that task completion is more nearly intrinsically rewarding. This seems to be a two-stage prescription. The first step in creating such a situation is to make sure that the task has a clearly marked point at which the worker recognizes that he has completed something. These periods of time should be neither so long that the task seems endless nor so short that it seems endlessly repetitive. The hypothesis is that tasks characterized by such completions acquire, in time, a more general interest and attractiveness (Ryan, 1970). The optimal task length has not been empirically determined, even as a hypothetical average, but it seems plausible that it would be between twenty minutes and an hour. Some tasks, such as conveyor work, may not be easily broken into smaller units; the best that can be done may be to mark off sections on the conveyor belt. Other tasks can be readily grouped or combined to permit a feeling of completion. The recycling of the task should provide activating change.

Are there black–white differences in the length of the optimal work cycle? If so, suitable variations in the supply of work or clear methods of signaling the completion of an artificially formed unit of work could be introduced for many jobs to facilitate job involvement. However, there is no answer to the question until the appropriate research is done, and any prescription for differential treatment of subgroups prior to finding the answers is quite premature.

The second step in increasing job involvement is to attach a reward for completion of meaningful units. Rewards may include money, praise, feedback of performance level by charts or other devices, or perhaps even a light or tone signalling completion. Once again the principles of behavior modification techniques seem applicable.

ETHNIC VARIABLES IN GOAL SETTING

The implications of the task-oriented view of motivation for practical problems of integration require careful formulation and research. Very little is actually known, in the sense of citable facts. Many inferences can be drawn from research done in other frames of references, and many more can be suggested intuitively, but all deserve to be viewed with a healthy skepticism.

We know that minority groups typically have experienced discrimination unknown to members of the white majority. A case in point in laboratory research was provided by Youssef (1968) in a study using the Buss aggression machines; blacks presumed to be on the receiving end of shock received heavier doses of shock than did whites from whites controlling the machine. More relevant is the shock that comes from the "last hired—first fired" history of blacks, Spanish-Americans, Indians, and (briefly) East European immigrants among other ethnic minorties. Perhaps even more significant is the history of enforced housing segregation, segregation of public facilities, and related Jim Crowism.

The history of discrimination may account for results reported by Katz and Benjamin (1960) in an experimental study using racially mixed four-man groups. They found that blacks, although given objective evidence of their equality in ability, nevertheless tend to exhibit feelings of inadequacy and a compliant orientation toward the white group members. Moreover, they were more susceptible to group influences.

We do not precisely know how such compliance influences intentions, but we can offer some rather safe hypotheses. One hypothesis is that people accustomed to discrimination will question the wisdom of setting competitive goals. Relevant evidence is given by Katz and Cohen (1962). When paired white and black students were put into a problem-solving situation without special training, blacks would not compete with whites even when the blacks' problems were presented in soluble form and the whites' were not. But with "assertion training" in which the blacks were given overwhelming evidence in favor of the correct solution, greater confidence and accuracy resulted (although whites showed decreased preference for these blacks as partners). The increased confidence transferred to an unrelated laboratory task. We do not know whether the confidence would transfer to a job, but it is worthy of investigation.

Another hypothesis is that minority members of high ability may nevertheless accept lower group goals, and therefore experience boredom on jobs where intrinsic motivation might have led to experiences of challenge and success. It is worth a trial to give training in the setting of increasingly more difficult goals in the hope of establishing a general desire for challenge.

Achievement and Fear of Failure

A common stereotype is that members of minorities tend to be low in achievement motivation and level of aspiration. A number of studies have been done on these topics over the last several years, with very little evidence to support the assertion (Gist and Bennett, 1963; Katz, 1967). There are occasional studies offering support (e.g., Mingione, 1965), and one of the more frequently cited studies found blacks relatively low on achievement motivation and the lowest of six ethnic samples on vocational aspirations (Rosen, 1959). In contrast, however, are studies reporting vocational aspiration and achievement motivation high among black students (Sain, 1966; Sexton, 1963). In a perhaps typical study, with Anglo-American and Mexican-American samples matched for intelligence, Barberio (1967) found no significant difference in need for achievement.

The differences in results may be due to differences in the method of measurement. As Dreger and Miller (1968) have pointed out, the evidence accumulates that, when measured by direct questions, the levels of aspiration of blacks are higher than those of comparable whites, but when measured by fantasy, lower or equal need for achievement is found. The important finding concerns expectation of future achievement, which is less for blacks than for whites.

An exception appears in the situation in which the goals of blacks are seen as related to success in a desired task. Lefcourt and Ladwig (1965b) showed that black inmates who were members of a jazz group persisted longer than a control group in a game with a white stooge (who always won) when they believed the task to be related to musical performance. The same authors, again with prisoners (1965a), showed that blacks had a greater expectancy that the results of their activities were not internally controlled but due to external influences beyond their control. It seems obvious that training programs should emphasize tasks in which individual efforts result in immediate and visible results.

Along with Katz (1967), we should be critical of the assumed generality of achievement motivation. It is widely recognized that various measures purporting to measure need for achievement or related constructs do not, in fact, correlate very well. Even in studies showing black pupils' disinterest in classroom learning, this may be less a matter of their lacking the achievement motive than of its being directed into nonintellectual pursuits. Achievement motivation at work may also appear lacking because it is directed elsewhere.

The research for a generalization about ethnic factors in achievement motivation seems to lead to a dead end. Without any special confidence in it, we can suggest that a potentially more fruitful approach will consider ethnic group membership as a moderating influence on the correlates of achievement motivation. Suppose that we identify a worker with a high achievement motivation (in our terminology, "intention to achieve"). A first question is very simple: how? By performing well on his job? By advancing to positions of authority and power? By accepting leadership in a civil rights organization? By excelling in athletics or the arts? By going to night school to prepare for a profession? Perhaps (and we offer this with no special conviction) there are ethnic differences in the probabilities of various answers.

Significance of mean differences aside, we feel that organizations should recognize the possibility or rather severe fear of failure, at least in individual cases. This fear certainly has implications for goal-setting behavior; all of the early level of aspiration studies made clear that failure experiences and anticipation of failure led to low goals. The black experience must lead to lower goals than those set by whites, who have a more rewarding experience. We return to the suggestion concerning more immediate rewards during the training period.

Social Evaluation and Self-Esteem

Minority group members typically have less formal education and less training in marketable skills than do whites. Moreover, a language barrier to effective communication with the majority is not uncommon. The dialect popularly associated with black speech is ungrammatical, with a limited vocabulary (Levin, 1965). Spanish-speaking Americans are frequently more nonlingual than bilingual; growing up in a home where only Spanish is spoken by undereducated parents and going to school where only English is used, they lack proficiency in either language. In social comparisons along these salient dimensions, minorities do not fare well; it is logical to expect minority group members in such situations to show low self-esteem, which would inter-fere greatly with setting significant goals.

However logical the expectation might be, it does not necessarily square with the available data. For example, a study of students of low socioeconomic class attending long-integrated Northern schools reveals that blacks consistently report higher self-esteem than whites (Wylie and Hutchens, 1967).

Care is needed in interpreting such data. There may be a large measure of defensiveness in survey responses. An individual's evaluation of himself is based in large part on his perception of how others evaluate him and on who is the evaluator. If that perception is negative, it may do some emotional good to say verbally that one has a high opinion of himself; after all, it's safe enough when one need set no goals on the strength of a purely verbal declaration. Katz gives as his example the fact that more blacks than whites report a desire to go to college, yet the proportion of blacks who had seen a college catalog or had written for information about college was lower. Such verbal overstate-ment on an anonymous questionnaire reveals "achievement values and achieve-ment standards that do not get reflected in actual achievement efforts" (Katz, 1967, p. 174). It also shows "awareness" of white organizational values, which should be related to those of blacks by a reward system during training.

Again, the fact is that at least some, and probably a disproportionate number, of those hired from low socioeconomic minority groups will suffer a low self-esteem, probably evidenced by excessive self-criticism and deprecation of their own efforts. Among school children, the highly self-critical children are typically low achievers, although the low achievement does not imply low standards for achievement. Quite the contrary; the standards are probably impossibly high. In a different context, Sexton (1963) spoke of black career expectations as "fantasies of ambition side by side with hopelessness."

It is a dangerous game to guess at the organizational effects and to make suggestions of what should be done to counter this situation. We could hypo-thesize that externally imposed goals of modest achievement, with extrinsic reward for attainment, could lead in small steps to more realistic standards and greater self-acceptance. But we can't be very sure, and we don't know what harmful side effects to anticipate.

Rewards and Incentives

Both rewards for past performance and incentives to achieve can be con-sidered as methods of changing intentions. Approval or disapproval of per-formance in a verbal learning task was offered as an incentive in a social rein-forcement study reported by Katz, Henchy, and Allen (1968). Subjects were grade-school black boys in a Northern city. Performance, particularly for boys with a strong expressed goal of approval, was greater when approval was given and when the examiner himself was black.

Black and white differences in choices of the kinds of gratifications they want have been studied. An experimental study of children, using candy as a reward, found that the willingness, to delay reward was due more to situational factors than to class or race (Seagull, 1966). A job satisfaction survey among underprivileged workers compared pair comparison rankings of sixteen motivational factors for blacks and for whites, with a median deviation of the resulting ranks of only one point (Champagne and King, 1967).

Do blacks and whites and Indians and Mexican-Americans want different things? We think not. In so far as working conditions, a fair boss, praise, pay, and respect from co-workers have anything to do with goal setting, their role is the same regardless of ethnic group.

Socioeconomic status may be another matter. Katz (1967) reported that poor children are better motivated when tangible rewards are offered, such as toys or money. On the other hand, middle-class children are motivated as well or better with feedback. If this generalizes to adults, in so far as integration of the organization implies hiring from applicants of low socioeconomic status, it may well be that tangible, extrinsic rewards will assist the goal-setting activity, especially during the training period.

Values

Race differences in values seem to be clearly identifiable. Mann (1962) reported on differences between whites and nonwhites in South Africa, labeling his results "commonplace in research of this sort." Whites were found to value personal satisfactions primarily, while nonwhites subordinated such satisfaction to community betterment. In this country, a comparison of black and white elementary-education students revealed a stronger economic value, as measured by the Allport–Vernon–Lindzey Study of Values, among the black students (Diener, 1967).

Bradford (1967) studied the attitudes of a group of 884 lower-class black youth, most of whom were high-school dropouts, who had voluntarily joined a retraining program. He commented on the degree of acceptance within this group of the so-called Protestant ethic. His subjects tended to hold the belief that work is important, that one ought to work hard, and that occupational advancement comes through hard work. The data, incidentally, are not defensive verbal responses to anonymous questionnaires; they were drawn from interviews with the subjects, their mothers, their job supervisors, and members of the training staff.

A group of graduate students at Bowling Green has developed a set of six scales to assess various aspects of the Protestant ethic; these scales have quite recently been administered by Olin and Patricia Smith to all employees in a large civil service installation. Small but statistically significant differences between responses of blacks and whites appear for four of the scales. Blacks were lower on scales measuring the value of social status, pride in work, and preference for being active. They were higher on job involvement, a component of the Protestant ethic that may have been especially strong in the Bradford (1967) interviews.

Again, we hesitate to assume very much from such sparse data, but it does appear that ethnic differences in value systems can be expected. It remains to see whether those differences influence the goal level set or merely the choice of a goal category.

CONCLUDING COMMENTS

Motivation at work is a difficult topic to summarize. We have chosen a frame of reference, intentional behavior, which is not widely used in the literature on motivation but which has, we think, especially important implications for the motivational problems that occur within organizations. Where the organization is being integrated there are special implications related to minorities such as blacks (e.g., setting low-level goals or setting none at all, fear of failure or lack of assertiveness or compensatory excessive assertiveness, or value systems that differ from those of the majority already in the organization) and other special implications related to the white majority (e.g., resistance to the admission of new black employees and resentment of the special treatment the newcomers may receive). If there is to be genuine integration, there must be something more than the physical presence of two or more identifiably dissimilar subgroups. There must be a common set of task-related goals. Moreover, there must also be a common set of social goals, at least to the extent of working toward reasonable harmony within the organizational setting.

Some of the implications of the literature for organizations seeking genuine integration have been mentioned before, but they seem worth repeating in summary.

1. Intrinsic motivation, where a worker or manager can set and generally attain his own goals, will result in higher performance levels than will be induced by extrinsic rewards. The latter, however, may be helpful to the inexperienced worker who must learn how to set goals rationally and specifically. Special training schools, whether company-sponsored or community-sponsored, seem indicated for several reasons: better environmental control, easier practice of the arts of goal setting, and, perhaps most critically, minimum disruption and threat to existing employees by the introduction of what they perceive as unqualified workers in their midst. Subsequent on-the-job training, with frequent attention and encouragement (as distinct from "close supervision"), should follow, and there is evidence to suggest that a "buddy system" or similar scheme might improve the transition with secondary benefits.[4]

[4] According to a study cited by Katz (1967), reading improvement was obtained among children in lower grades by having older students who also had reading problems serve as tutors; there were substantial gains in reading skills among the tutors as well.

2. Where the inexperienced worker fails to meet his goals, whether task or social, supervisory support is essential. The supervisor can help by analyzing the failure, helping to reset goals, and providing additional training to eliminate the skill deficiences that led to failure. Such positive approaches will protect the goal-setting activity. Conversely, disapproval of the person, or even indifference about the whole thing, will compound the loss of self-esteem and reduce the likelihood of specific and autonomous goal setting in the future. These factors suggest the need for supervisory training sessions with, of course, participation by the supervisors.

3. Goal-setting activity depends at least in part on the responsiveness or activity level of the worker. Such responsiveness may be increased in several ways, not the least important of which is the provision of a nutritional breakfast each day. Savings from absenteeism alone may justify the expenditure, even among the affluent malnourished.

4. All of these suggestions are actually suggestions for research; in no case can they be considered as supported either from field or from laboratory research. More specifically a suggestion for research, however, is the recommendation that extensive studies be made of the role of value in goal setting and of possible ways in which to change culturally determined values. The suggestion, it must be admitted, has serious ethical connotations and is made with some anxiety.

Most of these recommendations are expressed with reference to inexperienced workers. This is no accident. We are not convinced that there are important motivational differences between ethnic groups; rather, we think the important differences are between experienced and inexperienced workers. Prior to integration, there is one area in which the older established workers are inexperienced: the art of interracial collaboration. For inexperienced workers, whether the inexperience is in job tasks or in the tasks of interpersonal relations between races, the principal implication of our view is that special efforts should be made to assist people in learning to set goals with greater specificity. Efforts should include modifying jobs so that tasks group into meaningful wholes, formal promotional schemes, training programs for workers and for supervisors, and control procedures to be sure the training gets used. Such activity may produce improvements in the specificity of goal setting, and there should be corresponding increase in the levels of effort expended to move toward those goals. Changes in effort are, after all, what this is all about.

REFERENCES

Appley, M. H. Derived motives. *Annual Review of Psychology*, 1970, *21*, 485–518.
Barberio, R. The relationship between achievement motivation and ethnicity in Anglo-American and Mexican-American junior high school students. *Psychological Record*, 1967, *17*, 263–266.
Berkowitz, L. Social motivation. In G. Lindzey and E. Aronson, (eds.), *The hand-*

book of social psychology, (2nd ed.), Vol. III. Reading, Mass.: Addison-Wesley, 1968, pp. 50–135.

Borsook, H. Nutritional status of aircraft workers in Southern California. III. Effects of vitamin supplementation on absenteeism, turnover, and personal ratings. *The Milbrook Memorial Fund Quarterly,* 1945, *23,* 1–48.

Bradford, D. L. The formation of achievement attitudes among lower class Negro youth. *Dissertation abstracts,* 1967, *28* (1-A), 293–294.

Brozek, J., Guetzkow, G., Mickelson, O., and Keys, K. The effect of vitamin B deficiency on physical and psychomotor performance. *Journal of Applied Psychology,* 1946, *30,* 359–372.

Champagne, J. E., and King, D. C. Job satisfaction factors among underprivileged workers. *Personnel and Guidance Journal,* 1967, *45,* 429–434.

Diener, R. E. A comparative study of selected needs, values and attitudes of Negro and white elementary education students. *Dissertation abstracts,* 1967, *27* (9-A), 2825–2826.

Dreger, R. M., and Miller, K. S. Comparative psychological studies of Negroes and whites in the United States. *Psychological Bulletin Monograph Supplement,* 1968, *70,* Part 2, 1–58.

Duffy, E. *Activation and behavior.* New York: Wiley, 1962.

Fromkin, H. L., Klimoski, R. J., and Flanagan, M. F. Race and competence as determinants of acceptance of newcomers in success and failure work groups. *Organizational Behavior and Human Performance,* 1972.

Graen, G. B. Instrumentality theory of work motivation: Some experimental results and suggested modifications. *Journal of Applied Psychology Monograph,* 1969, Vol. 2, Part 2.

Gist, N. P., and Bennett, W. S., Jr. Aspirations of Negro and white students. *Social Forces,* 1963, *42* (1), 40–48.

Gurin, P., Gurin, G., Lao, R. C., and Beattie, M. Internal–external control in the motivational dynamics of Negro youth. In E. G. Epps (ed.), Motivation and academic achievement of Negro Americans. *Journal of Social Issues,* 1969, *25,* (3), 29–53.

Imperato, N. Survey of relations of nutrition and behavior. Unpublished manuscript, Bowling Green State University, 1969.

Katz, I. The socialization of academic motivation in minority group children. Lincoln, Neb.: *Nebraska symposium on motivation,* 1967, *15,* pp. 133–191.

Katz, I., and Benjamin, L. Affects of white authoritarianism in biracial work groups. *Journal of Abnormal and Social Psychology,* 1960, *61,* 448–456.

Katz, I., and Cohen, M. The effects of training Negroes upon cooperative problem solving in biracial teams. *Journal of Abnormal and Social Psychology,* 1962, *64,* 319–325.

Katz, I., Henchy, T., and Allen, H. Effects of race of tester, approval–disapproval, and need on Negro children's learning. *Journal of Personality and Social Psychology,* 1968, *8* (1, pt. 1), 38–42.

Keys, A. Brozek, J., Henschel, A., Mickelson, O., and Taylor, H. L. *The biology of human starvation,* Vol. III. Minneapolis: University of Minnesota Press, 1950.

Lefcourt, H. M., and Ladwig, G. W. The American Negro: A problem in expectancies. *Journal of Personality and Social Psychology,* 1965, *1,* 377–380. (a)

Lefcourt, H. M., and Ladwig, G. W. The effect of reference group upon Negroes' task persistence in a biracial competitive game. *Journal of Personality and Social Psychology,* 1965, *1,* 668–671. (b)

Levin, H. A. A psycholinguistic investigation: Do words carve up the world differently for Negro and white boys and girls from city and suburban junior high schools? *Dissertation abstracts,* 1965, *25* (12, Pt. 1), 7370–7371.

Lifson, K. A. Errors in time-study judgments of industrial work pace. *Psychological Monographs,* 1953, *67,* No. 5 (Whole No. 358).

Mann, J. W. Race-linked values in South Africa. *Journal of Social Psychology,* 1962, *58* (1), 31–41.

Mingione, A. D. Need for achievement in Negro and white children. *Journal of Consulting Psychology,* 1965, *29* (2), 108–111.

Mueller, E. F., Kasl, S. V., Brooks, G. W., and Cobb, S. Psychosocial correlates of serum urate levels. *Psychological Bulletin,* 1970, *73,* 238–257.

New Detroit Committee. *Progress report of the New Detroit Committee.* Detroit: Metropolitan Fund, Inc., 1968.

Rosen, B. C. Race, ethnicity, and the achievement syndrome. *American Sociological Review,* 1969, *24,* 47–60.

Ryan, T. A. *International behavior: An approach to human motivation.* New York: Ronald, 1970.

Ryan, T. A., and Smith, P. C. *Principles of industrial psychology.* New York: Ronald, 1954.

Sain, L. F. Occupational preferences and expectations of Negro students attending a high school located in a lower socio-economic area. *Dissertation abstracts,* 1966, *27* (4-A), 966.

Seagull, A. A. Sub-patterns of gratification choice within samples of Negro and white children. Papers of the Michigan Academy of Science, Arts and Letters, 1966, *51,* 345–351.

Sexton, P. Negro career expectations. *Merrill-Palmer Quarterly,* 1963, 9 (4), 303–316.

Smith, M. B. *Social psychology and human values.* Chicago: Aldine, 1969.

Smith, P. C., and Curnow, R. "Arousal hypothesis" and the affects of music on purchasing behavior. *Journal of Applied Psychology,* 1966, *50,* 255–256.

White, R. W. Motivation reconsidered: The concept of competence. *Psychological Review,* 1959, *66,* 297–333.

Wijting, J. P. Effects of task satisfaction on perception of the disparity between "preferred" and actual rate of work. Unpublished doctoral dissertation, Bowling Green State University, 1970.

Wylie, R., and Hutchens, E. B. Schoolwork ability estimates and aspirations as a function of socio-economic level, race, and sex. *Psychological Reports,* 1967, *21,* 781–808.

Youssef, Z. I. The role of race, sex, hostility and verbal stimulus in inflicting punishment. *Psychonomic Science,* 1968, *12,* 285–286.

CHAPTER SEVEN

Person Perception: A Review of the Literature and Implications for Training

Harry C. Triandis

INTRODUCTION BY THE EDITORS

Person perception focuses on how we see and respond to other persons. This chapter by Triandis examines three kinds of interpersonal responses in situations where persons are members of different racial groups: characteristics of the other person which provoke valid or invalid inferences about him or her; emotional responses to characteristics of the other person; and particular behavioral responses to the other person. For Triandis, the relevant variables are organized into the framework of relationships presented graphically in Figure 7–1. Analogies and predictions are developed throughout the chapter which have direct relevance for research and application to problems of integrating an organization.

If the present generation of minority members is to discover the organization as an agreeable environment, Triandis urges management to experiment with greater flexibility of operation—especially in relation to working conditions and pay schedules. He conceives of the organization as a dispenser of rewards

I am grateful to Jack Feldman, Fred Fiedler, and Roy Malpass for comments concerning an earlier draft of this chapter.

and costs. Rewards include financial rewards, such as pay, bonuses, and fringe benefits; status rewards, such as promotion and supervisory responsibility; information rewards, such as special training and skills; and goods and services, etc. He then observes the need both for rewarding behavior which is productive toward company goals and for punishing deviant behavior, such as stealing. Expected work norms and the contingent rewards and costs must be clearly and fully communicated (and understood) during training. In addition, an attitude of paternalism toward minority members is advocated in order to develop in them an emotional attachment to the organization. Research suggests one method of initiating a paternalistic attitude is to establish a race relations department whose function is to act as ombudsman to protect minority workers from discrimination which may occur inside or outside of the company. In the latter case, legal assistance or guidance regarding conditions in the home environment of the worker is seen as a way to reduce absenteeism and turnover. It is speculated that these procedures may develop greater company loyalty among lower-class minority members than nonminority members, because the former have more to gain. Another useful reform is the establishment of a system of interracial courts within the company to adjudicate misdemeanors of all employees and to apply appropriate sanctions as specified by company rules. All racial groups within the company, i.e., all workers, can be represented by frequently rotating people through the various roles which are required, such as "jury," "judge," and "lawyer."

The organization must also accept the responsibility for demonstrating that minority members are genuinely desired to succeed on the job. Pre-job training should include a series of experiences in which rewards depend upon the actions of the participants and for which rewards are immediately obtained. The training should continue until the minority worker has reached a level of competence which will allow him to compete successfully on the job. Also, the organization should be attuned to the need for training in the use of alarm clocks and transportation systems. Triandis also notes the need to train co-workers and supervisors, especially those who work in close proximity to the minority newcomers. Special approaches, such as self-insight exercises, can reduce conflict by identifying interracial similarities, by clarifying the nature and role of discrimination, and by providing opportunity to discuss advantages of integration. A recent volume of exercises by Fromkin and Sherwood (1973) is directed at these objectives. Last, as mentioned in other chapters, Triandis notes the importance of special training for minority supervisors.

Triandis applies some research findings about stereotypes to the design of training programs. He then argues that training programs should focus on (a) the recognition of behaviors by minorities which reinforce negative stereotypes and (b) the identification of alternative actions which are diametrically opposed to the uncomplimentary stereotypes. Similarly, training for competence in the technical aspects of the job is also crucial to the elimination of the unfavorable stereotype of incompetency. Last, Triandis offers suggestions regarding the need to train minority members for management positions—a strategy which may require many organizations to invest in fellowships for blacks in relevant undergraduate and graduate programs.

Triandis also raises the issue of changes required in the behavior of minority members themselves in order for them to become more viable assets to the organization. If minority members want to thrive in an industrial society, they must learn to adopt at least some of the perspectives of "the organization man," e.g., come to work on time. Coming to work regularly is not a white characteristic, but a characteristic of this industrial era. A recurrent theme throughout this volume is the notion of exchange between the organization and minority workers. If the organization is to provide a set of working conditions which are altered to meet the minority worker's needs for employment, the minority worker must be willing to alter some of his behavior in order to make a contribution to the survival and expansion of the organization.

How do people see each other and how does this affect the way they behave toward each other? What determines different ways of seeing other people? What are the consequences of such perceptions? What are the implications for organizational functioning of differences in perception of members of an organization? This chapter will try to answer such questions.

Questions of this type are central to a subfield of social psychology called person or social perception. This subfield has been important for forty years and there is a vast literature dealing with it. It touches on intergroup attitudes, stereotypes, and intergroup cooperation or competition. An administrator who is aware of some of this literature is likely to be able to analyze his personnel problems much more rationally and effectively. For example, he might improve his understanding of why some employees are evaluated one way by his subordinates and another way by his boss. If he learns to utilize some of the concepts developed by social perception theorists, he may find it easier to analyze a variety of personnel problems involving disagreements about the effectiveness, promotability, trainability, and desirability of certain employees.

The present chapter cannot cover all of the literature of person perception. It will concentrate particularly on the problems of social perception as they involve blacks and whites. These problems are particularly important, because when blacks and whites are members of the same organization, a number of phenomena relevant to social perception influence their behavior and experience and may function as barriers to organizational integration.

Person perception is concerned with the responses of individuals to person stimuli. There are three classes of such responses: attributive, affective, and overt. Attributive responses refer to inferences concerning the attributes of the other person; affective responses refer to emotions experienced in which the other person is the main stimulus; overt responses refer to particular behaviors which are elicited by the other person. The problem of this report is to examine the determinants of such responses in situations in which the two persons are black and white.

VARIABLES NEEDED TO UNDERSTAND THIS PROBLEM

The *input* in any analysis of social perception phenomena is the OTHER person. The perceiver (P) reacts to the other (O). The OTHER emits cues, some of which are noticed (categorized) by the perceiver. Which cues will be categorized depends on the nature of the relationship between P and O, the relevance of the cues for P's needs, values, and expectations, and the pre-existing categories available to P.

The *output* in any analysis of social perception phenomena is the response emitted by P. As we have already mentioned, there are three major classes of such responses—attributive, affective, and overt.

Ideally, a complete theory of social perception would consist of laws relating cues to output variables. Unfortunately, the problem is much more complex. The output variables are influenced by a variety of mediators, such as the values, needs, expectations, memories, stereotypes, interpersonal attitudes, implicit personality theories, hopes, norms, role perceptions, and expectancies of reinforcement of the perceiver. As a result a particular cue may produce a very different response, depending on the state of such mediators. The problem is further complicated by modifications of the relationships between inputs and outputs which can be traced to differences in culture and social setting.

The complexity of the problem can be perceived by anyone with a moderate familiarity with the American scene, if he considers how P might respond to O in the following dozen social relationships:

P is a black boss _____ O is a black subordinate
P is a black boss _____ O is a white subordinate
P is a black subordinate _____ O is a black boss
P is a black subordinate _____ O is a white boss
P is a black employee _____ O is a white fellow employee
P is a black employee _____ O is a black fellow employee
Repeat by changing the word "black" to "white" in the first column.

It is fairly obvious that a particular behavior of O will be seen quite differently in these situations. For example, if O were to spill a cup of coffee on P's trousers, we might expect that there would be a relatively simple way of extricating himself in the first situation, but in the second it might be seen as offensive, in the fourth it might be seen as exceptionally offensive, and in the fifth it could go anywhere from a mild embarrassment to a major offense.

In the next section we will examine some of the major theoretical systems that may provide ways of ordering the tremendous complexity suggested by this analysis.

THEORETICAL FRAMEWORK

One way to simplify the confusion suggested by the previous analysis is to attempt to guess how each of the variables mentioned in the previous section might be related to other variables. Such a system of relationship provides a framework within which we can examine the operation of particular variables on other variables. The framework of Figure 7–1, which is adapted from Triandis (1971, 1972), is such an attempt.

FIGURE 7–1.   *Antecedents and Consequents of Person Perception*

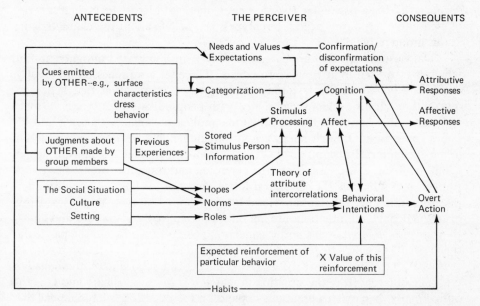

It is convenient to begin with cues emitted by the other. These cues are categorized; the act of categorization depends on the availability of particular categories. Availability is greater when P has an appropriate word, supplied by his language-culture community to categorize a cue, when he has established a habit of using a particular category, when he expects to use the category, and when his needs and values favor the use of the category. For example, in certain subcultures, some persons are said to be "swingers." A particular constellation of characteristics is involved in such a judgment, and the availability of this word facilitates the use of the cues. Furthermore, those who use this category very frequently, and whose values are particularly closely related to it, are more likely to use it in the future. The expectations that a person brings to the act of categorization are in part dependent on the judgments made by other people in his social group and in part on the confirmation or disconfirmation of expectations in previous encounters with similar people.

Several cues jointly lead to P's categorization of O. P categorizes O in categories which can be conceived as intersections of attributes. For example, assuming that P uses a theory of personality in which people are egocentric versus altruistic and dominant versus submissive, he will use four categories of people: egocentric, dominant; egocentric, submissive; altruistic, dominant; and altruistic, submissive. If his culture supplies labels for these four categories he will find it easier to use them; if he tends to use these categories frequently he will be more likely to use them; if his needs and values are particularly relevant to these two dimensions he will be more likely to use them.

The cues will be related to the use of attributes in lawful ways. For example, the cue "looks away from me" may be used as the sole determiner of the attribute "egocentric" for a particular P. Other cues, such as "black," may elicit a series of attributive responses, called stereotypes, i.e., beliefs about the characteristics of this group of people.

The various cues that are categorized by P are integrated into a cognition, which is expressed in attributive responses. The cues are processed differently, depending on the kinds of stored-stimulus person information that P has acquired through his previous experience with people like O, his theory of what traits go with what other traits (called his implicit personality theory), and his hopes concerning O. Such hopes are in part dependent on the social situation of the encounter. His cognition of O triggers emotion-related mechanisms, which result in affective responses. Both the cognition and the affect experienced with respect to O influence P's behavioral intentions about behaviors he will undertake in relation to O. Such behavioral intentions lead to overt responses. However, the behavioral intentions are not only affected by P's cognitions and affect; they are also affected by his norms concerning correct behavior in the particular social situation, which he learned in his culture, and his role relationship with O. It is clear, for instance, that if P is a boss and O is a subordinate, the behavior might be different from the situation in which P is the subordinate and O is the boss. Finally, behavioral intentions depend on the expected reinforcement that will be experienced for a particular behavior, and the value of this reinforcement for P.

The overt responses are not only influenced by the behavioral intentions of P with respect to O, but they are also influenced by previous habits elicited by some of the cues emitted by O.

Finally, the overt responses modify the expectations concerning O, and change the cognitions concerning O. For example, if P decided not to hire O, he is likely to change his expectations concerning O's competence and the attributes he will assign to O to make the total set of cognitive elements consistent with the cognitive element "I did not hire him." In short, after such a decision he will expect O to be less competent, to have many undesirable traits, and he will evaluate him more negatively than before the decision.

A good deal of empirical support for this framework can be found in analyses of person perception (Warr and Knapper, 1968), attitudes (Triandis, 1971) and the influence of cultural factors on such processes (Triandis, 1972). In the next several sections we will briefly cover two broad classes of theories—general and specific. This is to some extent an arbitrary distinction between those theories that employ constructs spread throughout Figure 7–1, and those dealing with more specific branches depicted in Figure 7–1. The latter theories deal with (a) the attributive responses, (b) the affective responses, (c) the overt responses, (d) implicit personality theories, and (e) stimulus processing.

GENERAL THEORIES

Consistency

In several recent publications the emphasis has been on notions of cognitive consistency. Basically these ideas emphasize that the cognitive elements represented in Figure 7–1, under THE PERCEIVER, must be coherent, and balanced. Major theoretical advances were made by Heider (1958), Newcomb (1968), Osgood and Tannenbaum (1955), Rosenberg (1956), Festinger (1957), Brehm and Cohen (1962), and others.

Of particular interest for our present concerns is a series of studies reviewed by Berscheid and Walster (1969) on the effect of treating another unjustly. They argue that an exploiter will justify his doing harm in order to reduce the dissonance created by his behavior. This is consistent with a number of empirical studies which they reviewed. Glass (1964) has further found that those high in self-esteem are more likely to derogate their victims than those low in self-esteem. Such deductions for cognitive dissonance theory are consistent with the analysis of prejudice presented by Triandis and Triandis (1960). According to these authors, black–white relationships have been characterized by exploitation in the economic, sexual, and status exchanges between the races, particularly in the past. Such exploitation is dissonant with the American ideal, as reflected in the Declaration of Independence and similar documents expressing basic values. One way to reduce this dissonance is to make a distinction between ingroup and outgroup members, on racial lines, and to develop cognitions, affect and behavioral intentions consistent with such a distinction. For example, one can argue that paying a black less for a particular job than one pays a white man, is all right because (a) blacks do not need as much money, since they live more modest lives, (b) blacks should get less because they are not as likeable as whites, (c) blacks do not deserve full payment because they are not as "human" as whites, etc. Man is capable of an infinite number of such rationalizations, most of which are completely irrational when subjected to an objective test.

Another derivation from dissonance theory is that people will be seen to get what they deserve. If they are poor this is because they are lazy, shiftless, and inefficient. Contact with people who have a lower standard of living tends to develop reliable stereotypes suggesting inability to get work done on time, inefficiency, etc. Specifically, Americans who come in contact with Greeks in the course of official duties connected with foreign aid show considerably greater stereotyping of Greeks along such lines than do Americans who have had no contact with Greeks. At the same time, the overseas Americans develop exceptionally favorable autostereotypes (Triandis and Vassiliou, 1967). A number of experimental demonstrations of such phenomena are reviewed by Berscheid and Walster (1969).

An exploiter's justification of his harmful acts is doubly harmful: not only does he see his own actions in a distorted way, but he is likely to commit further acts based on his distorted perceptions. One way to reduce derogation of the victim is to allow the victim to retaliate, as was done in an experiment by Berscheid, Boye, and Walster (Berscheid and Walster, 1969). This would suggest that as the blacks develop the means of retaliation for their economic exploitation, they will receive greater respect from the prejudiced whites. However, the difficulty with this prediction is that it assumes that the whites are aware of their exploitative behavior. In fact, it is most likely that most whites do not see exploitation in black and white relations. Under such conditions retaliation will lead to hardening of the conflict. Thus, the black power strategy is only good among the most liberal whites, who feel guilty about the present conditions of blacks. Most whites react to black retaliation the way innocent victims of aggression react to the aggressor.

Segregation from the victim makes it easier to derogate him than does intimate contact. The closer the contact, the more difficult it is to see the other person as "all bad" and deserving punishment. This suggests that integrated facilities should reduce the tendency to derogate. On the other hand, when integration brings the conflict of values, norms, roles, or facilities into sharper conflict, it can produce exactly the opposite effect.[1]

Similarity

Of particular concern in the special case of black and white interaction is the extent to which P and O are similar. Obviously, race is only one characteristic on which people may be similar or different. Other characteristics of some im-

---

[1] *Perspective*. Another strand of research originated from perceptual theorists concerned with the availability of categorization responses (Bruner, 1957), the influence of cultural factors on such categorization (e.g., Hallowell, 1958), the importance of the level of adaptation (Helson, 1964) on social judgments (Sherif and Hovland, 1961), and the importance of perspective (Ostrom and Upshaw, 1968) in the formation of personal reference scales (Upshaw, 1969).

portance are age, sex, and social class. However, all of these characteristics have an influence on social perception primarily because they imply similarities or differences on more fundamental aspects of the personality, namely one's values.

Man organizes his ways of thinking, or what is more formally called his cognitive categories, into hierarchical systems of abstraction—e.g., Scot terrier ⇛ dog ⇛ animal ⇛ living thing ⇛ thing. When we examine some of the most abstract of these categories we find some to be charged with affect (e.g., the category *freedom*), while others are quite neutral (e.g., the category *thing*). The abstract categories that are charged with affect are values. Relationships between such values are value orientations (Kluckhohn and Strodtbeck, 1961). Agreement on values between P and O leads to positive attributive and affective responses and to cooperative behaviors. Disagreement on values leads to an extremely strained relationship. For instance, if O values *cleanliness* and P considers it of no importance, if they have to live together this disagreement can produce a great deal of strain.

It is possible, however, for P and O to share similar values and to differ on norms. Norms are appropriate behaviors within a social situation. If P and O have similar values but different norms, the disagreement will produce considerable strain, but it will not be nearly as serious as in the case of disagreement on values. For example, if P and O agree that cleanliness is good, but they disagree on whether the dishes should be washed daily, this disagreement will lead to less conflict than disagreement on the merits of cleanliness.

It is also possible for P and O to agree on both values and norms but to disagree on roles. Roles are behavior patterns appropriate for persons holding a position in a social system. For example, P may be a wife and O a husband, and they may both agree that cleanliness is a good thing, and they may both agree that the dishes have to be washed, but they may disagree on *who* will wash them. Again, such disagreement is less severe than disagreement on whether the dishes should be washed, which is in turn less severe than disagreement on whether cleanliness is a good thing.

Smelser (1963) has proposed a theory of collective behavior which uses four "components of social action." Strain in any society may be found at the level of values, norms, roles, or facilities. Facilities are objects which may be used by persons to reach their goals. Disagreement on facilities is least conflict-producing, while disagreement on values is most conflict-producing. For example, if the husband disagrees with the wife on whether she should use the dishwasher or her own hands in washing the dishes, this would produce a conflict over facilities, which would be easy to resolve.

Turning now to the black and white relationships, these include relationships which involve disagreements over values. For example, the Black Muslims consider white people as devils and themselves as God's children. Separation from or destruction of the devils is appropriate on moral grounds. Under such conditions integration would be impossible and attempts to bring it about would be unrealistic. At the level or norms, blacks have adopted the point of view of the Declaration of Independence that all men are created equal and expect actions (norms) consistent with this view. Some whites have refused to adopt such norms in their interactions with blacks. Here we have an extremely severe strain, which may require major social changes before it is eliminated. At a less severe level there are disagreements about roles (e.g., who is going to do what job) and at a still less severe level about facilities (e.g., should we use this tool or that).

One major problem of the conflict between the two races is that there is a tendency to see every disagreement about facilities as reflecting a disagreement about values. For example, if a black delivery boy is made to use the rear door of an apartment building, this may be perceived by him to be a result of his inferior racial status, which refers to the basic value of *equality*. If a white employer refers to a black employee by his first name, it is possible that the black employee will see this as lack of respect and may again refer it to the value of *equality*. Vice versa, a black employee's too boisterous behavior may be seen as *disrespect* by his employer, or a legal challenge to a restricted clause in the operation of a club is likely to be seen by the members of the club as an attack on their *freedom* (of association).

Miscommunications between the races abound. One reason is that there is a history of conflict between the races, and conflict makes people think thoughts and feel emotions consistent with it. Thoughts such as "these people are dangerous, tricky, and untrustworthy" and negative feelings are likely to accompany conflict. In such settings, a relatively minor disagreement, such as a disagreement over facilities, is likely to be used as a cue for a major disagreement, such as a disagreement over values. In short, people have a tendency, when they are in conflict, to blow up a minor disagreement and to see it as a sample of a much more profound difference in point of view. This is why mediators are so helpful. Since they do not carry the "emotional baggage" of the parties in conflict, they can see each disagreement more realistically, and they can understand that the two sides are not in as much conflict as they think they are.

Typical of this point is the difference between ghetto dwellers and middle-class whites in the perception of what the white middle class calls *riots*. The ghetto dwellers define the *riots* as *protests*. The destruction of 40 million dollars worth of property in Watts was seen by many black participants as a way to make the message "noticeable." The message is that they are disillusioned with the progress they are making in the country in which the American dream is supposed to be accessible to all; they are tired of hearing promises and getting no results; they see themselves going nowhere—they are boxed in, just getting a welfare check, just looking at the rich people on TV. They feel condemned to insignificance. The protest was expensive, 34 dead and 1,032 injured, but to many blacks it was worth it. It gave them, for the first time, a feeling of potency, a feeling of being at the center of action and of attention, a feeling of importance. As one put it, "Negroes are willing to die for *respect*." It is unnecessary to elaborate the obvious point that for the white community the riot was a sign of aggression and of *disrespect* for life and property. Both sides saw it at the level of values.

From the point of view of our theoretical analysis, a riot which is limited to breaking windows and taking goods out of stores is a conflict over facilities. Different rioters, however, may define the situation differently. They might see it as a conflict at the level of facilities (here is my chance to get a new TV), roles (the black man needs this to express his protest), norms (if everybody did this the bad merchants would go out of business), or values (it's a good thing to do to gain respect from Whitey). The white middle class also could choose to see it at the level of facilities (this is a bunch of kids that got a chance to get a new TV), roles (blacks are telling us that they are dissatisfied), norms (they are breaking the law), or values (they show no respect for private property). It is important to notice that most blacks as well as most whites have typically employed explanations at the value level rather than at the lesser levels of analysis of conflict.

SPECIFIC THEORIES

The above theories deal with broad issues in social perception.[2, 3] Because of their generality they have been quite attractive to many students of the problem, but the empirical support for them has not always been overwhelming. Space does not allow further discussion of these theories, but the interested reader may find a review of Triandis (1971, Chapter 3) helpful in evaluating some of these theories. Less general theories, focusing more specifically on certain aspects of Figure 7–1, have been proposed by a number of recent writers. We turn now to these.

Attributive Responses

The most important theory in this category is attribution theory. This is a derivative of Heider's theorizing, which has inspired both Jones and Davis

[2] *Behavior theory.* Still another research tradition has emphasized the importance of reinforcement associated with O and has argued that the affective responses of P are a direct function of the frequency, duration, intensity, and nondelay of rewards. This school has argued that a variety of characteristics of P and O may act as reinforcements, the most important being their attitudinal similarity. This viewpoint can be seen in the work of Staats (1967), Lott and Lott (1968), Byrne and Clore (1967), Stapert and Clore (1969), and other recent writers.

A special kind of reward is provided by interaction with people who are similar. Similarity is likely to lead to greater amounts of positive interaction, hence to greater attraction.

[3] *Information theory.* Still another approach, information theory, was used by Bieri et al. (1966) to examine social judgment. In a rather elaborate theory they deal with such characteristics of the stimulus as its differentiation and articulation and focus, in particular, on the cognitive complexity of individual perceivers. They also examine the influence of the setting, including the type of interaction between P and O, and the effect of these variables on the particular response alternatives that P will select.

(1965) and Kelley (1967) to develop theory concerning which attributes of O are likely to make an impression on P. Of particular importance is the fact that this theory examines the conditions under which some event will be attributed to P or to O.

Consider, for example, the situation in which P is a white personnel director and O is a black applicant. Let us assume that in the course of the interview P sees that O's hands are trembling. What attribute of O might he infer from this observation? It is obvious that if all the people interviewed by P have trembling hands, P is not justified in attributing any characteristic to O (he should not infer, for instance, that O is anxious), because the uniformity of the responses of interviewees suggests that it is P who has the attribute (he is formidable) that causes the observation. On the other hand, if O is the only interviewee whose hands are trembling, there may be some justification for P to emit an attributive response (e.g., he is anxious).

Kelley argues that the attribution to the other rather than to oneself depends on the extent of differential responding toward the other. Thus, if P gives the same response to all others, the attribution must be assigned to P; on the other hand, if P responds differently to various others, the attribution must be assigned to the others. Differential responding can be seen either across others or across time or across modalities (social settings, etc.). Jones and Davis (1965) noted that when O acts in ways that are normal or typical, he does not impart information that P can use to make attributive responses about O. On the other hand, when O acts in unique and idiosyncratic ways he makes it possible for P to produce attributive responses. "The fewer distinctive reasons a person might have for an action (assuming he has some) and the less these reasons are widely shared in the culture, the more informative that action is concerning the characteristics of the person" (Kelley, 1967, pp. 208–209).

Attribution theory predicts the attributive responses from the consistencies between O's behavior and P's expectations, as well as from the variability in the cues emitted by O. It deals, then, with the upper left-hand corner of Figure 7–1. Functional theory, as proposed by Katz (1960) and others, also deals with that corner of the diagram but examines the utility of P's attitudes toward O for P's psychological functioning. Specifically, Katz argues that certain attitudes may help P maximize the rewards he receives from his environment, or they may protect him from acknowledging uncomplimentary basic truths about himself, or they may help him express a value, or they may help him understand the environment. For example, P may be particularly ready to see that O is a member of an organization in which P aspires to become a member, because this will give him an introduction to this organization; or, he may refuse to see that O is highly intelligent because this would lead to an unfavorable comparison; or, he may note that P is wearing an antiwar symbol on his lapel, because this agrees with his own sentiments about the war; or, he may notice that O is dark-skinned, because this helps him understand O's attitude toward blacks.

Jones et al. (1968) have examined the effect of different spacing of success and failure on person perception. They found that primacy is the rule: If a person has a series of successes followed by fewer and fewer successes he is perceived as more capable than if he has a series of failures, followed by more and more successes, even though the number of successes is the same. Streufert and Streufert (1969) examined the responses of subjects who were cognitively concrete or abstract, as originally defined in the writings of Harvey, Hunt, and Schroder (1961), in a situation in which the subjects were successful or unsuccessful in groups engaged in competition with opposing teams of subjects. They found that those who were successful attributed their success to themselves, while those who were unsuccessful attributed their failure to an equal extent to themselves and to actions of opposing teams. These findings were particularly clear in the case of subjects who were concrete, and low in cognitive complexity, and less pronounced in the case of subjects who were abstract and cognitively complex.

Another theory which deals with which characteristics of the stimulus will have an effect on the perceiver is one presented by Rommetveit (1960). He argues that the perception of other people tends to focus on covert rather than on directly observable attributes. A variety of overt stimulus events is integrated to form a covert attribution. Each overt event might mediate the attribution of several covert attributes. The basic idea of Rommetveit's theory is that the perception of attribute X is a function of the instrumental relevance of this attribute, i.e., depends on the extent to which discrimination of X is likely to increase the individual's goal achievement. Thus the higher the instrumental relevance of attribute X for P, the more important X will be in P's self, and the more probable it is that P will attribute X in O, if X-relevant cues are present. Rommetveit presented some evidence consistent with these predictions.

An example of the point made by Rommetveit can be found in the case of a white boss who notices that a black employee is late for work. The directly observable attribute is *lateness*, but the covert may be *lazy, unreliable,* or *irresponsible*. The theory states that the greater the importance of subordinate lateness for the supervisor's goal achievement, the more likely he will be to notice it and react to it by making covert attributions. A black who behaves, after he arrives late, in ways that are inconsistent with the characteristics lazy, unreliable, and irresponsible would block such attributions so that they would be less likely to occur. The trouble is that in order to block all possible attributions of lateness behavior he might have to be a veritable paragon of virtue. Thus, the simplest way to avoid such attributions is to arrive on time.

Rommetveit's point about overt stimulus events being used to predict covert attributes is reasonable enough, but it must be qualified in view of evidence from developmental studies of social perception, such as Lambert and Klineberg's (1967) study of stereotyping in eleven countries and Levy-Schoen's (1964) study of the relative importance of "dress" versus "expression" in social perception. These studies suggest that overt characteristics such as skin color, dress, type of hat worn, etc., play a predominant role in person perception among very young children, but after age seven personality characteristics are increasingly more frequently inferred from the superficial characteristics. Thus, a four-year-old will say that the stimulus person was *black*, while a nine-year-old might say that the stimulus person was *lazy*. Levy-Schoen's study also suggests that different cues are used by children of different ages, and that there is a developmental hierarchy of cue utilization. This point is in agreement with the study by Foa, Triandis, and Katz (1966), which argued that children first learn to differentiate between self and other, then on the basis of sex, and next on the basis of generation (older, same, younger). Which cues are used also depends on the context of judgment. For example, an American's nationality is not likely to become a cue in social perception in downtown Chicago, but it is more likely to become a cue in Rome, Italy.

Stereotyping

We will conclude this discussion of specific theories by examining some theoretical statements concerning stereotyping.

Stereotypes are beliefs about the characteristics of groups of people. Such beliefs should be distinguished from sociotypes, which are beliefs obtained from careful investigations. For example, to say that Northern blacks are Democrats rather than Republicans is a sociotype, since there is a good deal of evidence concerning their voting habits which supports this view.

Stereotypes often have a kernel of truth. A number of lines of evidence suggest that some stereotypes have validity. This is particularly true when the stereotype refers to an overt, easily observable characteristic such as *pious* (Schuman, 1966).

Contact between two ethnic groups does not necessarily lead to favorable stereotypes. The effect of contact is most clearly seen in changes in the clarity of the stereotype, i.e., the amount of consensus among members of one group concerning the characteristics of members of another group. Contact also increases the number of elements in a stereotype, the ambivalence of the elements (both bad and good elements are included), and the persistence of the elements (Triandis and Vassiliou, 1967; Vassiliou et al., 1972). Stereotypes change with different experiences, different political events, and the information that a person receives from his ingroup. There is good reason to distinguish between normative stereotypes, i.e., stereotypes that are cognitive norms received from one's ingroup, and direct experience stereotypes, i.e., stereotypes developed from direct observation. Vassiliou et al. have shown that the effect of contact on these two kinds of stereotypes is quite different.

In spite of the fact that stereotypes may have a kernel of truth, they are inferior judgmental processes because of their sense of absolutism, the perceiver's lack of awareness of selective distortion, the tendency to overstress the similarity among the members of the stereotyped group, the confusion concerning the causes of the attributes found in certain groups of people, and the role of internal motivational and value factors in providing distortions in perception (Campbell, 1967). In short, the kernel of truth is swamped by untruth.

Most people utilize stereotypes. Some people are more cautious in inferring characteristics on the basis of inadequate cues, but practically no one can think of other people without the use of stereotypes. Thus, the task of social scientists is not to eliminate the use of stereotyping, but to develop sufficient uncertainty, to reduce the subjective validity of stereotype-generating cues.

The greater the real contrast between two groups on a given attribute, the more likely it is that this trait will appear in the mutual stereotypes each has of the other (Campbell, 1967). This point implies that stereotyping is as much a function of the characteristics of P as it is a function of the characteristics of O, since it is the difference in their position on a given trait that determines stereotyping. Thus, a group that is abnormally clean will stereotype most groups that are average in cleanliness as dirty.

The more opportunities of observation, and the longer the exposure to the outgroup, the larger the role of the real differences in the stereotype. Attributes involved in intergroup interaction will be most likely to be represented in the stereotype. Those attributes that are most relevant to the needs and desires of P will be most likely to be found in the stereotype. Once a stereotype is established it requires little real difference to be re-evoked. Those attributes which are most strongly rejected within the ingroup will be most likely to be used in stereotyping the outgroup (Campbell, 1967).

While limitation of space does not allow the review of empirical studies supporting these propositions, it is sufficient here to state that there is considerable evidence congruent with these points.

One factor that may have a considerable influence on stereotyping is the probability of reward or costs associated with different stereotypes. Consider, as an example, Clark's statistic that about twice as many young men in the black ghetto are classified as deliquent as those outside the ghetto. Of course, this statistic cannot be taken on its face value, because we know that in middle- and upper-class neighborhoods delinquent behavior is often not reported, or when it is reported it is excused. However, since we do not know exactly how much inaccuracy there is in delinquency statistics, let us assume, for the sake of the present argument, that a 10 percent delinquency rate is correct for the ghetto and a 5 percent rate is correct for the white neighborhoods. Now suppose that a young lady finds herself alone in a relatively deserted street, carrying a pocketbook containing $100. Further suppose that she sees either a black young man or a white young man approaching her at a rather determined pace. Given the assumed validity of the statistics and the situational constraints operating on the young lady, it would make sense for her to be more alarmed when she sees the black than when she sees the white youth. The point to be made here is simply that running away from the young man if he is not a thief involves relatively little cost, but not running away involves at least $100. Thus, false stereotyping has consequences that are less unpleasant than veridical perception (90 percent of such young men are perfectly harmless). In short, it pays to assume that 100 percent of the young men are dangerous, in spite of the fact that one is wrong in making this assumption 90 percent of the time, simply because one is rewarded the remaining 10 percent of the time.

In an early social perception study Ichheiser (1949) pointed out that false social perception is rather typical, as is stereotyping. He pointed out that cues that are taken for granted are not attended to, frames of reference distort perception, naive persons assume that they perceive others accurately, overemphasize the unity of the personality, and underestimate the effects of the situation on social perception. He further argued that perceivers have poor implicit personality theories that simply conform to stereotypes held in their culture. This probably happens because we are rewarded for our false perceptions.

Overt Action

While attribution theory, functional theory, and Rommetveit are concerned with the attributive responses of the individual, Triandis (1967) and Triandis, Vassiliou, and Nassiakou (1968) have proposed a theory concerned with his overt responses.

Interpersonal behavior is a function of (a) whether P and O belong to the same ingroup (e.g., the same family or group of friends); (b) whether O is of higher, equal, or lower status than P; and (c) the length of acquaintance and familiarity of P and O. Specifically, if P and O belong to the same ingroup, responses will tend to be associative and will be characterized by solidarity and cooperation. If they belong to outgroups the responses will be either suspicious or antagonistic. The definition of the size of the ingroup differs from culture to culture. For example, white middle-class Americans define their ingroup as "people like me." This is a broad ingroup, but it explicitly does not include people who are very different in political views, culture, or race. Ghetto blacks define their ingroup in rather more narrow terms, often limiting it to their immediate family and friends. The result is that there is considerable antagonism and aggressive, exploitative behavior among ghetto blacks, as well as between ghetto blacks and whites.

When O is of higher status than P he evokes respect, admiration, and subordination responses. If he is of low status he evokes protection or superordination responses. If he is of equal status he evokes friendship, gaming, and joking responses.

When P and O are extremely familiar with each other, the behaviors that occur between them are of considerable intensity and are often intimate. When they do not know each other the behaviors are cautious and remote.

In this theory any behavior can be represented by three coordinates, one for each of the three dimensions of interpersonal behavior described above. We can scale the extent to which the behavior is appropriate within the ingroup, for persons of various status relationships and for persons of different levels of intimacy. We can similarly rate any O–P relationship on the same three dimensions. The theory predicts that the behaviors that have coordinates most similar to those of the coordinates of the O–P relationship would be the most appropriate. For example, if we look at Table 7–1, which is a crude dichotomous representation of the theory, and we know that O is a girl who belongs to P's ingroup, P and O know each other very well, and they are of equal status, it would be appropriate to predict that *to marry* is a probable behavior; or behaviors that have a similar position in Table 7–1, such as *to kiss and to cuddle*, are more likely than behaviors located far from that cell such as *strike with fist*. On the other hand, if O is not in P's ingroup, is of lower status, and P and O do not know each other, we might expect behaviors such as *exclude from the neighborhood* to be more probable than behaviors such as *admire the ideas of*.

In short, Triandis's theory specifies the conditions under which some behaviors are more probable than others. The three dimensions (ingroup–outgroup, status, familiarity) were obtained inductively, from factor analyses of the behavioral differential (Triandis, 1964) and the role differential (Triandis, Vassiliou, and Nassiakou, 1968), but it is impressive that they correspond very closely to the dimensions found in other kinds of investigations. Thus, Ardrey (1961) reviews a vast array of paleontological and anthropological findings to conclude that our remote animal ancestors were characterized by two basic behavior patterns: territoriality and dominance. Under territoriality he includes the defense of the territory from invasions by outgroup bands of other animals of the same species, protection of the weaker members of one's ingroup, grooming, cooperation in hunting, etc. Dominance behavior can be seen in the pecking orders established by many animals. Schlosberg's (1954) analysis of emotions employed three dimensions corresponding to association, dominance, and activity (pleasant, controlling, and active) (see Osgood, 1966). Osgood's work with the semantic differential has repeatedly found the dimensions evaluation, potency, and activity. Roger Brown's (1965) work with forms of address has found that solidarity and status were the two main dimensions. LaForge and Suczek's (1955) personality descriptions utilized association, dominance, and activity dimensions. In short, this pattern of dimensions has considerable generality in many areas of psychology from animal social psychology to conceptual functioning.

Other people are perceived in terms of (a) their good–bad qualities, (b) power, (c) the extent to which they *intended* to behave well or poorly, and (d) their responsibility for what happened (Taguiri, 1968). Two of these dimensions also correspond to some of the dimensions mentioned above.

If ingroup–outgroup, status, and familiarity are the basic dimensions of social behavior and they occur in all human groups, the task of understanding black and white interactions becomes one of exploring the exact meaning of these dimensions for each cultural group. Triandis, Vassiliou, and Nassiakou (1968) have demonstrated that such meaning may be quite different across

TABLE 7-1 *Examples of Behaviors That Fit the 8-Cell Typology Described in Text*

TYPE OF GROUP	STATUS RELATIONS			FAMILIARITY (INTIMACY)
	O Higher Than P	O Equal to P	O Lower Than P	
Ingroup	Admire the ideas of	Marry	Help him choose a mate	High
	Invite to dinner	Play bridge with	Teach him	Low
Outgroup	Show contempt toward	Ridicule	Criticize	High
	Go on strike against	Strike with fist	Exclude from the neighborhood	Low

cultural groups. Thus, for instance, one does not *argue with* an unknown person in certain cultures, while he is quite likely to do so with an old friend.

Different definitions of the ingroup can produce misunderstandings, as when a white person assumes that he is accepted in a black's ingroup, but the black, who we suspect has a narrow ingroup, does not react to him as an ingroup member. Similarly, a white person may consider status a very important dimension, while the black militant might reject it and say: "Who are you to tell me what to think or what to do?"

A line of research that is now being developed by Triandis is an attempt to study the way blacks and whites perceive their social environment and to determine differences among such groups in the perception of the above mentioned dimensions. One finding will illustrate the point. There appear to be different degrees of differentiation among blacks and whites in the ingroup and outgroup categories. Specifically, white appear to differentiate many kinds of ingroup members—family, friends, acquaintances, other people like me, colleagues, etc.; outgroups are coarsely differentiated—people not like me, enemies. Blacks seem to have a more highly differentiated outgroup—people you can cheat, suckers, enemies, etc. Corresponding to this, middle-class professors assign grades like A, B, C, and D, and then Failure to their students; maybe blacks consider more kinds of failure—justifiable and not so justifiable, etc. Furthermore, whites seem to differentiate more on the status dimension. Since more of them are in the middle, they must discriminate both upwards and downwards. Blacks react to status in a more undifferentiated manner. Finally, whites differentiate degrees of familiarity and formality which most ghetto blacks do not bother with. Thus, some misunderstandings among the races may be traceable to different degrees of differentiation of the basic dimensions of social interaction.

Affective Responses

We have already mentioned a number of general theories that are concerned with the determinants of affective responses. Points of view based on behavior theory, such as those of Staats, Lott, and Lott, Byrne and others deal specifically with such responses. We will now turn to some specific theories dealing with this class of response.

A particularly interesting class of theories deals with the affective responses of people to status inconsistency. While status is a relatively simple matter in animal social relations, in humans it has features that complicate prediction in many cases. One of the problems is what has been referred to as *status congruence* (for a recent review, see Sampson, 1969). When a person has high status on some dimensions of status such as age, income, and race and low status on some other dimensions of status, such as education and sex, the person is status incongruent. Status incongruent people produce conflicting responses in others, since others feel confused and uncertain about the correct way to behave toward them. Frequently, the perceiver feels negative emotions in the presence of status incongruent persons. A related concept is concerned with the *inputs* that P brings to the social situation and the *outputs* that he sees himself obtaining from it. For example, a P that is very attractive will expect to have a date with a highly attractive O. If O is relatively unattractive, P will feel cheated because his inputs (qualifications, investments, etc.) exceed his outputs (rewards).

The implications of these theories for black–white interactions are considerable. For example, when a black who, according to many whites, is supposed to be of low status has positive characteristics (he is intelligent, wealthy, educated, or what have you), he is likely to be status incongruent for such whites. The affective response of these whites to this particular black will be even more negative than their response to status congruent blacks. This explains the particularly negative behavior of Southern white policemen to black physicians, as documented in the experiences of the black professionals in the South.

Similarly, those white workers who are racists will react to a status incongruent black more negatively than they will to an ordinary black. This is a bit of information that blacks might utilize when interacting with prejudiced whites, by hiding those of their characteristics which increase their status incongruence.

Adams (1965) has proposed the theory of inequity to account for such phenomena. The theory of inequity deals with a broad problem of exchange and is thus related to Thibaut and Kelley's (1959) analysis of social exchange.

Recent extensions of this theory by Foa and Foa (1969) promise to be extremely fruitful. Basically, exchange theorists argue that there is a tendency for P to give to O rewards proportional to the rewards he received from O; similarly with costs, if O inflicts punishment and costs on P, there is a tendency for P to retaliate. However, Foa and Foa consider the fact that such exchanges occur in six different forms: there are exchanges of love, status, information, money, goods, services. These forms are conceived as qualitatively different in a systematic way, with love and money at opposite sides of a circle as follows:

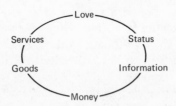

The Foas argue that the laws of exchange are most different when something on one point of the circle is exchanged with something in the opposite pole of the circle. More specifically, love and money are exchanged under very different rules, while love and status (which are close to each on the circle) are exchanged under similar rules. For example, you cannot usually pay the bill in the restaurant by telling the owner that you love him, or that you admire his ideas; money is the appropriate form of exchange. On the other hand, you cannot pay a hostess with money; love or status ("Oh! What a wonderful cook you are") is the appropriate exchange. The implication of the Foa theory is that interpersonal satisfaction depends on the extent to which exchanges follow the proper rules. If whites deprive blacks of status and attempt to quiet them down with money, the exchange will fail, because it involves qualitatively different entities. The only direct way to remedy the black man's status deprivation of 300 years is to give him status. A related entity such as love could do the job, but money never will. Whites tend to think that money is synonymous with status, but a rich black who is treated disrespectfully will not think so.

Implicit Personality

Bruner and Tagiuri (1954) suggested that different people have different implicit personality theories. The idea of an implicit personality theory can be found, in part, in the early work of Asch (1946) in which it was argued that certain traits, such as "warm" or "cold" are more central than other traits in social perception. Wishner (1960) showed that the centrality of a trait is a function of its intercorrelations with other traits. Warr and Knapper (1968) have done several studies which show a variety of traits to be central. People have implicit personality theories that are independent of the characteristics of the persons whose personality they judge, as suggested by Passini and Norman's (1966) finding that the same structure of personality traits is obtained when subjects judge close acquaintances or unknown stimulus persons. Some personality differences in the type of implicit personality theory utilized by various types of subjects have been uncovered. For example, both Steiner (1954) and Pederson (1965) found that highly authoritarian subjects differ from less authoritarian in their implicit personality theories. Specifically, Steiner found that authoritarian subjects reject the possibility that highly desirable and undesirable traits can coexist within the same person.

The evidence concerning implicit personality theories may be used to advantage by blacks who interact with whites. Since the characteristic "warm" has been found to be quite central and to relate to many other desirable traits, and since warmth and spontaneity are valued in the black culture and are quite highly developed for ingroup interactions, one pattern of behavior that blacks might find quite advantageous is the path of warm and friendly interactions with fellow workers. A major problem, of course, is that blacks feel anxious about being rejected by prejudiced whites, so they are less likely to initiate such interactions with whites. Furthermore, as newcomers to the industrial organization they may be unwilling to "go all out" and display such warmth. However, managements may be able to facilitate the emission of such behaviors by encouraging the development of groups of black and white buddies who have warm and friendly relationships during training. Once such groups are formed, they might become the nuclei for larger groups within the factory.

Numerous other personality characteristics have been found to influence person perception. For example, Taylor and Oberlander (1969) found that "people-oriented" persons, as measured by personality attributes such as high tendency for self-disclosure, high need-affiliation and being firstborn, are more sensitive to person cues and discriminate incomplete faces better than non-people-oriented subjects. Harvey and Clapp (1965) found that self-esteem influences social perception. Harvey et al. (1968) found differential susceptibility to negative, positive, and neutral cues among persons who differ in conceptual level, as conceptualized by Harvey, Hunt, and Schroder (1961).

BLACKS AND WHITES ON VARIABLES OF THE CONCEPTUAL SCHEME

Very few studies have utilized representative samples of blacks and whites and have focused on variables relevant to those mentioned in the conceptual scheme. Most studies utilized samples of convenience, such as students (Lott and Lott, 1963), and are of limited applicability for our present analysis. Impressionistic studies abound, but they cannot be reviewed here. The best studies on black culture that we have been able to find so far are those of Clark (1965), Keil (1966), Liebow (1967), and Maruyama (1969). An important critique of such studies by Valentine (1968) plus a variety of books by black revolutionaries such as Malcolm X (1964) and Julius Lester (1968) were also helpful.

Black ghetto culture has some characteristics that remain from the relatively remote African past of the black man but is mostly a modern development. It is deeply rooted in the experience of slavery, and its present form is a reaction to ghetto life as it exists today. In a very real way ghetto black culture has been molded by the particular environment that the white man has imposed on the ghetto.

Consider some of the major characteristics of certain subgroups of ghetto blacks, as found repeatedly in empirical investigations—low self-esteem, short time perspective, external rather than internal focus of control (Lefcourt and Ladwig, 1965; Escoffery, 1968). In sections of this cultural group there is little concern with time, low interpersonal trust (Erskine, 1969), low ingroup boundary stability, high suspicion and a good deal of "rapping" (Kochman, 1969). There is an underdevelopment of cooperative skills, and conflict is handled with overt hostility rather than with persuasion.

Objectively, Clark states, the black ghetto is characterized by overcrowding, deteriorated housing, high infant mortality, crime, and disease; subjectively, by resentment, hostility, despair, apathy, and self-depreciation, as well as compensatory grandiose behavior. The mass media penetrate and invade it with upper-middle-class values and aspirations. Since attainment of upper-middle-class goals is often blocked, the response of some blacks is to reject these values and to engage in behaviors which defy the white majority. A black man who makes $20,000 per year selling marijuana is likely to see an ordinary job as obviously inadequate. Furthermore, in terms of some of the values of the larger society, he is doing well and his "success" is looked up to by the young.

Clark suggests that deliquency and other forms of antisocial behavior are forms of protest against the white order, as can be seen from the dramatic decrease in such behaviors during periods of other forms of protest, such as was observed in Montgomery, Alabama, during the bus boycott.

One of the frequently mentioned characteristics of the ghetto is the matriarchal family and the absent father. Much has been made about this feature of the ghetto (Moynihan, 1965). Perhaps its importance is not as great as claimed by Moynihan (Valentine, 1968), in view of the fact that there are perfectly viable cultures in other parts of the world which employ similar family organizations, and lower-class black women are able to play both the instrumental and expressive roles in bringing up their children (Nobers, 1968). But as long as blacks consider whatever is white as superior, as reflected in their aesthetic judgments (Martin, 1964) and their judgments of black and white personality (Bayton, Austin, and Burke, 1965), the deviation of this pattern from the dominant white is likely to produce envy and dissatisfaction among black youngsters. The lack of stability in family life, the extremely demanding schedules of black women who often hold full-time jobs outside the house and at the same time must take care of several youngsters, and the absence of the father result in understimulation of intellectual development (Deutsch, Katz, and Jensen, 1968), school failure, and the development of less willingness to delay gratification (Mischel, 1961).

The accomplishment of most middle-class goals does, of course, require willingness to delay gratification, to work toward relatively long-range goals, and to plan. None of these characteristics can be developed to an optimal degree in the ghetto environment.

Basically, the ghetto environment is characterized by conditions in which the individual receives little reward for his efforts. Just as the upper-class environment often provides conditions in which the child receives much reward for little effort, the lower-class environment provides conditions in which effort and rewards are unrelated. In both cases effort will not become connected with rewards, and the person will develop expectations of external control of reinforcement. By contrast, the middle-class child is likely to connect his behavior with its outcomes.

Consider three hypothetical case studies which do fit, however, data collected by observers (e.g., Maruyama, 1969). A ten-year-old, in the black ghetto, gets a job at 50 cents an hour, works for forty hours and takes $20 home. In the street outside his home he gets involuntarily involved in a fight; a policeman intervenes and searches his pockets, finds the money, and takes it away. It is perfectly consistent with policeman thinking that a black ghetto ten-year-old who has $20 in his pockets must have stolen it. In this example, the constructive behavior—work—was followed by punishment—loss of $20. Now consider the same sequence in a middle-class neighborhood. The policeman finds the money and asks the boy where he got it; the boy tells him, the policeman believes him, or if he does not believe him, checks and finds that the boy's story is accurate. Here, the constructive behavior is followed by reward ($20). Now consider an upper-class child who asks his father for some money; the father has no change, so gives him a $20 bill. No effort, in this case, was followed by reward ($20). In short, the ghetto and the upper-class environments both do not maximize the probability that constructive behavior, such as work, will be followed by reward. If "good things" do not happen because of what you do, but they just happen, then mysticism, reliance on fate and change are more likely to develop in the upper class and the ghetto and least likely to develop in the middle class. The current fad with mystical cults is frequently popular among upper-class students. Preachers, mystics, and evangelists have been most successful among the lower classes. Finally, the background of most hippies and yippies is upper-middle-class or lower-lower class; there are few from the sort of background where they had to struggle to make ends meet. At any rate, the ghetto environment suffers from the same social pathology that afflicts the spoiled upper-class child—however, without the protection of an influential father who can save the family name from the disgrace of the son's going to prison.

In the case of the lower-class blacks the resentment of "the system" is likely to be translated into suspicion and hostility of both white society and other blacks who are competing for the scarce resources of the ghetto. Thus, the ingroup is small, and there is suspicion and hostility toward all who are outside of this narrow ingroup.

The repeated failures in life may result in low self-esteem and self-depreciation or in escape through drugs or in self-aggrandizement in fantasy. There is little concern for time, since action occurring in time fails to lead to rewards. Delinquent behavior is often the only kind of behavior that leads to reinforcement. Aggressive behavior has considerable survival value and is so functional in the ghetto that if one is not sufficiently aggressive he is likely to be physically molested or robbed (Maruyama, 1969).

Liebow (1967) details how life after life in the ghetto is characterized by experiences of failure, expectations of failure, and more experiences that confirm the expectations. The kinds of jobs some ghetto men can get depress their self-esteem; their experiences depress it further. Finally, it seems as though they are incapable of doing anything. Liebow's subjects spent their time at the street corner. Here the measure of a man is considerably smaller, weaknesses are turned upside down and transformed into strengths, and he is once again a man among men.

It is easy to see how the frustrations detailed by Clark in his description of life in the ghetto would predispose aggression. In fact, what is remarkable is not that 10 percent of the black young men are criminals, according to the definitions of middle-class society, but that 90 percent are not!

These highly unfavorable contemporary conditions are superimposed on a cultural tradition that goes back to the dark days of slavery. At that time the slaves came from cultures with highly developed kinship systems. This situation confronted the slaveowners with potential opposition, strengthened by ingroup ties. By making all forms of ingroup ties, such as marriage, illegal, the slaveowners laid the foundation of modern black culture's family structure. For a slave, work was something that was good for other people, since he did not obtain any rewards from it. Thus, he worked as little as possible and took as much time as he could. The present conditions of the ghetto perpetuate this pattern.

SOME RESEARCH PROBLEMS SUGGESTED BY THIS ANALYSIS

It is reasonable to expect that changes in facilities and roles will be relatively easy, but changes in norms and values will be quite difficult. We do not know, as yet, how to change values, because most of the social psychological research so far has been directed toward changing non-ego-involving attitudes.

At the present time we do not know about the extent of dissimilarity in values, norms, and roles among blacks and whites in our society. A study by Lott and Lott (1963) shows considerable agreement between black and white Kentucky high-school students on fundamental values. The total pattern of values was similar, with both groups giving most emphasis on religious and least emphasis on esthetic values. On the other hand, the whites were higher on economic values and the blacks were higher on social values on the Allport–Vernon scales. Black girls scored "in the male direction," showing few differences from black boys, while white girls were quite different from white boys. The Lotts suggest that regional values account for such similarities, but the fact that 52 percent of the black and 40 percent of the white children attend movies more than once a week, and 19 percent of the black and 13 percent of the white watch TV for more than 20 hours per week, suggests a considerable exposure to the values of the outside world, particularly Hollywood, which may produce a certain amount of homogeneity in values. We have little information about the extent of disagreement, the focus of disagreement, and the heterogeneity of responses within each of the two cultural groups, or within each of the domains of concepts. It is most likely that when enough research is done we will find a very complex pattern of results, with various parts of each social group showing dissimilarities in particular values, norms, roles, and particular facilities.

Even if we had enough knowledge about such dissimilarities we would not know to what extent it is moral to apply this knowledge to changing the two cultures in question. The ethical questions involved in changing cultures must be worked out.

We need to do some more research about ways of changing values, norms, roles, and facilities. Much of the research done in social psychology has been concerned with changes in non-ego-involving attitudes, which change easily, particularly in the laboratory. The situation is not as optimistic in the field (Hovland, 1959).

We need to study a variety of procedures designed to change aspects of a person's way of perceiving his environment. Among the more promising are (a) ways to impart information about the other culture, such as culture assimilators (Fiedler, Mitchell, and Triandis, in press): these are programmed learning procedures which instruct a person about the fundamental ways in which his culture differs from another culture; (b) T-groups, a way to increase the interpersonal sensitivity of the individual; (c) role playing, a way to provide the experience of "being in the shoes of the other guy" which, incidentally, produces a good deal of attitude change (Janis, 1968); (d) simulations, a way to stimulate interaction with members of other cultures, including the experience of interacting with a person whose culture is totally different from our own—e.g., the notion of the contrast American (Stewart et al., 1968).

Wight (1969) has compiled a *Handbook for Cross-Cultural Interaction Training* which summarizes these and many other procedures. This handbook examines a variety of training methodologies, such as the use of small groups, T-groups, role playing, cross-cultural exercises, cultural immersion, third-culture experience, and studies of one's own culture. Within each of these types of training, there are numerous procedures. For example, the cross-cultural exercises might include doing an intensive description of a community, interviewing people to make a list of critical incidents involving conflict between two cultural groups, developing case studies, becoming exposed to nonverbal communications from another culture or to persons whose behavior contrasts sharply with the kind one is accustomed to. One of the most promising techniques is the use of culture assimilators, programmed learning experiences involving incidents of cross-cultural interaction. A person reads about each incident and attempts to evaluate it and to explain why it happened. He then receives feedback, consisting of an evaluation of his own explanation, and instruction on how to analyze similar cross-cultural interactions. Each incident is selected to make some particular point and to force the person to develop ways of thinking about other cultures which lead to understanding, suspension of judgment, and which avoid overreaction to cultural differences.

Still more techniques need to be developed and tested. A new technique needs to be developed to train people in the "de-escalation of conflict" by systematically moving the locus of conflict from the level of values to the level of facilities. It is easier to handle conflict at that level. It is also important to perceive the conflict as a non-zero-sum game and to adopt a problem-solving set when negotiating with the "other group." In a zero-sum game, what one wins the other loses, e.g., in bargaining over the price of merchandise. A non-zero-sum game is one where both can win. For example, if a boss agrees to raise the salary of a subordinate by 30 percent and the subordinate responds by producing 30 percent more, both the boss and the subordinate gain. Many conflicts can result in agreements that benefit all parties, but such solutions require creativity.

Hypothesis. 1. Conflict is resolved most easily when the situation is perceived as a non-zero-sum game over facilities, in which both sides are to blame for the conflict; it is most difficult to resolve when the situation is perceived as a zero-sum game over values, and each side blames the other for the conflict.

Notes: As a suggestion to researchers (which may be skipped by the administrators, who can just read the hypotheses), one can see a 2×4×2 factorial study in which ten negotiation teams, each consisting of two black and two white students, attempt to reach agreement. The 16-cell design would require 160 teams of four students each.

The manipulation of the game as zero-sum versus non-zero-sum may involve reaching agreements structured on only one dimension, versus agreement involving several dimensions, on some of which both can obtain satisfactory outcomes. The manipulation of facilities, roles, norms, and values would involve different topics of negotiation. The manipulation of the focus of guilt might be made by having neutral observers state to each side either "You are to blame as much as the other side" or "The other side is to blame for this conflict." The dependent variable would be the number of agreements reached. The prediction is that in the easy case several of the teams in that cell will reach agreement; in the difficult case few agreements will be reached.

Corollary. If hypothesis 1 is supported and if we know the kinds of disagreements that are found among blacks and whites differing in social class and sex, we would be able to predict specific difficulties in reaching agreement that are likely to occur in boss-subordinate and employee-employee pairs in industry.

Hypothesis 2. Each of the procedures currently employed in cross-cultural training, e.g., Wight (1969) makes some contribution to the reduction of conflict.

Notes: A sample of five training methods could be selected from the Wight handbook. The method of subtraction could be used in training both blacks and whites. Thus, each subject could be exposed to a different set of four training experiences, but one group of subjects would be exposed to all five training experiences, as follows:

Group   I: A, B, C, D, E
Group II: B, C, D, E
Group III: A, C, D, E
Group IV: A, B, D, E
Group V: A, B, C, E
Group VI: A, B, C, D

If ten pairs of trained negotiators are given negotiation tasks of considerable difficulty, as determined by the previous study, after they are trained in each of these groups, it will be possible to measure the effect of omitting one method on the percentage agreements reached. The total experiment would require 120 subjects.

Another set of studies should examine the extent to which one can train subjects to employ "cognitive algorithms," that is, particular ways of thinking about issues, which change behavior. One is encouraged by the results of McClelland and Winters (1969), who had some success in changing need achievement behaviors, to hope that cognitive training may have some effect. A separate study may be needed to assess the effectiveness of each of these cognitive algorithms:

(a) "As a human I have a natural tendency to project conflict to the level of values. I must bring it down to the level of facilities.'

(b) "As a human I tend to stereotype others. Most stereotypes are extremely inaccurate. What do I think about my opponent? What I think is probably quite wrong."

(c) "What is my subjective estimate of the validity of the black cue? It is probably exaggerated by a factor of 5. I should make my decisions by discounting this cue to a much greater extent than I usually do."

(d) "I am probably justifying my previous unfair actions toward him by saying to myself that he is getting what he deserves, in order to feel more comfortable with myself."

Hence, *Hypothesis 3:* It is possible to train people to think in ways that reduce conflict and to increase the frequency of negotiation agreements.

Another series of studies might examine other forms of content for training programs. The culture assimilators, tested in hypothesis 2, are constructed on the assumption that learning the point of view of another culture improves the likelihood of agreement, communication, and attraction toward members of this other culture. One could also test the effect of insight, as suggested by Katz's functional theory, as well as the effects of different types of contact on stereotyping. For example, we might test *Hypothesis 4:* If prejudice serves an ego-defensive function for an individual, providing this person with insights concerning the extent to which his prejudiced responses are due to defensive reactions will lead to a reduction in his prejudice.

A variety of hypotheses can be tested concerning the way the environment is structured and the effects of such structuring on liking for the other race. For example, *Hypothesis 5:* The more frequently rewards (phenomenological definition) are received in the presence of the other race, the greater the liking for the other race.

Hypothesis 6: The greater the frequency of behavior directed toward superordinate goals (common between whites and blacks), the greater the liking for the other race.

The hypotheses presented above are but a small sample of the hypotheses that may be derived from the theories we reviewed in the first part of this chapter. They are illustrative of what needs to be done. Many more studies, some quite exploratory, are needed. For example, we know very little about the implicit personality theories of blacks and whites concerning blacks and whites. A few studies suggest that blacks have unusually favorable views concerning the effectiveness of the personality adjustment of whites, but such information is probably dated (it was obtained in the early 1960s).

IMPLICATIONS FOR ADMINISTRATIVE POLICY

There is a fundamental difference in the outlook of the researcher and the administrator. The researcher examines his data, finds gaps and alternative interpretations, and formulates new studies. By a gradual process of elimination of alternative interpretations he arrives at a clear understanding of the nature of the relationships he is interested in. This process takes time. The administrator needs answers now; he cannot wait for the researcher to carry out ten or twenty years of research in order to give him the answer. This conflict can be eliminated if the researcher is willing to *guess* which administrative actions might prove effective and the administrator is willing to *test* his policies, in the manner described by Campbell (1969). The administrator's approach to social change is usually very weak, because he *assumes* that the guesses of scientists are "the truth." Let us dispel any such notions. We are willing to guess, but such educated guesses need to be tested. It is a fundamental error to *assume* that a reform is going to be successful. We must carry out reforms the way we carry out experiments: to guide our next round of reforms.

Campbell has correctly pointed out that we must shift our emphasis from the advocacy of specific reforms, such as changes in policy or organizational structure, to the advocacy of the seriousness of a problem that might be solved with the reform. We must first recognize a problem and then carry out *several* kinds of reforms, if possible on matched groups; otherwise, we use the variety of quasi-experimental designs reviewed in Campbell's paper. It is possible to collect a broad range of data so as to be able to reject a variety of plausible rival hypotheses that might explain a particular set of results associated with a reform. We need to measure each outcome in many different ways, to ensure that our measurements really reflect the quality we think we are measuring. We must plan our reforms in such a way as to permit multiple measurement over time, so as to obtain several measures of outcomes both before and after the reform. We must guard against all kinds of methodological mistakes in the selection of the groups we reform which might lead to incorrect conclusions due to regression effects. If the reforms are carried out in this experimental spirit, our educated guesses may be useful. In this section we propose several reforms.

Changing the Organization

Managements wishing to integrate their organizations should conceive of them as providing rewards and costs. A variety of rewards are dispensed by the organization. Over and above the financial rewards, the bonuses, and the fringe benefits, there are status rewards, information rewards (such as providing special training and developing special skills), goods and services, etc. In spite of the long tradition against paternalism, which is in very good standing in American society, there may be good reasons to assume a paternalistic attitude toward black employees. There is a theoretical reason to expect that this policy will be greatly appreciated by blacks: namely, they have experienced very small ingroups, and the affective attachment to a larger ingroup, such as a company, may be welcomed. For the white employee whose ingroup is larger than the company, paternalism implies restriction of freedom and is typically resented. The point is that this may not be true for the black employee. There is also evidence from studies done abroad that paternalistic American companies succeed much more in countries in which a small ingroup is typical (e.g., Sears of Peru) than do nonpaternalistic companies. One way to provide such a paternalistic service is to establish a "race relations" department whose function is to protect the company's black workers. There is ample evidence (Jacobs, 1968; Grossman, 1969) that blacks are treated unfairly by the white establishment, particularly the police. This department should trace complaints by black workers. It should give them legal advice, and it should ensure that political and other pressures are exerted to change the conditions of the ghetto. Such a department, properly staffed with aggressive young lawyers, could be the most effective way to reduce black absenteeism and turnover. Once the black workers have developed a sense of loyalty to the organization which is protecting them and a feeling that the organization is ensuring that their rights as citizens are respected, they will be as loyal as the most loyal white employees —perhaps even more loyal since they have more to gain.

The reduction of delinquency and deviant black behavior may require firm paternal handling and an emphasis on a particular sequence: (a) a large sense of reinforcement for being a member of the particular company, and (b) instant dismissal if deviant behavior is observed. In short, deviant behavior must acquire connections with negative reinforcements of such magnitude that it cannot be seen as "paying off," under any conditions. During black training the whole issue must be discussed openly and the employee may be told (if appropriate): "We know you have a criminal record. That is forgotten. But we have certain rules and we cannot operate this factory if we do not follow these rules. Even if you are caught stealing an item worth 1 cent you will be instantly dismissed, the way we instantly dismiss any white employee who is caught doing something illegal." Another useful reform would be for the management to provide for a system of interracial "courts" which will judge the misdemeanors of all employees, both black and white, and would dismiss those who steal, etc., as specified by company rules. It is important that the worker's black peers participate in the decision of dismissal. It is also desirable to give each worker the experience of sitting in such a court, as the jury, at the earliest opportunity, so he can experience the system from the inside. The important thing is to eliminate the conditions under which delinquent behavior is a form of protest.

The industries of the future may have to experiment with greater flexibility in operation, as well as in working conditions and schedules of payment. For example, they may give employees greater freedom to come and go, or pay them according to different schedules, giving people a chance to select the schedule that they find most agreeable. Granted, such changes are going to be expensive. The question is whether the benefits that will be derived in increased morale among all workers might not balance these costs. Such changes may be essential if the current generation of black employees is to find modern industry an agreeable environment.

Training the Black Employee

Many of the characteristics of the black ghetto are considered undesirable by most ghetto dwellers. It is therefore ethical to change them. Many of the psychological characteristics of blacks who come to work in white-controlled industry will be reactions to the racism of white society. It is up to management to adopt administrative policies that will counteract these traits, will modify the black stereotypes of whites, and will make the work environment moderately enjoyable for the black worker.

Ghetto blacks think of whites as superhuman exploiters, intelligent, cold, calculating manipulators, and as supremely selfish. A young black answered a sentence completion "White men are . . ." by inserting "going to do anything to keep black men down." This stereotype needs to be changed. However, most supervisors concerned with efficiency are likely to be seen as confirming this stereotype. For this reason it is important to provide special training to supervisors of blacks, such as the culture assimilator training discussed earlier, and special bonuses for working with black workers.

At the same time the ghetto workers must change. While there is much that needs changing in the white establishment before blacks can feel comfortable in it, it is important to stress also the changes that must occur among blacks. This is a point which black militants often overlook. They talk much about changing white society and the establishment, but they do not realize that the gap is much more one of social class than of race. Specifically, they overlook the tremendous homogeneity of the middle and upper class in the industrialized countries. Only Malcolm X, toward the end of his life, reached the insight that is discussed here: that there is no such thing as a white culture versus a black culture, but an urban industrial culture versus a rural agricultural culture. The skilled worker in Western Europe, Russia, India, Japan, Australia, or the United States lives in ways which are strikingly similar to the skilled worker in Nigeria; the professionals in these countries are even more similar; those who belong to the jet set in these countries cannot be distinguished by any test other than what is their preferred language for communication within their families (at work they often use English). In short, industrial man, not white man, is a special type. It is with that man, who admittedly is more frequently white than black, that the black man must learn to live. If he wants to live in an industrial society, just as his Nigerian cousins want to, he must develop the perspectives of industrial man. The Chinese Communists are changing their peasant society into an industrial society the quickest and perhaps the most painful way, but nevertheless they are changing it fast. The Chinese are neither white nor capitalists, but they learn to come to work on time! Coming to work on time is a bit of behavior which is typical of industrial man; it is not a white characteristic (vast numbers of whites in South America never come to work on time). In short, while industry must change to make a home for the black man, it is also clear that the black ghetto dweller will have to change in order to hold a job in industry. Some changes may be superficial, but others will be of greater importance.

It is the responsibility of industry to give to black employees the kind of training that will demonstrate to them that the company genuinely wishes to have them as employees. This training should include a variety of experiences designed to raise self-esteem, to lengthen time perspective, and to provide a feeling that constructive behavior leads to positive outcomes. It should be recognized that most of the black employee's past experience dissociated his own actions with good outcomes, and he should be told that things will be different from now on. Black infants, less than twelve months old, may acquire a feeling of helplessness because their mothers are too busy to attend to them when they cry. When this happens the child stops crying but becomes apathetic. One might hope that if the black worker is given a series of exercises in which outcomes are made to depend on his actions and rewards are obtained immediately, he will begin to see that action leads to rewards, that such sequences *exist* "in nature" and should be sought. Of course, we need experiments here to determine if providing such exercises can reverse a process which can be traced all the way back to infancy. Let us hope a reversal is possible.

A good deal of training will be required before the black employees can be introduced to the factory floor. Basic skills like using the public transportation system or an alarm clock are sometimes lacking. Most importantly, blacks often lack the motivation to stay on the job. They feel aversion for the whole white environment, which they associate with oppression, anxiety, defeat, failure. Much training is required to be provided to overcome such feelings.

The training should also concentrate on rewarding punctuality. It might use models (blacks who are on time and are rewarded) and also information (those late are fired.) Anecdotal evidence suggests that very few trials are needed to learn to be on time, provided the motivational framework is clear. The Chicago bus drivers are fired if they report for work but two minutes late. Most of the drivers are black, and they are extremely prompt in arriving for work.

Blacks are highly suspicious in interpersonal relations—and with good reason. This pattern must again be broken. It requires a series of experiences in which trust responses are evoked and rewarded. In the pre-work-training sessions trust might be evoked.

There are certain games, called prisoner-dilemma games, which might be used as part of the training experience. In these games a person may choose one of several responses, and his opponent also chooses one of several responses. The games are geared in such a way that some of the responses are essentially "cooperative"—i.e., they lead to small rewards for both—and some are competitive. As an example, consider the following matrix with responses A and B that P might make and C and D that O might make. The numbers in the matrix represent the gains and losses for P under each diagnoal and for O over each diagonal.

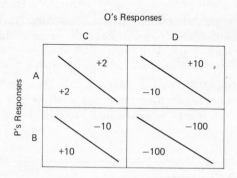

The best way for P and O to make money, in this game, is for both of them to make the cooperative response—A for P and C for O. Then both will make $2. On the other hand, if P makes the response B, while O makes the cooperative response, then P wins $10 while O loses $10. Similarly, if O decides to play D, he might make $10, provided P was cooperative. Disaster befalls both if they decide to be greedy simultaneously, since in that particular game they both lose $100. Now it is possible to manipulate the values in the matrices of such games so as to encourage trusting (cooperative) behavior, and thus give to a person extensive experience with a segment of life in which when he is cooperative he gets rewarded, and when he is nasty he gets punished. If such games are structured so that cooperative and trusting responses are reinforced, it should be possible to teach such responses to the black workers. It should also be helpful to acknowledge, when training them, that trust is indeed inappropriate in the ghetto, so that what they learn in the job setting should not necessarily be used in the ghetto. This kind of development of separate systems of behavior, one for the job and one for the ghetto, may not be any more difficult than learning two languages. Bilinguals switch from one language to another with great ease, and there is no reason to expect, on the basis of present knowledge, that this cannot also be done with other kinds of behavior patterns.

During training some elements of attribution theory, with demonstrations, might be included to help the blacks understand the reactions of whites. According to this theory, reviewed in the first part of this chapter, any deviation from "normal" behavior is likely to lead to attribution of particular traits. Thus, a particular deviant behavior which the black finds highly rewarding may actually be counterproductive, in terms of his long-term goals, because it creates or reinforces uncomplementary stereotypes. The best way to change un-complementary stereotypes is to behave in ways which are unexpected, and hence will be noticed, but which are diametrically opposed to the stereotypes. Thus, a man who has the reputation of being stingy can change the stereotype by behaving generously, and so on. In a study by Davis and Triandis (1965) naive white students negotiated with confederates of the experimenters who were well-trained blacks. The blacks were chosen to be highly articulate and were supplied with an impressive array of arguments backed up with statistics. The effect on the prejudiced whites was shattering. Never before had they seen a black speaking such excellent English, arguing his case with such eloquence, and backing it up with such solid evidence. The white subjects showed a large and highly significant change in their affective responses and their attributive responses; on the other hand, their behavioral intentions changed very little. One implication from this study is that there is a need for careful selection of the blacks who are first brought into a particular department.

Selecting the Black Employee

A recent study by Fromkin, Klimoski, and Flanagan (1970) showed that highly competent persons are preferred co-workers. The race of such people is not important if they are highly competent. On the other hand, people who are incompetent *and* black were generally seen as less desirable co-workers. It seems important, then, to provide excellent technical training to blacks so that their preparation for work in industry will be better than average. Under such conditions, their race may be ignored, and they may be accepted. One way to ensure adequate preparation is to select blacks that are already well trained. Furthermore, deductions from Jones et al. (1968) would suggest that when blacks are introduced into a new company they must be seen as having a number of successful experiences. This condition would be dissonant to current stereotypes and would also lead to the perception of blacks as competent. An anecdote, told by an industrial consultant, supports this suggestion. In integrating a railroad, he hired blacks to train them for the *most* difficult job. Most white employees were ready to walk out, but they stayed on the job because their stereotypes were so strong that they did not believe the blacks would be able to handle such complex jobs. When the well-chosen blacks succeeded, the opposition dissolved.

It follows that an exceptionally effective way to integrate organizations is to hire black management. Unfortunately, the limited numbers of qualified blacks for top-level positions in American industry make this suggestion of limited practicality, but efforts must be exerted. One might, for example, seriously consider a substantial increase in scholarship aid to qualified black students planning to go to engineering school, followed by a Master's in Business Administration, since this is one of the most effective routes of entry into top management.

Training the White Employee

A successful program requires also the training of the white workers. They must see the essential similarities of blacks and whites and their common humanity. They must realize something about the unity of mankind, the way racial and cultural differences develop, the role of their ancestors in creating a culture which leads to several forms of discrimination, the need for integration and the reduction of conflict. Some of the basic defense mechanisms which they employ and which feed their prejudice must be made clear to them. Such defense mechanisms have been found to be relatively impervious to conventional information approaches to attitude change. Special approaches are needed, including the so-called self-insight approach (for a review of relevant studies see Triandis, 1971a, Chapter III). The reduction of the instrumental relevance of the black cue must be accomplished in such training. The white workers must learn that a "successful black" is not a status incongruent stimulus. Training exercises, in which rewards follow friendly, constructive behaviors in interracial settings, should be useful.

Black Work Assignments

Great care must be taken with the matching of the black's ability and training with the difficulty of the job. Since blacks have low self-esteem, it is essential to structure the situation so that they will rarely fail and will experience success very frequently. At the same time, the jobs should not be too easy, since such jobs are low in prestige and often boring. Optimal matching requires jobs of intermediate complexity. Of course, training, overlearning, the availability of counseling help and the activities of the race relations department will also be important in keeping the worker from becoming discouraged and in ensuring that he does not quit.

Structuring the Environment

Administrative action can also be directed toward structuring the jobs, so that blacks and whites will have superordinate goals, will experience a good deal of equal-status contact under rewarding conditions, and special bonuses will be dispensed when interracial groups cooperate and develop interdependence.

CONCLUSION

In this chapter we surveyed the most significant theories of social perception and examined the most important findings concerning black and white differences. From a juxtaposition of these two sets of findings we derived some suggestions for social action. Many of these suggestions are dramatic, such as the casting of the company as the protector of the rights of the black employee, but only dramatic shifts in present policy are likely to lead to significant improvements in interracial relations and to the integration of the organization.

REFERENCES

Adams, J. S. Inequity in social exchange. In L. Berkowitz (ed.), *Advances in experimental social psychology.* New York: Academic Press, 1965, pp. 267–300.

Ardrey, R. *African genesis.* New York: Delta Books, 1961.

Ash, S. E. Forming impressions of personality. *Journal of Abnormal and Social Psychlogy,* 1946, *41,* 258–290.

Bayton, J. A., Austin, L. J., and Burke, K. R. Negro perception of Negro and white personality traits. *Journal of Personality and Social Psychology,* 1965, 1, 250–253.

Berscheid, E., and Walster, E. H. *Interpersonal attraction.* Reading, Mass.: Addison-Wesley, 1969.

Bieri, J., Atkins, A. L., Briar, R. L., Leaman, R. L., Miller, H., and Tripodi, T. *Clinical and social judgment.* New York: Wiley, 1966.

Brehm, J. W., and Cohen, A. R. *Explorations in cognitive dissonance.* New York: Wiley, 1962.

Brown, R. *Social psychology.* New York: Free Press, 1965.

Bruner, J. S. On perceptual readiness. *Psychological Review,* 1957, *64,* 123–152.

Bruner, J. S., and Tagiuri, R. The perception of people. In G. Lindzey (ed.), *Handbook of social psychology.* Reading, Mass.: Addison-Wesley, 1954, 634–654.

Byrne, D., and Clore, G. L. Effectance arousal and attraction. *Journal of Personality and Social Psychology Monograph,* 1967, *6,* No. 4, 1–18.

Campbell, D. T. Stereotypes and the perception of group differences. *American Psychologist,* 1967, *22,* 817–829.

Campbell, D. T. Reforms as experiments. *American Psychologist,* 1969, *24,* 409–429.

Clark, K. B. *Dark ghetto: Dilemmas of social power.* New York: Harper, 1967.

Davis, E. E., and Triandis, H. C. An exploratory study of intercultural negotiation. Urbana, Ill.: Group Effectiveness Research Laboratory. University of Illinois, 1965. (Also in *Journal of Applied Psychology,* 1971, *1,* 240–262.)

Deutsch, M., Katz, I., and Jensen, A. R. *Social class, race and psychological development.* New York: Holt, 1968.

Erskine, H. The polls: Negro philosophies of life. *Public Opinion Quarterly,* 1969, *33,* 147–158.

Escoffery, A. S. Personality and behavior correlates of Negro American belief in "fate-control." *Dissertation Abstracts,* 1968, *28,* (8-A), 3261–3262.

Festinger, L. *A theory of cognitive dissonance.* Stanford, Calif.: Stanford University Press, 1957.

Foa, U. G., and Foa, E. Resource exchange: Toward a structural theory of inter-personal communication. In A. W. Siegman and B. Pope (eds.), *Studies in dyadic communication*. Long Island City, N.Y.: Pergamon Press, 1969.

Foa, U. G., Triandis, H. C., and Katz, E. W. Cross-cultural invariance in the differentiation and organization of family roles. *Journal of Personality and Social Psychology*, 1966, *4*, 316–327.

Fromkin, H. L., Klimoski, R. J., and Flanagan, M. F. Race and competence as determinants of acceptance of newcomers in success and failure work groups. *Organizational Behavior and Human Performance*, 1972, 7 (1), 25–42.

Glass, D. C. Changes in liking as a means of reducing cognitive discrepancies between self-esteem and aggression. *Journal of Personality*, 1964, *32*, 531–549.

Grossman, P. Police behavior in the black ghetto. In L. Horstman (ed.), *Urban features USA*. Houston, Tex.: Center for Research in Social Change and Economic Development of Rice University, 1969, pp. 118–138.

Hallowell, A. I. Ojibwa metaphysics of being and the perception of persons. In R. Taguiri and L. Petrullo (eds.), *Person perception and interpersonal behavior*. Stanford, Calif.: Stanford Univerity Press, 1958, pp. 63–85.

Harvey, O. J., and Clapp, W. F. Hope, expectancy and reactions to the unexpected. *Journal of Personality and Social Psychology*, 1965, *2*, 45–52.

Harvey, O. J., Hunt, D. E., and Schroder, H. M. *Conceptual systems and personality development*. New York: Wiley, 1961.

Harvey, O. J., Reich, J. W., and Wyer, R. S. Effects of attitude direction, attitude intensity and structure of beliefs upon differentiation. *Journal of Personality and Social Psychology*, 1968, *10*, 472–478.

Heider, F. *The psychology of interpersonal relations*. New York: Wiley, 1958.

Helson, H. *Adaptation-level theory*. New York: Harper, 1964.

Hovland, C. I. Reconciling conflicting results derived from experimental and survey studies of attitude change. *American Psychologist*, 1959, *14*, 8–17.

Ichheiser, G. Misunderstandings in human relations: A study in false social perception. *American Journal of Sociology*, 1949, 55, No. 2, Part 2.

Jacobs, P. *Prelude to riot: A view of urban America from the bottom*. New York: Random House, 1966.

Janis, I. L. Attitude change via role playing. In R. P. Abelson, E. Aronson, W. J. McGuire, T. M. Newcomb, M. J. Rosenberg, and P. H. Tannenbaum (eds.), *Theories of cognitive consistency: A sourcebook*. Chicago: Rand McNally, 1968, pp. 810–819.

Jones, E. E., and Davis, K. E. From acts to dispositions: The attribution process in person perception. In L. Berkowitz (ed.), *Advances in experimental social psychology*. New York: Academic Press, 1965, pp. 220–266.

Jones, E. E., Rock, L., Shaver, K. G., Goethals, G. R., and Ward, L. W. Pattern of performance and ability attribution: An unexpected primacy effect. *Journal of Personality and Social Psychology*, 1968, *10*, 317–340.

Katz, D. The functional approach to the study of attitudes. *Public Opinion Quarterly*, 1960, *24*, 163–204.

Keil, C. *Urban blues*. Chicago: Chicago University Press, 1966.

Kelley, H. H. Attribution theory in social psychology. In D. Levine (ed.), *Nebraska symposium on motivation*. Lincoln, Neb.: University of Nebraska Press, 1967, pp. 192–240.

Kluckhohn, F., and Strodtbeck, F. L. *Variations in value orientations*. Evanston, Ill. Row, Peterson, 1961.

Kochman, T. "Rapping" in the black ghetto. *Transaction*, 1969, *6*, 29–34.

Lambert, W. E., and Klineberg, O. *Children's views of foreign people: A cross-cultural study*. New York: Appleton-Century-Crofts, 1967.

LaForge, R., and Suczek, R. The interpersonal dimension of personality. III. An interpersonal checklist. *Journal of Personality*, 1955, *24*, 94–112.

Lee, R. E., III, and Schroeder, H. M. Effects of outward bound training on urban youth. *Journal of Special Education*, 1969, 3, 187–205.

Lefcourt, H. M., and Ladwig, G. W. The American Negro: A problem in expectancies. *Journal of Personality and Social Psychology*, 1965, *1*, 377–380.

Lester, J. *Look out Whitey! Black power's gon' get your mama!* New York: Grove Press, 1968.

Levi-Schoen, A. *L'image d'autrui chez l'enfant.* Paris: Presses Universitaires de France, 1964.

Liebow, E. *Tally's corner: A study of Negro streetcorner men.* Boston: Little, Brown, 1967.

Lott, A. J., and Lott, B. E. *Negro and white youth: A psychological study in a border-state community.* New York: Holt, 1963.

Lott, A. J., and Lott, B. E. A learning theory approach to interpersonal attitudes. In A. G. Greenwald et al. (eds.), *Psychological foundations of attitudes.* New York: Academic Press, 1968, pp. 67–87.

Malcolm X. *The autobiography of Malcolm X.* New York: Grove Press, 1964.

Martin, J. G. Racial ethnocentrism and judgment of beauty. *Journal of Social Psychology*, 1964, *63*, 59–63.

Maruyama, M. The ghetto logic. (Mimeo, 1969.)

McClelland, D. C., and Winter, D. G. *Motivating economic achievement.* New York: Free Press, 1969.

Mischel, W. Delay of gratification, need for achievement and acquiescence in another culture. *Journal of Abnormal and Social Psychology*, 1961, *62*, 543–552.

Moynihan, D. P. *The Negro family: The case for national action.* Washington, D.C.: U.S. Department of Labor, 1965.

Newcomb, T. M. Interpersonal balance. In R. P. Abelson et al. (eds.), *Theories of cognitive consistency: A sourcebook.* Chicago: Rand McNally, 1969, 28–52.

Nobers, D. R. The effects of father absence and mother's characteristics on the identification of adolescent white and Negro males. *Dissertation Abstracts*, 1968, *29*, 1508–1509.

Pederson, D. M. The measurement of individual differences in perceived personality-trait relationships and their relation to certain determinants. *Journal of Social Psychology*, 1965, *65*, 233–258.

Osgood, C. E. Dimensionality of the semantic space for communication via facial expressions. *Scandinavian Journal of Psychology*, 1966, *7*, 1–30.

Osgood, C. E., and Tannenbaum, P. H. The principle of congruity in the prediction of attitude change. *Psychological Review*, 1955, *62*, 42–55,

Ostrom, T. M., and Upshaw, H. S. Psychological perspectives and attitude change. In A. C. Greenwald et al. (eds.), *Psychological foundations of attitudes.* New York: Academic Press, 1968, pp. 217–242.

Rommetveit, R. *Selectivity, intuition and halo effects in social perception.* Oslo: Oslo University Press, 1960.

Rosenberg, M. Cognitive structure and attitudinal affect. *Journal of Abnormal and Social Psychology*, 1956, *53*, 367–372.

Sampson, E. E. Studies of status congruence. In L. Berkowitz (ed.), *Advances in experimental social psychology*, Vol. 4. New York: Academic Press, 1969, pp. 225–270.

Schlosberg, H. Three dimensions of emotion. *Psychological Review*, 1954, *61*, 81–88.

Schuman, H. Social change and the validity of regional stereotypes in East Pakistan. *Sociometry*, 1966, *29*, 428–440.

Sherif, M., and Hovland, C. I. *Social judgment.* New Haven: Yale University Press, 1961.

Smelser, N. J. *Theory of collective behavior.* New York: Free Press, 1963.

Staats, A. W. An outline of an integrated learning theory of attitudes. In M. Fishbein (ed.), *Readings in attitude theory and measurement.* New York: Wiley, 1967, pp. 373–376.

Stapert, J. C., and Clore, G. L. Attraction and disagreement-produced arousal. *Journal of Personality and Social Psychology,* 1969, *13,* 64–69.

Steiner, I. D. Ethnocentrism and tolerance for trait "inconsistency." *Journal of Abnormal and Social Psychology,* 1954, *49,* 349–354.

Stewart, E. C., Danelian, J., and Foster, R. J. *Simulating intercultural communication through role-playing.* Washington, D.C.: HumRRO, George Washington University, 1968.

Streufert, S., and Streufert, S. C. Effects of conceptual structure, failure and success on attribution of causality and interpersonal attitudes. *Journal of Personality and Social Psychology,* 1969, *11,* 138–147.

Tagiuri, R. Person perception. In G. Lindzey and E. Aronson (eds.), *The handbook of social psychology,* Vol. III. Reading, Mass: Addison-Wesley, 1969, pp. 395–449.

Taylor, D. A., and Oberlander, L. Person-perceptions and self-disclosure: Motivational mechanisms in interpersonal processes. *Journal of Experimental Research in Personality,* 1969, *4,* 14–28.

Thibaut, J. W., and Kelly, H. H. *The social psychology of groups.* New York: Wiley, 1959.

Triandis, H. C. Exploratory factor analyses of the behavioral component of social attitudes. *Journal of Abnormal and Social Psychology,* 1964, *68,* 420–430.

Triandis, H. C. Towards an analysis of the components of interpersonal attitudes. In Carolyn and Muzafer Sherif (eds.), *Attitudes, ego envolvement and change.* New York: Wiley, 1967, pp. 227–270.

Triandis, H. C. *Attitudes and attitude change.* New York: Wiley, 1971.

Triandis, H. C. *Analysis of subjective culture.* New York: Wiley, 1972.

Triandis, H. C., and Fishbein, M. Cognitive interaction in person perception. *Journal of Abnormal and Social Psychology,* 1963, *67,* 446–453.

Triandis, H. C., and Triandis, L. M. Race, social class, religion and nationality as determinants of social distance. *Journal of Abnormal and Social Psychology,* 1960, *61,* 110–118.

Triandis, H. C., and Vassiliou, V. Frequency of contact and stereotyping. *Journal of Personality and Social Psychology,* 1967, *7,* 316–328.

Triandis, H. C., Vassiliou, V. and Nassiakou, M. Three cross-cultural studies of subjective culture. *Journal of Personality and Social Psychology Monograph Supplement,* 1968, *8,* No. 4, 1–42.

Upshaw, H. S. The personal reference scale. In L. Berkowitz (ed.), *Advances in experimental social psychology,* Vol. IV. New York: Academic Press, 1969, pp. 315–372.

Valentine, C. A. *Culture and poverty.* Chicago: The University of Chicago Press, 1968.

Vassiliou, V., Triandis, H. C., Vassiliou, G., and McGuire, H. Reported amount of contact and stereotyping. In H. C. Triandis (ed.), *The analysis of subjective culture.* New York: Wiley, 1972.

Warr, P. B., and Knapper, C. *The perception of people and events.* New York: Wiley, 1968.

Wight, A. R. *Cross-cultural and community involvement training.* Estes Park, Colo.: Center for Research and Education, 1969.

Wishner, J. Reanalysis of "impressions of personality." *Psychological Review,* 1960, *67,* 96–112.

CHAPTER EIGHT

Communication: Structure and Process

Lyman W. Porter

INTRODUCTION BY THE EDITORS

Unless an organization can foster a work atmosphere with adequate information exchange, it will be unable to coordinate the activities and efforts of individual components, the skills of individual members will be underutilized, and, as a consequence, it will probably be at a competitive disadvantage in the industrial world. Effective communication is vital to the organization's survival. However, Porter cautions against optimism about achieving genuine communication at the moment of integration, and then he offers some guidelines to help reduce barriers in interracial communication within organizations. Noting the absence of relevant research, he offers suggestions both for research and practice—the latter stemming from inferential leaps Porter was courageous enough to make.

The critical element is the opportunity for members of different races to discover there is value to be gained by accepting and agreeing with communications from members of the other race. Porter hypothesizes that mutual perception of attitude similarity between members of different races increases the receptivity of both persons to what the other is saying. Particularly crucial is whether or not members of the two races discover that they share some common

The author wishes to acknowledge the valuable assistance of Jerry Kaiwi in the preparation of this chapter.

216

attitudes at least toward relevant aspects of the work environment, such as attitudes toward the boss, the fairness of the pay, etc. The organization can design some pre-job training which helps employees become aware of these similarities. In addition to pre-job training opportunities discussed in chapters by Hellervik and Triandis, the organization can provide on-the-job opportunities to discover attitude similarities by designing small interracial work groups in which goal achievement requires cooperative interaction on tasks and where different race members have equal status and equal competence.

Porter also notes the need to distinguish between comprehension and acceptance as two components of the communication processes. Comprehension involves the accuracy of the transfer of meaning from sender to receiver. Acceptance involves the receiver's willingness to act in response to the sender's message. Comprehension is necessary but not a sufficient condition for acceptance. There are several factors which inhibit comprehension. Of primary importance are differences in the subcultures which characterize members of different races. Training can focus attention on generating common sets of language symbols for topics or objects which are organizationally relevant. Acceptance seems to be a function of a large number of variables, not the least of which are communicator credibility and communicator attractiveness. Two factors have been established as determinants of communicator credibility, i.e., the communicator's perceived expertise or competence or objectivity. Both expertise and objectivity enhance the acceptance of messages, but competence seems to be more potent than objectivity. Similarly, a number of factors can enhance the attractiveness of a communicator and thereby increase the persuasive impact and acceptance of his messages. The more the communicator and recipients share common attitudes which are relevant to the topic of the message, the more recipients tend to accept his message. Of importance to organizational integration is the finding that irrelevant similarities in attitudes among members of the same group seem to have little effect upon acceptance of communications.

Porter's insightful analysis of laboratory and field research on vertical communication provides a number of relevant suggestions about interracial communication in organizations. Both upward and downward communication in organizations is greatly influenced by the fact that supervisors have greater control and power to reward. This difference in status affects both the amount and type of messages which are sent between levels. For example, there is a strong tendency for subordinates to filter their upward communications to present themselves in a favorable light. The degree of filtered inaccuracy is a function of the degree of their trust or confidence in the supervisor's intentions toward them and their careers. Subordinates also perceive their upward-bound messages as more important than their superiors do. Supervisors should be attuned to this distortion and take care that their subordinates feel they completely understand and appreciate what has come from below. An interesting finding is the tendency of subordinates to search for more meaning in messages and to search for hidden meanings in messages from their superiors. Porter calls this the "iceberg effect." The supervisor should pay more attention to his com-

munication and be aware of how much interpretation goes into his messages. It is advisable for a superior frequently to check out the meanings which are attached and discover the aspects of his style or his relationships with particular employees where misinterpretations are most likely to occur. Then, he can choose appropriate steps to improve the accuracy of his communications. It is likely that all the above phenomena are exaggerated when the subordinate and the superior are members of different races or different social classes. In biracial work situations, the supervisor needs to be particularly sensitive and aware of biases in communication. It seems wise for organizations to train their best supervisors in effective communication and assign them work groups with new minority employees or where the proportion of minority members is high. At the same time, it is helpful for supervisors in such situations to have a narrow span of control.

There are also some special considerations in horizontal communications, e.g., those communications occurring between members of the same work group or between people on the same level within an organization. One variable is the size of the work group. Biracial work groups should be kept as small as economically feasible to promote opportunities for better communication within the work group and between the work group and their supervisor or upper levels of management. Staff roles, when they have status equal to line positions, may offer minority members special communication opportunities which will enhance the speed of smooth integration.

> The greatest problem of communication is the illusion that it
> has been accomplished.
>
> (G. B. Shaw)

If organizations are to become truly integrated, and at the same time retain a capacity for goal achievement, they will need to devote considerable attention to the quality of communication. Unless an organization can develop a work environment that can maintain and foster an adequate degree of information exchange, the skills of individual members of an interracially composed work force will be underutilized. This in turn can lead to profound dissatisfaction among employees. Furthermore, no organization can long survive in a competitive and challenging world if it is unable to coordinate the activities and efforts of its different components. Effective communication is vital to this task of coordination.

Let us be clear that we expect that in the immediate future the goal of genuine communication in integrated organizations will be exceedingly difficult to achieve. Anyone considering the amount and quality of communication between members of different races in present day organizations should be under no illusions concerning the barriers that would impede such communication. In fact, if one is not careful, it is easy to become quite pessimistic about the probability of very much real communication—the transfer of meaning from sender to receiver—taking place. Nevertheless, we believe that this kind of communication is possible, even if at the moment we have few guidelines or aids to help it flourish.

Unfortunately, to be able to make any reasonably sound conclusions or recommendations in regard to the present topic, numerous extrapolations from the literature will be required. The reason for this is simple: there is a scarcity of directly relevant research studies bearing on communication in integrated organizations. There are many studies of communication in organizations (though not nearly so many as on the topic of leadership or motivation in organizations), and there are a few studies on the functioning of interracial groups. But there are virtually no studies on communication between members of biracial groups in organizations. The investigations dealing with communication in organizations ignore race (and, by implication, are studies of whites communicating with whites), and the studies of the functioning of interracial groups tend to ignore communication. (Exceptions to this latter statement are several experiments by Katz: e.g., Katz and Benjamin, 1960; Katz, Goldston, and Benjamin, 1958.) Thus, if one were to depend upon specifically relevant research findings to write this particular chapter he would be left with nothing to say. Consequently, in the remaining sections of the chapter we will rely on tangential evidence that will require some rather generous "inferential leaps" in order to be able to draw any pertinent conclusions at all.

The general focus of this chapter will be on the problem of communication in organizational settings, as such communication is affected by work forces composed of different racial backgrounds. The analysis will emphasise the process of communication taking place in a socially structured environment—namely, organizations in which people are employed and work takes place. We thus are narrowing the scope from the broader topic of interracial communication per se. We are limiting it to the *organizational* setting—to the world of orders, bosses, ranks, performance, decisions, inspection, goals, and the like. This locale would seem to be as good a crucible as any to see if blacks and whites can, indeed, communicate effectively.

The next section of the chapter will discuss the interracial context of communication, drawing upon some of the available literature dealing with such questions as attitudes toward different races and the effects of racial comparisons on the performance of minority group members. The following section will look at the nature of the communication process and will examine factors affecting the comprehension and acceptance of messages. The succeeding section will examine organizational structural factors as they affect the communication process. In all of these three sections, particular attention will be paid to variables that are presumed to facilitate or inhibit communication when it involves members of different races working together. The final section of the chapter will specify some conclusions and implications for practice and will suggest some lines for needed future research.

THE INTERRACIAL CONTEXT OF COMMUNICATION

The research relevant to aspects of the interracial context of communication generally falls into two categories: factors determining social attraction to members of other races and behavior in biracial task situations. Since aspects of each of these topics are covered in more detail elsewhere in this book, only examples of the findings and conclusions that have implications for organizational communication will be mentioned here.

Factors Determining Social Attraction to Members of Other Races

A number of studies carried out in the past ten years have attempted to determine the key factors involved in the acceptance or rejection by an individual of a member of a different racial group (e.g., Byrne and Ervin, 1969; Byrne and McGraw, 1964; Byrne and Wong, 1962; Rokeach and Mezei, 1966; Rokeach, Smith, and Evans, 1960; Stein, Hardyck, and Smith, 1965; Triandis and Davis, 1965; Triandis, Loh, and Levin, 1966). Most of these studies have centered on the so-called "race–belief" controversy set off by Rokeach (1961) and followed up by the research of Byrne, Triandis, and others. The race versus belief question refers to whether attraction or rejection of members of other races is more determined by attitude similarities and dissimilarities or by the fact of same or different group (i.e., race) membership. Rokeach's original hypothesis was that the attitude factor was the more important one—that is, that close similarity in attitudes between two members of different races will outweigh racial differences and will result in attraction rather than rejection. Subsequent research has generally confirmed Rokeach's notion, although it has also demonstrated that a number of other variables—such as an individual's initial degree of prejudice, the status of the two individuals vis-à-vis each other, etc.— will modify the impact of attitude similarity. Particularly important are the *degree* of attitude similarity and the *relevance* of attitude similarity to the particular behavioral situation. The research on the race–belief question is well summarized in a recent review by Simons, Berkowitz, and Moyer (1970), and the reader is referred to their article for additional details.

The implications of the several studies dealing with the race–belief controversy for communication in organizational settings would seem to be rather direct: to the extent that an individual of a given race (whether the majority or a minority race) perceives that the person of the other race with whom he is communicating has attitudes similar to his own, he is more likely to be receptive to the content of that communication. Thus, prior information about each other's attitudes may set the stage for improved communication in the future that deals with work-related topics. Of course, the whole sequence can work in reverse: once two members of different races in the work force find out that they have *different* attitudes, the climate for effective communication is thereby made that much more difficult. (Other aspects of attitude similarity and credibility will be discussed in a later section of this chapter.) The main point here is that if members of biracial work teams do not have the opportunity to find out the attitudes of their fellow employees, they are likely to assume that members of a different race have attitudes divergent from their own. Such untested assumptions will be likely to inhibit communication across the races.

Behavior in Biracial Task Situations

Findings of studies carried out in the late 1950s and early 1960s, in which the performance of blacks was observed in actual or simulated biracial situations, suggest several trends that have implications for communication. Before briefly reviewing these studies, we must stress that extreme caution needs to be exercised in extrapolating from them. As noted, they all took place prior to 1965 or 1966. Given the changing nature of the civil rights movement and the rise of black militancy in the latter half of the 1960s, it is quite possible—even probable —that were these identical studies to be repeated now the results would be markedly different. Furthermore, one is reluctant to give too much weight to the specific findings because of the nature of the samples—almost all were limited to college students, both black and white—and because of the fact that all of the studies were conducted outside of real-life organizational situations. None of them involved circumstances in which the subjects were employed on actual jobs. Nevertheless, they constitute most of what evidence there is on the interaction of adult blacks and whites in task-type situations.

One category of findings in these studies indicated that when blacks are placed in intellectual-type task assignments, their performance tends to be affected adversely if they are led to believe that it is being compared with that of equivalent white groups (Katz and Greenbaum, 1963; Katz, Epps, and Exelson, 1964), particularly when other elements of anxiety may be present. A second set of findings concerned apparent compliant behavior on the part of blacks in biracial task situations. Examples of the latter type of behavior specifically concerned communication activities, as it was found that in biracial teams working on intellectual-type problem-solving tasks blacks spoke less than whites and blacks spoke more to whites than to other blacks (Katz, Goldston, and Benjamin, 1958; Katz and Benjamin, 1960). (One is prompted to speculate whether, if the studies were replicated in the early 1970s, the results might not be precisely the reverse.) This type of behavior has been interpreted by some as "failure-avoidant." For example, Lefcourt and Ladwig, commenting on the Katz studies, state: "... it can be tentatively concluded that when Negroes enter biracial, competitive, achievement-motivation eliciting tasks they will have high expectancies of failure and consequently will behave in a failure-avoidant manner" (1965, p. 688). A third aspect of the findings indicates that both of the above-mentioned tendencies can be modified by changing certain elements in the environmental situation. Thus, for example, Katz and Cohen (1962) found that by supplying what they called "assertion training" they could produce more confident behavior by blacks in the biracial situation. Likewise, Lefcourt and Ladwig (1965) were able to induce more task persistence by blacks when the task was presented as one relating to behavior areas where they could draw on previously acquired competence. Both of these latter studies are encouraging in that they indicate that overly compliant behavior by any group of individuals —black or white—can be altered by some fairly direct changes in the environmental circumstances.

Perhaps the major implication of these types of studies for communication is that, taken at a very broad level of generality, they demonstrate that such factors as blacks' concern about comparisons with whites (and, probably today, whites' concern about comparisons with blacks) in achievement-type tasks add to the complexity of communication within would-be integrated organizations. That is, additional "noise" or transmission interference between sender and receiver is added beyond that which is normally there anyway in organized social situations. Communication in nonintegrated organizations is difficult. Such difficulty is probably multiplied by a factor or two or three in organizations that are attempting to become completely integrated.

PROCESS FACTORS IN COMMUNICATION

In this section we proceed to an analysis of the communication process in order to develop a better understanding of what may take place in the interactions between communicators and receivers when they are of different races. Throughout, it will be useful to keep in mind the usual paradigm of communication for this analysis: communicator—message—channel—recipient. These elements have been labeled by McGuire (1969) as antecedent or independent variables in the communication process. Equally important, however, are distinctions among the consequent or dependent variables. In detailing the results of the attitude change literature, McGuire (1969) lists five components or steps in the change process: attention, comprehension, yielding, retention, and action. For our purposes here, where we are concerned with implications for the communication process in organizations rather than for attitude change per se, we shall collapse these components into two broad types of dependent behavioral variables: comprehension and acceptance. These two variables form the basis of the following subsections.

In any communication situation, but particularly so in the organizational setting involving integrated work forces, distinguishing between comprehension and acceptance should aid in our analysis. This is because it is quite possible to have the former without achieving the latter. Accordingly, of course, if comprehension is not present, then acceptance is made difficult if not impossible. Comprehension can be defined as the degree to which the receiver understands what is sent by the communicator, and it involves the accuracy of the transfer of meaning from sender to receiver. The important point, though, is that when we speak of comprehension we are not talking about any necessary subsequent motivated behavior of the recipient. Comprehension, then, can be thought of as (ordinarily) a necessary but not a sufficient condition for the communicator to affect the attitudes and behavior of the recipient. For the latter to happen, the receiver must accept the content or import of the message. Thus, acceptance can be defined as a willingness to change one's attitudes or to act in response to the communicator's message. If acceptance is achieved, it implies the existence of a particular motivational state on the part of the recipient. (Of course, certain behaviors or acts may never take place despite acceptance because other factors present in the situation act to counter or prevent this.) As a general hypothesis, we can assume that both comprehension and acceptance will be more difficult to achieve within newly integrated organizations than within non-integrated organizations or ones that have been interracial for some time.

In the two subsections that follow, we have been greatly aided by several recent major reviews of the literature: particularly, McGuire (1969), who reviewed the broad range of attitude research; Mehrabian and Reed (1968), who dealt with determinants of accuracy; Simons, Berkowitz, and Moyer (1970), who covered similarity, credibility, and attitude change; and Giffin (1967) who surveyed investigations dealing with source credibility and interpersonal trust.

Comprehension in Communication

In their excellent review of the research literature concerned with determinants of communication accuracy, which bears directly on comprehension, Mehrabian and Reed (1968) organize the results of relevant studies around five elements in the typical communication paradigm: attributes of the communicator; the recipient; the channel; the communication (message); and the referent (subject matter). For the next few paragraphs we shall follow their outline and report the nature of some of their conclusions that seem particularly relevant to comprehension of communication within integrated organizations.

COMMUNICATOR AND RECIPIENT ATTRIBUTES. In Mehrabian and Reed's analysis, the most significant attribute of the communicator and recipient (addressee) are the subcultures from which they come. Thus, Mehrabian and Reed state that:

> For most of the . . . communicator attributes, a communicator's subculture or reference group is assumed to provide a readily obtainable index of the attribute, since a communicator's attitudes and prejudices probably reflect a salient characteristic of this subculture. Similarly, the kinds of coding rules [i.e., methods of putting information into symbols] used by a communicator may be assumed to be largely determined by his subculture (1968, p. 366).

If one accepts this viewpoint, the implications for communication between members of two different races in the work situation would appear to be obvious. If, as appears likely, the communicator and receiver in such instances do indeed come from different subcultures, the chances of comprehension occurring are thereby reduced. In particular, accuracy is presumed to be reduced when the two parties do not share the same coding rules for "cognizing the referents about which they are communicating"—that is, when they do not have a common set of symbols to refer to particular objects or topics. (This conclusion is particularly supported by the laboratory research findings of Triandis, 1960a, 1960b.) It would appear that attempts to generate common coding rules for key objects in the environment might help to alleviate this type of comprehension inaccuracy.

Among other attributes of the communicator (and of the recipient, since the two are linked together in a reciprocal manner when comprehension is being considered) that affect accuracy, according to Mehrabian and Reed, are: (1) the level (absolute) of cognitive development of the two communicators; (2) the depth or magnitudes of positive or negative feelings the communicator or receiver has toward the referent; and (3) the depth or magnitude of positive or negative feelings the communicator (recipient) has towards the recipient (communicator). The former factor is found to be positively related to communication understanding and the latter two to be inversely related. All three aspects might well be present in an integrated work setting. If, in a biracial work situation, some or all of the blacks have grown up in an educationally and culturally deprived background, then one could assume that cognitive development might be affected which in turn would make it more difficult for comprehension of communications to take place at work. In the case of the attributes dealing with the strength of the communicator's feelings about the referent, one could infer that many of the topics that might be discussed in biracial situations—particularly in those organizations undergoing the process of being integrated—would indeed tap deep-seated attitudes that would interfere with comprehension. As to the third factor, the magnitude of the communicator's feelings about the recipient, much would depend upon the extent to which the communicator classified an addressee as part of a stereotyped group about which he has some definite feelings. In such instances, still another barrier to accuracy has been erected that would be hard to remove.

One other attribute of the communicator is mentioned by Mehrabian and Reed: the rate at which he sends information. Thus, the more information he sends per unit of time, the harder it is for the addressee to decode accurately. This could become important in biracial work teams if employees become highly emotional or involved in their interactions with members of a different race. As Mehrabian and Reed point out: "A high drive is a source of information which is attended to in varying degrees. It follows that a communicator in a high-drive state is on the average less accurate in his communications than one in a low-drive state" (1968, p. 375).

CHANNEL ATTRIBUTES. Perhaps the most important attribute relating to channels (i.e., the media through which the message is sent—spoken words, written words, gestures, touch, etc.) insofar as the topic of this chapter is concerned, is that which relates to feedback information available to the communicator. To the extent that the communicator is deprived of one or more channels of feedback information, the chances for comprehension are decreased. In the biracial work situation, members of either racial group can be predisposed not to use all available channels when receiving communications from a member of the other race, thus depriving the communicator of useful feedback. An example would be where the recipient presents a completely impassive facial expression and also says nothing, while at the same time he is failing to understand some aspects of the communication. Evidence of certain behavioral patterns existing in ghetto life (Kochman, 1969) would seem to indicate that this kind of situation might frequently arise when whites are initiating communications to blacks. The apparent relatively low degrees of interpersonal trust and high degrees of suspicion that pervade the ghetto might lead to a habitual pattern of concealment of feelings on the part of some blacks when receiving communications from a white fellow worker. In this case, in the absence of correct feedback due to channels not being used, the white communicator would continue to give messages that would not be responsive to errors of decoding. One can imagine this type of inaccuracy being magnified when the communicator is a white supervisor and the recipient a black subordinate. (Such superior–subordinate situations will be discussed in more detail in a later section.)

COMMUNICATION ATTRIBUTES. The two chief aspects of the communication itself that, according to Mehrabian and Reed, affect its accuracy or comprehension are its redundancy and its objectivity. Redundancy can be further subdivided into two types: simultaneous and serial. The former refers to all aspects of the communication being consistent with each other. Thus, a sarcastic remark is less redundant than a nonsarcastic comment, since it conveys one type of information via the verbal channel and an opposite type through the intonational channel. If sarcasm is more prevalent in biracial work teams than in single-race teams, then this could be a factor leading to a reduction in communication accuracy by inserting additional confusion into the situation. (The other kind of redundancy, serial, refers to the organization of the parts of the communication.) Especially important in the integrated work setting is the "objectivity" of the communication, which is defined by Mehrabian and Reed as "the degree to which a communication has a well-defined meaning independent of the situation or context in which it is presented." Thus, if a given communication means something quite different in context A and in context B, it possesses low objectivity. This could be a crucial factor affecting the comprehension of communications across employees of different races in a work situation, if there are certain words, phrases, or expressions that have a quite distinctive meaning for one of the racial groups but not for the other. For instance, one needs to look no further than the word "rap" (defined by Kochman, 1969, as ". . . a fluent and a lively way of talking, always characterized by a high degree of personal style") for an illustration of a communicated expression likely to have low objectivity in some organizational circumstances.

REFERENT ATTRIBUTES.   The chief characteristics of referents that affect the accuracy of comprehension of communications, according to Mehrabian and Reed, are their ambiguity and their complexity. Citing the well-known Macy, Christie, and Luce (1953) "noisy marbles" study, they note the great difficulty introduced into communications when the object of a message cannot be easily encoded or decoded and is thus "ambiguous." It is probably a fairly safe prediction that if members of two different races start working together in situations where they have not had much previous experience with each other, there will be initially a number of referents that would fit the "ambiguous" label and hence be a cause of reduction in comprehension. If the referent is especially complex, comprehension can also be reduced. In certain work situations, the degree or type of technology could introduce some quite complex referents that would necessarily have to be discussed in the course of carrying out production operations. While such complexity would hinder communication whether or not a work group was racially mixed, it could be expected to put an additional strain on communication comprehension in a biracial situation where other factors hindering accuracy were already present. The faster such groups could come up with simplified definitions or descriptions of common referents, the more likely this source of potential inaccuracy could be reduced.

Acceptance and Agreement in Communication

Up to now in this section we have been talking about various factors or variables that could operate to interfere with comprehension in the communication process. Even if we assume, however, that communications have been received accurately, there is no guarantee that the two parties to them will be in agreement on issues and willing to accept the point of view of the other and even act on that viewpoint. It is to this question of acceptance that we now turn our attention.

Analysis of the factors involved in the acceptance of communications can again utilize the basic elements in the communication process: sender—message —receiver. It would appear, however, from a review of the research evidence that, for the purposes of understanding how acceptance might be achieved in communication episodes that take place in organizational settings, the primary emphasis must be centered on the *communicator* and how he is perceived by the recipient. This orientation will form the basis for the discussion that follows.

The available research literature establishes the concepts of *credibility* and *attractiveness* as the major conceptual variables involved in whether a receiver accepts or agrees with a communicator's message. (McGuire, 1969, utilizing Kelman's [1961] ideas, also includes the variable of power in his "tricomponental analysis" of source valence. However, since power is chiefly concerned with obtaining compliance to communication it will not be considered further here, because it falls outside of the main purview of this section; it will be dealt with in a later section where superior–subordinate communication is considered.) Of course, saying that credibility and attractiveness are the chief factors in influencing acceptance merely pushes the analysis back one step, because we must next ask: what variables affect the perception of a communicator as a credible source of information?

CREDIBILITY. When we use the term credibility, we are concerned with whether the receiver views the sender and his message as capable of being believed. To the extent that this state exists, message acceptance is enhanced. Two major factors have been identified as crucial in determining the perception of a communicator as credible—his expertise or competence, and his objectivity or trustworthiness (McGuire, 1969). The attitude-change evidence seems clear in supporting the notion that degree of perceived expertise of the communicator is positively correlated with belief in his credibility (e.g., Fromkin et al., 1970). This in turn is correlated with greater likelihood of message acceptance.

The question of communicator trustworthiness or objectivity hinges on the receiver's perception of the motives and intent of the message sender. Although it would seem obvious that communicators who are seen as more "objective"— that is, who have no vested interest in the content of the communication or any position advocated in it—would be more persuasive, the attitude-change literature leaves this conclusion somewhat in doubt (McGuire, 1969). There appear to be some particular situations, in fact, when partiality rather than impartiality actually enhances acceptance possibilities. However, since much of this research was carried out in laboratory rather than field situations, caution needs to be exercised in extrapolating to real-life work situations. In fact, although sufficient research evidence is not available to justify it, we would make the prediction that perceived trustworthiness of the communicator will have positive effects on the acceptance of messages in organizational environments. Most important, though, is the question of whether the communicator's expertise is more or less influential than his objectivity and trustworthiness in gaining acceptance. In this regard, McGuire views the available evidence as fairly clear-cut in its implications: "At present, the literature on source credibility can be summarized by saying that the perceived-competence aspect adds to persuasive communications more than the trustworthiness aspect does" (1969, p. 187).

ATTRACTIVENESS. Turning to attractiveness of the communicator as a factor in message acceptance, we find three variables identified by McGuire (1969) as critical: similarity between source and receiver, familiarity, and liking. As previously mentioned in an earlier section of the chapter where the "race-belief" controversy was discussed, similarity between communicator and receiver can be of two major types: that based on common membership in a group and that based on a commonality of attitudes. Clearly, the two do not necessarily always go together. Two members of a similar group can have different attitudes toward a number of referents, and two individuals having a host of common attitude similarities can be members of different groups (i.e., races, in the present context). Again, recalling our earlier discussion, attitudinal similarity appears to be the more important of the two types of similarity.

In their review, Simons et al. find that, generally speaking, sources perceived by receivers as more similar to themselves are also regarded as more attractive. The important point, however, is that while similarity may generate attraction to, or a feeling of commonality with, a source, it does not always produce agreement with or acceptance of the source's message. Put another way, it means that a communicator who generates strong feelings of attractiveness on the part of those with whom he works cannot be sure that he will also be a persuasive communicator to them.

A crucial element in the determination of whether attitude similarity will result in acceptance of a communicator's message is the degree of *relevancy* of the similarity in relation to the topic of the message. As Brock (1965), Berscheid (1966), and Byrne and Rhamey (1965) have shown, if the attitude similarities of the two communicating parties appear to be highly relevant (i.e., logically related) to the communicator's message, there will be a strong tendency toward increased acceptance (Simons et al., 1970). On the other hand, if the attitude similarities appear to the receivers *not* to be relevant, then the evidence indicates that there will be little impact of the communicator on gaining acceptance of his messages. Relevancy also appears to be critical in determining whether membership similarities will affect acceptance, according to Simons et al. They postulate that "irrelevant membership-group similarities have little or no effect on attitude change." Furthermore, they state that "evidence that non-member sources may be more persuasive than members on relevant issues is provided by a number of studies ..." (p. 10).

Familiarity has long been a highly researched variable with respect to its relationship to message acceptance and attitude change. Much of this research, especially as it relates to ethnic relations, was recently reviewed by Amir (1969) under the heading of the "contact hypothesis"—i.e., the hypothesis that increasing the contact between members of two different groups (e.g., races) improves their attitudes toward each other. Amir concludes that intergroup contact does change attitudes but that the direction of change "depends largely on conditions under which contact has taken place" (p. 338)—that is, on whether the conditions are "favorable" or "unfavorable." Favorable conditions would include situations in which the contact is pleasant, the status of the two members or groups are equal, the social climate is supportive, and so forth; unfavorable conditions would include highly competitive situations, those involving tension, and the like. Thus, it appears that under the right kinds of conditions receivers will react more favorably to messages from communicators with whom they have had some previous contact, though there is no certainty that this will always occur.

The variable of "liking," as it affects acceptance of communications, is somewhat difficult to untangle from similarity and familiarity, since it would seem that the latter two variables are often causal in determining liking. In any event, the evidence as reviewed by McGuire (1969) appears to support the conclusion that the more the communicator is liked by the receiver—for whatever reasons—the more likely he is to be persuasive.

Instrumentality of the Source's Communications

The overall thrust of the research material on credibility and attractiveness appears to support the kind of interpretation that is suggested by Simons et al. (1970): namely, it is the *instrumental* value of the communications coming from the source that is the determining factor in acceptance. That is, the message is more likely to be accepted and acted upon the more the receiver perceives that his acceptance will lead to positively valued outcomes. Thus, even though the receiver views the sender as different from himself, he will still tend to accept communications from the source if he feels that something will be gained by doing so. An obvious example would be a situation where a lower-middle-class patient is receiving advice from an upper-class physician. Even though the patient views the doctor as quite different from himself, and even holding different views on the nature of an illness, the patient is likely to accept the advice because by doing so he believes he will obtain a positive outcome (i.e., faster recovery). Of course, it should be stressed that in most situations similarities in membership groups and in attitudes will be seen as more instrumental than will dissimilarities; the point, however, is that this is not always so. A source perceived as dissimilar can still also be perceived as being able to send a communication that has instrumental value for the receiver.

We can continue to utilize the concept of instrumentality to translate the general conclusions of the preceding pages into an analysis specific to the context of an integrated work force. The critical element in this situation is an *opportunity* for the members of each of the races to find out or learn that there is reward value to be gained by accepting or agreeing with communications from the other race. There needs to be, in other words, a chance for receivers of one race to observe those things—such as expertness, good intentions, and attitude similarities—that can lead to the development of attraction to, and trust in, the communicator. Particularly crucial will be whether or not members of the two races are able to discover that they hold more or less common attitudes toward relevant aspects of the work environment, such as the nature and value of the tasks themselves, the quality of the boss, the fairness of the organization, and the like. We can speculate that in a great many work situations there will be a wide band of general agreement about relevant objects in the immediate environment, since everyone is likely to be affected similarly by them. (Even in autocratic boss, for example, can be expected to generate strong reactions that are irrespective of the racial differences of the subordinates. In such a case it should not take too long for these reactions to begin to be shared and for common group norms to develop.) If such shared attitudes are uncovered and brought to light it increases the likelihood that membership (i.e., racial) differences will recede more into the background as a factor affecting perceptions of communicator credibility and attractiveness. Individual differences should begin to outweigh racial differences in impacting communications.

ORGANIZATIONAL STRUCTURAL FACTORS IN COMMUNICATION

Up to the present point, we have been analyzing the communication process without regard to the organizational positions of the communicator and recipient—that is, without regard to the effect of the structure of the organization. Before explicitly considering organizational structural factors we will first digress somewhat to examine several key facets of the literature dealing with laboratory studies of communication networks. While such investigations do not deal with total organization contexts as such, they do serve to emphasize certain structural features of communication—particularly as they relate to the functioning of small groups. Following this brief consideration of the network research we will focus on the vertical dimension of organizational structure, where communication is between individuals occupying different hierarchical or status positions. In the latter part of this section we will look at the horizontal dimension where communicator and recipient are on more or less equivalent levels within the organization structure.

Laboratory Studies of Communication Network Structures

Communication network research has been concerned primarily with the effects on small group communication processes of two basic types of communication structures generally labeled as "centralized" networks and "decentralized" networks. Early research utilized several variations of each; however, the wheel has become most representative of the centralized networks, and the circle or comcon (complete communication) has become most representative of the decentralized networks. The wheel is characterized by a central person who may communicate with all other members, these members being on the spokes of the wheel and each able to communicate only with the central person or through him to other members; the circle is characterized by the lack of a structurally determined central position with each member able to communicate with the person to either side. The comcon, like the circle, has no structurally determined central position but unlike the circle, allows all members to communicate freely with all other members. Experiments with these basic types of networks (e.g., Bavelas, 1950; Bavelas and Barrett, 1951; Christie et al., 1952; Heise and Miller, 1951; Leavitt, 1951; and Shaw, 1954a), all detected differences in measures of group performance and individual satisfaction between centralized and decentralized networks. In addition, these experiments suggested that other variables (e.g., type of task) interacted with the communication pattern to affect group behavior.

In his review of the network literature, Shaw (1964) suggested that two general concepts can be used to account for most of the effects of networks on communication in groups. These are "independence" (Leavitt, 1951; Shaw, 1954b) and "saturation" (Gilchrist et al., 1954). Independence, as originally defined by Leavitt, refers to differences in "answer-getting potential" among positions in the network. That is, for example, in wheel networks the structure determines the identity of the leader or decision maker with the requirement that all information be funneled to him. This creates high independence for this position but low independence for the peripheral positions (since they have little or no "answer-getting potential"). In contrast, the circle network does not structurally determine a decision maker and thus does not automatically assign dependent or independent roles to the various members. Therefore, all members of the circle start with an intermediate degree of independence.

Saturation was a concept introduced to deal with the notion of optimal levels of communication activity as they relate to particular network positions. Where an optimal level is surpassed for a given position, saturation is said to exist. As Gilchrist et al. (1954) have noted, saturation may take two forms: "channel saturation," referring to the number of channels connected to an individual position, and "message saturation," referring to the volume of information fed into or exiting from a given position. The degree of saturation will also include information-manipulation requirements and other "task demands." Given the types of tasks usually dealt with in work-type situations, saturation would be expected to be higher in centralized positions (as in the center of a wheel) and lowest in peripheral positions.

Attempts to extrapolate from the basic notions and findings of the small-group network studies carried out in laboratory settings to groups performing work in real-life organizations would appear to be extremely hazardous. This is because so much of the psychological context that surrounds a person's work role in organizations is absent in the typical network experiment. Without going into the larger question of how well one can generalize from such lab studies to organizations (Weick, 1965), it seems apparent that most extrapolations would be in the nature of pure speculation. With this caveat in mind, we might anticipate the following kinds of situations arising:

In small-group work situations that approximate a wheel-type of structure, placing a member of one race in the central position and members of a different race in the peripheral positions could result in excessive saturation impact on the former type of position. If the peripheral members tended to be distrustful of the central member and were not convinced of his credibility as a communicator, they might well withhold vital information. This in turn would cause an above-optimum level of communication activity (in order to gain the needed information) on the part of the central person that would decrease the overall effectiveness of the group. Independence differences between the central and peripheral positions, in such a situation, might be reduced because the withholding of information by those on the periphery would reduce the "answer-getting potential" of everyone. Such potential communication difficulties might be alleviated by the organization's adoption of more decentralized network structures, particularly where there appears in advance to be a high level of prejudice or distrust. Decentralized networks tend to provide alternate passages for blocked communication links and thus could be utilized to reduce the hazards of overload or saturation on any given position. Also, there might be more likelihood of avoiding extremely low levels of independence which tend to lead to low satisfaction with communication.

The Vertical Dimension

Upward and downward communication in organizations is dominated by the fact that superiors have differential reward power in relation to subordinates. This difference in power, and therefore control, affects both the amount and the types of messages that are sent from one level to a receiver at a different level. Documentation of this has come from both controlled laboratory-type experiments (e.g., Kelley, 1951; Cohen, 1958; Haber and Iverson, 1965; and Watson, 1965) and from field studies (Maier et al., 1963; Read, 1962; and Slobin, Miller, and Porter, 1968).

The results of these studies, some carried out on small groups and others carried out in larger organizations, present a rather coherent picture of the process of communication across levels. Perhaps the most common finding concerns what happens in upward communication. There seems to be a strong tendency for the lower-status person—i.e., the subordinate—to structure his communications in such a way as to present himself in the most favorable light possible to his superior (the reward-controller). This tendency appears to be intensified when the lower-level sender has strong aspirations toward a higher-level position or at least has a good possibility of moving up in the organization. For example, in his widely cited laboratory study, Cohen (1958) found that if a person was in a situation that allowed future upward mobility he was much more likely than a nonmobile person to restrict the amount of negative information he sent upward. Thus,

> In the present experiment the Low Mobiles [as compared with Low Non-Mobiles] appear to be behaving in a way guaranteed to promote their chances of being rated favorably by the powerful highs and therefore being moved to the higher group. They are careful about criticism, stay more with the task and center their attention less on their own group (Cohen, 1958, p. 49).

Much the same sort of result was obtained by Read (1962) in his field study carried out in three organizations. He found that the accuracy of upward communications concerning work-related problems of the subordinates was inversely related to the upward mobility strivings of the communicator. Presumably, this means that upward-oriented subordinates either neglected to report negative information and/or distorted it in such a way that it preserved a favorable image but gave the boss a misleading picture of the actual situation. Of even greater potential significance for the question of upward communication in integrated organizations is Read's additional finding that the tendency toward inaccuracy was greatly exacerbated if the subordinate held a low degree of trust or confidence in the superior's motives and intentions toward the subordinate and his career. This kind of finding again emphasizes that perceived trust is probably a critical factor in the communication process.

One other finding that tends to hold up across experimental investigations (e.g., Hurwitz, Zander, and Hymovitch, 1960) is the tendency for low-status individuals, when given a free choice concerning whom to communicate with, will tend to send more communications to high-status receivers than to fellow low-status colleagues. If this kind of result is coupled with the one discussed above dealing with distortions in upward communication, it would appear to indicate that lower-level individuals do not avoid contacts with high-status and high-power individuals—in fact may seek out such contacts—but when they do have interactions they structure them in a manner designed to enhance positive evaluations of the sender by the receiver. It must be noted, however, that field studies carried out in actual work organizations have not found any overwhelming tendency for subordinates to communicate far more often with a boss than with their superiors or subordinates. In fact, there is evidence (Burns, 1954; Dubin and Spray, 1964; Lawler, Porter, and Tenenbaum, 1968) that executives initiate interactions more often with subordinates than with superiors. Of course, in most cases they will have several subordinates and only one superior, so it is difficult to draw a base line in this connection. The key point is, though, that both small-group and organizational studies indicate that lower-level individuals do not avoid contacts with superiors and indeed must have them if they are to have influence in how they will be rewarded and reacted to by those in power.

In the upward communication process the superior, naturally, does not play a passive role but reacts to the messages he is receiving constantly from below. In fact, in a small-group laboratory study, Alkire et al. (1968) found that high-status individuals receiving communications from low-status senders were more interventionist in terms of interrupting and clarifying communications sent upward than were low-status individuals receiving communications downward from high-status senders. Apparently, the relatively greater status and power of the individuals occupying the higher position permitted more intervention without consequences than was the case where the lower-status person was the receiver. The study illustrates the opportunities that higher-level individuals in organizations have to influence and affect the type of communications they receive from below.

Whether such opportunities will be used wisely by superiors will depend upon many situational circumstances as well as the boss's perception of the sender. Two recent studies, Lawler, Porter, and Tenenbaum (1968), and Tenenbaum (1970), both find a consistent tendency among managerial-type personnel for superiors to evaluate communications received from below less positively than do the subordinates who send the messages. In other words, there is a tendency in upward communication in work organizations for subordinates to regard their messages sent upward as more important than do their superiors. If this turns out to be a widespread type of finding, it has some interesting implications for such communications situations. It could imply that bosses, by their tendency toward placing lower value on upwardly sent messages, are in effect discouraging upward communication behavior on the part of their subordinates. This would be true to the extent that the superior's reaction is made known—whether intentionally or not—to the subordinate. The subordinate learns, so to speak, that "the boss doesn't really care about what I think is important." From an instrumental point of view, the finding that the superior places a lower evaluation on messages from subordinates than does the sender makes sense. The subordinate often is not highly influential in determining the boss's rewards. Hence, messages coming upward from the subordinate can be ignored more safely than can messages coming down from a boss.

Downward communication has generally not been the focus of as much research attention as has upward communication. We can hypothesize, however, that subordinates will have a tendency to search for meanings in messages coming from above that may not be put there or intended by the sender (the boss). We might, in fact, label this the "iceberg effect," in that the subordinate may direct his attention as much to what is hidden in a message as to that which is apparently open and obvious. The reason would be that it is important to him to get a complete message because of the relative influence the boss has on what happens to him in his job. Searching for meaning in communications from above is, in a word, instrumental to the subordinate's attainment of rewards and satisfaction.

While, as we said, the evidence concerning downward communication practices is skimpy, the previously referred to studies of reactions to communications episodes by Lawler, Porter, and Tenenbaum (1968) and Tenenbaum (1970) indicate that subordinate receivers attach at least as much importance to boss-sent messages as do the superiors themselves. Considering that there is a general tendency for the initiator to have a more positive feeling toward his communication than the receiver, the fact that subordinates attach as much importance to downward-sent messages as do the initiators indicates that they are paying close attention to what is communicated from above. In some instances, in fact, it could be hypothesized that the boss in sending a communication downward fails to appreciate how much interpretation the subordinate is attaching to his message. When this occurs, it can be the basis for inaccuracy and thus a factor contributing to superior–subordinate difficulties in working together.

If we put together all of the information we have concerning organizational communication in the vertical dimension and apply it to the analysis of integrated organizations, we must first consider the question of the consequences produced by members of different races occupying the positions of superior and subordinate. We have, in effect, four possible situations: (1) Communication upward from a black subordinate to a white superior, (2) Downward from a white superior to a black subordinate, (3) Upward from a white subordinate to a black superior, and (4) Downward from a black superior to a white subordinate. (Presumably, almost all studies cited in this section involved communication between white superiors and white subordinates.)

Given current employment patterns—resulting from past employment practices—we can probably assume that for the next few years, at least, the two most common vertical communication situations in organizations will involve white superiors and black subordinates. In such situations, an important modifying condition may well be the proportion of blacks among the subordinates reporting to a given superior. We can speculate that if it is one out of ten we will have a different communication situation from that for a proportion of, say, six out of ten. In the first instance, the lack of presence of other black peers would probably tend to increase the frequency of black subordinate–white superior communication, relatively speaking, because of the decreased (or zero) opportunities for black-to-black peer communication. Also, if the white superior is inclined to feel threatened (in terms of his ability to handle the situation) by the presence of black subordinates, he is presumably less likely to feel so in a situation with one such subordinate as compared with five or six. Feeling lower threat should be a factor helping to improve the accuracy of communication. Hence, we might be able to assume that the greater the proportion of blacks reporting to a white supervisor the less frequent and less accurate will be the communication between them, especially during the early phases of the group's existence. If this is so, it would imply that from a communication point of view, organizations should give particular attention to placing their best white supervisors (especially those high in self-confidence) in those situations where the proportion of minority members is high.

If we disregard the proportion of minority subordinates, for the moment, we can consider the general nature of upward black-to-white and downward white-to-black communication. The evidence noted in the literature concerning subordinate filtering and structuring of upward communications designed to be instrumental for the subordinate's attainment of rewards, would lead us to predict that this tendency would be greatly enhanced or reduced depending upon how much the black subordinate values the rewards available in the work situation. If he does not value these rewards (such as promotion into the managerial hierarchy) highly, then there may not be much filtering. For that matter, in such cases there may not be much communication at all, if the supervisor is seen as relatively unimportant in terms of the kinds of rewards the black values. "Why bother" might be the prevalent theme. If the available rewards are highly valued, considerable filtering might occur simply because the supervisor would be seen as even more in control of rewards than in the case of a white subordinate viewing a white supervisor. The white supervisor, who is used to supervising other whites, may well be unaware of the more extensive filtering going on and thus operate on a set of rather unrealistic assessments of the situation. Also, in line with the research evidence concerning the lowered importance supervisors attach to subordinate communications, the white supervisor may tend to place too little emphasis on what he is hearing from below—especially so if he views the black as clearly a low-status and low-power person in the situation. This would tend to increase the supervisor's ignorance of what is "really" going on below him in the organization.

In downward communication from the white supervisor to the black subordinate, much will depend again on the degree to which the receiver values the rewards to be gained in the work situation. If he (the subordinate) identifies strongly with the job and with the organization, he is likely to attend to such communications. To the extent that he is alienated from the situation or feels that there is little he can do to influence his fate in it, he will be likely to be unresponsive to the supervisor's communications. Of course, depending on the degree of social pressure from his peers, this latter tendency can be amplified even more in some situations.

Switching attention to the (up-to-now) not very common situation of a black supervisor with at least some white subordinates, we may anticipate increased upward filtering of communications as compared to a white–white or black–black situation. It is not too hard to imagine that in many such circumstances the white subordinate will assume that he is at least as qualified as the black for the supervisory position and hence may be quite competitive in his interactions with his black boss. If so, he might well withhold vital information in his upward communication. It appears then that white-to-black upward communication could well present more than normal difficulties for the receiver. But, in this kind of a situation the black supervisor may be more prone to spend effort on interpreting correctly than would a white supervisor receiving communications from black subordinates. This would tend to be so where the black supervisor has had to demonstrate more than the usual qualifications to reach the position and thus feels less certain about being able to stay in it or to move ahead (as compared with a white supervisor counterpart).

In downward communication from a black superior to a white subordinate, there may be a tendency toward overcompliance on the part of some whites. The study mentioned earlier by Katz and Benjamin (1960) is relevant here in that he found that authoritarian whites (college students) in an experimental task situation reacted in a compliant manner toward blacks when having to arrive at mutual group decisions. Though there were no experimenter-controlled status or power inequities (and, hence, the study is more directly pertinent to peer-peer interactions) and thus no superior–subordinate kinds of interactions, the results nevertheless suggest that some whites, when put into a circumstance involving a black supervisor, will attempt to respond in a compliant manner thereby introducing additional "noise" into the communication process. Of course, without knowing more about the distribution of authoritarianism in the employed population in given organizations, it will be difficult to make specific predictions as to how often this will occur. For those whites who are less authoritarian-oriented, reactions to communications from black supervisors may resemble the white-to-white situation: a search for meaning in messages from a source that has reward control power.

Influencing all four of the vertical-type communication situations just discussed—upward black-to-white, downward white-to-black, upward white-to-black, downward black-to-white—will be the factors we have mentioned in the earlier part of this chapter. Particularly, the extent to which the superior of one race and the subordinate of another race are able to discover that they hold some common beliefs should facilitate communication by increasing mutual acceptance and, therefore, trust. Of course, the very circumstance that the two parties in vertical communication occupy different levels in the organization tends to militate against the development of a completely shared frame of reference. The fact that power is *not* equalized makes it more than ordinarily difficult to uncover opportunities for the establishment of communicator credibility. Nevertheless, it is possible for this to develop, and there may be aspects of organization structure that will assist in this. As just one example, the size of the span of control might play an important role. Although the literature tends to show no general advantage for either a narrow or wide span (Porter and Lawler, 1965), in an integrated work situation one might hypothesize that a narrower span would provide increased opportunities for superior and subordinate to find out that they do hold at least some common beliefs. If the span is too wide, chances for this kind of discovery to occur might be much less prevalent. Clearly, here is an area where more relevant research is needed, not only on the effects of span of control but also on other aspects of the structure of organizations as it affects communication in integrated situations.

The Horizontal Dimension

A number of writers (e.g., Simpson, 1969; Landsberger, 1961; and Strauss, 1962) have commented on the fact that organizational theorists and investigators have concentrated their attention on vertical communication to the neglect of horizontal or lateral communication. Indeed, even though the imbalance was noted as long as ten years ago, the situation remains relatively unchanged today: we have considerably more research evidence available for analysis of the vertical dimension than we do for the horizontal one. Even so, there remains little doubt as to the frequency or importance of lateral-type communication in organizations, and thus it is necessary to consider this dimension in discussing communication in integrated organizations.

The horizontal dimension is made up of at least several major types of communication interactions: those occurring among peers within work groups, those occurring across major units within the organization, and those occurring between line and staff types of positions. Each of these types will be looked at in turn, in an attempt to discover implications for the integrated work situation.

Peer-Peer Communication in Work Groups

Commonsense observation tells us that this type of lateral communication is prevalent in almost all types of work situations. This is particularly so for informal—i.e., nonorganizationally specified—communication. In fact, in many work situations the opportunity to engage in interactions with one's peers is regarded as a major source of job satisfaction. Since we can assume there is a strong tendency for this kind of communication to occur within work situations, the major analytical question becomes one of determining which organizational factors affect the amount and kinds of such interactions.

Research addressed to this question has focused for the most part on the factor of work-group size. As might be expected, the empirical evidence indicates that deleterious effects occur when group size becomes too large. As Hare (1962) in his review of research findings put it, when there is an increase in group size "there is a more mechanical method of introducing information, a less sensitive exploration of the point of view of the other, and a more direct attempt to control others and reach a solution whether or not all group members indicate agreement." Similarly, several studies (e.g., Hare, 1952) have shown that group cohesiveness is weakened as group size increases. Furthermore, as Porter and Lawler (1965) have noted in their review dealing with job attitudes and behavior, "the literature on subunit size shows that when blue-collar workers are considered, small size subunits are characterized by higher job satisfaction, lower absence rates, lower turnover rates, and fewer labor disputes."

Clearly, it would seem from the above type of evidence that small size of work group (where size in terms of numbers of individuals is at least four or five) contributes to a facilitation of communication among peer group members. They come to work more often, and they are likely to feel more free to initiate communications with one another. For those situations, such as work teams composed of members of different races, where communication difficulties might be anticipated in advance, it would seem to be appropriate to take steps to hold the size of groups to as small a number as possible. Like any other measure the organization might take, this will not ensure real communication. It should, however, contribute to it in many work situations, and it should help prevent some unnecessary problems from developing.

Communication Between Members of Different Units

Studies of lateral communication across different units have focused largely on the question of interdepartmental rivalries and conflicts in relation to the work flow (e.g., Landsberger, 1961; Strauss, 1962; Dutton and Walton, 1965). The primary issue has been one of how the individual member of one department, who has loyalty to that department and whose immediate fate is bound in with its success or failure, is able to interact effectively with a member from another department who has similar loyalties and feelings toward his own work unit. Since, as noted, most of this literature dealing with such horizontal interactions has been concentrated on aspects of conflict rather than on communication per se, it tends to be peripheral to the present topic. However, again, we can proceed to some tenuous extrapolations: It would seem likely that where interdepartmental conflicts exist, having members of two different races be the primary communicators between departments would probably accentuate an already difficult situation. In those cases where this type of climate exists already, it would seem prudent for the sake of communication to fill the communication roles with members of like races. Of course, this may not be possible, especially if one unit is composed mostly of whites and the other mostly of blacks.

On the other hand, however—as Dutton and Walton (1965) illustrate in their account of interdepartmental conflict and cooperation within two different plants—if a conflict type of climate has not developed, then two departments with clearly distinctive and potentially conflicting roles in the work flow may work harmoniously together. For these kinds of situations, where a spirit of cooperation has been strongly established in the past, having members of different races on the communication boundaries between the units may actually facilitate integration. That is, in such a circumstance communication would be taking place in a positive atmosphere which could engender feelings of trust and credibility between two individuals who might not otherwise have opportunities to realize they shared some common belief systems. Thus, while lateral communication interactions across departments may hold perils for communication in biracial work forces, they may also present some otherwise overlooked opportunities. Here, as in other instances, the question of how good the communication is between members of different races cannot be separated from the question of how much of a general level of trust and cooperation has existed previously throughout the organization.

Communications Between Line and Staff

The third variety of horizontal communication is that between members of the line, or direct chain of command, and the members of staff or support units. Here again, as was the case with interactions across departments, much has been made of the kinds of conflict that can exist between line and staff (e.g., Dalton, 1950). Regardless, however, of the potential for such conflict, there seems to be one particular characteristic of line–staff communication that tends to be found rather consistently in different kinds of work situations: the greater communication activity and the greater knowledge of organization events on the part of staff employees compared with their counterparts in the line (Davis,

1953; Burns, 1954; Zajonc and Wolf, 1963). Presumably, this is due to the nature of the jobs undertaken by staff members which generally give them more opportunities for geographical mobility in their day-to-day activities in the organization. In any event, this regularly obtained finding provides an important suggestion to a company that wishes to increase communication between members of different races within its work force: namely, the organization should search for chances to have members of minority races serve in staff-like roles, because this will increase the likelihood that they will be integrated into the communication networks that exist within the enterprise. In other words, here is an opportunity for the organization to take a step that should decrease minority members' isolation and increase their inclusion within the total work force. Naturally, such moves would not lead to success in those cases where extensive and severe line–staff conflict exists in the organization, such that staff members are clearly regarded as intruders in the affairs of the line or are completely powerless. In these instances, however, there are probably other communication problems in the organization, anyway, that would mitigate against the success of any moves to improve communication between members of different races.

CONCLUSIONS AND IMPLICATIONS FOR PRACTICE

The bulk of this chapter has been devoted to an analysis of the process and structure of communication in integrated work situations. Since there is so little directly relevant research, much of the preceding analysis has involved extrapolations from the data of studies carried out in single-race situations. Thus, we have been forced to generate a high ratio of speculation to hard, empirical data. With this reservation in mind, we can proceed to try to summarize our major conclusions, and then follow this with several basic implications for practice.

Summmary of Conclusions

1. There is an extreme scarcity of directly relevant research concerned with interracial communication in *organizational* settings.

2. Racial membership differences may be less important than assumed attitude or belief differences in determining the quality of communication in biracial work situations.

3. Several sets of factors have been found that affect communication accuracy and appear to have direct relevance to the integrated work situation:

(a) Attributes of communicators and recipients brought to the work situation that will aid or hinder accuracy of communications. These include: (1) subcultural differences; (2) levels of cognitive development; and (3) strength of feelings about common objects (including the communicator and/or recipient) in the work environment.

(b) Failures of individuals to use available channels for providing feedback to the communicator (of a different race) hinder him in detecting errors in reception accuracy.

(c) Building redundancy into communication aids accuracy and should be especially important in biracial work situations.

4. Similarities between source and recipient must be perceived as relevant by the two communicating parties if there is to be a favorable impact on the acceptance of communication.

5. Even where obvious differences—rather than similarities—exist between communicator and recipient, the establishment of credibility can improve the quality of communication. Particularly helpful to the building of such credibility are conditions that increase the perception of the communicator as (1) having good intentions toward the recipient, and (2) being competent and possessing expert knowledge.

6. Messages from dissimilar sources will be accepted as long as the receiver believes acceptance will have instrumental value for him—that is, will help him obtain what he wants or needs.

7. Evidence from a variety of research situations documents the fact of highly filtered communications when messages are sent upward from low-rank individuals to higher-ranking superiors. This tendency appears to be accentuated where the lower-status individual has high mobility aspirations. In integrated work situations, where a subordinate of one race is communicating upward to a supervisor of another race, such filtering should occur to the extent that the subordinate values the kinds of rewards that the superior has available to administer in the work situation.

8. Persons in higher-level positions in organizations are able to have a strong influence over the type and quality of communication received from below, in that they can reinforce upward communications behavior or discourage it. This impact of the supervisor on upward communication should be particularly true in biracial work situations, where the subordinate of one race is likely to be extremely alert to the reactions of the supervisor of a different race.

9. In downward communication, it is hypothesized that subordinates will focus as much on what is covert in messages from above as on what is direct and overt. Again, this tendency may be accentuated in vertical communication between members of different races.

10. It is hypothesized that the proportion of minority members reporting to a given white supervisor will affect the quality and quantity of vertical communication within a work group.

11. In vertical communication situations involving a black supervisor and a white subordinate, some whites may react with overcompliance that adds "noise" to the situation.

12. Work-group size has been shown to be a key factor in affecting employees' attitudes, their participation in the work force, and the quality of their communication: the larger the group size, the more negative the effects. Thus, in integrated work situations, there appear to be advantages to keeping the size of work groups as small as possible.

13. Lateral communication situations involving interdepartmental interactions present problems but also opportunities for communication between members of different races, depending on the general climate of cooperation existing in the situation.

14. Staff roles, if they represent reasonably equal status vis-à-vis line positions, may provide special communication opportunities for minority employees.

Implications for Practice

1. Organizations should give attention to creating opportunities for individuals of different races to discover that they may share some degree of attitude similarity concerning aspects of the work situation. This should help to decrease the salience of membership (i.e., racial) differences in affecting employees' behavior in their day-to-day contacts on the job.

2. Organizations should take steps to help provide members of each race with pertinent information on any factors that would lead to the establishment of conditions of credibility in communication situations. In other words, to the extent that the organizations—i.e., its supervisors and managers—can help individuals to demonstrate their expertise, good intentions, etc., better communication should result.

3. Those in supervisory positions should be alert to excessive compliance on the part of any subordinates, but particularly those of a different race from themselves. This kind of subordinate behavior probably provides a clue to the supervisor that he is not obtaining adequate or accurate feedback to his communications.

4. Supervisors, and those in higher-level positions, will need to realize the powerful influence they have over the types and quality of communications they receive from subordinates of a different race. Supervisors' failure to be aware of their impact will likely result in highly filtered upward communications.

5. Recognizing the importance of perceived instrumentality as a factor contributing to individuals' motivation to communicate, organizations should make every effort to demonstrate to all of their members—both whites and minority employees—the reward value of effective communication. Organizations could, in fact, specifically incorporate the area of interracial communication behavior into their existing appraisal and reward systems in order to increase the likelihood of perceived instrumentality.

6. Organizations need to give attention to the size of work groups— keeping them as small as economically feasible—if they wish to promote opportunities for good communication within biracial work groups.

7. Placing minority group members in certain organizational positions—such as those staff roles that require geographical mobility of action throughout the organization—may facilitate communication between them and white employees. Likewise, however, placing minority group members in other roles —such as departmental representatives in situations that have traditionally had a high degree of conflict—may hinder their integration into the organization.

RESEARCH NEEDS

Given the great paucity of relevant research on aspects of the present topic, one is tempted to conclude that almost any kind of research in this area will make a contribution to our knowledge. Indeed, such is probably the case. The topic is "wide open," as it were, for soundly conducted research projects. For some years hence, at least, no one doing research in the field will need to worry about duplicating what someone else has investigated previously.

Below are listed briefly a sample of the more obvious possibilities for research projects in this area. The list is only a starter and by no means exhausts the possibilities for meaningful contributions to knowledge and to the goal of truly integrated organizations.

Research is needed in the following areas, among others, on:

1. Organizational structural configurations that may be able to facilitate communication. This kind of research is needed at both the level of the work group and of the total organization (or large unit within the organization).

2. The effects of different proportions of racial composition within work groups on: (a) vertical communication between subordinates and superiors, and (b) horizontal communication across peers within the groups.

3. The effects of different kinds of job designs as they impact interracial communication within work units. For example, do vertically enlarged jobs have as one of their important side benefits the better integration of the minority member into the organization? Does job rotation facilitate more frequent interracial communication and thus foster movement toward integration?

4. The effects of various types of training on the communication behavior of supervisors. Particularly important to measure in terms of results would be acts of communication omissions as well as commissions. Is T-group-type training the only, or the major, kind of training that will have any positive effects on improving the communication of supervisors who are in charge of biracial work units?

5. Comparative studies of two major types of vertical communication situations: white supervisors with black subordinates, and black supervisors with white subordinates. Are the problems faced in each situation similar, or are there distinctive types of problems in one situation that do not occur to the same extent in the other situation?

6. Longitudinal studies of work groups undergoing stages of integration of minority members into formerly all-white groups. What are the changing patterns of communication that occur across time in such situations? Are there factors in the situation that can be isolated as facilitating or inhibiting communication in such groups?

7. Characteristics of communicators in interracial groups with good communication (i.e., frequent and accurate) versus those in groups with poor communication. To what extent are demographic characteristics, experience, personality traits, and other such variables factors in the development of good communication in integrated organizations?

REFERENCES

Alkire, A. A., Collum, M. E., Kaswan, J., and Love, L. R. Information exchange and accuracy of verbal communication under social power conditions. *Journal of Personality and Social Psychology*, 1968, 9, 301–308.

Amir, Y. Contact hypothesis in ethnic relations. *Psychological Bulletin*, 1969, 71, 319–342.

Bavelas, A. Communication patterns in task-oriented groups. *Journal of the Acoustical Society of America*, 1950, 22, 725–730.

Bavelas, A., and Barrett, D. An experimental approach to organizational communication. *Personnel*, 1951, 27, 366–371.

Berscheid, E. Opinion change and communicator–communicatee similarity and dissimilarity. *Journal of Personality and Social Psychology*, 1966, 4, 670–680.

Brock, T. C. Communicator recipient similarity and decision change. *Journal of Personality and Social Psychology*, 1965, 1, 650–654.

Burns, T. The directions of activity and communication in a departmental executive group: A quantitative study in a British engineering factory with a self-recording technique. *Human Relations*, 1954, 7, 73–97.

Byrne, D., and Ervin, C. R. Attraction toward a Negro stranger as a function of prejudice, attitude similarity, and the stanger's evaluation of the subject. *Human Relations*, 1969, 22, 397–404.

Byrne, D., and McGraw, C. Interpersonal attraction toward Negroes. *Human Relations*, 1964, 17, 201–213.

Byrne, D., and Rhamey, R. Magnitude of positive and negative reinforcements as a determinant of attraction. *Journal of Personality and Social Psychology*, 1965, 2, 885–889.

Byrne, D., and Wong, T. J. Racial prejudice, interpersonal attraction, and assumed dissimilarity of attitudes. *Journal of Abnormal and Social Psychology*, 1962, 65, 246–253.

Cohen, A. R. Upward communication in experimentally created hierarchies. *Human Relations*, 1958, 11, 41–53.

Christie, L. S., Luce, R. D., and Macy, J., Jr. Communication and learning in task-oriented groups. Technical Report No. 231, 1952, M.I.T., Research Laboratory of Electronics.

Dalton, M. Conflict between staff and line officers. *American Sociological Review*, 1950, 15, 342–351.

Davis, K. A method of studying communication patterns in organizations. *Personnel Psychology*, 1953, 6, 301–312.

Dubin, R., and Spray, S. L. Executive behavior and interaction. *Industrial Relations,* 1964, *3,* 99–108.

Dutton, J. M., and Walton, R. E. Interdepartmental conflict and cooperation: Two contrasting studies. *Human Organization,* 1965, *25,* 207–220.

Fromkin, H. L., Klimoski, R. J., and Flanagan, M. F. Race and competence as determinants of acceptance of newcomers in success and failure work groups. Paper No. 279, Institute for Research in the Behavioral, Economic and Management Sciences, Purdue University, 1970.

Giffin, K. The contribution of studies of source credibility to a theory of interpersonal trust in the communication process. *Psychological Bulletin,* 1967, *68,* 104–120.

Gilchrist, J. C., Shaw, M. E., and Walker, L. C. Some effects of unequal distribution of information in a wheel group structure. *Journal of Abnormal and Social Psychology,* 1954, *49,* 554–556.

Haber, L., and Iverson, M. A. Status maintenance in communications from dyads with high and low interpersonal comparability. *Journal of Personality and Social Psychology,* 1965, *1,* 596–603.

Hare, A. P. A study of interaction and concensuses in different sized groups. *American Sociological Review,* 1952, *17,* 261–267.

Hare, A. P. *Handbook of small group research.* New York: Free Press, 1962.

Heise, G. A., and Miller, G. A. Problem-solving by small groups using various communication nets. *Journal of Abnormal and Social Psychology,* 1951, *46,* 327–335.

Hurwitz, J. I., Hymovitch, B., and Zander, A. F. Some effects of power on the relations among group members. In D. Cartwright and A. F. Zander (eds.), *Group dynamics.* Evanston, Ill.: Row, Peterson, 1960, pp. 800–809.

Katz, I., and Benjamin, L. Effects of white authoritarianism in biracial work groups. *Journal of Abnormal and Social Psychology,* 1960, *61,* 448–456.

Katz, I., and Cohen, M. The effects of training Negroes upon cooperative problem solving in biracial teams. *Journal of Abnormal and Social Psychology,* 1962, *64,* 319–325.

Katz, I., Epps, E. G., and Axelson, L. J. Effect upon Negro digit-symbol performance of anticipated comparison with whites and with other Negroes. *Journal of Abnormal and Social Psychology,* 1964, *69,* 77–83.

Katz, I., Goldston, J., and Benjamin, L. Behavior and productivity in biracial work groups. *Human Relations,* 1958, *11,* 123–141.

Katz, and Greenbaum C. Effects of anxiety, threat, and racial environment on task perfomance of Negro college students. *Journal of Abnormal and Social Psychology,* 1963, *66,* 562–567.

Kelley, H. H. Communication in experimentally created hierarchies. *Human Relations,* 1951, *4,* 39–56.

Kelman, H. C. Processes of opinion change. *Public Opinion Quarterly,* 1961, *25,* 57–78.

Kochman, T. "Rapping" in the black ghetto. *Trans-Action,* 1969, *6* (4), 26–34.

Landsberger, H. A. The horizontal dimension in bureaucracy. *Administrative Science Quarterly,* 1961, *6,* 299–332

Lawler, E. E., III, Porter, L. W., and Tenenbaum, A. Managers' attitudes toward interaction episodes. *Journal of Applied Psychology,* 1968, *52,* 432–439.

Leavitt, H. J. Some effects of certain communication patterns on group performance. *Journal of Abnormal and Social Psychology,* 1951, *46,* 38–50.

Lefcourt, H. M., and Ladwig, G. W. The effect of reference group upon Negroes task persistence in a biracial competitive game. *Journal of Personality and Social Psychology,* 1965, *1,* 668–671.

Macy, J., Jr., Christie, L. S., and Luce, R. D. Coding noise in a task-oriented group. *Journal of Abnormal and Social Psychology,* 1953, *48,* 401–409.

Maier, N. R. F., Hoffman, L. R., and Read, W. H. Superior–subordinate communication: The relative effectiveness of managers who held their subordinates' positions. *Personnel Psychology*, 1963, *16*, 1–11.

Mehrabian, A., and Reed, H. Some determinants of communication accuracy. *Psychological Bulletin*, 1968, *70*, 365–381.

McGuire, W. J. The nature of attitudes and attitude change. In G. Lindzey and E. Aronson (eds.), *Handbook of social psychology* (2nd ed.), Vol. III. Reading, Mass: Addison-Wesley, 1969, pp. 136–314.

Porter, L. W., and Lawler, E. E., III. Properties of organization structure in relation to job attitudes and job behavior. *Psychological Bulletin*, 1965, *64*, 23–51.

Read, W. H. Upward communication in industrial hierarchies. *Human Relations*, 1962, *15*, 3–16.

Rokeach, M. Beliefs versus race as determinants of social distance: Comment on Triandis' paper. *Journal of Abnormal and Social Psychology*. 1961, *62*, 187–188.

Rokeach, M., and Mezei, L. Race and shared belief as factors in social choice. *Science*, 1966, *151*, 167–172.

Rokeach, M., Smith, P., and Evans, R. I. Two kinds of prejudice or one? In M. Rokeach, *The open and closed mind*. New York: Basic Books, 1960.

Shaw, M. E. Some effects of unequal distribution of information upon group performance in various communication nets. *Journal of Abnormal and Social Psychology*, 1954, *49*, 547–553. (a)

Shaw, M. E. Group structure and the behavior of individuals in small groups. *Journal of Psychology*, 1954, *38*, 139–149. (b)

Shaw, M. E. Communication networks. In L. Berkowitz (ed.), *Advances in experimental social psychology*, Vol. I. New York: Academic Press, 1964, pp. 111–147.

Simons, H. W., Berkowitz, N. N., and Moyer, R. J. Similarity, credibility, and attitude change: A review and a theory. *Psychological Bulletin*, 1970, 73, 1–16.

Simpson, R. L. Vertical and horizontal communication in formal organizations. *Administrative Science Quarterly*, 1959, *4*, 188–196.

Slobin, D. I., Miller, S. H., and Porter, L. W. Forms of address and social relations in a business organization. *Journal of Personality and Social Psychology*, 1968, *8*, 289–293.

Stein, D. D., Hardyck, J. A., and Smith, M. B. Race and belief: An open and shut case. *Journal of Personality and Social Psychology*, 1965, *1*, 281–289.

Strauss, G. A. Tactics of lateral relationships: The purchasing agent. *Administrative Science Quarterly*, 1962, 7, 161–186.

Tenenbaum, A. Dyadic communications in industry. Unpublished doctoral dissertation, University of California, Berkeley, 1970.

Triandis, H. C. Cognitive similarity and communication in a dyad. *Human Relations*, 1960, *13*, 175–183. (a)

Triandis, H. C. Some determinants of interpersonal communication. *Human Relations*, 1960, *13*, 279–287. (b)

Triandis, H. C., and Davis, E. E. Race and belief as determinants of behavior intentions. *Journal of Personality and Social Psychology*, 1965, *2*, 715–725.

Triandis, H. C., Loh, W. D., and Levin, L. A. Race, status, quality of spoken English, and opinions about civil rights as determinants of interpersonal attitudes. *Journal of Personality and Social Psychology*, 1966, *3*, 468–472.

Watson, D. L. Effects of certain social power structures on communication in task-oriented groups. *Sociometry*, 1965, *28*, 322–336.

Weick, K. E. Laboratory experimentation with organizations. In J. G. March (ed.), *Handbook of organizations*. Chicago: Rand McNally ,1965, pp. 194–260.

Zajonc, R. B., and Wolfe, D. M. Cognitive consequences of a person's position in a formal organization. Technical Report No. 23, 1963, University of Michigan, Institute for Social Research, Research Center for Group Dynamics.

CHAPTER NINE

Leadership, Power, and Influence

Donald C. King and Bernard M. Bass

INTRODUCTION BY THE EDITORS

The concept of leadership is central to management and is crucial to the effective organization of people. King and Bass review the literature and reveal the absence of blacks in leadership positions in modern industry—an open indictment of the policies and discrimination of social institutions in this country. At the same time, there is a notable shift in concern on the part of blacks away from mere increments in the number of minority members who are hired toward greater demands for full representation in all levels of the organization hierarchy. King and Bass propose a hierarchy of black concerns regarding integration which proceeds in a step-wise fashion until each concern is satisfied; entry into the organization, access to skilled jobs within the organization, and access to power in managerial positions within the organization. They propose that the demand for management positions is in its infancy and warn against devoting an inordinate amount of attention to lower-level entry problems, while ignoring the need for recruiting and training minority members for managerial positions. They speculate that blacks will gain greater access to managerial positions: when a high-level decision to recruit blacks into key management is made in organizations in which the structure and values require strict compliance with top management decisions, e.g., the recent integration of blacks into the higher ranks of the military; when the decision for promotion is made on the basis of professional expertise and other objective criteria, such as seniority; and when the organization is concerned with social responsibility and social change.

247

Bass and King's review is addressed to variables in leadership theory and research which seem most likely to affect or be affected by the racial composition of supervisor–subordinate teams. It is noted that individual, situational, and cultural variables interact with leadership to affect the production and satisfaction of work groups.

Foremost among potential problems of leadership is the black subordinate's perception that his black supervisor has been coopted by the white power structure. The conflict of values and the man-in-the-middle problems which face black supervisors can become a formidable dilemma, unless the organization is willing to allow black supervisors to retain non-work-related values which are uniquely black (i.e., to be promoted and to continue to be black). Furthermore, visible upward influence is particularly critical for black supervisors in order for them to maintain their credibility and role potency. Gaps in the educational experiences of black supervisors should be filled through training by participative educational approaches, rather than directive or didactic activities.

Next, attention is given to problems of black supervision of white subordinates. The small number of black supervisors in most organizations is most likely to create a fishbowl atmosphere for the black supervisor. This can result in greater drive and anxiety about success, general rather than close supervision, and a reluctance on the part of the black supervisor to initiate interaction with his white subordinates. Other leadership problems arise with a white supervisor of black employees. Typically, white supervisors of minority group members tend toward exaggerated or inappropriate responses, greater censoring of responses, less spontaneity in supervisor–subordinate relationships, and less certainty about how rigidly to enforce company rules and procedures.

King and Bass raise other important issues concerning interracial leadership in organizations. For example, are current supervisory practices such as management by objectives and participatory theories transferable to supervisors of the disadvantaged employee? Although there is an absence of relevant data, there is some cross-cultural research which documents the need for cautious generalization of these standard practices. However, in agreement with some of the findings reported in other chapters in this volume, it seems reasonable to recommend that supervisors should intensify their efforts to increase the reliability in the performance of black subordinates by simple manipulation of rewards and by developing their perception that they are an integral part of the organization with some control over what happens to them. The organization may be attuned to tendencies of white supervisors to undervalue performance capabilities of subordinates and, therefore, believe more directivity with them is required. Some research suggests that these notions can be reduced through the design of small work groups which set their own performance standards and sanctions for violations of these standards.

King and Bass stress the need for assessment of leadership potential. Foremost among the relevant variables are interpersonal skills, i.e., consideration for others and motivating others through concern for their needs. It is also proposed that the black supervisor is effective to the extent to which he can adapt to change and be sensitive to changes in the work environments. They caution that effort toward greater power equalization will face stern tests of an organization's willingness to be flexible and adopt multiple-goal strategies. The organization will have to spend more time and give more support to supervisors of biracial work groups and provide opportunities for team-building activities with the leader and his group.

Finally, organizational policies concerning interracial selection and promotion must be clear and monitored and enforced consistently with adequate sanctions for violations. If the organization can be flexible and follow the recommendations in this chapter, while it will endure some short-run costs, it is likely that longer term benefits will be substantial.

The concept and the actuality of leadership occupies a key position in any consideration of integration in organizations. The absence of blacks in leadership positions is startling and is an open indictment of the policies and prejudices of social institutions in this country. Consider professional athletics, an area to which blacks have had relatively free access in recent years. Until the fall of 1969 Bill Russell was the sole example of a black manager of a major professional team in any sport. Add to this the paucity of black quarterbacks, the key leadership position in college football.

Turning to business and industry, a recent article reports that there are only about 150 blacks among the 100,000 CPAs in this country (Mitchell, 1969). Further, there is only one black in over 3,000 partners of fifty-two of the country's largest CPA firms (and he is a native of the West Indies). The largest division of one of our giant corporations in 1969 had seventeen black supervisors among the thousands of managerial employees in the organization. Most of its plants, by the way, are located in urban areas with large black populations. Finally, Dr. Martin Luther King, in an address before the American Psychological Association in September, 1967, stated ". . . there are no studies, to my knowledge, to explain the absence of Negro trade union leadership. Eighty-five percent of Negroes are working people. Some 2,000,000 are in trade unions but in 50 years we have produced only one national leader—A. Philip Randolph" (1968, p. 7).

While some areas of research in this book may be relatively "mature" and well researched, issues of race and leadership in organizations are just beginning to grow in importance. Indeed, one can rather easily document a shifting concern on the part of blacks away from a mere increase in the number of black employees on the payroll to a greater concern for full representation in the various levels of the organizational hierarchy.

A report in the *Wall Street Journal* (Dec. 23, 1969) of the experiences of Chase Manhattan Bank illustrates this shift. Chase Manhattan Bank has made intensive efforts to recruit blacks and Puerto Ricans for over seven years. These two groups now comprise about 30 percent of the bank's employees, up from 8 percent in 1963. The article states,

> It is generally agreed that Chase has done much better than other members of the New New York financial community . . . in opening both clerical jobs and other higher ranking positions to non-whites. And in business circles, few, if any, concerns are thought to have a keener sense of "corporate responsibility" than Chase.

But only thirteen of 1,365 officers at Chase are black or have Spanish surnames. Bitterness, primarily over the perceived lack of opportunity for advancement, led some of the nonwhite employees to file formal charges of racial bias against Chase in 1967. A bank official is quoted as conceding that the organization, "probably wasn't as aggressive as it might have been" in promotiong nonwhites.

The initial struggle of the black was for entry into the business and industrial organization. Then came the long push toward access to skilled jobs. Now we see the early stages of the battle for access to managerial positions.

We might propose a hierarchy of concerns about integration in organizations similar in its functioning to Maslow's (1954) postulation of a hierarchy of motives. The hierarchy can be diagrammed as follows:

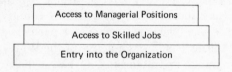

In the absence of any of these opportunities the lowest-level concern for mere access to work was prepotent and the source of greatest attention by minority group members. But as this first concern becomes more satisfied it ceases to be both a dominant issue and a source of satisfaction. Then the concern for better, more skilled jobs becomes central. The recent effort to break restrictive job-entry practices in the skilled construction trades illustrates the point. The thrust toward management is in its infancy but will increase particularly as skilled jobs become more available to blacks.

Behavioral scientists have found a "cultural lag" between the motives of many American workers and the motives attributed to them by management, as judged by managements' policies and behavior. Much organizational research has noted how the policies of most organizations are addressed to economic needs and that relatively little has been done to mobilize employees' needs for ego satisfaction and self-actualization (e.g., Likert, 1967).

We see a similar "cultural lag" in the area of integration of organizations. Management may well find itself devoting great attention to lower-level entry problems while ignoring the emergence of higher-order concerns about opportunities for positions of leadership and influence within the organization.

FACTORS AFFECTING THE MOVEMENT OF BLACKS INTO MANAGEMENT

Before turning to a more specific discussion of racially influenced issues in leadership, we will briefly discuss some of the situational and organizational factors which influence the extent to which blacks have access to managerial positions.

A first factor is the extent to which organizational structure and values require strict compliance with top-management decisions. If the decision is made to increase the number of blacks in leadership positions, can parts of the organization circumvent such directions if they wish to? In our society the foremost example of real integration at managerial levels within large organizations is in the military. This has occurred in the face of the fact that Lt. General Benjamin Davis, who recently retired, was spoken to only in the line of duty when he was the first black cadet at West Point. Political forces pushed integration early in the military and structural and normative variables permitted a more rapid opening-up of leadership positions to blacks than in other institutions.

A second factor which should influence the accessibility of leadership positions to blacks is the base on which such decisions are made. In organizations where they are based primarily on professional expertise and/or objective data such as seniority, positions should be more accessible. Where such decisions are based primarily on more subjective factors such as "leadership qualities," they should be less accessible.

A third factor involves the extent to which a particular organization wishes to appear to the rest of society to be responsive to social concerns and social change. Organizations to a greater or lesser degree are currently seeking blacks as "window dressing," which in turn has led to the many bitter charges of tokenism on the part of members of the black community.

A fourth factor is that blacks will be more likely to be nominated for positions of leadership in temporary, less valued social systems than in permanent highly valued systems. In fact, Fenelon (1966) suggests that in temporary social settings, such as laboratory experiments in psychology, blacks may be over selected as leaders. His study involved pairs of high- and low-dominant white and black coeds. They performed a clerical task in which one subject assumed the role of leader, the other of follower. Contrary to expectations, blacks assumed the leader role twice as often as white girls no matter what their relative dominance scores.

RACE AND LEADER–SUBORDINATE RELATIONS

In looking at the effect of race in leader–subordinate relations in organizations, no attempt will be made to survey the massive research literature in the field of leadership (such as found in Bass, 1960) for two reasons. First, as noted by Hollander and Julian, ". . . a disproportionate amount of our current knowledge about leadership in social psychology comes from experiments which are methodologically sophisticated but bear only a pale resemblance to the leadership that engages people in persisting relationships" (1969, pp. 394–395). And second, much of the research about black–black and black–white interaction prior to the mid-1960s may have little relevance to understanding the young college black, following the black revolution in the United States.

Our approach will be to address ourselves to those variables within the area of leadership research and theory which would appear to be particularly sensitive to or affected by the racial composition of supervisory–subordinate teams. The focus will be on those variables which can be influenced by the way in which groups are composed and structured or which might present reasonable targets for change agents in attempts to improve the functioning of groups.

Implicit in our discussion is the view that individual, situational, and cultural differences all influence the productivity and satisfaction of work groups. A classical illustration of the interaction of individual and situational factors is the study by Vroom and Mann (1960) in which leader authoritarianism was found to be negatively related to work-group effectiveness in one part of an organization but positively related to effectiveness in another part of the same organization where work-group size was larger and opportunities for leader-subordinate interaction were quite limited. Fiedler (1967) has proposed a model in which he attempts to specify the relationship between measures of the leader and measures of group performance. The key variable in his model is situational favorability which, in turn, is determined by assessing these factors: task structure, position power (of the leader), and leader-member relations. Bass (1968) points out that the effectiveness of democratic or authoritarian leadership depends upon cultural differences. Democratic supervisors are more favored in such countries as the United States, the United Kingdom, Holland, and the Latin world than in Greece, for example.

Marrow (1964), in a similar vein, reports that the manager of a new Harwood Manufacturing plant in Puerto Rico actively began to encourage employee participation in problem-solving meetings. Soon turnover increased sharply. An investigation revealed that the workers had decided that if management was so ignorant of the answers to its problems that it had to consult employees, the company was badly managed and would not survive.

We will next consider the following racial combinations of supervisors and subordinates in turn:

black superior — predominantly black subordinates
black superior — predominantly white subordinates
white superior — predominantly black subordinates

In each case we will discuss individual, situational, and/or cultural variables which would appear to be salient in affecting the particular superior–subordinate relations.

Black Supervisor—Predominantly Black Subordinates

Status differences and problems among blacks, as among members of any group, are a fact of life. Martin Luther King stated:

> Every riot has carried strong overtones of hostility of lower class Negroes toward the affluent Negro and vice versa. No contemporary study of scientific depth has totally studied this problem. Social science should be able to suggest mechanisms to create a wholesome black unity and a sense of peoplehood while the process of integration proceeds (1968, p. 7).

A central problem is one of trust. How can blacks in leadership positions develop trust on the part of their black subordinates while, at the same time, they have "bought into" the establishment by striving for and accepting a position of leadership? The concern about being coopted by the power structure is a prevalent and perplexing one for the black leader.

Delbecq and Kaplan (1968) studied the managerial effectiveness of local leaders in neighborhood opportunity centers in an urban ghetto. Members of the communities served by the centers saw the directors as conservative, unwilling to permit community involvement and influence in decision making, and ineffective in negotiations and discussions with leaders in the wider community. Subordinates in the centers were predominantly social activists desiring immediate change and action. They viewed social protest in the form of marches and rallies as a prime vehicle to promote change. The directors in turn tended to see vigorous subordinate disagreement as a threat to their own self-esteem and to their leadership position. They knew that the downtown office (higher management) took a dim view of demonstrations and the directors tended to regard demonstrations as "unprofessional." While the perceptions of the directors by community members and subordinates become more understandable in the light of such differences in role demands and values, the stress engendered by such conflicting role demands is intense and pervasive.

We feel then that "man-in-the-middle" problems, which all supervisors face, are particularly severe for black leaders who supervise groups consisting of predominantly black members. Stemming from this we predict that organizations, which demand and stress "company loyalty" among supervisors, create serious problems for black supervisors. For example, the majority of blacks in this country currently support many of the goals of the Black Panthers, though they may not support their methods. Companies which either overtly or subtly (a) take a strong law-and-order and respect-for-property stand, and (b) expect their manager to accept and promulgate such a position, could alienate black managers from their black subordinates.

Resolution of conflicting role demands and identity problems through identification with management may be less viable for a black than for a white supervisor. When a white worker is promoted to foreman, he often "acts out" his joining management by leaving his worker identification behind. He often moves his family to a new neighborhood. The new black foreman may experience greater difficulty disassociating himself from worker associates and may find it impossible to move his family at all. Thus resolution of the man-in-the-middle dilemma may be more difficult for him.

A second prediction is that upward influence is a more critical variable for black supervisors. Pelz (1952) documented the importance of perceived upward influence as a factor in effective leadership. Couple with this the long-standing feeling of impotence and powerlessness of large segments of the black subculture (Baron, 1968; Sloan, 1968). As a result of a study of black citizens in Chicago, Baron states: "Negroes remain second-class citizens partly because of the discrimination of individual Whites but mainly because of the way Whites control the major social institutions of our society" (p. 27). The interaction of these two variables should make it particularly important for black supervisors to have upward influence in their organizations and for this influence to be visible to their subordinates. An experience of a black plant manager in a new Westinghouse plant in the Pittsburgh ghetto which was related to one of the authors illustrates this point. Shortly after company personnel occupied the plant two militant community leaders entered the plant and asked to see the man in charge. They were referred to the plant manager but said, no, they wanted to see the *man in charge*. They found it hard to believe that the black to whom they were referred could have any real authority.

A third more speculative and tentative prediction is that verbal skills of black leaders will correlate more highly with subordinate regard than will verbal skills of white leaders. "Rapping skills have been well documented as a source of prestige and influence within the black subculture" (Kochman, 1969). Extending this finding to organizations, one would expect such skills to have a higher correlation with success in a leadership position when the segment of the organization in question has predominantly black members.

A fourth prediction is that, in firms with predominantly black managers and workers, directive, didactic management-education activities designed to improve managerial performance will meet with little success. Black managers will be more prone to resist being "lectured at" by white consultants or educators about how to handle black subordinates. Even more than for white managers of whites, participative educational approaches will be required.

A fifth prediction is that compared with white managers, there will be unexpected gaps in the educational experiences of black managers that may have to be filled through deliberate training or practice. Thus, a newly formed black company with an all-black management team arranged the first airplane trip for its newly appointed managers, none of whom had ever flown before.

Black Supervisor—Predominantly White Subordinates

Our earlier discussion of access of blacks to managerial positions suggested that such advancement is most likely to occur in organizations in which promotion decisions are (a) made on "rational," objective bases, and (b) based upon technical or professional expertise. This suggests few, if any, special problems for the black leader in supervising technical or professional work groups.

In other groups we would predict that, when compared with white supervisors, black supervisors would (a) be more likely to exercise general rather than close supervision, and (b) would be more likely to permit or encourage subordinate initiation of interaction with them rather than initiate such interaction themselves. These predictions are based upon two assumptions. First, close supervision and initiation of interaction are behaviors which spotlight the leadership position. Second, we assume that most blacks supervising whites will attempt to minimize any feelings of status incongruity on the part of white subordinates by making their supervisory status less conspicuous.

The small number of black leaders in organizations—particularly blacks who supervise whites—makes for a fishbowl atmosphere for people in such positions. (Mayors Hatcher of Gary and Stokes of Cleveland are much more widely known than the mayors of Fort Wayne and Cincinnati.) Predicted consequences of such a fishbowl environment are (a) a greater drive and greater anxiety about succeeding—about making it: the black plant manager from Westinghouse previously mentioned states that he and his plant *must* succeed and that any other outcome is intolerable; (b) greater sensitivity to negative data regarding the activities supervised and possible overreaction to such data; (c) as a corollary of (b), more of an external orientation—greater need for external confirmation of the value of the group's and the leader's performance.

White Supervisor—Predominantly Black Subordinates

A major change has taken place in most parts of this country in the attitude of whites toward black subordinates. Historically whites tended to treat blacks as nonpersons whose interests, problems, and sensibilities were of little import or concern. A contemporary carryover of the feeling was reported to the first author by a manager of one of our large corporations. During a recent regional meeting of the organization in South Carolina, he experienced acute embarrassment when one of his fellow managers told a crude "nigger" story in the presence of two young black waiters. He was told later that they "didn't mind" by a local manager of the firm. While examples of this kind are still far too numerous, concern and uncertainty are more typical contemporary attitudes of whites regarding black–white relations.

The current confusion on the part of many whites in this country over when to refer to "them" as Negroes, blacks, or Afro-Americans is a trivial and often funny example of our uneasiness in race relations. Whites supervising blacks often reflect, if not "for the record," in private conversations, a feeling of walking on eggshells. This feeling may well be reflected in (a) greater censoring of responses and reactions by white supervisors when most of their subordinates are black, (b) less spontaneity in supervisory–subordinate relations, and (c) less certainty on the part of white supervisors as to how rigidly to enforce company rules on procedures.

Reciprocally black subordinates may be less willing to discuss personal problems with a white as opposed to a black supervisor. This statement is consistent with Sattler's (1970) research review, which indicates that black clients prefer black counselors.

A second problem area centers on white racism and/or lack of knowledge about and empathy with black values and sensibilities on the part of white leaders. When a complex social system is not functioning well, it is always difficult to determine the factors contributing to the problem and how such factors interact. Thus when organizations such as inner-city schools fail to meet the needs of students, parents, teachers, and the wider community, a natural place to "fix the blame" is with school leadership, particularly if the leaders are white. Such a view may be realistic, or it may be misdirected. The real difficulty comes in validating or invalidating such accusations. The net result is to make the diagnosis of organizational problems and the development of action programs for change still more difficult than they usually are.

ORGANIZATIONAL ISSUES OF CONSEQUENCE

We will now turn to other issues involving race and leadership in organizations, *viz.*, supervising blacks in traditionally white-dominated organizations, leader selection, differences in leadership style in integrated organizations, leadership succession, and the impact of integration on personnel practices and power distribution in organizations. We will close with some specific recommendations regarding how racial changes in the composition of management of an organization can be handled most constructively.

Supervising Blacks in Traditionally White-Dominated Organizations

The type of supervision we receive is related to job success, motivation, and morale, independent of whether or not we have suffered ethnic and or economic discrimination. But we lack knowledge about whether currently accepted, effective supervisory practices, emphasizing participation, management-by-objectives, and other techniques appropriate to the culture of the middle-class white, are completely transferable and applicable to the supervision of the disadvantaged employee, particularly those from black and other minority groups.

It may be that what is known about effective supervision generally is completely applicable to supervising the disadvantaged. However, cross-cultural studies suggest otherwise. For instance, as previously mentioned, the usual emphasis on participative practices has been found less satisfactory in some cultures (Bass, 1968). Recent events suggest that the disadvantaged, many representing a third generation of welfare clients, many from minority groups, form distinct subcultures. It follows that special practices may be required, such as early and continued success experiences, closer supervision,[1] extra attention to building esteem, different principles for reward, and sensitivity to cultural differences by supervisors.

But there is almost a complete absence of research information. We can only pose questions and speculate about answers.

If we look at the pre-black-revolution data, one line of discourse suggests that the tough no-nonsense approach was most effective for maximizing productivity. For example, this was seen in a Detroit bumper grinding and polishing shop. Workers were marginal, required little skill, and turned over rapidly (Goode and Fowler, 1949). Similar results appear in underdeveloped countries with large labor surpluses (Bass, 1968). Currently, the situation is quite different. The formerly disadvantaged employee has been actively recruited. There is much pressure from outside agencies and upper management to see that he is retained in a productive capacity and is personally satisfied with his role. The disadvantaged employee has greater expectations than his marginal, older brother of 1949. Other workers may be disturbed by the special treatment given the disadvantaged. The white or black supervisor is thus again caught as a man in the middle, with additional new pressures on himself coming from above and below, for he still "must get out the work." Ultimately, he still will be judged on this. He must juggle these many interests with tact and skill.

The research literature does provide some descriptions of the attitudes and feelings of black disadvantaged citizens as a subset in our population. These data make it possible to speculate about what might be more efficacious in supervising them in order to increase such outcomes as the reliability of their performance on the job.

Common attributes discriminating blacks have included: pessimism about achieving aspirations (Bowerman and Campbell, 1965); negative self-concepts (Ausubel, 1958); less potent determiners of own fate (Battle and Rotter, 1963); more anxious and less effective when competing (Katz and Benjamin, 1960).

The work attitudes of black employees may be quite different from those held by middle-class white management. Centers and Bugental (1966), for

---

[1] Close supervision of one small sample of migrant cherry pickers was found far more productive than distant supervision of a not-too-comparable second sample (Friedland, W. H., 1969).

example, found that the extent to which intrinsic and extrinsic job components are valued is a function of occupational level. At higher levels the intrinsic components, such as self-expression, interest, and the value of the work, were more highly valued, while such extrinsic components as pay and security were the more important factors at the lower levels—the location of most disadvantaged employees.

Beyond the issue of attitudes toward work, more globally, the black disadvantaged tend toward a unique degree of alienation. Alienation from middle-class values has its roots in the ghetto psychology. As a result of the constant rejections by the larger society, children grow up doubting their own worth. While traditional middle-class values stress hard work, getting ahead, etc., the values of the ghetto residents emphasize beating the system (Clark, 1965).

An individual is sensitive to his environment only when he thinks that he can affect it. He will respond to environmental cues only when he feels that it will benefit him to do so (Coleman, 1964). If the findings of feelings of powerlessness among ghetto residents are accurate, then perhaps efforts of a supervisor to increase the reliability of performance of black subordinates by reasoning or simple manipulation of rewards and punishments is ineffective because the alienated workers feel that whatever they do is irrelevant and that they will not be promoted or get a rise, even if they do report to work regularly and turn out excellent production.

We hypothesize that to promote more reliable performance among alienated workers, a supervisor needs to make them feel an integral part of the operation and help them to realize that they do have some control over what happens to them.

An apparently successful effort among these lines has been reported by MacDonald (1967). In the Job Corps Centers it was found that verbal chastisement and other punishments, as well as positive rewards, were of little value in shaping behavior. However, when groups were formed, and these groups set goals and applied sanctions for rule infractions, these infractions dropped 60 percent in two weeks. This suggests that if supervisors organized their employees into groups which set performance standards for members and applied sanctions for violations of these standards, reliability and conscientiousness could be greatly increased.

Elsewhere, Bass has detailed the relationships among a supervisor's directivity, his own personal attributes, those of his subordinates, the external environment of the organization, the organizational climate, and the nature of the work to be done (Bass and Barrett, 1971). Extrapolating from this exhaustive analysis we propose the following:

Where subordinates are black, supervisors are more likely to undervalue their subordinate's capabilities and, therefore, will tend to be more directive with them. As a consequence of racist attitudes—conscious or unconscious— white supervisors of blacks will also believe such directivity to be more legitimate in comparison with participation. They will also tend to be more directive consistent with an expectancy of high turnover among their black subordinates, which in turn will contribute to such turnover. White supervisors of blacks will more often want to be respected by their black subordinates rather than liked by them and, again, will choose to be more directive with them. In addition, white supervisors will be more directive with black subordinates because they, the supervisors, are more concerned about being valued by their most probably white boss than by their black subordinates. Such directivity will also be fostered because it will be seen as less risky and more likely to enhance quantity of output. On the contrary, black supervisors will be more concerned about how their black subordinates feel about them and will tend toward less directivity. Such differences in directivity should, in turn, influence productivity and job satisfaction. The direction and magnitude of this influence will be moderated by such variables as the extent to which work tasks are well defined and structured, group size, and organizational norms about how directive a supervisor should be.

Actual racial characteristics of subordinates will influence how their supervisor, black or white, behaves toward them. We guess that a mixed black-and-white group of subordinates will tend to be low in cohesion and as a consequence will foster more directive behavior by their supervisor. All things equal, where all workers are of one race, cohesion is likely to be higher and a participative style more common among supervisors. The lower status accorded blacks will generally foster more directive approaches among their white supervisors. We guess that black subordinates compared with whites will be more prone to avoid risk, uncertainty, and involvement, again promoting more directive behavior by their supervisors, black or white.

Much of what we have said so far will be conditioned by the external environments in which the organization operates. Political pressures may be exerted in the black community to increase opportunities for participation in decision processes, even though supervisors would prefer to be directive. Relations between supervisors and black subordinates might more resemble negotiations, where each party collectively acts according to how much it perceives itself to have more or less power than the other party. Collectively, all supervisors—black or white—may push for directivity. Collectively, all black subordinates will push for participation. Resolution may be through bargaining, with outside black politicians, for example, playing a role in organizing black power.

Assessment of Leadership Potential

Repeatedly, success as a supervisor has been forecast by a battery of assessments which included a test of intelligence and related aptitudes. Supervisors are likely to be in the upper portion of the population in intelligence. They must have the learning ability to keep up with new technological and economic developments. They also have to be able to solve problems effectively, even if much of their assignment is routine and problems mainly concern which rules apply in a given case. Particularly among higher-level supervisors, planning skills, analytical abilities, and judgment are predictive of success (Randle, 1956). If supervisors are to lead employees, they need technical competence and some understanding of the tasks of their group, as well as human relations skills to deal with their people and administrative skills to deal with their organization. Will the fact that those led are black make any difference in these aptitude requirements?

Some information is already available on this issue. Abegglen (1958) found that interpersonal skills were important to supervisory effectiveness, particularly in organizations that are widely dispersed. Carp, Vitola, and McLanathan (1963) uncovered strong relationships between human relations skills and volume of productivity in a routine work situation. A supervisor's lack of consideration was strongly associated with employee withdrawal from the job in the form of absence, lateness, and quitting (Fleishman and Harris, 1962).

Some way of assessing interpersonal competence adds to the accuracy of the forecast of success in management. For instance, Arbous (1953) accurately predicted for 529 South African administrative trainees the trainees' salary increases per unit length of service and the job grade they eventually attained, by means of intelligence tests combined with a test which required the candidate to interview a female applicant and to contribute to a group discussion. While most studies to identify potential managers have found that intellectual traits are as important as interpersonal competence, studies in some companies have shown that intellectual ability is more likely to forecast successful performance in the first years of employment, while interpersonal factors become more significant in later years (Ferguson, 1964).

Interpersonal competence does not necessarily imply the need for close relations with others. On the contrary, the typical supervisor is likely to avoid what those concerned only with interpersonal interaction are seeking—namely, gratification from close relations with other persons. What interpersonal competence does imply is consideration for others and motivating others through concern for their needs. Particularly difficult will be identification of the needs of black subordinates by their white supervisors. Interpersonal competence of the type required for leadership potential seems to be assessed consistently with most accuracy by peer ratings and on occasion by information tests about supervisory practices.

OTHER APPROACHES. Specially keyed Biographical Information Blanks (BIB) have been able to forecast success as a supervisor. Such results depend on an extensive biographical survey which asks questions about home, family, education, vocational planning, finances, leisure time, health, and social and community relations.

Self-esteem, self-rated sense of confidence, and self-perceived competence have also proved predictive of aspects of supervisory behavior. For example, Bowers (1963) reported that the self-esteem of a foreman correlated highly with the extent to which he was supported by his boss and how well he perceived his own subordinates' attitudes toward him. At the same time, the foreman with high self-esteem was less likely to use group approaches to supervision.

As said earlier, the many studies suggesting lack of self-esteem among blacks compared with whites suggest, then, that black supervisors will be more group-oriented and faced with greater barriers to success as a consequence of the lack of esteem they are accorded by themselves or others. Needed are BIB analyses for identifying factors contributing to the success of supervisors with black subordinates. Comrey, High, and Wilson (1955) found that those aircraft production supervisors who felt confidence in their company and their subordinates and who felt they had adequate authority and responsibility were more likely to operate more efficient departments. Again, among 577 Standard Oil of New Jersey managers, a self-appraisal of performance contributed to the prediction of their success.

The evidence is mixed on the extent to which empathy tests can forecast success as a supervisor, although theoretically we would expect that supervisors would be more effective who were empathic as revealed by tests, who could accurately make judgments about the needs and likely actions of others, and who could understand what others wanted. We would guess that empathy will be less across the races, further increasing the supervisory difficulties of blacks supervising whites or vice versa.

Identifying supervisors with potential for promotion is particularly fraught with subtle errors, because the job and personal requirements are likely to vary from one position to another and from one organization to another. In a highly authoritarian firm, interpersonal competence may be quite different from that in a more democratically operated business. A dilemma is posed. One can choose to select new supervisors to fit into the old organization—but suppose the old organization leaves much to be desired? The criteria of success as a supervisor may shift markedly as an organization begins the integration of its workers and management. Then a different approach may be suggested in which supervisors are selected who do not conform to what has been seen as the successful executive in the old organization (Bass and Barrett, 1971).

Building on Fiedler's (1967) ideas, we hypothesize that interpersonal rather than intellectual competence is more effective when the situation is neither extremely "favorable" [2] nor unfavorable to the superior. If we can determine how the black worker affects the favorableness of the situation, then we could forecast, using Fiedler's theory, how much "human" or task concern is optimal.

Differences in Management Style Between Black and White Leaders

There are likely to be systematic differences in the leadership style of the typical black and the average white supervisor which are independent of the

[2] A highly "favorable" situation is one in which leader–member relations are good, i.e., the leader is esteemed by his subordinates. In addition, the task is highly structured. A highly unfavorable situation is one in which members do not esteem the leader, and the task is unstructured. Fiedler has found repeatedly that the considerate leadership emphasizing interpersonal relations is most effective when the situation is moderately unfavorable. With extreme favorability or unfavorability, the controlling, active, task-directed leader is more effective.

nature of the group supervised. We suggest, for instance, that to survive in our society and eventually occupy a leadership position, blacks generally have needed greater flexibility than most whites. Among black leaders yesterday's radical may well be today's moderate and tomorrow's Uncle Tom. Consequences stemming from such flexibility may be posited to have both functional and dysfunctional value for the successful performance of leadership roles in organizations.

Functionally the typical black supervisor might exhibit greater adaptability to change and more sensitivity to the immediate dimensions of the work environment. That is to say, he might be more aware of and responsive to many of the situational moderators of effective work group performance.

Dysfunctionally, learned and previously reinforced desires to avoid becoming locked into positions may be perceived by subordinates as lack of predictability or fuzziness in establishing goals and in structuring activities. King and Clingenpeel (1968) found that supervisory effectiveness was positively correlated with agreement among supervisors themselves, their superiors, and their subordinates regarding the supervisor's job attitudes and behavior. Selznick (1957) has stated that the leader's most important function is, "to define the ends of group existence, to design an enterprise distinctively adapted to these ends, and to see that the design becomes a living reality" (p. 37). Early experience, particularly among older black leaders, may result in a degree of "trained incapacity" to provide the amount of initiation of structure and clarity of their own position which subordinates need to (a) feel comfortable with their supervisor, and (b) more importantly, to work together with a common purpose.

Leadership Succession

The increased social integration of leadership positions in organizations will, of course, involve the process of leadership succession. Blacks will assume positions formerly held by whites and vice versa. Ziller (1965) states that, in organizations in which responsibility for group action is shared by the members, the attitudes and productivity of the group tend to be perpetuated after a change in formal leadership.

On the other hand, in organizations in which power is centralized, severe changes often occur after leadership succession. A change in leadership appears to be more traumatic in more hierarchically controlled, authoritarian organizations. If we assume that a difference in the race of the new and the old leader makes the change more dramatic and visible, we would predict more extensive adjustment problems in organizations where power is centralized. We might also speculate that the perceptions of how and why a black was appointed to a position formerly held by a white might be radically different among subordinates.

A common belief among blacks is that a black must not only be as competent, but more competent than a white to be selected for a responsible position. This view is shared by some whites. (In England, black physicians report that many white patients seek them out because the patients feel they must be extra bright to obtain the M.D.) Currently other workers may well feel that blacks are being given special considerations for supervisory jobs, just as many white workers feel blacks are currently being given undue consideration for skilled jobs. Such differences in the expected or perceived competence of new supervisors is always present, but it may be greater when leadership succession crosses racial lines. This, in turn, would make it more difficult for the new supervisor to establish an influence base with his subordinates.

We predict that managements composed of a mix of blacks and whites will have more progressive personnel policies than all-black or all-white managements. This is predicted on Ward's (1965) survey, which showed that where top management of a firm were mixed Catholic, Protestant, and Jew, the firm was more progressive than if all were from a single faith.

Various attributes of an organization's climate outside the work group will favor official endorsement of participative, democratic, supervisory behavior toward racially mixed or black subordinates. This will be more true, for instance, where top management is trying to convey an image of liberalism and progressivism to the public in its institutional advertising. As blacks appear in company advertising in roles which used to be reserved to whites, expectations of both blacks and whites within the firm build toward black participation at all levels. Participation at all levels by blacks will be favored where objectives are clear and easy to measure, so that white management's fear, mistrust, and uncertainty about black capability will not be able to form the basis of excluding them from various organizational roles.

Departments will make a difference. We guess that staff rather than line positions will be more readily open to blacks. In white management's eye, blacks will have less authority if relegated to staff.

However, we judge that directivity will be more likely by supervisors where races are mixed in the ranks of supervisors and/or subordinates. This will be due to the relatively low interaction potential likely when communication must cross racial lines. Mixed groups, whether supervisors or subordinates, will be less intimate and familiar with each other and less "connected." Tendencies to interact will be lower, and direction rather than participation will be more common among supervisors. For example, Sattler (1970) summarized the research literature in the influence of race on behavior in interviews. Respondents tend to give socially desirable responses to interviewers of races other than their own. That is to say, they tend to give responses which are socially "correct" or acceptable, whether or not they reflect their true feelings. Sattler further states that lower-class respondents are more likely to be sensitive to the interviewer's race than are middle- and upper-class respondents.

This latter prediction relates directly to Leavitt's (1965) discussion of power equalization. He points out that a major focus of behavioral scientists interested in organizational change has been the greater equalization of power in organizations. He states:

> Besides the belief that one changes people first these power-equalization approaches also place major emphasis on other aspects of the human phenomena of organizations. They are, for example, centrally concerned with affect; with morale, sensitivity, psychological security. Secondly, they value evolutionary, internally generated change in individuals, groups, and organizations over externally planned or implemented change. Thirdly, they place much value on human growth and fulfillment as well as upon task accomplishment; and they often have stretched the degree of causal connection between the two. Finally, of course, the power-equalization approaches, in their early stages at least, shared a normative value that power in organizations should be more equally distributed than in most existent "authoritarian hierarchies." Operationally, this belief was made manifest in a variety of ways: in encouraging independent decision-making, decentralization, more open communication, and participation (p. 1154).

From our earlier discussion many areas of possible conflict should be apparent between the emphases just cited and, at least, the immediate effects of integration. We have suggested that mixed racial groups will tend to be less cohesive, for example. We have outlined a plethora of problems facing the leader, black or white, of groups while racial integration is in process. These problems relate both to his relationship with his subordinates and to higher management. Lastly, we have suggested that the impetus for such integration must often come from a source external to the immediate group and that differences among group members and management may have to be adjudicated by outside community leaders. All these factors indicate that efforts toward greater power equalization will face stern tests as integration proceeds. While most of us would, we imagine, positively value both increased integration and increased power equalization, in the short run they do not appear to be mutually enhancing goals. The solution to this dilemma involves constant attention to multiple goals in organizations. Blacks in our society have recently expressed concerns that the "year of the black" has been replaced by the "year of ecology" or the "year of women's liberation" in the minds of many people, although little or no real progress has been achieved in the lot of most black citizens. Organizations cannot afford to be faddist or to concentrate only on single dimensions if they hope to achieve real social progress. They must develop the capacity to address concomitantly a multiplicity of important goals.

Black–White Similarities and Differences

The emphasis of this chapter has been upon variables which may be affected by the racial composition of people in a particular work environment.

As a consequence of this emphasis we have focused a good deal on predicted differences in reactions or problems between blacks and whites. Blacks do form a significant ethnic subgroup of our pluralistic society and difficult change issues are raised both for white-dominated organizations and for blacks as organizational integration proceeds. These issues should be considered openly and as objectively as possible. Many people attempt to "will" away such issues by saying basically we are all alike or that the problem is white racism. Both of these positions have a good deal of validity, but they oversimplify the issues, tend to focus on the assignment of guilt or fault rather than questions of change, and ignore the impact on all of us of growing up in a race-conscious society.

Given people as they actually are at this moment in history, accurate perception of the other person seems to be fundamental to effective interpersonal relations. We can be at one of three levels in interpersonal perceptual accuracy (Carr, 1965).

Minimally, we can be at the level where we are unable to differentiate between ourselves and others. We predict what others will do based on what we perceive in ourselves. Here, if we are wrong, we are committing the error of *unwarranted assumed similarity*. For instance, if a white is at this low level of interpersonal perception, he predicts that a black will feel the same way about matters as he feels. He may be right; he may be wrong, but it's the best he can do if he has no other information to go on.

If the perceiver can differentiate himself from others, he may achieve a bit greater accuracy. But such accuracy is based on the modal response he believes, as a whole, other people or subsets of other people make; subsets might be blacks but not whites, disadvantaged people in general, or disadvantaged blacks. Here he makes predictions based on stereotypes. Stereotyping is regarded pejoratively. It runs counter to our values of recognizing and responding to others in terms of their unique individuality. Nevertheless such predictions are accurate on the average to the extent that (a) there are, in fact, modal differences in the responses of the subsets, and (b) his stereotypes match the true modal responses of the subset. And whether we like it or not, much of the accuracy of our perceptions of subsets of strangers depends upon our knowledge of their modal responses. Again, this is true if we have nothing else to use. We hopefully strive for a better interpersonal understanding than this, which only occurs when we can differentiate among persons in the same subset. As Dunnette (1969) points out, this is an empathic level requiring learning much idiosyncratic information about specific other persons, a level which is not only more accurate but which involves more respect for the uniqueness of the other person. Unfortunately, this level is difficult to attain. It represents much more of a laudable goal than a realistic starting point.

The modal responses of blacks and whites may be far apart, as is often true of responses in many different cultures to questions about human relationships. For example, the average black is far more convinced about the past and continuing injustices being perpetrated upon blacks than is the average white.

Here considerable interpersonal accuracy can be promoted through the learning of such modal responses coupled with learning to avoid the error of automatically assuming similarity.

FACILITATING CHANGE IN ORGANIZATIONS

In this concluding section we will briefly suggest some avenues of affecting change in the racial mix of people in leadership positions in organizations. Our suggestions will be designed to minimize dysfunctional conflict at the intrapersonal, interpersonal, group, and intergroup levels in organizations. They are based on the assumption that destructive and growth-producing opportunities for confrontation and conflict will remain at all the levels mentioned.

Reducing Conflicts within the Leader

We suggest that a leader, be he white or black, will need more than the usual amount of time to establish mutually satisfying and productive relationships with subordinates when his subordinates are either racially mixed or of a different racial composition than he. Thus time and support are two prerequisites to the development of such relationships. Higher management, which expects and demands strict loyalty to values at variance with those of the people the leader supervises, may prevent any real working-through of the supervisory–subordinate relationship.

Team Development

Relationships between members of work groups of different races and between the group and their leader may well stabilize and become frozen at a shallow, unsatisfying, and minimally productive level unless direct efforts are made to improve such relationships.

Team-building activities can assist the group leader and members to communicate openly about (a) the nature of the group processes within the team, and (b) the quality of the interpersonal relationships among group members and between leader and members. Such efforts are integral parts of the organizational development (OD) programs which are gaining increasing favor in organizations (e.g., see Bennis, 1969). They would appear to be particularly appropriate in racially mixed teams.

Organizational Policies

Finally, organizational goals in the area of racial integration must be clear, unambiguous, and escapeproof. Over fifteen years after the Supreme Court's school desegregation decision, some parts of the country still do not see school integration as a national policy which they must follow. Organizations must show that they are doing more than reluctantly complying with government requirements if they expect real change. Commitment to a more fully integrated organization must be real, and such commitment must be supported in two major ways. First, the organization must not only develop clearly stated non-discriminatory selection and promotion procedures, but it must also monitor these procedures and back them up with adequate sanctions. Second, there must be a willingness to incur some short-run costs in the form of temporary dissatisfaction and loss of efficiency in the service of longer-run social goals.

REFERENCES

Abegglen, J. C. *The Japanese factory.* Glencoe, Ill.: Free Press, 1958.

Arbous, A. G. *Selection for industrial leadership.* New York: Oxford University Press, 1953.

Ausubel, D. P. Ego involvement among segregated Negro children. *Mental Hygiene,* 1958, *42,* 362–369.

Banking on blacks. *Wall Street Journal,* December 23, 1969, *50,* 1.

Baron, H. M. Black powerlessness in Chicago. *Trans-Action,* 1968, *6*(1), 27–33.

Bass, B. M. *Leadership, psychology, and organizational behavior.* New York: Harper, 1960.

Bass, B. M. A preliminary report on manifest preferences in six cultures for participative management. Technical Report 21, N00014–67(A), University of Rochester, June, 1968.

Bass, B. M., and Barrett, G. V. *Industrial psychology.* Boston: Allyn and Bacon, 1971.

Battle, E., and Rotter, J. B. Children's feeling of personal control as related to social class and ethnic group. *Journal of Personality,* 1963, *31,* 482–490.

Bennis, W. *Organization development: Its nature, origins, and prospects.* Reading, Mass.: Addison-Wesley, 1969.

Bowerman, C. E., and Campbell, E. Q. Aspirations of southern youth: A look at racial comparisons. *Trans-Action,* 1965, *2*(2), 24.

Bowers, D. G. Self-esteem and the diffusion of leadership style. *Journal of Applied Psychology,* 1963, *47,* 135–140.

Carp, F. M., Vitola, B. M., and McLanathan, F. L. Human relations knowledge and social distance set in supervisors. *Journal of Applied Psychology,* 1963, *47,* 78–80.

Carr, J. E. The role of conceptual organization in interpersonal discrimination. *Journal of Psychology,* 1965, *59,* 159–176.

Centers, R. and Bugental, D. E. Intrinsic and extrinsic job motivations among different segments of the working population. *Journal of Applied Psychology,* 1966, *50,* 193–197.

Clark, K. B. *Dark ghetto.* New York: Harper, 1965.

Coleman, J. S. Implications of the findings on alienation. *American Journal of Sociology,* 1964, *70,* 76–78.

Comrey, A. L., High, W. S., and Wilson, R. C. Factors influencing organizational effectiveness. VII: A survey of aircraft supervisors. *Personnel Psychology,* 1955, *8,* 245–257.

Delbecq, A. L., and Kaplan, S. J. The myth of the indigenous community leader: A case study of managerial effectiveness within the "War on Poverty." *Academy of Management Journal,* 1968, *11*(1), 11–25.

Dunnette, M. D. People feeling: Joy, more joy, and the "slough of despond." *Journal of Applied Behavioral Science*, 1969, *5*, 25–44.

Fenelon, J. R. *The influence of race on leadership prediction*. Unpublished master's thesis, University of Texas at Austin, 1966.

Ferguson, J. L. Social scientists in the plant. *Harvard Business Review*, 1964, *42*(3), 133–143.

Fiedler, F. *A theory of leadership effectiveness*. New York: McGraw-Hill, 1967.

Fleishman, E., and Harris, E. Patterns of leadership behavior related to employee grievances and turnover. *Personnel Psychology*, 1962, *15*, 43–56.

Friedland, W. H. Labor waste in New York: Rural exploitation and migrant workers. *Trans-Action*, 1969, *6*(4), 48–53.

Goode, W. J., and Fowler, I. Incentive factors in a low morale plant. *American Sociological Review*, 1949, *14*, 618–624.

Hollander, E. P., and Julian, J. W. Contemporary trends in the analysis of leadership processes. *Psychological Bulletin*, 1969, *71*, 387–397.

Katz, I., and Benjamin, L. Affects of white authoritarianism in biracial work groups. *Journal of Abnormal and Social Psychology*, 1960, *61*, 448–456.

King, D. C., and Clingenpeel, R. E. Supervisory effectiveness and agreement among superiors, supervisors, and subordinates regarding the supervisor's job behavior. *Proceedings of the 76th Annual Convention of the American Psychological Association*, 1968, 559–560.

King, M. L., Jr. The role of the behavioral scientist in the civil rights movement. *Journal of Social Issues*, 1968, *24*, 1–12.

Kochman, T. "Rapping" in the black ghetto. *Trans-Action*, 1969, *6*(4), 26–34.

Leavitt, H. Applied organizational change in industry: Structural, technological, and humanistic approaches. In J. G. March (ed.), *Handbook of organizations*. Chicago: Rand McNally, 1965, pp. 1144–1170.

Likert, R. *The human organization*. New York: McGraw-Hill, 1967.

MacDonald, W. S. Responsibility and goal establishment: Critical elements in Job Corps program. *Perceptual Motor Skills*, 1967, *24*, 104.

Marrow, A. J. Risks and uncertainties in action research. *Journal of Social Issues*, 1964, *20*, 5–20.

Maslow, A. H. *Motivation and personality*. New York: Harper, 1954.

Mitchell, B. N. The black minority in the CPA profession. *Journal of Accountancy*, 1969, *128*, 41–48.

Pelz, D. C. Influence: key to effective leadership in the first line supervisor. *Personnel*, 1952, *24*, 209–217.

Randle, C. W. How to identify promotable executives. *Harvard Business Review*, 1956, *34*(3), 122–134.

Sattler, J. M. Racial "experimenter effects" in experimentation, testing, interviewing, and psychotheraphy. *Psychological Bulletin*, 1970, *73*, 137–160.

Selznick, P. *Leadership in administration*. Evanston, Ill.: Row, Peterson, 1957.

Sloan, E. L. Negro community leadership in a Northern City. (Doctoral dissertation, Michigan State University). Ann Arbor, Mich.: University Micro Films, 1968, No. 68–4216.

Vroom, U., and Mann, F. Leader authoritarianism and employee attitudes. *Personnel Psychology*, 1960, *13*, 125–140.

Ward, L. B. The ethics of executive selection. *Harvard Business Review*, 1965, *43*(2), 6–28, 171–172.

Ziller, R. C. Toward a theory of open and closed groups. *Psychological Bulletin*, 1965, *64*, 164–182.

CHAPTER TEN

The Impact of Social Structure on Organizational Change

Ord Elliott and Donald D. Penner

INTRODUCTION BY THE EDITORS

In a society of organizations which are dominated by white culture and white expectancies about minority behavior, there is bound to be some initial conflict during integration of minority members who share a common and somewhat different set of expectancies. The level of organizational integration and the degree of conflict which may attend integration are postulated to be a function of the degree to which both the white majority and nonwhite minority are able to unfreeze existing expectancies and proscriptions concerning appropriate values and behavior. Significant black work expectancies are likely conditioned by the statistics reported by these authors which show that blacks are more likely to be unemployed than whites and black unemployment is almost double the rate of white unemployment. These figures hold relatively true for all skill and occupational levels. Similarly, current statistics are reported which show that blacks typically fall into lower income levels than whites, and blacks achieve lower educational levels than whites, and so forth. As a result, blacks are disproportionately overrepresented in the lower socioeconomic classes and have less access to the tools which may be necessary to achieve in the current competitive society. Similarly, environmental constraints which are associated with poverty and lower social classes provide an alternative to the pathological explanation for the high crime rates in black ghettos. Frequently, administrators inappropriately attribute such characteristics to blacks, when they are not linked to race but rather to social class.

The set of white expectations which are based upon the above statistics tend to become a self-fulfilling prophecy—i.e., the expectations themselves strengthen the probability that blacks will not progress, and instead, will exhibit the expected behaviors. Such expectations counter any positive effects of training programs and serve to inhibit blacks' performance within the organization. In such cases, blacks in a white organization will tend to measure their performance against the low levels of performance expected of them, instead of against criteria which would contribute to their successful performance on the job. The organization and its management must be prepared to reject the white stereotype of generalized and inflexible inferiority which they project onto blacks and, at the same time, be willing to accept a pluralistic society of black and white values without attempting to modify the unique cultural and racial identity of black people.

> Now, there is simply no possibility of a real change in the Negro's situation without the most radical and far-reaching changes in the American political and social structure.
>
> (James Baldwin, *The Fire Next Time*, 1962)

SOCIAL STRUCTURE: WHAT IS IT? WHO NEEDS IT?

Baldwin is not alone in criticizing the existing social structure, yet one might well ask, what is it? "Social" implies interaction. "Structure" implies order. "Social structure" suggests that there is some ordered way of perceiving human behavior. From this perspective one can look at and analyze black–white relations. If there is indeed a pattern to their interaction, then there are reasons for it. If these reasons can be identified, then the possibility of improving organizational integration is increased.

Social structure is a broad term, referring to any social behavior that recurs regularly (Moore, 1963). Differences between classes and ethnic cultures become part of this system, which is nothing more than a way of defining the relationship between individuals and groups (Udy, 1968). It is human nature to categorize, not only others but oneself as well. The extent of this categorization, while not always conscious, is a focal point for the lives of both black and white Americans. As Ralph Ellison, a black writer, said:

> Unfortunately many Negroes have been trying to define their own predicament in exclusively sociological terms, a situation I consider quite short-sighted. Too

many of us have accepted a statistical interpretation of our lives and thus much of that which makes us a source of moral strength to America goes unappreciated and undefined. Now, when you try to trace American values as they find expression in the Negro community, where do you begin? To what books do you go? How do you account for Little Rock and the sit-ins? How do you account for the strength of those kids? You can find sociological descriptions of the conditions under which they live but few indications of their morale (Ralph Ellison, *Shadow and Act*, 1964).

Thus the very existence of the construct, social structure, implies that man has a need for a certain degree of order, that this order helps him confront the chaos of life, and that, as a consequence, this same order becomes one of the forces which determines behavior. Man's perception of order becomes an expectancy, his expectancy an act, his act a pattern of actions (Moore, 1963).

In our society, where organizations are nearly always white dominated, the black subculture with its unique characteristics confronts the pervasive white middle class with its own recipe for behavior. Each group has a perception of social structure in terms of the variables that have some bearing on their interaction. Thus organizations reflect the social structure as it is perceived by the white middle class. These same organizations have expectancies about how white organizations will treat them.

This chapter examines these very expectancies, their basis, their validity. Secondly, are there differences between blacks and whites? If so, what are they? Do these differences affect behavior or expectations of behavior? Are they actual or matters of perception? In addition the implications of expectancies in determining organizational change are explored.

In the United States relative status is determined primarily by socioeconomic variables such as employment, occupation level, income, and education. These data, as they characterize individuals or groups, become a force which maintains the *status quo*. Kurt Lewin hypothesized that the *status quo* is a balanced state maintained by numerous opposing vectors (Deutsch, 1969). The level of discrimination in a particular organization is determined by the intensity and direction of these forces (Loye, 1971). In Lewin's view, social change occurs in three steps: (1) unfreezing, (2) moving to a new level, (3) refreezing. Thus the level of discrimination may be lowered by actions which unfreeze the existing *status quo* and then move to and refreeze the level at a lower point.

In this chapter the role of the black as defined by Lewin's force field is considered first in terms of socioeconomic variables. Other important normative characteristics ascribed to blacks by the white middle class are then looked at as they modify this series of socioeconomic forces. Finally the norms and values which epitomize treatment of the black in American organizations are critically examined with a view toward a reformation of certain of these norms and values which would facilitate integration.

THE FORMATION OF A ROLE: SOCIOECONOMIC STATISTICS

Unemployment

Unemployment Rates

	1930	1940	1950	1960	1962	1964	1969	1970
Ratio, nonwhite to white	.92	1.20	1.76	2.04	2.24	2.13	2.06	1.80

SOURCE: Department of Labor 1970; Department of Commerce, 1971.

As blacks shifted from agricultural occupations to the cities, the ratio of nonwhite to white unemployed increased steadily through 1962. Although the trend seems to have been reversed during the last decade, a projection into the 1970s is difficult to make. One might predict that the ratio has increased during the 1970–1971 economic recession since blacks, who typically fill the lower jobs in most organizations, would probably be the first let go in the event of a layoff. However, the U.S. Department of Labor (1970) reported that the increase in unemployment during the summer and fall of 1969 applied about equally to white and black workers, and in 1970 the increase in white unemployment was somewhat sharper than that of blacks and other races, the black rate being slightly less than double the white rate for the first time since the early 1950s (U.S. Department of Commerce, 1971). Further, the percentage change in unemployment rates from 1961 to 1969 was essentially equal for whites and nonwhites. During this period of decreasing unemployment the rate for whites decreased from 6.5 percent to 3.1 percent, an actual drop of 48.3 percent. The nonwhite ratio decreased from 12.4 percent to 6.4 percent, a 48.4 percent actual decrease (Department of Labor, 1970).

These somewhat heartening statistical trends are considerably dampened under closer scrutiny. Black males are more likely to be unemployed than black females, whereas the reverse is true for whites. Beyond this, black unemployment is double that of whites, while, at the same time, the duration of unemployment for blacks is significantly longer. Though some maintain that lack of education and skill accounts for the disproportionately high unemployment of blacks, one finds that all black occupational levels fall below the white norm. For example, in 1962, 11 percent of all nonwhite professional and technical workers with work experience were unemployed, compared with 6 percent of whites.

As the skilled labor force increases, both black and white workers who would ordinarily qualify for semiskilled jobs will assuredly be pushed into the unskilled labor force or become unemployed in the face of increasing competition with those who are better trained. If a tradition of prejudice excludes blacks, the greater portion of this potentially larger unemployed group will be black.

Occupational Level

Nonwhites as Managers, Officers, or Proprietors

1955	1960	1968	1969
2.3%	2.6%	2.9%	3.2%

Source: Department of Labor, 1970.

In contrast to unemployment patterns, statistics show that nonwhites have moved to jobs of higher occupational status with more ease. The greatest changes have occurred since 1940, largely resulting from the enactment by Federal and state governments of laws forbidding traditional discriminatory employment practices. Although professional and technical jobs are opening at significantly increased rates for nonwhites, they still hold far less than their proportional share. In 1969, of all those employed, aged sixteen years or older, 49.8 percent of the whites were in white-collar jobs as compared with 26.2 percent for nonwhites. Thus occupational distributions have not yet been greatly affected. Within each broad occupational group, nonwhite workers are more likely than white to be employed in the least skilled categories and at the lowest levels of the well-paid jobs.

Income

The patterns of black unemployment are closely correlated with income (see Table 10-1). Black family incomes continue to be lower than those of white families—they were 64 percent of white incomes in 1970, an increase from the 53 percent ratio in 1961–1963 (Department of Commerce, 1971). In general the incomes of black females are closer to those of white females than are those of black males to white. In 1963 the median income of nonwhite males was $2,507 as compared with $4,816 for whites (Moynihan, 1965).

TABLE 10–1 *Distribution of Family Income, by Color, 1959 and 1968*[a]

QUINTILE	WHITE			BLACK AND OTHER RACES			WHITE–BLACK INCOME DIFFERENCE	
	Median Income		Percent Change,	Median Income		Percent Change,		
	1959	1968	1959–68	1959	1968	1959–68	1959	1968
Lowest Fifth	$2,199	$3,196	45.3	$856	$1,723	101.3	$1,343	$1,473
Second Fifth	4,806	6,447	34.1	1,999	3,564	78.3	2,807	2,883
Middle Fifth (Overall Median)	6,742	8,937	32.6	3,482	5,591	60.6	3,260	3,346
Fourth Fifth	8,801	11,789	34.0	5,263	8,283	57.4	3,538	3,506
Highest Fifth	13,031	19,341	48.4	8,483	13,000	53.2	4,548	6,341

[a] Numbers in constant 1968 dollars.

Source: Based on data from the Department of Commerce, Bureau of the Census, Current Population Reports, Series P-60.

As the amount of education increases, the income of white workers tends to increase far more than the income of black workers. During the 1960s black men who completed college received an income only 70 percent that of white college graduates—which was about the same percentage gap visible between blacks and whites who had fewer than eight years of school. Not surprisingly, the median income of nonwhite high-school graduates ($3,821) in 1963 was about the same as that for white males who had only completed elementary school ($3,749) (Moynihan, 1965). Comparisons of family income of whites and nonwhites for the years 1959 and 1968 show that while non-whites have gained more in family income on a percentage basis between 1959 and 1968, on an actual dollar basis whites have increased considerably more. At each of the five median points on the chart above (with the exception of the fourth fifth) the actual dollar differences between white and nonwhite family income were larger in 1968 than in 1959. Additionally, 1968 medians for non-whites at each fifth of the distribution are lower than the comparable 1959 medians for whites. One way to interpret these data is that nonwhites are over ten years behind whites in income level.

Education

Proportions of People Who Have Completed at Least Four Years of High School

Age Group	White	Black	Black to White Ratio (in Percentage)
	Percentage		
20–21	82	58	71
22–24	81	56	69
25–29	77	56	73
30–34	73	50	68
35–44	66	37	56
45–54	59	29	49
55–64	45	15	33

SOURCE: Adapted from *Manpower Report of the President,* U.S. Department of Labor, March, 1970, p. 93.

Although the disparity between white and black educational attainment has apparently decreased in more recent age groups, the actual percentage of blacks in the youngest group who finished high school is still far from the white norm. While black literacy rates, school attendance, and the extent of education have increased substantially over the past few decades, by 1965 the median number of years of school completed for blacks was 9.0 compared with 12.0 for whites (Pinkney, 1969).

The three-year gap in educational attainment fails to illustrate the extent of the differences. Nearly a tenth of whites (9.9 percent) have completed four or more years of college compared with only 4.7 percent of blacks. Over one-half (50.5 percent) of blacks discontinued their education after elementary school or earlier, as compared with 31.2 percent of whites. And, of course, the statistics ignore the quality of education; black and predominately black schools have long resided at the lower end of this spectrum (Pinkney, 1969).

Importance of Status

Employment, occupation level, income, and education in composite form become a well-used abstraction, namely the socioeconomic index, America's major symbol of status. As such, the status of the black falls far below white comparisons. The average black earns about half of the average white's income. His rate of unemployment is double, and when unemployed, he is likely to remain out of work twice as long. Most black jobs are low-paying, unskilled, and menial. Nearly half of all blacks live in slums. Infant mortality is twice the rate for white Americans. Education is of inferior quality and less often obtained. In short, when viewed in terms of the dimensions of status, the black finds himself with only half the stature of a white.

Black socioeconomic class structure is pyramidal in shape, with a large lower class, a somewhat smaller middle class, and a very small upper class. In contrast the white majority forms a diamond shape class structure with small lower and upper classes and a large middle class (Drake, 1965). The black is frequently physically isolated in "black belts," becoming in his own mind and to the white mind just so much more dissimilar.

Because of his lower status relative to the white middle class, the black has fewer of the tools which may be fruitfully used in a competitive society. As this deficiency reduces opportunities for advancement, so do white perceptions of his lower status further diminish his chances. Inferiority in status may be transcribed to inferiority of a more universal or nondescript nature. What organization values inferiority or, for that matter, condones it? If a class "doesn't have it" the prevailing logic, so easily bred, is that the man "doesn't have it." A role is formed—that is, a set of expectations shared by most.

A CONSIDERATION OF SOME CHARACTERISTICS FREQUENTLY ASCRIBED TO BLACKS BY WHITES

Intelligence

The role of the black does not end with socioeconomic data. If the socioeconomic role is adhered to, it follows that the black must be less intelligent. Enough men have gathered data to support this point of view, and today it remains unresolved in many minds whether the black is biologically less intelligent or whether his deprived background has rendered him that way.

The biogenetic point of view as espoused by Jensen (1968) maintains that genetic factors account for some 80 percent of the individual differences between blacks and whites. He suggests that socioeconomic status may, consequently, be used to measure intelligence because occupational hierarchy coupled with educational requirements act as screening devices for the less intelligent. Thus, where a society permits and in fact requires a high level of social mobility, socioeconomic status invariably becomes correlated with the genetic basis of intelligence. However, even Jensen concludes that the measurement of intelligence by socioeconomic status is very difficult with respect to race, since skin color has no determining influence on intelligence. It is even more difficult to divine any correlation when one considers that the social mobility of blacks is significantly more restricted than for comparable whites. Thus to the extent that blacks are deprived social mobility, measurement of their intelligence on the basis of socioeconomic status will become increasingly inaccurate.

The most infamous measure of intelligence is the IQ test. A quick glance at the extensive literature in this area illustrates that there are many factors which have been correlated with intelligence. Gottesman (1968) mentions a number of them: basal metabolism rate, EEG alpha frequency, height, weight, anxiety level, race and warmth of examiner, father's occupation and years of schooling, mother's attitude toward achievement, home cultural level, mother's concern with language development, degree of anoxia at birth, desire to master intellectual skills, and more. What IQ tests do measure is current performance on a test based on success as defined by a very specific culture, and certainly not innate intellectual potential. What is more interesting is that given the IQ distributions of a sample of normative Southeastern white and black school children, the two frequency distributions overlap to such an extent that to predict intelligence from skin color or race involves only chance accuracy (Gottesman, 1968).

Figure 10-1 is illustrative of a typical intelligence distribution. In this case 25 percent of the blacks tested show greater performance than half of the whites tested. More importantly the range of the two distributions are virtually the same. Thus the lowest and highest in intelligence of both black and white are similar. Individual differences totally overshadow any difference that exists between races, which means that in reality there is always an individual who

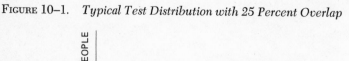

FIGURE 10–1. *Typical Test Distribution with 25 Percent Overlap*

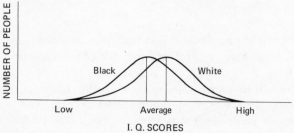

SOURCE: Pettigrew, 1964.

can fulfill the intellectual components of a specific job regardless of his ethnic origin.

This conclusion is drawn from a test whose validity is already of questionable value. The mean differences, then, may be attributable to characteristics of the test, to basic genetic differences, or to environmental factors. Of the three, modern psychology largely concludes that the mean difference in IQ results from the deprivation of greatly differing environments characteristic of racial segregation. While it is admitted that there may exist small differences in genetic abilities between races, neither race is pure and separate genetically by any means, and, hence, genetic arguments which seemingly validate the cause of segregation become spurious.

A study done by Sherwood and Nataupsky (1968) found that biographical data collected from the investigator can be used to predict conclusions of black–white intelligence research. Thus one might well question the impact of such heated controversy about intelligence. The mere existence of the dialogue separates black from white beyond the color difference. Is it really important that the black is less intelligent by virtue of genetic factors or by environmental deprivation? To the organization which must meet the needs of *immediacy* both arguments demand the same solution. Inferiority can hardly be expected to breed the best profits, and in either case the people who have decided on the demarcation of inferiority have been members of the privileged class, a position whose preservation is dependent to a large degree on the maintenance of a status differential.

A study conducted by Rosenthal and Jacobsen (1968) manipulated expectations of performance in a classroom situation. Although the experiment has since been criticized for lack of adequate controls (Barber and Silver, 1968), the results are, nevertheless, pertinent to industrial black–white relations. When teachers expected that certain children would show greater intellectual development, these children, in fact, did show this very improvement.

Thus for the organization that accepts any theory of racial inferiority, genetic or cultural, the relationship between blacks and whites will demonstrate consistent distance. Again and again the organization will try to deal with an "inferior being" by expecting inferior work, and in so doing, very likely getting just that.

Pathology

To the black of inferior status and intellectual ability is attributed excessive criminal activity, drug addiction, and other signs of personal instability, precisely what Kenneth B. Clark (1965) has labeled the "pathology of the ghetto." Statistics support a higher incidence of crime emanating from the ghetto, yet the predominant white conclusion is that such criminality is to be expected from an inferior being.

Indeed, black crime rates are high, particularly for aggressive acts, such as aggravated assault and homicide, and for escapist crimes including drug addiction, gambling, and drunkenness (Pettigrew, 1964). Racial discrimination within the judicial system, while clearly existing, does not account for the obviously excessive black incidence of crime. The cause of white supremacists is further dignified by uniting criminality with genetic inferiority. However, environmental explanations most often proffered by social scientists more realistically define the roots of this problem.

Blacks are generally confined to those areas of lower socioeconomic status from which the high crime rates emanate regardless of race. Consider a man in the lower class, poor, living in a slum in a large metropolitan city, unemployed, belonging to a disorganized family. Each of these factors has been correlated with crime apart from race and especially so in the case of the crimes typically ascribed to blacks (cf. Pettigrew, 1964).

While blacks have generally accepted the culture of white America, replete with the ideology of equality and happiness for all, they have been unable to realize the happiness or socioeconomic stability of their counterparts in white Middle America. This special type of discrimination, which blocks them almost irrevocably from a chance for success within the larger culture, may lead to crime as a vehicle of escape, of ego-enhancement, of a mobility otherwise unachieved, or of frustration denied aggressive release (Pettigrew, 1964).

In a study of civil rights activity and reduction of crime among blacks, Solomon, Walker, O'Connor, and Fishman (1965) reported that blacks release long-dammed-up resentment of segregation by asserting themselves (directly or vicariously) in direct action for civil rights. When this type of emotional expression occurs in a framework of community organization the need for aggressive outbursts of a violent sort is reduced.

But again the real question is, given the higher crime rate among blacks by reason of pathology or by reasons of environment, how does this man stand in the white world—low! Crime may be only one way of reacting to environment. To the white world it is pathology, it is deviance, it is bad. From another perspective the very homogeneity of Middle America—with its neatly trimmed lawns, its struggle for material possessions, its measure of men based on those very possessions, its infernal emphasis on conformity and sameness as somehow equated to godliness—has been interpreted by others to be beyond madness, beyond pathology. One might well ask to whom does pathology belong, and who has the right to assign it.

Matriarchy

In 1965, a Department of Labor bulletin (largely the effort of Daniel Moynihan) was released which stated "beyond equivocation" that the root of the black problem could be found in their broken, matriarchal family structure (Rainwater, 1965). Since that time the frequently voiced white conviction has been that black families are characterized by disorganization, that the mother totally dominates a family devoid of male guidance, that this produces boys with feminine characteristics and girls with masculine traits, that proper education of children is impossible to achieve in such a climate, and that such a family is necessarily supported by welfare (Billingsley, 1970).

Moynihan's (1965) thesis assumes that the transient male who only occasionally lives at home is incapable of providing the necessary income, discipline, or direction to his children. Moynihan further argues that the situation has been getting worse and not better despite all the civil rights legislation and numerous poverty programs. The black has simply not taken on the stable father-directed orientation of middle-class America. Therefore national policies should be redirected to promote this goal.

In essence Moynihan is excusing any defects in the social system from blame for black problems and is instead blaming the blacks themselves for failing to provide the family stability which would surely cure their deviance. Whether Moynihan's intent to redefine the civil rights program was political expediency or sincere reformation is not of issue here. As the report became public through extensive journalistic coverage, white visions of black entrapment in a symbolic ghetto of inferiority solidified.

Criticism of Moynihan's report has been slow to follow (cf. Rainwater, 1965; Hyman, 1969) and certainly has never reached the level or intensity of coverage it achieved shortly after release. Nevertheless, social scientists noted that the data were not false but that the selection and interpretation of the data were somewhat one-sided. In short, they felt that Moynihan failed to control for economic and educational variables which would have necessitated comparisons with whites, that data which may have contradicted his conclusions were not included, and that the conclusions themselves were unwarranted and speculative.

More thoughtful research has shown that broken families are not so much a product of racial differences as of socioeconomic factors, and that ghetto white families are often without fathers in residence. Outside slum areas, family stability tends to be the rule rather than the exception. And what is family stability, anyway? One might hypothesize that even in white Middle America the father tends to be a forgotten figure. Forgotten also is the fact that no one really knows very much about the father's influence in either black or white families. It may well be that the stable black family is more patriarchal than its white counterpart.

Data recently released by the U.S. Census Bureau show signs of increasing dissolution of the black family, which if Moynihan's assumptions are to be believed would indicate more "pathological" behavior. The percentage of black children living with both parents declined from 75 to 67 percent during the decade. The white rate remained at 91 or 92 percent (Department of Commerce, 1971). Further, black women appeared more likely to encounter marital discord than whites. In 1970, 19 percent of all black women who were at one time married were either divorced or separated as compared with 6 percent of white women (Department of Commerce, 1971).

In a report on "The Strengths of Black Families" (1971) issued by the National Urban League, data such as that presented in the recent census report were countered as a misrepresentation. The report identifies and analyzes five strengths of black families: their adaptability of family roles, strong kinship bonds, strong work orientation, strong religious orientation, and strong achievement orientation. About 90 percent of the black babies born out of wedlock were kept by the parent and kin in existing families; 67 percent of the illegitimate white babies, compared with 7 percent of the black illegitimate babies, were formally adopted or placed. Further, the report states that most assertions about widespread desertion in black families are not based on actual desertion rates (National Urban League, 1971).

Farley and Hermalin (1971) conclude that the majority of both black and white families are in the statuses indicative of family stability and that most black families maintain a sound husband–wife relationship, with the children residing with both parents. Mack (1971), in addition to reaffirming that social class is too often neglected in examining the black matriarchy, investigated the complexities of the husband–wife power relationship, which, she concluded, was far more important in determining family stability than attempts at ethnic differentiation. Mack stresses that most of the research has looked at the white community and seen that education, occupation, and income are important sources of power. This kind of power is perceived as residing with the female in black families, where a black female schoolteacher, for instance, might well be married to a janitor. On the basis of this socioeconomic bias, it is presumed that black women retain the power within the family. Such a conclusion is unwarranted solely on the grounds of this one orientation, for the black male may use sex as a power vehicle in the same manner that a white may use his socioeconomic status.

THE IMPACT OF THE ROLE

It is unfortunate that only recently have social scientists come to realize that what is different is not necessarily inferior. Black deviations from white norms have been viewed on a vertical basis with, as one might suspect, a bottom bias. To view difference on a horizontal plane has not been easy for either social scientists or politicians, which may be some indication of the strength of traditional viewpoints reflected from the mass of white Middle America.

Once a role has been formed, as in the case of the black in which a set of expectations about his behavior becomes normative, the man who by virtue of his blackness falls into this role tends to fulfill the characteristics demanded of it. To the extent that a man holds values divergent from his role, problems of identity result. The American black was first a slave, deprived of a culture, history, and language, unique only in the things he did not possess, outside and below the "human" social structure. Despite the American ideology of equality, his role incorporated inferiority, passiveness, and servility. Not surprisingly then, in so many cases the black's self-image not only reflects this role structure but also confirms and supports it. Managers might well ask why they should hire a man who is low in self-esteem or has low expectations of achievement. In a study by Lott and Lott (1963), black boys showed somewhat exaggerated or unrealistic aspirations in their desires to enter professional or business fields; 41 percent of the boys and 46 percent of the white boys wanted a professional or business career. However, only 30 percent of the blacks, in contrast with 41 percent of the whites, actually expected to attain this type of job. Dreams and expectations are not the same thing. Dreams or desires function to transcend reality as a salve against the pain of existence, while expectations operate strictly in reality, reflecting the world as it is and not as it might be.

The typical black sees in the white world the middle-class occupations associated with success, prestige, and pride. Undoubtedly, his own job bears little resemblance, yet whether employed or unemployed he measures himself against the aura of white success, constantly reminded of just where he stands. The black world is not so separate, not so different as one might suspect (cf. Frazier, 1966; Liebow, 1967). If in truth black culture is really different, then as a culture it should be self-generating and self-sustaining, with clear boundaries marking it off from the larger society, impervious to the values and norms of white culture. Different as it may be in some respects, the black subculture is just that—a subculture, irrevocably tied to the institutions which move America (Liebow, 1967).

The black subculture is by no means homogeneous but has its own socioeconomic structure with an upper middle class made up largely of professional and business men. As Frazier (1966) describes this black "high society," he characterizes it by conspicuous consumption and excessive club formations. Because this group of blacks has been excluded from social interaction with white society of comparable status, they have imitated the behavior of the white upper class as far as possible, maintaining and participating in their own social cosmos. Thus, the black professional has a special kind of identity problem. He wants somehow to be respected for what he has achieved in America, yet his color ties him to the typical lower-class black. In an effort to break this demeaning image, he has formed a distinct society within the black community because he could not make ties with his white socioeconomic equals. His exclusion from the white world has meant that despite his efforts to succeed (as defined by the larger culture), he is regarded as of no real consequence.

PREJUDICE AS A TRADITION

"I've been scuffling for five years," he said. "I've been scuffling for five years from morning till night. And my kids still don't have anything, my wife don't have anything, and I don't have anything" (Liebow, 1967).

While it is not new knowledge that the American black is excluded in many ways from the movement of American economic and social life, the perpetuation of this group exclusion remains slightly more mysterious. Are groups bad? Everyone has a need for group belongingness, a place to anchor. Without the stable relationships that family or peer groups provide, individuals become insecure, uncertain of their identities. It is from within the homogeneity of groups that one learns codes of behavior toward other members and other groups, that one learns of group antipathies and conflicts. To the extent an individual finds his education within a group reliable and rewarding, he learns to give credence to opinions sponsored by that group (cf. Bem, 1970).

In today's complex society individuals are likely to be members of several groups, but for the black, his ethnic group is the overpowering characteristic of his role (E. U. Essien-Udom, 1966), primarily because ethnic distinctions are embedded into the cultural definitions and norms in our social system (Banfield and Wilson, 1966). This prejudice is not a product of demented or psychotic minds so much as it is characteristic of the normal personality. Unfortunately, when prejudice is normal in a society, its most respected and powerful members are most committed to maintaining the legitimate organizations which cannot help but reflect the normal personality. In a study by F. K. Heussenstamm (1971) Black Panther bumper stickers were placed on the cars of fifteen exemplary drivers with no moving traffic violations within the last twelve months. The appearance (straight, hippie) and the race (black, white, Mexican-American) of the drivers were varied. Drivers were instructed to observe all traffic regulations. All together, the participants received thirty-three citations in seventeen days—a result of unwarranted police provocations. The appearance of the drivers had no effect on the number of citations received.

In *Native Son* (1940) Richard Wright, a black novelist, tries to capture the nature of extended prejudice. In the following selection, Mr. Max, a white lawyer, presents closing arguments to the jury in defense of his black client, Bigger Thomas:

If only ten or twenty Negroes had been put into slavery, we could call it injustice, but there were hundreds of thousands of them throughout the country. If this state of affairs had lasted for two or three years, we could say that it was unjust; but it lasted for more than two hundred years. Injustice which lasts for three long centuries and which exists among millions of people over thousands of square miles of territory, is injustice no longer; it is an accomplished fact of life. Men adjust themselves to their land; they create their own laws of being; their notions of right and wrong. A common way of earning a living gives them a common attitude toward life. Even their speech is colored and shaped by what they must undergo. Your Honor, injustice blots out one form of life, but another grows up in its place with its own rights, needs, and aspirations.

Feeling the capacity to be, to live, to act, to pour out the spirit of their souls into concrete and objective form with a high fervor born of their racial characteristics, they glide through our complex civilization like wailing ghosts; they spin like fiery planets lost from their orbits; they wither and die like trees ripped from native soil.

Your Honor, remember that men can starve from a lack of self-realization as much as they can from a lack of bread! . . . . Excluded from, and unassimilated in our society, yet longing to gratify impulses akin to our own but denied the objects and channels evolved through long centuries for their socialized expression, every sunrise and sunset make him guilty of subversive actions. Every movement of his body is an unconscious protest. Every desire, every dream, no matter how intimate or personal, is a plot or a conspiracy. Every hope is a plan for insurrection. Every glance of the eye is a threat. His very existence is a crime against the state!

Only a few doubt the depth of existing black prejudice, although there are fewer who care to accept the institutional and traditional nature of it. One might well ask that if prejudice is so deeply a part of our social structure—rooted in fact in its very foundations—how then can it be extirpated? There are some who feel that color consciousness is so firmly embedded in both black and white psyches, that the only way to free ourselves from its bonds is for color differences to disappear: complete physical assimilation. Gottesman (1968) writes that in an admittedly speculative extrapolation Glass and Li calculated that the R° gene frequencies in the two populations would be matched in 60.7 generations, or 1,669 more years (3622 A.D.). For all practical purposes the populations would be indistinguishable in about 39 generations, or 3025 A.D.

Thirty-nine generations is a long time to wait for racial harmony. There are others who believe in and are committed to pluralism, that in American society it is fully possible for separate class or ethnic groups to retain distinctive characteristics. Although these distinct groups may sometimes form coalitions and at other times be in conflict, within the framework of a complex society it is presumed that large organizations and associations are more concerned with their own purposes and administrative problems than with preserving status differentials. The liberal mind conceives of society as individuals who confront a neutral body of law and a neutral institutional complex. This idealistic expectancy is part of the American dream. For the black, at least in the present, the expectancy is more of a dream. As James Baldwin has stated:

The idea of rising expectations is part of the American experience: you leave the famine-ridden farm in Ireland, you come to America, you fit into the American scene, you rise, you become a part of a new social structure. But that is only the European immigrant's experience. It is not the black experience. I did not one day decide to leave my farm and come to America. I was brought here. I did not want to come. And when I got here, I did not, like the Irish and the Jews and the Russians and the Poles and the Greeks and the Italians, immediately find myself in a slum and then by hard work and saving my pennies rise out of the slum into a position of relative economic security so that my idea of reality changed. That is not the black experience in this country, and there is no point in pretending to ourselves on any level whatever that it is. The black experience is entirely different. You find yourself in a slum and you realize at a certain point that no amount of labor, no amount of hard work, no amount of soap is going to get you out of that slum. . . . If you are a Negro, you understand that somehow you have to operate outside the system and beat these people at their own game (1966, p. 473.)

Social structure as perceived by the black is not the perception of white Americans. There has been no structural assimilation, yet the black has tasted the values and norms of the American Dream, so completely in the case of middle and upper-class blacks that they are barely distinguishable from whites of similar social-class level in cultural patterns (Pinkney, 1969). In fact the evidence frequently points to black overconformity to middle-class standards of behavior (Pinkney, 1969). As Baldwin implies, blacks have adopted the cultural pattern of the dominant white society. They are not different by virtue of African origin, for that part of their history is buried under the weight of American custom. They are different chiefly because American society has somehow decided that they should be different. It is, in short, in the American tradition.

CHANGING TRADITION

It seems unlikely that the black will willingly allow the social structure as it now stands to exist. The norms which govern acceptance in and rewards from America's institutions incorporate exclusion. Knowingly or unknowingly, even many white liberals have been unable to divest themselves of the concept of white supremacy. As James Baldwin has said:

> In order for the Negro to become an American citizen, all American citizens will be forced to undergo a change, and all American institutions will be forced to undergo a change too. These institutions, which are established, can only begin to operate to free me and all other Americans by changing. There is no possibility, for example, of the Church in this country accepting me into it as a Christian without becoming a different institution itself (1966, p. 489).

By scrutinizing the components of social structure, it is possible to gain a perspective of one's own interactions and the interactions of other groups. This detachment is arrived at through knowledge, through an ability to lift oneself from role prescriptions and group affiliations, in an increasingly larger and universal context. From this perspective the problem of integrating an organization becomes clear. The black is set apart somehow because he is seen as representing different goals and values from those of most organizations which admittedly have values characteristic of the white middle class. His role is perceived as different because the forces of social structure serve the *status quo*. It seems that each trait assigned blacks is merely a synonym for different, repeated over and over, gathering reinforcement and momentum along the way. Difference becomes inferiority. Inferiority becomes intolerable.

The specifics of this generalized inferiority under analysis have the solidity of water. Black values are startlingly similar to the normative white middle-class values. As for intelligence, there is great overlap and large within-culture difference; therefore there is no way of predicting that one black man will be less intelligent than one white man. As for family structure or pathology, who judges, by what authority, and for what necessity? Stereotypes vary more as a function of class than of race, while prejudice is related to real or perceived differences in belief systems and not to color (Hyman, 1969). Furthermore, Klineberg (1971), in reviewing black–white relations from an international perspective, concludes that "conflict may occur without color differences, and that where such differences exist they may play little or no part in conflict. The notion of high visibility appears to me to contribute very little to the analysis. It is tempting to conclude that color is unimportant, and that 'black and white' represent a false dichotomy."

The American manager cannot wait sixty generations for the physical assimilation of the races. He must decide first and foremost that a pluralistic society is possible and that structural assimilation of the black is possible. If organizations have not tended to act on problems beyond their perceived self-interest because leaders are reluctant to initiate sociopolitical action, then the leaders must recognize that the *status quo* may be a threat to this very self-interest. Without change, the kind of stability upon which organizations depend may vanish, for the *status quo* is now in turmoil and stability requires change.

Organizations are in a position to affect the social structure by redefining the structures of their own organizations to include structural assimilation of blacks without modifying their unique identity. This is quite simply a prescription for recognizing and practicing equality. In a study by Fromkin, Klimoski, and Flanagan (1971), it was shown that highly competent newcomers are the most preferred co-workers, regardless of race. If the competitive demands of many highly competent blacks are met, then more doors for all blacks might open. A black in an executive position reduces the novelty of a black line supervisor or a black secretary. Thus, the penchant of white Americans to characterize blacks as a group might be used to further integration, as blacks in high-status jobs generate respect for their race as an entity.

The job of closing the opportunity gap is facilitated by shifting the role of the black from that of social inferior to that of social equal. This shift is easiest in a cohesive group in which the altered behavior can be made the principal focus of the group, by expecting and reinforcing it constantly to the point that status within the group is dependent upon it (cf. Bem, 1970). The man who was once a bigot may become the inveterate egalitarian.

This structural approach aims for coincident interpretations of black and white roles within the organization. This does not mean that a given black should be expected to share the personality traits of a given white, but does mean that the structure of the various roles within the organization will exclude all color focus and will include pressure to exhibit equalitarian behavior. The structural approach realizes that the outside community is different, that the larger external structural forces will encourage a different set of role expectations which will be brought to the job. Nevertheless, the larger social structure can be changed by effecting change within the organization. Tension cannot be removed as long as the larger external structure is different, but the goal of racial nondifferentiation can be stressed so strongly that, at least within the workings of that particular organization, color will not be the chief distinguishing characteristic of any individual.

The greatest danger is to expect that given this structural emphasis of equality there will be no racial differences. Remember that a commitment must be made to a pluralistic society, that differences must be accepted. The black cannot become the white completely and should not be expected to—in fact, that is not a desirable goal. A black man, in entering a predominately white organization, very likely brings with him a personal history of discrimination which becomes, in the present, skepticism. A white man brings his own special skepticism, a distrust of difference.

Some social scientists (in particular those from the psychoanalytic school) believe that even if all external structural blocks to black advancement were removed, the black's own values, attitudes, and habits would still confine him to an inferior position. The preponderance of experimental psychology, however, favors the structural approach—that is, situational pressures to act in a nondiscriminatory fashion (Katz and Gurin, 1969). Furthermore, K. B. Clark found resistance "to be associated with ambiguous or inconsistent policies, ineffective action, and conflict between competing authorities. Efficient desegregation is dependent on the unequivocality of prestige leaders, the firm enforcement of changed policy, the willingness to deal with violations, the refusal of those in authority to tolerate subterfuges, and the readiness to appeal to morality and justice" (Harding, Proshansky, Kutner, and Chein, 1969).

CONCLUSION

Organizations and their leaders must be committed to the goal of integration, fully cognizant that the end result is worth reaching—and, more importantly, worth suffering for. If the commitment is made, then the process is twofold. The role of the black must be altered, structured so that in terms of the interactions within that organization color is not the primary basis of differentiation. Secondly, realizing that the external and internal structures are not the same, the organization must educate its employees to see apparent differences for what they are—differences not to be judged on a good–bad continuum, on the basis of socioeconomic status or intelligence or family structure, not to be labeled with trademarks of inferiority, but simply differences and nothing more. Change cannot be a passive experience for any organization. Integration will not happen. It must be made to happen. The slavery that exists in the mind must be lifted by

the very mind that contains it, must be forced from the edge of consciousness
to the center of rationality, where the folly of its existence will be found.

> *For Who*
> *Besides God*
> *Would claim a black face*
> *To lift his withered soul*
> *From the measure of white dust*
> *And say too late*
> *You could have*
> *Been a man*

(Ord Elliott, Easter, 1971)

REFERENCES

Baldwin, James. *The fire next time.* New York: Dell, 1962.
Baldwin, J., Glazer, N., Hook, S., Myrdal, G., and Podhoretz, N. Liberalism and the Negro: A round-table discussion. In B. E. Segal (ed.), *Racial and ethnic relations.* New York: Thomas Y. Crowell, 1966, pp. 459–492.
Banfield, E. C. and Wilson, J. Q. The Negro in city politics. In R. J. Murphy and H. Elison (eds.), *Problems and prospects of the Negro movement.* Belmont, Calif.: Wadsworth, 1966, pp. 376–393.
Barber, T. X., and Silver, M. J. Fact, fiction, and the experimenter bias effect. *Psychological Bulletin,* 1968, 70 (6, Part 2), 1–29.
Bem, D. J. *Beliefs, attitudes, and human affairs.* Belmont, Calif.: Brooks/Cole, 1970.
Berelson, B., and Steiner, G. A. *Human behavior: An inventory of scientific findings.* New York: Harcourt, 1964.
Billingsley, A. Black families and white social science. Professionals and the poor. *Journal of Social Issues, 26,* No. 3, 1970, 127–142.
Blake, J. and Davis, K. Norms, values, and sanctions. In R. L. Faris (ed.), *Handbook of modern sociology.* Chicago: Rand McNally, 1964, pp. 456–484.
Brink, W., and Harris, L. What whites think of Negroes. In R. J. Murphy and H. Elinson (eds.), *Problems and prospects of the Negro movement.* Belmont, Calif.: Wadsworth, pp. 24–34.
Broom, L., and Glenn, N. D. The occupations and income of black Americans. In N. D. Glenn and C. M. Bonjean (eds.), *Blacks in the United States.* San Francisco: Chandler, 1968, pp. 24–42.
Clark, K. B. *Dark ghetto.* New York: Harper, 1965.
Cleaver, E. *Soul on ice.* New York: McGraw-Hill, 1968.
Deutsch, M. Field theory in social psychology. In G. Lindzey and E. Aronson (eds.), *Handbook of social psychology,* Vol. I. Reading, Mass.: Addison-Wesley, 1969, pp. 412–487.
Drake, St. C., and Cayton, H. The world of the urban lower-class Negro. In R. J. Murphy and H. Elinson (eds.), *Problems and prospects of the Negro movement.* Belmont, Calif.: Wadsworth, 1966, pp. 59–79.
Dreger, R. M., and Miller, K. S. Comparative studies of Negroes and whites in the

United States: 1959–1965. *Psychological Bulletin Monograph Supplement 70,* 1968.

Edwards, G. F. Community and class realities: The ordeal of change. In T. Parsons and K. B. Clark (eds.), *The Negro American.* Boston: Houghton Mifflin, 1965, pp. 280–302.

Ellison, R. Reflections of a writer. In R. J. Murphy and H. Elinson, (eds.), *Problems and prospects of the Negro movement.* Belmont, Calif.: Wadsworth, pp. 257–273.

Erikson, E. H. The concept of identity in race relations: Notes and queries. In T. Parsons and K. B. Clark (eds.), *The Negro American.* Boston: Houghton Mifflin, 1965, pp. 227–253.

Essien-Udom, E. U. The appeals and challenges of the black nationalist movement. In R. J. Murphy and H. Elinson (eds.), *Problems and prospects of the Negro movement.* Belmont, Calif.: Wadsworth, 1966, pp. 274–282.

Farley, R., and Hermalin, A. Family stability: A Comparison of trends between blacks and whites. *American Sociological Review,* 1971, *36,* 1–17.

Fein, R. An economic and social profile of the Negro American. In T. Parsons and K. B. Clark (eds.), *The Negro American.* Boston: Houghton Mifflin, 1965, pp. 102–133.

Frazier, E. F. "Society": Status without substance. In R. J. Murphy and H. Elinson (eds.), *Problems and prospects of the Negro movement.* Belmont, Calif.: Wadsworth, 1966, pp. 294–305.

Fromkin, H. L., Klimoski, R. J., and Flanagan, M. F. Race and competence as determinants of acceptance of newcomers in success and failure work groups. *Organizational Behavior and Human Performance,* 1972, *1,* 25–42.

Ginzberg, E. Findings and directions. In E. Ginzberg (ed.), *Business leadership and the Negro crisis.* New York: McGraw-Hill, 1968, pp. 171–175.

Glenn, N. D. Changes in the social and economic conditions of black Americans during the 1960's. In N. D. Glenn and C. M. Bonjean (eds.), *Blacks in the United States.* San Francisco: Chandler, 1968, pp. 43–54.

Gordon, M. M. Assimilation in America: Theory and reality. In R. J. Murphy and H. Elinson (eds.), *Problems and prospects of the Negro movement.* Belmont, Calif.: Wadsworth, 1966, pp. 223–256.

Gottesman, I. D. Biogenetics of race and class. In M. Deutsch, I. Katz, and A. Jensen (eds.), *Social class, race, and psychological development.* New York: Holt, 1968, pp. 11–51.

Gottlick, D., and Campbell, J. Winners and losers in the race for the good life: A comparison of blacks and whites. In N. D. Glenn and C. M. Bonjean (eds.), *Blacks in the United States.* San Francisco: Chandler, 1958, pp. 65–74.

Grier, W. H., and Cobbs, P. M. *Black rage.* New York: Basic Books, 1968.

Harding, J., Proshansky, J., Kutner, B., and Chein, I. Prejudice and ethnic relations. In G. Lindzey and E. Aronson (eds.), *Handbook of social psychology,* Vol. V. Reading, Mass.: Addison-Wesley, 1969, pp. 1–61.

Hauser, P. M. Demographic factors in the integration of the Negro. In T. Parsons and K. B. Clark (eds.), *The Negro American.* Boston: Houghton Mifflin, 1965, pp. 71–101.

Heussenstamm, F. K. Bumper stickers and the cops. *Trans-Action,* 1971, *8,* 32–33.

Hoffer, E. The Negro is prejudiced against himself. In R. J. Murphy and H. Elinson (eds.), *Problems and prospects of the Negro movement.* Belmont, Calif.: Wadsworth, 1966, pp. 35–44.

Hyman, H. Social psychology and race relations. In I. Katz and P. Gurin (eds.), *Race and the social sciences.* New York: Basic Books, 1969, pp. 3–48.

Jensen, A. R. Introduction: Biogenetic perspectives. In M. Deutsch, I. Katz, and A. Jensen (eds.), *Social class, race, and psychological development.* New York: Holt, 1968, pp. 7–10.

Johnson, R. B. Negro reactions to minority group status. In B. E. Segal (ed.), *Racial and ethnic relations.* New York: Thomas Y. Crowell, 1966, pp. 251–270.

Katz, I. and Gurin, P. Race relations and the social sciences: Overview and further discussion. In I. Katz and P. Gurin (eds.), *Race and the social sciences.* New York: Basic Books, 1969, pp. 342–376.

Killingsworth, C. Jobs and income for Negroes. In I. Katz and P. Gurin (eds.), *Race and the social sciences.* New York: Basic Books, 1969, pp. 194–273.

Klineberg, O. Black and white in international perspective. *American Psychologist,* 1971, *26,* 119–128.

Leach, E. R. Social structure: The history of the concept. *International encyclopedia of the social sciences,* Vol. 14. New York: Macmillan, 1968, pp. 482–489.

Liebow, E. *Tally's corner.* Boston: Little, Brown, 1967.

Lincoln, C. E. Color and group identity in the United States. *Daedalus,* 1967, *96,* 527–541.

Lott, A., and Lott, B. *Negro and white youth: A psychological study in a border state community.* New York: Holt, 1963.

Loughney, J. *An evaluation of three black novelists: Richard Wright, Ralph Ellison, and James Baldwin.* Unpublished manuscript, Department of American Studies, Purdue University, January, 1971.

Mack, D. E. Where the black-matriarchy theorists went wrong. *Psychology Today,* 1971, *24,* 86–87.

McDaniel, P. A., and Babchuk, N. Negro conceptions of white people in a northeastern city. In B. E. Segal (ed.), *Racial and ethnic relations.* New York: Thomas Y. Crowell, 1966, pp. 230–238.

McKnight, J. Community action. In E. Ginzberg (ed.), *Business leadership and the Negro crisis,* New York: McGraw-Hill, 1969, pp. 161–168.

Metzger, P. L. American sociology and black assimilation: Conflicting perspectives. *American Journal of Sociology,* 1971, *76,* 627–647.

Moore, W. E. Social structure and behavior. In G. Lindzey and E. Aronson (eds.), *Handbook of social psychology,* Vol. IV. Reading, Mass.: Addison-Wesley, 1969, pp. 283–322.

Moore, W. E. *Social change.* Englewood Cliffs, N.J.: Prentice-Hall, 1963.

Moynihan, D. P. Employment, income, and the ordeal of the Negro family. In T. Parsons and K. B. Clark (eds.), *The Negro American.* Boston: Houghton Mifflin, 1965, pp. 134–159.

National Urban League. *The strengths of black families.* July, 1971.

Parsons T. *Structure and process in modern societies.* Glencoe, Ill.: Free Press, 1960.

Parsons, T. Full citizenship for the Negro American? A sociological problem. In T. Parsons and K. B. Clark (eds.), *The Negro American.* Boston: Houghton Mifflin. 1965, pp. 709–754.

Perrow, C. *Organizational analysis: A sociological view.* Belmont, Calif.: Wadsworth, 1970.

Pettigrew, T. F. *Profile of the Negro American.* Princeton, N.J.: Van Nostrand, 1964.

Pettigrew, T. F. Complexity and change in American racial patterns: A social psychological view. In T. Parsons and K. B. Clark (eds.), *The Negro American,* Boston: Houghton Mifflin, 1965, pp. 325–362.

Pinkney, A. P. *Black Americans.* Englewood Cliffs, N.J.: Prentice-Hall, 1969.

Podhoretz, N. My Negro problem—and ours. In B. E. Segal (ed.), *Racial and ethnic relations.* New York: Thomas Y. Crowell, 1966, pp. 239–250.

Price, D. O. Occupational changes among whites and nonwhites, with projections for 1970. In N. D. Glenn and C. M. Bonjean (eds.), *Blacks in the United States.* San Francisco: Chandler, 1969, pp. 55–64.

Proshansky, H., and Newton, P. The nature and meaning of Negro self-identity. In M. Deutsch, I. Katz, and A. Jensen (eds.), *Social class, race, and psychological development.* New York: Holt, 1968, pp. 178–218.

Rainwater, L. Crucible of identity: The Negro lower-class family. In T. Parsons and K. B. Clark (eds.), *The Negro American*. Boston: Houghton Mifflin, 1965, pp. 160–204.

Rainwater, L., and Yancey, W. L. *The Moynihan report and the politics of controversy*. Cambridge, Mass.: M.I.T. Press, 1967.

Rosenthal, R., and Jacobson, L. Self fulfilling prophecies in the classroom: Teachers expectations as unintended determinants of pupils' intellectual competence. In M. Deutsch, I. Katz and A. Jensen (eds.), *Social class, race, and psychological development*. New York: Holt, 1968, pp. 219–253.

Sarbin, T. R., and Allen, V. L. Role theory. In G. Lindzey and E. Aronson (eds.), *Handbook of social psychology*, Vol. I. Reading, Mass.: Addison-Wesley, 1969, pp. 488–567.

Schneider, E. V. *Industrial sociology*. New York: McGraw-Hill, 1957.

Schulz, D. A. Variations in the father role in complete families of the Negro lower class. In N. D. Glenn and C. M. Bonjean (eds.), *Blacks in the United States*. San Francisco: Chandler, 1968, pp. 134–142.

Sheatsley, P. B. White attitudes toward the Negro. In T. Parsons and K. B. Clark (eds.), *The Negro American*. Boston: Houghton Mifflin. 1965, pp. 303–324.

Sherwood, John J., and Nataupsky, M. Predicting the conclusions of Negro–white intelligence research from biographical characteristics of the investigator. *Journal of Personality and Social Psychology*, 1968, 8, 53–58.

Solomon, F., Walker, W. L., O'Connor, G. J., and Fishman, J. R. Civil rights activity and reduction in crime among Negroes. In R. J. Murphy and H. Elinson (eds.), *Problems and prospects of the Negro movement*. Belmont, Calif.: Wadsworth, 1966, pp. 337–354.

Thompson, D. The formation of social attitudes. In B. E. Segal (ed.), *Racial and ethnic relations*. New York: Thomas Y. Crowell, 1966, pp. 97–110.

Toynbee, A. J. *A study of history*, Vol. I. London: Oxford University Press, 1934.

Udy, S. H. Social structure: Social structural analysis. *International encyclopedia of the social sciences*, Vol. 14. New York: Macmillan, 1968, pp. 489–495.

United States Department of Commerce. *The social and economic status of Negroes in the United States, 1970*, BLS Report No. 394, July, 1971.

United States Department of Labor. *The Negroes in the United States: their economic and social situation*, Bulletin No. 1511, June, 1966.

United States Department of Labor. *Manpower report of the president*, March, 1970.

Van den Berghe, P. L. Paternalistic versus competitive race relations: An ideal-type approach. In B. E. Segal (ed.), *Racial and ethnic relations*. New York: Thomas Y. Crowell, 1966, pp. 44–52.

CHAPTER ELEVEN

School Desegregation and Ethnic Attitudes

James A. Green and Harold B. Gerard

INTRODUCTION BY THE EDITORS

Green and Gerard report some preliminary findings from their large-scale and longitudinal study of school desegregation of black, Mexican-American, and Anglo children in six different grades of elementary schools. Pre-measures and post-measures were taken before desegregation and then again one year and three years afterwards. Data about ethnic identity and racial awareness are presented. There are at least two major findings with implications for organizations. First, interracial stereotyping for all races and related differences in scholastic performance became exaggerated both with increments in the age of the children and with desegregation. These researchers hypothesize that these effects may be attributable to the self-fulfilling prophecy of the stereotypic roles that parents and teachers impose on their children. Similarly, several authors in this volume have cautioned against white supervisors fulfilling their own stereotypic perceptions of minorities and their expectations of poorer performance from minority workers.

Second, the data on racial awareness and ethnic identity reveal an increase in choosing to be with one's own group and an enlarged cleavage between the different races. Green and Gerard note the relatively short time period during which their measures were taken and hypothesize that the cleavage would dissipate with more time. It is difficult to determine if this enhanced racial identity and separatism are attributable to the effects of desegregation or to the current trends toward enhancing the esteem for one's own group; nevertheless, foremen and supervisors might be aware of these early effects of desegregation and take steps to assuage, but not aggravate, the tensions and separatism.

The purpose of this chapter is to describe a large-scale longitudinal field study of school desegregation in a medium-sized city in southern California and to present data from one of the measures used in the assessment procedures. Studies of school desegregation and their problems have unique characteristics that can be related to the problems and solutions in integrating organizations on the total social scale. The problems encountered in desegregating school systems are the same or nearly the same as the problems encountered in desegregating any organization. Perhaps the effects are accentuated with children, since children respond more openly to stress. Therefore, by knowing what happens in the classroom, we may be in fact, in an advantageous position relative to studying the process with adults in some social system. Children, because of their naiveté, provide a very fertile ground for such studies. We found that preschool children are aware of racial and ethnic differences and tend to be frank both in their responses to children of other ethnic groups and to psychological instruments designed to measure ethnic attitudes. Adults tend to be much more cautious in expressing their feelings when responding to people and to psychological questionnaires.

What we are saying is that an examination of the process of school desegregation enables us to get an accentuated picture of the stresses, strains, and benefits that might accrue from mixing people from different backgrounds. Eventual integration of American society depends upon what happens in the early years of a person's growth and development. Mixing adults of different racial backgrounds who have heretofore lived separate lives cannot be a completely effective solution. Eventual integration of adult members of society will depend on their early formative experiences. With this long-term perspective, the study of school integration looms as having number one priority.

The depressed social position of blacks, Mexican-Americans, and other minorities in the United States will only be improved through institutional changes, such as school integration. Employment and education, in contrast to housing, are the settings in which changes are taking place. As communities end de jure and de facto segregation, the need for information becomes increasingly vital. We need to know what factors contribute to successful or unsuccessful desegregation and what short-term and long-term effects are to be expected as a consequence.

Most of the testimony considered by the Supreme Court for the 1954 ruling to outlaw segregation consisted of statements made by expert witnesses on both sides of the issue. Little in the way of empirical evidence was presented or available at that time. In 1965 the U.S. Office of Education made a survey, the results of which were published as the Coleman Report (1966), which contains the evidence that was lacking in 1954. Coleman sampled about 650,000 children in over 4,000 elementary and high schools throughout the country. The teachers, principals, and district superintendents participated in the study as well. The original report was followed by one published by the U.S. Commission on Civil Rights (1967), which reported a further analysis of the same data. The main finding that emerges in these two reports is that the greater the proportion of white pupils in a mixed classroom, the higher the achievement of black pupils in that classroom. The Coleman data also reveal that the achievement of both white and black pupils is positively related to the social-class background of the school neighborhood. In the light of this latter finding, the investigators for the U.S. Commission on Civil Rights attempted to determine the influence of racial composition of the school on achievement, holding constant (by statistical means) the quality of educational services available, the academic ability and social background of classmates, and the academic and home background of the teachers. The relationship between racial composition of the school and achievement of minority children reported by Coleman exists even when these other factors are controlled.

What process or processes mediate the effect on a minority child's achievement of being in a classroom in which the majority of the children are white? Is it mediated by teacher attitudes, by changes in self-attitudes or achievement-related attitudes of the minority child? Does the minority child become more competitive? Are there group standards in the white subculture that are different from those in the minority subculture and that become internalized by the minority child? Our study takes an intensive look at a single school district in an attempt to discover mediating mechanisms. Our strategy has been to follow children who have been desegregated through the grades, taking periodic measurement of factors that might reveal what variables account for changes in adjustment and achievement.

The data from the study reported here were collected one year before and again one year after desegregation; the population sample consisted of approximately 1,800 elementary-grade children who were either black, Mexican-American, or Anglo.

THE COMMUNITY OF RIVERSIDE

Historically, the Riverside School District favored the development of neighborhood elementary schools, as most communities do. Because of a high degree of residential segregation in the community and flagrant gerrymandering of attendance areas, this policy fostered the development of three de facto segregated schools containing only black and Mexican-American children. About eleven years ago, the Riverside School District began a program of compensatory education for the three minority schools. This program, however was rejected by a group of black parents, who felt that compensatory education was too slow and would not solve the problems that their children were having in school as effectively as would total and immediate desegregation.

In the summer of 1965, shortly before school was to start, one of the segregated schools was partially destroyed by an arsonist. Faced with the problem of not having enough classrooms for the majority of students in that school, the school board made a tentative decision to bus those children out of the area and into neighboring all-white schools. At an open meeting of the school board in late September, 1965, the members of the board went much further; they committed themselves to developing a plan for complete integration for the entire school district to be implemented the following fall (1966). The decision was made in the face of some vigorous protests from a sizeable segment of the Anglo community.

The Mexican-American parents were not active in the drive to integrate, nor were they generally favorable toward the idea. They tended to view the desegregation program as a threat to the preservation of the Mexican subculture. Currently, however, the Mexican-American community is very involved in the school district, is very vocal regarding school decisions, and is much more aggressive about the needs of members of their own community.

Riverside is a city 75 miles east of Los Angeles, with a population of approximately 140,000 people, 11 percent of whom are Mexican-American and 6 percent black.

TABLE 11-1   *Characteristics of Anglo, Mexican–American, and Black Households in Riverside, California, Summer, 1963*

	Anglo %	Mexican–American %	Black %
Characteristics of Head			
Works as Laborer or Domestic	12.7	45.0	50.0
In Lowest Two Categories of			
Duncan SES Index	17.9	68.4	67.0
Jr. High or Less Education	15.9	61.1	32.7
Foreign Born	4.5	27.7	0.0
Born in Riverside	5.7	39.8	8.8
Born in Southeastern U.S.	12.6	7.4	60.8
Characteristics of Family			
Speak English Only Half the Time or Less	0.0	55.9	0.0
Rental Under $90 Per Month	58.1	94.7	93.3

SOURCE: From a survey conducted in 1963 as part of an epidemiological study of mental retardation. For a more comprehensive report on this study, see Jane Mercer, *Labeling the Mentally Retarded.* Berkeley, Calif.: University of California Press, 1973.

When the Riverside black population is compared with the Anglo population, it is clear that the black wage earners have significantly less formal education, are more likely to have been born in the South, are employed in much lower-level occupations, and live in less expensive dwellings. Mexican-American heads of households have even less formal education than blacks, are more likely to be natives of Riverside or to have been foreign born than either of the other two groups; they also have jobs at a level comparable to that of the blacks and live in less expensive dwellings. In addition to their economic and educational disadvantages, Mexican-American families face additional cultural barriers, best indexed by the fact that almost 56 percent of the families report speaking Spanish at home most of the time. In general, Mexican-Americans in Riverside were found to be more economically disadvantaged than either Anglos or blacks.

DESIGN OF THE STUDY

Our sample includes 712 Anglo, 651 Mexican-American, and 406 black children. Virtually all of the minority children bused into the Anglo schools when the program began are in the sample, plus a group of Anglo children matched for age with the minority children. The children were distributed fairly evenly by grade from kindergarten through grade six.

Pre-measures were taken on the children in the spring of 1966, before the main plan of desegregation was implemented in the Riverside schools. The second set of measurements was taken one year after desegregation (in the spring of 1967); a third set of measurements was completed in the spring and summer of 1969. Additionally, data about the desegregation process were gathered from the child's parents; each parent was interviewed in his home. Demographic information, parents' attitudes toward specific childrearing practices, and their attitudes toward desegregation in particular were collected. We also asked the child's teacher to assess him relative to other children in his class on a number of performance dimensions, and we collected sociometric evaluations in each classroom.

Thus, we have four perspectives on the child: his parents, his teacher, his classmates, and himself as evidenced by his performance on our test battery. In addition, we have each child's scores on a number of standardized achievement tests that are given each year in the California public schools. These test scores provide the main criterion variable regarding the effects of desegregation.

METHODOLOGICAL CONSIDERATIONS

There were certain contaminants over which we had no control. These act to obscure and blunt many of the conclusions which we might hope to draw. We will only mention a few. First, total desegregation did not take place all at once; it happened over a period of three years. Eight percent of the black and Mexican-American children were bused to formerly all-Anglo schools in 1965,

77 percent of the minority children were moved in September, 1966, and the remainder, who were mostly Mexican-American, were bused to receiving schools in 1967. This turns out to be a cloud with a silver lining in one respect, since we are able to make cross-group comparisons between children who were and were not desegregated initially.

Second, because of time pressures to go into the field and collect data on the children, we hired the most available people for interviewers—graduate students, wives of graduate students, and people who had been associated with the schools. We therefore are unable to estimate an important effect, that of the ethnic group of the interviewer on the child's responses to the test battery. Most of our interviewers were white; black and Mexican-Americans were not available as psychometrists for a number of reasons. Some preliminary analysis indicates that this is not as severe a limitation as one might expect. By the time of the summer measurements, we were able to hire a group of minority interviewers.

After desegregation, school principals were given considerable autonomy over hiring and firing of teachers and over the design of curricula. This created considerable diversity of atmosphere and programs within the district. Distinguishing the effects of these changes from desegregation effects is not an easy problem. Our most serious handicap is that we do not have a segregated district against which to compare the effects of desegregation. It was just not feasible to take measurements on some comparable school district. Without another school district, of course, we cannot account for the effects of changes other than desegregation that may have affected the city of Riverside and its children. Many events occurring within, as well as beyond, the boundaries of the city may have had effects that would tend to influence the attitudes and behavior of children in the Riverside schools.

In addition to these general problems which plague the study, many of the individual measures have their own peculiar difficulties. In spite of this, there is sure footing for drawing certain conclusions. In this chapter we present some data from a test which attempts to measure feelings of ethnic identity and racial awareness.

Each child was administered a variety of measures of attributes which we thought would mediate adjustment and achievement in the mixed classroom and which might be affected by either desegregation and/or maturation.

ETHNIC ATTITUDES

Most of the research conducted in the area of racial identification and awareness has been done with preschool children, using black or white dolls or pictures of black or white children as stimuli (Morland, 1958, 1962, 1963; Goodman, 1958; and Clark and Clark, 1947). The findings of these studies provide a relatively consistent picture of the development of racial identity of the minority child.

Clark and Clark (1947) report that black children in racially mixed schools (black and white) tended to identify themselves as being black less frequently than did black children in segregated schools. In both groups, a larger proportion of four-year-olds correctly identified themselves with pictures of their own race than did three-year-olds. Black children were asked to express a preference for a black or white doll in answer to various questions in order to study: (1) the development of the childs' ability to identify race by skin color, (2) his racial preferences, and (3) his acceptance or rejection of his racial identity.

The results show that at age three, 77 percent of the black subjects correctly identified the "colored" and "white" dolls, but by a ratio of two to one they did not choose the black doll as looking like themselves. By age seven, 100 percent of the black children correctly labeled the "race" of the dolls, and 87 percent of them chose the "colored" doll as looking like themselves, but a majority still preferred to play with the white doll and identified it as the "nice" doll. At age five, 78 percent of the children identified the black doll as "bad," while by age seven, only 43 percent chose the black doll as the "bad" doll, but 40 percent refused to express a preference for either doll in response to this question.

Morland's series of studies, which concentrated on regional differences in race awareness of nursery-school children, showed consistently that blacks are less likely than whites to make correct racial self-identifications. Morland also found that black children prefer white children as playmates but not vice versa. When black and white children were divided into categories of high, medium, and low racial recognition ability, a majority in each category preferred whites. For both black and white children, the percentage preferring whites was greater for subjects of high recognition ability.

Goodman attempted to test the hypothesis that separate-but-equal schools cause personality damages to black children. On the basis of certain observational data, she classified the children into categories of high, medium, and low racial awareness and found differences in behavior and self-perception among the three groups. The most interesting differences indicated that blacks who are highly aware are most insecure about their racial status, while whites in the same category are most secure about their racial status. Also, the differences in the medium awareness category suggest that the blacks are more uneasy about the topic of race than the whites. Goodman suggests that peer influences are more important than parental values in determining racial or color awareness and that parents' behavior, rather than their attitudes, shape the child's attitudes. Goodman also found, as did Clark and Clark and Morland, that black and white children become aware of racial differences as early as age three or four, and that within this racial awareness lies an understanding of the values placed on color by the larger society.

Self and ethnic attitudes were chosen as the main focus of this chapter because we suspect, on the basis of previous work reported in the literature, that this attitude will be crucial in determining the overall success of the desegregation experiment, as well as the way in which the individual child fares in the mixed ethnic environment. Changes in interethnic attitudes ought also to be a good indicator of how well or poorly desegregation is going.

THE ETHNIC PICTURES TEST

The child was first shown six pictures of elementary-school-age boys: two Anglo, two black, and two Mexican-American. The interviewer said, "These are pictures of six boys who are just about your age. I know that you don't know any of them, but I want you to play a game and guess what they are like. Which of these boys do you think is the *kindest?*" The interviewer then turned the selected pictures face down and asked the child; "Now which of these boys who are left do you think is the *kindest?*" and so forth until the child had rank-ordered the six pictures. This same procedure was followed for rankings of the pictures as to happiness, strength, speed, and scholastic performance. The entire procedure was then repeated with a set of six pictures of elementary-age girls. Finally the child was shown the picture set corresponding to his own sex and asked to indicate which of the six children was most like him, which of the six he would most like to be, and which he would most like to have as a friend.

RESULTS

Adjective Rankings

The data, which are the sums of the rankings across four faces (two of each sex) representing each ethnic group, are presented in Table 11–2. Each child gave a rank (from 1—first choice to 6—sixth choice) to each picture for each dimension. The ranks across the four pictures were summed to yield a score which describes the child's evaluation of each ethnic group on each of the five dimensions (kind, happy, strong, fast, best grades). Since the scores are based on ranks, they are not independent, since if a child ranks the faces of one ethnic group on a particular dimension, the rankings for the faces of the other two ethnic groups will necessarily be depressed. The rankings between dimensions do not affect each other and are therefore independent.

The data in the table are presented by ethnic group and grade. Grade is used because it gives an indication of age in the desegregated classroom.

Comparing the mean rankings on the kindness dimension, the Anglo pictures were considered kindest by all the children for both pre- and post-desegregation years. Comparing the mean rankings by grade, the significant trends for the 1966 rankings of the Anglo faces are quadratic; the linear trend is non-significant. There is a significant linear trend by grade ($F = 12.54$, $p < .01$), such that as grade increases, the ranking of the Anglo faces becomes more unfavorable. Overall, the ranking of the Anglo faces is more unfavorable after than

TABLE 11-2   *Average of Summed Rankings of Ethnic Group Pictures*[a]

Kindest—Photographs of Black Children

	K	1	2	3	4	5	6	7
Anglos								
1966	16.56	16.42	16.32	16.67	14.90	14.81	13.83	—
1967	—	18.10	17.03	16.61	17.14	14.96	15.74	14.70
Mexican–American								
1966	16.56	17.76	17.62	18.02	16.93	17.35	16.74	—
1967	—	18.05	18.33	18.53	17.50	17.55	17.24	16.93
Blacks								
1966	15.25	15.24	14.90	14.64	15.44	14.60	16.11	—
1967	—	15.18	15.08	15.35	14.69	14.41	15.59	14.52

Kindest—Photographs of Anglo Children

	K	1	2	3	4	5	6	7
Anglos								
1966	9.95	8.85	9.57	9.72	11.02	11.95	11.77	—
1967	—	8.09	8.81	10.35	9.29	11.05	11.35	11.32
Mexican–American								
1966	11.30	10.33	10.04	9.77	9.67	9.13	9.49	—
1967	—	9.83	9.73	10.22	9.52	9.21	9.95	9.51
Blacks								
1966	12.03	12.32	11.95	10.66	11.42	11.14	9.77	—
1967	—	11.98	11.57	11.88	10.72	12.10	10.25	10.95

Kindest—Photographs of Mexican–American Children

	K	1	2	3	4	5	6	7
Anglos								
1966	16.15	16.71	16.14	15.55	15.95	15.23	16.36	—
1967	—	15.80	16.31	15.02	15.56	16.08	14.89	15.98
Mexican–American								
1966	14.75	13.95	14.33	14.26	15.39	15.50	15.76	—
1967	—	14.17	13.92	14.00	14.98	15.46	15.18	15.55
Blacks								
1966	14.70	14.41	15.61	16.73	15.12	16.25	16.11	—
1967	—	14.96	15.33	15.22	16.58	15.47	16.15	16.52

Happiest—Photographs of Black Children

	K	1	2	3	4	5	6	7
Anglos								
1966	15.89	16.28	16.27	16.55	16.15	16.03	16.02	—
1967	—	16.62	17.42	16.50	16.80	15.82	16.27	15.00
Mexican–American								
1966	15.41	16.38	17.12	16.97	17.26	17.43	17.05	—
1967	—	15.65	17.20	16.76	16.91	17.31	16.72	16.89
Blacks								
1966	15.58	15.55	16.01	15.75	16.22	16.28	16.22	—
1967	—	15.35	15.96	16.18	15.95	15.33	15.90	15.52

[a] Each cell entry represents the average sum of rankings given to four pictures of each ethnic group. The smaller the number, the more positive is the evaluation.

TABLE 11–2   (continued)

Happiest—Photographs of Anglo Children

	K	1	2	3	4	5	6	7
Anglos								
1966	11.09	10.34	11.07	11.31	11.55	11.93	11.82	—
1967	—	9.91	9.64	11.77	11.00	11.93	11.57	12.43
Mexican–American								
1966	12.09	11.06	10.70	10.94	10.85	10.29	11.09	—
1967	—	11.20	10.65	11.57	10.98	10.55	11.03	11.34
Blacks								
1966	12.19	11.82	11.98	11.49	11.44	11.65	11.29	—
1967	—	11.75	11.77	11.77	12.13	12.93	11.78	11.21

Happiest—Photographs of Mexican–American Children

	K	1	2	3	4	5	6	7
Anglos								
1966	15.70	15.33	14.72	14.09	14.28	13.96	14.05	—
1967	—	15.45	15.15	13.71	14.20	14.24	14.15	14.56
Mexican–American								
1966	15.10	14.59	14.18	14.07	13.87	14.25	13.84	—
1967	—	15.13	14.22	13.98	14.09	14.21	14.32	13.76
Blacks								
1966	14.22	14.61	14.47	14.75	14.33	14.05	14.48	—
1967	—	15.11	14.33	14.03	13.90	13.95	14.31	15.26

Strongest—Photographs of Black Children

	K	1	2	3	4	5	6	7
Anglos								
1966	15.33	14.51	13.42	12.87	13.28	12.06	12.31	—
1967	—	14.37	13.67	12.50	11.97	11.85	12.00	11.25
Mexican–American								
1966	14.93	14.45	14.22	13.05	12.39	11.37	11.00	—
1967	—	14.89	15.04	14.04	12.29	11.63	11.03	10.42
Blacks								
1966	14.29	14.17	12.84	12.33	11.72	11.77	11.81	—
1967	—	14.71	14.20	13.09	12.11	11.54	11.21	10.91

Strongest—Photographs of Anglo Children

	K	1	2	3	4	5	6	7
Anglos								
1966	12.70	14.55	16.53	16.73	17.10	18.10	17.92	—
1967	—	14.17	15.48	17.56	18.53	18.40	18.06	18.95
Mexican–American								
1966	13.89	14.85	15.37	16.92	17.60	17.78	17.86	—
1967	—	14.28	15.24	16.21	17.72	18.51	18.63	19.06
Blacks								
1966	14.17	15.03	16.63	17.18	17.16	17.28	16.59	—
1697	—	15.05	15.50	16.42	17.18	16.97	17.96	18.08

TABLE 11–2 (continued)

Strongest—Photographs of Mexican–American Children

	K	1	2	3	4	5	6	7
Anglos								
1966	14.65	12.93	12.11	12.39	11.61	11.82	11.75	—
1967	—	13.45	13.11	11.92	11.49	11.85	11.93	11.90
Mexican–American								
1966	13.80	12.90	12.36	12.00	12.00	12.83	13.13	—
1967	—	12.94	11.81	12.66	11.97	11.94	12.33	12.51
Blacks								
1966	13.51	12.79	13.30	12.47	13.11	12.97	13.51	—
1967	—	13.22	12.66	12.48	12.69	13.47	12.81	13.00

Fastest—Photographs of Black Children

	K	1	2	3	4	5	6	7
Anglos								
1966	14.93	15.18	14.01	14.65	13.55	12.76	12.78	—
1967	—	15.70	14.75	13.77	13.97	12.90	13.52	12.28
Mexican–American								
1966	15.40	15.04	14.84	13.54	12.30	11.46	11.25	—
1967	—	15.63	15.36	14.13	13.08	11.64	10.55	9.65
Blacks								
1966	14.48	15.00	13.30	12.73	12.46	11.45	12.74	—
1967	—	13.96	14.46	13.77	12.55	12.14	10.71	12.95

Fastest—Photographs of Anglo Children

	K	1	2	3	4	5	6	7
Anglos								
1966	12.85	12.36	13.03	13.22	14.60	15.50	16.03	—
1967	—	12.19	13.07	13.85	15.26	15.56	15.81	17.05
Mexican–American								
1966	13.06	13.47	13.52	14.27	15.04	15.09	15.37	—
1967	—	12.94	13.40	14.60	14.50	16.10	16.34	18.21
Blacks								
1966	13.51	13.86	14.49	15.22	14.75	16.88	15.44	—
1967	—	14.18	13.83	14.74	15.41	15.47	16.87	16.47

Fastest—Photographs of Mexican–American Children

	K	1	2	3	4	5	6	7
Anglos								
1966	14.90	14.42	15.02	14.11	13.81	13.73	13.17	—
1967	—	14.20	14.61	14.37	12.76	13.52	12.79	12.66
Mexican–American								
1966	14.15	13.57	13.61	14.16	14.63	15.44	15.37	—
1967	—	13.42	13.28	13.65	14.41	14.67	15.10	14.12
Blacks								
1966	14.00	13.11	14.77	14.01	14.77	14.60	13.81	—
1967	—	13.98	13.97	14.29	14.02	14.37	14.40	14.00

TABLE 11–2　(continued)

Best Grades—Photographs of Black Children

	K	1	2	3	4	5	6	7
Anglos								
1966	15.72	15.22	15.51	16.47	15.73	15.89	15.63	—
1967	—	15.96	16.24	15.58	16.77	15.78	16.47	16.10
Mexican–American								
1966	15.61	15.85	16.68	16.27	15.52	16.17	15.80	—
1967	—	16.32	16.68	16.91	16.44	16.83	16.83	17.08
Blacks								
1966	15.00	14.61	14.80	14.69	15.61	15.00	15.44	—
1967	—	14.81	14.15	14.74	15.39	15.18	15.40	15.56

Best Grades—Photographs of Anglo Children

	K	1	2	3	4	5	6	7
Anglos								
1966	11.50	10.77	10.90	10.46	10.62	10.42	10.11	—
1967	—	10.39	10.30	11.31	9.66	9.90	9.30	8.93
Mexican–American								
1966	12.70	12.78	11.74	11.54	11.30	9.90	9.70	—
1967	—	11.78	11.43	11.92	10.70	10.00	9.83	8.53
Blacks								
1966	12.20	13.05	13.15	12.07	11.66	11.22	10.66	—
1967	—	13.03	13.13	12.75	11.44	11.85	10.43	11.04

Best Grades—Photographs of Mexican–American Children

	K	1	2	3	4	5	6	7
Anglos								
1966	15.45	15.99	15.63	15.05	15.63	15.68	16.25	—
1967	—	15.63	16.02	15.41	15.56	16.31	16.22	16.95
Mexican–American								
1966	14.29	13.42	13.56	14.18	15.08	15.89	16.47	—
1967	—	13.89	13.95	13.67	14.85	15.13	15.32	16.38
Blacks								
1966	14.79	14.29	14.42	15.22	14.70	15.77	15.70	—
1967	—	14.28	14.76	14.50	15.16	15.33	16.15	15.39

before desegregation, the post-desegregation unfavorableness increasing with age (grade).

A different pattern emerges for the kindest ranking of the black pictures. Both the linear and quadratic trends are significant in 1966; only the linear trend is significant in 1967. The linear trends for both years account for almost 90 percent of the variance. Generally, the rankings of the black pictures increase in favorability as grade increases. In 1967, black faces are perceived as kinder with increasing grade, a trend which is also present in 1966 but which is not quite as strong.

For the Mexican-American faces, the statistically significant trend for grade is linear for both years, with the rankings becoming more unfavorable as grade increases, except for second and fifth graders, who saw an increase. The Mexican-American pictures are ranked less kind as grade increases. The data seem to indicate that black and Mexican-American children think that being white is good and white is kind; therefore the Anglo is perceived as having a more valuable quality than being black or being Mexican-American.

The linear trend for both years is steeper for the black faces than it is for the Mexican-American faces. It is difficult to say what this means, since the rankings are correlated, and we do not know whether the trend of age is due to a downgrading of whites or an upgrading of blacks.

The rankings of the pictures on the dimension of "happiest" yield many of the same patterns as reported on "kindest," although the grade and ethnic differences are not as striking. The conceptual difference between the two is that "kind" is an interpersonal trait whereas "happy" is not. Specifically, the Anglo faces are ranked "happiest" by all the subject children for both years. The linear trend is not significant for 1967, but the quadratic trend is. The quadratic trend means that a direct relationship between favorability of attitude and grade is not evident; instead some grades increase in favorability (see Table 11–2). For 1966, the significant trend is linear with the kindergarten children showing more favorable rankings and the sixth-grade children showing the most unfavorable rankings. Rankings of the black faces for "happiest" show a statistically significant linear trend for 1966 but not for 1967. The trend is such that the older children rank the black faces as less happy than the younger children. These results are different from the results for the "kindest" rankings of the black faces. The "kindest" rankings show a significant linear trend for both years, whereas the results of the "happiest" rankings for the black faces show a significant linear trend only for 1966.

The rankings of the Mexican-American faces for "happiest" show a significant linear trend for both 1966 and 1967. It is interesting to note that the stereotypic picture of the "happy Mexican-American" is not evident in these data. One would assume that the Mexican-American faces might be ranked "happier" than the Anglo or black faces if certain stereotypes are maintained among the children. However, the data show that the above is not correct, because the Anglos are ranked "happiest," while the Mexican-Americans are ranked next happiest and the blacks ranked least happy.

Analyzing the results by taking the percentage of subjects whose first choice was either an Anglo, black, or Mexican-American face, we find the percentage who pick Anglos as "happiest" decreases sharply from 1966 to 1967 across all subjects as compared with change in percentage of those who pick Anglos on the "kindest" dimension. Anglos are perceived as less happy (an intrapersonal trait) after a year of desegregation, but there is no change in their being perceived as kinder after a year. That perception remains the same.

The rankings of the children's faces on the dimension of "strongest" show some of the clearest trends. The faces of the blacks are perceived as "strongest," and this perception increases linearly with age. The Anglo faces, on the other hand, are perceived as least strong, and this tendency increases with grade. The Mexican-American pictures are given a ranking that falls somewhere in between the Anglo and black rankings. In all cases, for all pictures, the linear trend for grade is significant.

Obviously, being strong has its advantages in grade school. It implies that a child could use this strength to manipulate or wield power over peers. From other data that we have, it would seem that minority children are able to use their strength as a source of power. It is reasonable to assume that minority children put in a desegregated situation would feel anxious and uncomfortable in that new situation and would use their strength to express whatever frustrations they may be feeling.

For the rankings of the "fastest" dimension, the data reveal almost the same pattern as they do for the "strongest"; that is, black pictures tend to be ranked as "fastest," and these rankings tend to become more extreme and disparate as grade increases. The linear trend is the significant one for the black faces for 1966 and 1967, this trend accounting for almost 90 percent of the variance. The statistical linearity holds for the Anglos, but instead of the rankings increasing in favorability, they decrease. The linear trend is not significant for the Mexican-American faces.

The last ranking that the subject children completed was on a dimension of "best grades." The divergence of the rankings of the faces between Anglos, Mexican-Americans, and blacks is very striking. The Anglos are ranked as receiving best grades by all sample children over grade and time. The rankings given to the Anglo faces is best described as a linear trend across grade; the linearity accounts for almost all of the variance. The rankings of the Mexican-American faces on "best grades" becomes less favorable as grade increases for both 1966 and 1967. This trend is linear and is statistically significant; that is, most of the variance is accounted for by the linear trend. There is no linearity for the rankings of the black faces on "best grades." It is interesting to see the strong trend by grade for Anglos in the favorable direction and for Mexican-Americans in the unfavorable direction. If the rankings along this dimension are somewhat indicative of what is really happening in desegregated situations, the Anglos are achieving and getting better grades, whereas the minority children are not faring as well academically.

Ethnic Differences

Looking at the results of "kindest" first from Table 11–3, it shows that the Anglo pictures, in comparison with the black and Mexican-American pictures, are rated "kindest" by all ethnic groups, with the most favorable rankings manifested by the Mexican-American subjects. There is little or no significant change of these rankings as a function of desegregation. The differences among the rankings of the pictures on the "happiest" dimension exhibit very much the same pattern. However, there is one exception: the subjects give more favorable rankings to the Anglo faces on the dimension of "kindest" than they do on "happiest."

The minority faces are ranked "stronger" than the Anglo faces. This is the

TABLE 11–3 *Average of Summed Rankings of Ethnic Group Pictures*[a]

Kindest

	Anglo Pictures		Mexican–American Pictures		Black Pictures	
	1966	1967	1966	1967	1966	1967
Anglo subjects	9.87	9.87	16.06	15.76	15.74	16.39
Mexican–American subjects	9.74	9.74	14.69	14.03	17.29	17.83
Black subjects	11.48	11.48	15.31	15.59	15.12	15.01

Strongest

	Anglo Pictures		Mexican–American Pictures		Black Pictures	
	1966	1967	1966	1967	1966	1967
Anglo subjects	11.16	11.01	14.66	14.62	16.15	16.44
Mexican–American subjects	10.98	11.03	14.30	14.37	16.70	16.75
Black subjects	11.75	11.94	14.41	15.20	15.83	15.78

Happiest

	Anglo Pictures		Mexican–American Pictures		Black Pictures	
	1966	1967	1966	1967	1966	1967
Anglo subjects	15.92	17.08	12.52	12.34	13.55	12.66
Mexican–American subjects	16.04	16.79	12.68	12.30	13.25	13.09
Black subjects	15.99	16.39	12.99	12.87	12.99	12.97

Fastest

	Anglo Pictures		Mexican–American Pictures		Black Pictures	
	1966	1967	1966	1967	1966	1967
Anglo subjects	13.67	14.49	14.18	13.68	14.13	13.95
Mexican–American subjects	14.07	14.82	14.27	14.03	13.63	13.26
Black subjects	14.53	14.92	13.96	14.13	13.49	13.26

Best Grades

	Anglo Pictures		Mexican–American Pictures		Black Pictures	
	1966	1967	1966	1967	1966	1967
Anglo subjects	10.67	10.01	15.65	16.01	15.65	16.13
Mexican–American subjects	11.55	10.81	14.47	14.57	15.96	16.69
Black subjects	12.28	12.27	14.75	14.95	14.92	14.86

[a] By year, ethnic group of child, ethnic group of picture, and dimension.

most significant difference on the dimension of "strongest." This difference does not appear on the dimension of "fastest."

The Anglos are overchosen in terms of "best grades" and the Anglos overchoose themselves in comparison with the Mexican-American and black subjects' self-choices. The trend of each ethnic group to overchoose themselves on the "best grades" dimension is obvious from the table of means.

In sum, the Anglo pictures are ranked most favorably on the dimensions of "kindest," "happiest," and "best grades." There is little or no change on the dimensions of "kindest" or "happiest" in the rankings of the Anglo pictures after one year of desegregation, but the rankings of the Anglo faces on "best grades" becomes more favorable. The minority faces are rated most favorably on the dimensions of "strongest" and "fastest." What is striking about these results are the clear age trends, unaffected by a year of desegregation. For instance, the rankings of the Anglo pictures on the dimension of "best grades" are clear in this respect. Also, the rankings of the black pictures on the dimension of "strongest" become more favorable over age and show no difference over time.

Overall, the data for the adjective rankings indicate that certain stereotypes (i.e., ranking of Anglo faces are receiving best grades and black faces as strongest and fastest) become more extreme with increasing age, the increase being more marked for the minority children. The children are responding to the content of the questions and not to the form of the questions. Also, they do not seem to be responding in terms of experimenter demands or any variables irrelevant to the questions being asked. On the contrary, it seems that the children are discriminating quite clearly along the five dimensions just discussed.

"Most Like You," "Most Like to Be," and "Most Like for a Friend"

The pre-desegregation data for "most like me" are comparable to those reported by Clark and Clark (1947).

TABLE 11–4   *Ethnic Pictures, 1966–1967 Data*

	MOST LIKE ME		MOST LIKE TO BE		MOST LIKE FOR A FRIEND	
	Prop.[a] 1966	Prop. 1967	Prop. 1966	Prop. 1967	Prop. 1966	Prop. 1967
Anglo Male Subjects						
Anglo Pictures	.82	.82	.79	.73	.55	.61
Mexican–American Pictures	.11	.11	.15	.17	.23	.19
Black Pictures	.07	.08	.05	.10	.21	.20
Anglo Female Subjects						
Anglo Pictures	.82	.75	.68	.66	.44	.56
Mexican–American Pictures	.10	.14	.19	.25	.30	.28
Black Pictures	.09	.10	.14	.10	.26	.16
Mexican–American Male Subjects						
Anglo Pictures	.44	.37	.55	.54	.46	.48
Mexican–American Pictures	.51	.57	.43	.42	.34	.37
Black Pictures	.05	.05	.02	.04	.20	.15
Mexican–American Female Subjects						
Anglo Pictures	.49	.39	.64	.58	.57	.50
Mexican–American Pictures	.46	.56	.31	.36	.29	.37
Black Pictures	.04	.04	.05	.07	.14	.13
Black Male Subjects						
Anglo Pictures	.29	.24	.51	.39	.48	.42
Mexican–American Pictures	.13	.17	.23	.32	.23	.22
Black Pictures	.59	.58	.26	.29	.23	.35
Black Female Subjects						
Anglo Pictures	.24	.22	.42	.37	.41	.32
Mexican–American Pictures	.23	.23	.19	.24	.28	.30
Black Pictures	.53	.55	.39	.40	.31	.38

[a] Proportion of subjects picking pictures.

Approximately 82 percent of the Anglo children picked Anglo pictures as being "most like me"; approximately 48 percent of the Mexican-American children picked Mexican-American faces; and approximately 56 percent of the black children picked black faces. Thus, the data show that the Anglo children used ethnic group membership to classify themselves to a much greater extent than did the minority children. This same general trend is repeated for 1967 data, one year after desegregation (the exception is that Mexican-Americans increase from 48 percent to 56 percent in their choice of the Mexican-American faces as being most like them).

TABLE 11–5 *Proportion of Children by Ethnic Group and Grade Choosing a Picture of Someone in Their Own Ethnic Group as "Most Like Me"*

Grade	Anglo	Black	Mexican–American
K	72 (.85)	26 (.58)	29 (.36)
1	116 (.88)	45 (.63)	43 (.42)
2	68 (.93)	36 (.77)	41 (.46)
3	74 (.84)	29 (.67)	44 (.54)
4	75 (.81)	31 (.72)	44 (.58)
5	48 (.76)	21 (.70)	65 (.70)
6	45 (.58)	17 (.77)	31 (.66)
	498	205	297

Within both the 1966 and 1967 data for the minority children, we found that there were fewer cross-group choices with increasing age; that is, the older the child, the more likely will he choose a picture of his own ethnic group as being "most like me." The reverse, however, seems to be true for Anglo children. This suggests that for the minority child, the older he becomes, the more likely he is to use ethnicity as a basis for identifying himself. This effect may be due to the increasing clarity of his own status as a minority group member, but that this effect is in the opposite direction for the Anglo children seems a bit puzzling. It may indicate that ethnicity becomes less of a basis for classification for the Anglo child as he grows older since, for him, there is no growing awareness of any sort of unique racial identity. The world is becoming just as complex for him as it is for the minority child, but it seems that he begins to use other cues (e.g., in this limiting instance—shape of head, smile or frown, clothing, etc.) more often than the minority child as a basis of classification.

In general, it may be that people tend to be aware of features of others that they themselves possess uniquely. Thus, redheads tend to be much more attentive to hair color in others, very short or very tall people attentive to height. Any feature that tends to mark a person as somehow different may become a salient basis for classifying himself and others. Recent work by Freedman and Doob (1968) and Goffman (1963) indicates that this is the case. The explanation, therefore, for increasing tendency to use race as a classification may reflect the growing awareness of the fact that the minority child sees himself as different from the population at large. The data for the Anglo children, following the same argument, reflect a desensitization to race as a classification since, as they grow older, they find that they look like most of the rest of the population. There are many other plausible interpretations for the interaction between age and ethnicity on self-identification, but the one suggested here seems like the most parsimonious. It's easy to find other explanations for the age trend for the minority children, but it's hard to interpret those trends as well as the trend for the Anglo children by invoking a single principle, as has been done. Where the child isn't using ethnicity as a basis for classification, he may be saying that the child has a red sweater like mine or big ears like me.

There are several other trends in the data that we would like to mention. First of all, the questions concerned with self-attribution (most like me, most like to be) reveal a clearcut status hierarchy. That is, the largest percentage of Anglo children pick Anglo pictures, the males more than the females. There are relatively few outgroup choices. A fairly large proportion of Mexican-American subjects, on the other hand, choose out. However, their outgroup choices are almost exclusively limited to the pictures of the Anglo children. An extremely small percentage of Mexican-American subjects choose black pictures. The blacks, when choosing out, pick Anglo as well as Mexican-American pictures. This differential pattern of choices between the ethnic groups seems to demonstrate a status hierarchy, with the Anglos on top and the blacks on the bottom.

An interesting pattern emerges with the choices of the black males. This group, more than the females, picks Anglo pictures in response to the first two questions; however, the proportion of black males choosing Anglo pictures decreases after one year of desegregation. These results seem to indicate that the black males are upwardly mobile before desegregation. After desegregation, they become less so and are less likely to choose an Anglo face; they thus appear to be evaluating Anglo children less positively. This may, in part, be due to negative experiences with Anglos.

The blacks, as well as the Mexican-Americans, choose Anglo faces less often on all three questions one year after desegregation. (The only exception to this is the Mexican-American males, who increase their choice of Anglo faces from 46 percent to 48 percent when asked, "Who would you most like for a friend?") In general, both minority groups tend to pick more faces of their own ethnic group one year after desegregation. This trend is evident on all three questions.

It would seem from these results that the three groups, Anglos, blacks, and Mexican-Americans, tend to separate themselves within the mixed classroom. This pattern is abundantly evident in the sociometric data, where we find actual choices of friends to occur along ethnic lines. It would seem that desegregation initially serves the function of separating the three ethnic groups.

IMPLICATIONS

In this chapter we have reported the results of two kinds of measures taken from the ethnic pictures. The first group of data falls under the heading of racial attitudes and reveals some very clearcut trends. The second group of data deals with racial awareness and racial identity.

Racial attitudes were assessed by having children rank the ethnic pictures along five dimensions: kindest, happiest, strongest, fastest, and best grades. The main findings are as follows: the Anglos are rated kindest of all; however, as the children grow older, the Anglos are ranked as less kind. This trend also occurs with the rankings of the faces along the dimension of happiest, although it is not as striking. The minorities, on the other hand, are rated stronger and faster than the Anglos, and this difference increases with age. The Anglos are perceived as getting the best grades before desegregation and this perception increases with age and with year of desegregation. It is obvious from these data that stereotypes become more exaggerated with age and also that time in a desegregated situation has an effect on perception of scholastic performance of Anglos. One reason these stereotypes increase may be due to the roles that parents and teachers force on children. The self-fulfilling prophecy may be working if parents and teachers reward minority children for being strong and fast and white children for achieving scholastically and for being kind.

Three questions were asked of the children, having to do with racial identity and awareness. They were shown the pictures again and asked, "Which child is most like you?"; "Which child would you most like to be?"; and "Which child would you most like for a friend?". For "most like me" 80 percent of the Anglos picked themselves in response to that question, whereas only 50 percent of the minorities pick a face of their own ethnic group. The data also indicated that Mexican-Americans will pick an Anglo if they are picking out, whereas blacks will pick both Anglo and Mexican-Americans if they are picking outside of their own ethnic group. The older Anglos seem to "pick out" more, and the older minorities seem to pick "in" more. It also appears that the minority children, as a function of desegregation, pick more faces from their own ethnic group in response to the three questions.

The data on identity and awareness seem to indicate a tightening and a cleavage between the ethnic groups into three distinct groupings within the desegregated school system. If the groups were to continue this way, they could be more distinct and separate, and little or no interaction between them would be a result. On the other hand, they could begin coalescing at some point, and the children would begin to interact with each other. At this point, the benefits of interacting with children from other ethnic groups would be evident. This chapter refers to change that has occurred after one year of desegregation. It is impossible to say whether the linear effect will persist or, after the encapsulation reaches some critical point, a widening will occur.

This initial encapsulation of the groups could be highly beneficial. It is more than likely that this encapsulation could lead to group cohesiveness among the minority groups and that this cohesiveness could then serve to promote certain salutory effects. For instance, Guttentag (1970) points out that cohesiveness can lead to more power for members of the group, greater learning for individual members, and more freedom in expressing a diversity of behaviors. Pettigrew (1969), on the other hand, feels that the movement toward ethnic cohesiveness may not be beneficial. For him, separateness has primarily negative consequences. He feels that the ultimate goal of this society is integration at *all* levels—housing, education, religion, employment, etc. One of the most important consequences of separateness is that it prevents each group from learning which set of beliefs and values it has in common. Secondly, isolation leads to the development of real differences in beliefs and values.

Whether increased interaction or increased separateness is the result of a desegregated system is largely predicated on the resiliency of that system or organization. Any system, whether industrial or school, needs to have built into it a certain amount of flexibility. Besides the changes that the organization makes before desegregation, it should also be prepared to make quick and necessary changes after desegregation. The organizational administrators must have fairly realistic expectations about the changes that will take place and, most importantly, realistic expectations about the *rate* of change.

Any change to a system has unanticipated consequences. These may take longer than expected. In the case of the Riverside school district, the decision to desegregate resulted from pressure by a group of minority parents and a fairly liberal school board. The desegregation experiment could not have been initiated had not the decision to change been made with unity, certainty, and a willingness to tolerate and deal effectively with conflict.

Directly analogous to this situation is the one for industrial organizations. It would be advisable to have people in positions of authority able to understand and deal with the rising conflicts. As the teacher in the schoolroom can subtly and perhaps unintentionally influence the interactions that children from different ethnic groups have, so the foreman or supervisor can assuage or aggravate the tensions arising from industrial desegregation.

There is a tendency for minority members to separate into their own ethnic groups and to develop a stronger sense of ethnic identity in the initial stages of desegregation. The cause of the increased ethnic and consequent self awareness is very difficult to pinpoint. It could be the effect of desegregation, or it could be the result of current trends among minority groups toward increased group esteem and militancy. Desegregation is the catalyst of change, and the schoolroom is the outside world in microcosm.

REFERENCES

Clark, K. B., and Clark, Mamie P. Racial identification and preference in Negro children. In T. M. Newcomb and E. L. Hartley (eds.), *Readings in social psychology*. New York: Holt, 1947, pp. 169–178.

Coleman, J. S., et al. *Equality of educational opportunity*. Washington, D.C.: U.S. Government Printing Office, 1966.

Deutsch, M., and Collins, Mary E. *Interracial housing: A psychological evaluation of a social experiment*. Minneapolis: University of Minnesota Press, 1951.

Freedman, J. L., and Doob, A. *Deviancy: The psychology of being different*. New York: Academic Press, 1968.

Goffman, Erving. *Stigma.* Englewood Cliffs, N.J.: Prentice-Hall, 1963.

Goodman, M. E. *Race awareness in young children.* Reading, Mass.: Addison–Wesley, 1952; New York: Collier, 1964.

Guttentag, M. Group cohesiveness, ethnic organization, and poverty. *Journal of Social Issues,* 1970, *26,* 105–132.

Morland, J. K. Racial recognition by nursery school children in Lynchburg, Virginia. *Social Forces,* 1958, *37,* 132–137.

Morland, J. K. Racial acceptance and preference of nursery school children in a southern city. *Merrill Palmer Quarterly,* 1962, *8,* 271–280.

Pettigrew, T. Racially separated or together? *Journal of Social Issues, 25,* 43–69.

U.S. Commission on Civil Rights. *Racial isolation in the public schools,* Vol. 1. Washington, D.C.: U.S. Government Printing Office, 1967.

Weinberg, M. *Integrated Education.* Toronto: Glencoe Press, 1968.

Yarrow, Marian Radke, Campbell, J. D., and Yarrow, L. F. Interpersonal dynamics in racial integration. In Eleanor E. Maccoby, T. M. Newcomb, and E. L. Hartley (eds.), *Readings in social psychology.* New York: Holt, 1958, pp. 623–636.

CHAPTER TWELVE

Laboratory Research and the Organization: Generalizing from Lab to Life

Howard L. Fromkin and Thomas M. Ostrom

INTRODUCTION BY THE EDITORS

Fromkin and Ostrom note the glaring absence of research on race relations within organizations and, in particular, research studies on the process of integrating organizations. In contrast, there is a tremendous volume of laboratory studies on race relations. Yet, when attempts are made to apply laboratory research data to decision making, it is frequently accompanied by apprehension or rejected entirely. While present day experimentation within integrating organizations is of prime importance, it is clear that such data are currently unavailable and many considerations hinder its rapid accumulation. This chapter provides a perspective which helps bridge the gap between laboratory-derived findings and problems of integration in organizations. The unique role of laboratory experimentation is discussed in relation to its yield of useful data on organizational behavior. A perspective is provided which aids in generalizing laboratory findings to organization settings. The major feature is the degree of

The authors gratefully acknowledge the comments of Donald C. King on an earlier draft of this paper, which was written while the authors were supported by a grant from the Krannert Graduate School of Industrial Administration and The Free Press to Fromkin and an NSF grant (GN534.1) from the Office of Science Information Service to Ostrom.

overlap between the critical elements that influence behavior in laboratory set-tings and those present in the particular applied setting. The identification of critical elements, which are similarities and differences between the deter-minants of behavior in any two environments, is the foundation of the perspec-tive. The focus is on those variables which determine behavior in one setting and which are absent from the other setting. Fromkin and Ostrom provide a number of examples of how the concept may be used. We encourage you to read through the latter section of the chapter for some generalizations from laboratory research which have implications for integrating the organization.

One of the major purposes of the present volume is to examine social psycho-logical research on race as it relates to problems of integrating organizations. The usefulness of such research is, unfortunately, limited, for as Katz (1970, p. 71) suggests, "Until now, most social psychological research on race has been narrowly concerned with the study of verbal prejudice." Verbal prejudice plays only one part in the complex of organizational problems that require at-tention. The marked extent to which social action research on integration has been neglected is further revealed in a recent review of the literature on race and ethnic relations by Harding, Proshansky, Kutner, and Chein (1969).

In spite of this indigent literature on race relations in organizations, many social scientists and administrators exhibit extraordinary reluctance to pursue the alternative approach of drawing upon basic laboratory research. The re-search may not be specific to race or organizations, yet, knowledge has accumu-lated at this level for such relevant phenomena as social influence processes (e.g., persuasion and attitude change); status differences; cooperation and con-flict; leadership; and other group processes. For Lewin (1945) and others (cf. Cartwright and Zander, 1968, pp. 37–41), problems of race relations are best understood as an example of more basic phenomena such as the effect of group status on group living and so forth.

When attempted, application of laboratory findings to organizational problems are frequently accompanied by apprehensive statements about the relevance of such research. A more extreme position is to reject laboratory-derived results entirely as a legitimate empirical base for knowledge in the social sciences. Recently, a number of critical articles have raised questions about the applicability of laboratory findings for the solution of practical problems. The questions receive encouragement from several instances in which the results of laboratory studies failed to predict how people behave in specific applied situations such as monitoring radar displays (e.g., Kibler, 1965), space travel (e.g., Simons, 1964; Chapanis, 1967), and education (e.g., Mackie and Chris-tensen, 1967; Elliott, 1960). In addition, the identification of a number of "artifacts" associated with laboratory experiments has provided support for the charge that the laboratory method is "artificial" and has sometimes been mis-taken as armor for alternative research methods (cf. Argyris, 1969).

While it is certain that direct experimentation with integrating organizations is of paramount importance in arriving at solutions, it is equally clear that such data are currently unavailable and that a multitude of practical considerations hinder their rapid accumulation. The absence of field experimental data in combination with recent invidious rejections of laboratory data constitute a practical dilemma to the administrator, who, therefore, is unable to profit from the rich resources of social science. The present chapter proposes a perspective that helps bridge the gap between the data of laboratory experiments and the problems faced by organizations, with special emphasis on integration. It is based on the presumption that laboratory data have considerable value for understanding and predicting behavior in the organization but that certain "cautions" are in order when attempting to apply the results of laboratory research. In lieu of the customary general warnings about the inapplicability of laboratory research, warnings that do not afford the administrator an avenue to use available data, this approach focuses on some bases for judgmental processes which render laboratory findings serviceable in organizational settings. In sum, the following perspective provides a structure for the bridge by (a) separating the specious from the valid criticisms of laboratory research, and (b) specifying cautionary guidelines that should be followed when moving from laboratory data to any given domain of application.

LABORATORY EXPERIMENTATION

The aim of laboratory research is to identify stimulus-response relationships. In general, the experimenter casts his expectations in the form of a stimulus–response hypothesis. For example, high-competent black newcomers are more acceptable to white co-workers than low-competent black newcomers (e.g., Fromkin, Klimoski, and Flanagan, 1971). The stimulus side of the postulated relationship, i.e., competency of the black newcomer, becomes the variable to be manipulated, i.e., the "treatment" variable, or the "independent" variable. The investigator decides how to vary competency so that high-competent black newcomers will be introduced to some groups and low-competent black newcomers to others. The manipulated variable, perceived competency of the black newcomer, is but one of the stimuli that determine subjects' reactions to the newcomer. At the same time, the researcher decides which variables to hold constant across the high-competent and low-competent groups, factors such as the duration, intimacy, and quality of interracial contact.

The response side of the postulated relationship is the variable to be measured, or the dependent variable of the experiment. The perceived acceptability as co-worker is only one of the response domains which may be measured. The term "variable" is well chosen because a persons' responses may vary according to the different kinds of social and organizational changes he encounters.

Although these defining features of laboratory experimentation are well known, it will be helpful to digress for a moment to emphasize the characteristics that are relevant to the present analysis. All laboratory experiments involve the manipulation and control of stimulus conditions. A research site is selected so that the experimenter can actively intervene in the lives of his subjects. This permits him to assign randomly a level of the independent variable to each subject. The control feature of the research site refers to the ability of the experimenter to hold constant over all groups any other stimulus conditions that effect the behavior under observation. This combination of manipulation and control of stimulus conditions permits a more precise identification of causality in explaining relationships.

These characteristics of laboratory experimentation do not involve designation of any particular setting, but instead refer to "situations" where systematic variation and precise measurement of variables are possible. Thus, the laboratory component of the above phrase does not imply any restriction to environments that contain particular equipment configurations (e.g., microphones and tape recorders, etc.), subject populations (college sophomores), or awareness of being a "subject," but can include a diversity of locations, such as industrial organizations (e.g., Morse and Reiner, 1956; Coch and French, 1948), paint departments (e.g., Brock, 1965), and university dormitories (e.g., Siegel and Siegel, 1957).

The term "laboratory experiment" has two components that must be clearly distinguished. The variation and control requirements, i.e., the "experimentation" component, refer to a *research strategy* that espouses the intentional variation of stimulus conditions believed to determine the occurrence of an event (as contrasted with the passive observation of events *in situ*). The "laboratory" component refers solely to the *research setting*. This is not necessarily determined by the research strategy, and it should be considered independent of the experimentation component. Consequently, criticisms of laboratory experimentation that are traceable to characteristics of the research setting do not vitiate the valuable contributions of experimental strategies to theory and administrative practice. For purposes of generalization, these two components have quite different implications.

The Experiments' Strength

The greatest advantage in using experimental research as an empirical base from which to generalize is the confidence one can place in the validity of experimentally verified relationships. For the administrator concerned with organizational change, it is preferable to base such decisions on data which can pinpoint the specific stimulus conditions that are responsible for a relationship. Paraphrasing Kurt Lewin, one cannot be confident in the validity of a relationship until it can be shown that actual changes of the stimulus lead to the predicted changes in the response. Availability of only correlational data, as is obtained in most descriptive and survey research, permits a greater variety of alternative explanations to stand. The entire class of explanations appealing to individual differences in age, personality, sex, mood, etc., are eliminated from consideration when subjects are randomly assigned to different levels of the independent variable.

An issue of vital relevance to integrating the organization is the validity of the contact hypothesis. This is the hypothesis that contact between members of different races, i.e., the opportunity to interact and communicate, is likely to bring about a reduction in prejudice. Amir (1969) reviews a number of studies that show amount of interracial contact to be positively related to favorable interracial attitudes. These field studies and their correlational data do not answer the causal question of whether interracial contact produces a reduction in prejudice. Such data are equally supportive of the conclusion that less-prejudiced individuals engage in more interracial contact. The discovery of a correlational relationship between two variables, X and Y, does not guarantee either that X causes Y or that Y causes X. A more distressing possibility is that contact does not cause more favorable attitudes nor do favorable attitudes cause increases in contact. Instead, some third variable may cause both increased contact and more favorable interracial attitudes. For example, it may be that individual differences in the degree of interpersonal "sociability" (cf. Williams, 1964) mediate the relationship. Persons who are highly sociable are likely to seek a wider variety of social activities that may, in turn, result in increased interpersonal contacts, including members of different races. At the same time, persons who are highly sociable are most likely to "express" interpersonal attitudes such as unprejudiced beliefs when such expression maintains or increases social interaction and social rewards.

An experimental approach to the contact hypothesis would circumvent these interpretive difficulties (cf. Cook, 1969). The experimenter would manipulate the contact variable by exposing some groups to high frequencies of interracial contact and other groups to low contact. Such systematic variation of frequency of contact would ensure that the stimuli presented to the several groups are similar in all other respects, differing only along dimensions associated with brief versus lengthy contact. By assigning subjects in a random manner to the different treatment groups, one is assured that such subject differences as initial attitudes or dispositional sociability are not confounded with the contact variable. With this approach, obtaining a positive relationship between contact and attitude would allow one to conclude confidently that contact causes a reduction in prejudice. The experimental approach does not deny the importance of such dispositional antecedents; in fact, it may be quite important to include them as factors in the experimental design. For example, the direction of initial attitudes (positive or negative) has been shown to affect the contact relationship: initially positive interracial attitudes tend to become more favorable and initially negative attitudes tend to become more unfavorable as a result of contact (cf. Deutsch and Collins, 1951; Sapir, 1951).

The above considerations lead to the conclusions that laboratory experiments provide the best available empirical basis from which to assert the validity of a causal relationship. One can usually be confident that a literal replication of an experiment would produce substantially the same findings. What such research, or any research for that matter, does not tell us is whether the observed relationship would hold under all other circumstances. Nor is it immediately informative as to which conditions strengthen, weaken, or reverse the relationship. It becomes an important activity, once a causal relationship is reliably obtained, to use experimental methods in determining the limiting conditions that bound the relationship.

The question of whether or not causal conclusions can be drawn is not the sole issue involved in the generalization problem. But it is as central to the problem of practical application as it is to theory construction. Nonetheless, asserting the superiority of laboratory experimentation over field surveys on these grounds does not imply it is superior on all grounds (cf. McGuire, 1969).

The Experiment's Limitations

Many of the variables that decision makers, along with all others interested in applications of social science findings to society, are concerned with cannot be studied using laboratory experimental procedures. A variety of nonexperimental procedures have been examined by Campbell and Stanley (1963) for use in these circumstances. Quasi-experimental designs can be found which maximize the ability of the researcher to draw causal inferences on the basis of the data they produce.

One class of problems that cannot be studied using manipulation techniques are those variables which are impossible to manipulate by any human agency. One cannot study peoples reaction to earthquake disasters, to erupting volcanos, to tornadoes and typhoons in an experimental fashion. But just as astronomers approach their discipline in a passive, nonmanipulative fashion, so can the social scientist examine such natural events and profit thereby. Unfortunately, whereas the number of variables which astronomers need to consider is relatively small, the social scientist is faced with a multitude of interrelationships when examining natural events in the human area. There also exists at the individual level a variety of variables for which the experimenter finds it impossible to manipulate experimentally. Sex, race, physical features, and the genetic basis of intelligence are all outside the realm that experimenters can control. So if we are to acquire any systematic knowledge of the effects of these variables on human behavior, we must do so employing nonexperimental designs.

Practicality places a second limitation on kinds of variables the experimenters can employ experimental manipulations on. While it may be technically feasible to examine leadership hierarchies over a variety of different organizations, the expense in human time, money, and effort to meet all the requirements of the manipulation experiment would be so massive that it becomes absolutely impractical. If one wished to study the contact hypothesis over periods of time extending up to four years, one could introduce such a manipulation into a school system or industrial organization, but once again practical matters would make this very difficult and very expensive.

The use of the manipulation experiment is further limited by ethical and moral concerns. One cannot subject human subjects to manipulations that would lead to physical or psychological harm. It would be totally unacceptable to study human grief by deceiving subjects into believing that a loved one had just passed away.

An entirely different class of limitations to the use of the laboratory experiment stems from difficulties that are not inherent in the use of manipulation as a research strategy, but rather are addressed to the laboratory as a site. These de facto limitations deal with such problems as location of the laboratory, use of nonvolunteer subjects, awareness of subjects that they are being studied, limited time perspective, and restriction in the subject population.

The Experiment's Setting

Experimental research strategies do not prescribe any particular kinds of settings. Yet, in practice the vast majority of laboratory experiments in social psychology are performed in settings which, because of their particular characteristics, can be classified as "standard laboratories." Standard laboratories are those maintained for research purposes and identified as such to subjects. Characteristics associated with standard laboratories may vary from requesting subjects to appear at the "Behavioral Science Laboratory in Herman Webster Hall" to equipment configurations such as microphones, cameras, and one-way mirrors (cf. Fromkin, 1969). One important property of such laboratories is that any or all of the above characteristics promote in subjects an awareness that they are participants in research, i.e., they may impel subjects to believe that, for this time period, their welfare is protected and their behavior is being observed, measured, and/or evaluated. This awareness and related phenomena raise a central issue surrounding laboratory experimentation. Can relationships established in standard laboratories be expected to occur unchanged in nonlaboratory settings (e.g., organizations)?

Awareness of being a research participant can also occur in laboratory settings that are other than "standard." Although most criticisms (cf. Friedman, 1967) of laboratory experiments have been directed toward research conducted in such standard sites (indeed, most published laboratory research has been conducted at such sites), they also apply to some field-based research settings. Concern over unobtrusive and nonreactive measures (Webb, Campbell, Schwartz, and Sechrest, 1966) applies no matter where research is conducted.

This philosophical question of generality has provoked many individuals to advocate abandonment of laboratory experimentation because it is "artificial." However, it is obvious that criticisms of "unrealism," "artificiality," and "irrelevance" are more an indictment of characteristics of the standard laboratory setting and less a condemnation of the experimental research strategy.[1] Since characteristics of laboratory settings are susceptible to modification, laboratory experiments may vary in their degree of applicability according to which stimuli are present during the study. It appears that the "artificiality" shortcomings of standard laboratories are being unjustly elevated to the status of a fatal flaw.

GENERALIZING FROM THE LABORATORY

Once a relationship between two variables, X and Y, has been demonstrated under very specific laboratory conditions, potential applied consumers of this information are faced with many problems of evaluation.[2] Of central concern is the question of generality. Generality refers to the likelihood that experimental findings will recur unchanged in the larger untested universe. By definition, generalization always requires extrapolation to realms not represented in one's sample, e.g., to other populations, to other representations of the treatment variable (X), to other representations of the measurement variable (Y), and so forth. It is clear that generality may have several different meanings (cf. Campbell and Stanley, 1963, pp. 17–34; Kaplan, 1964; Sidman, 1960, pp. 46–67). For example, are the findings obtained with a particular sample of college students useful for accurately predicting the behavior of managers? Are the findings obtained under a particular treatment variable X (e.g., high frequency of interracial contact) useful for accurately predicting behavior under other nonidentical representations of X (e.g., contact between worker and supervisor)? Are the findings obtained under a particular measurement variable Y (e.g., favorability of interracial attitude) useful for predicting behavior under other representations of Y (e.g., cooperative behavior)?

Although it is important to determine if a relationship is applicable outside the confines of a particular laboratory experiment, one is faced with the reality that such generalizations are never logically justified. Furthermore, there are no objective criteria by which one can assess the degree of generality any laboratory experiment possesses.

But we do attempt generalization by guessing at laws and checking out some of these generalizations in other equally specific but different conditions. In the course of the history of science we learn about the "justification" of generalizing by the cumulation of our experience in generalizing, but this is not a logical generalization deducible from the details of the original experiment. Faced by this, we do, in generalizing, make guesses as to yet unproven laws, including

[1] It may be noted that these same "artifacts" have been found to operate in a variety of field settings (cf. Argyris, 1968, pp. 190–191; Kroger, 1967; Page and Lumia, 1968; Rosen, 1970; Rosen and Sales, 1966; Sherwood and Nataupsky, 1968).

[2] Similar problems of generality occur with other methods of research (e.g., field and survey methods) and are not unique to laboratory methods (cf. Adams and Preiss, 1960).

some not even explored. The sources of external validity are thus guesses as to general laws in the science of a science: guesses as to what factors interact with our treatment variables, and, by implication, guesses as to what can be disregarded (Campbell and Stanley, 1963, p. 17).

Evaluation of generality then, e.g., the decision to act or not act administratively upon the organizational implications of any particular relationship demonstrated in laboratory experiments, is a matter of judgment. The basis for such judgments resides in the identification of critical differences between a specific research setting and a specific organizational setting. Of the many differences between the two environments, only some of the dissimilarities are likely to be critical. A difference is "critical" when a particular variable is present in only one of the two environments and is absolutely essential to the unaltered occurrence of a particular stimulus–response relationship in that environment. Censorious descriptions of laboratories as artificial are based on perceived differences which are claimed to impose limitations on the generality of laboratory experiments. Careful examination, however, reveals that most of the contended differences are either not *true* dissimilarities or are not *critical* dissimilarities. Examples of the former are presented below under "Artifacts," and examples of the latter are presented below under "Realism."

Artifacts

Artificiality, as it is commonly used, encompasses stimuli present in the standard laboratory setting that lead the subject to be sensitive to the experimenter's intent (Campbell and Stanley, 1963) and/or expectancies (Rosenthal, 1969) or that arouse evaluation apprehension in the subject (Rosenberg, 1969). To the extent that the subject's behavior is determined by such extraneous conditions, it is viewed as artificially produced, and any observed relationship should not be generalized. Riecken (1962, pp. 33–34) proposed a similar view of the laboratory as a social situation where

> The subject has more than one problem. One is the "task" that the E sets. Another is what we may, for convenience, call his "deutero-problem," meaning his personal problem as defined by three aims. . . . First, he wants to accomplish his private purposes or get his rewards—e.g., pay, course credit, satisfaction of curiosity, self-insight, help with a problem and so on; second, he wants to penetrate the E's inscrutability and discover the rationale of the experiment—its purposes and the types of judgment that will issue from it; and, third, he wants to accomplish this second aim in order to achieve a third, namely in order to represent himself in a favorable light or "put his best foot forward"!

Thus, it is reasonable to expect that subjects' responses in laboratory settings will not be determined solely by the treatment variable, and instead may be attributed, at least in part, to subjects' motivations to confirm the experimenter's hypothesis (e.g., Orne, 1969), to disconfirm the experimenter's hypothesis (cf. the "screw you effect" discussed by Masling, 1966, p. 96), or to acquire a favorable evaluation from the experimenter (e.g., Rosenberg, 1969). Such motives are considered "artifacts" which increase the artificiality of observations obtained in the laboratory, because their arousal is generally unintended and potentially confounded with the independent variable. According to this view, laboratory settings are a source of nonrepresentativeness because subjects' awareness of participation in research provokes motivations and behaviors unlike the motivations and behaviors in nonlaboratory settings, e.g., organizations.

In order for the above "awareness" phenomena to jeopardize the usefulness of laboratory findings for predicting organizational behavior, it is necessary to assume that the motivations and behavior related to awareness are unique only to laboratory settings. The validity of this assumption seems, at the very least, questionable. While it may be true that people don't ordinarily encounter experimenters in their day-to-day life, they do encounter people and situations that lead them to examine the motives of others and suffer evaluation apprehension. Does not the black entering an organization experience evaluation apprehension, are there no demand characteristics he responds to, are not suspicions present about the "true" reason he has been recruited, and hasn't he talked with friends about the organization and the possibility of his being duped by it?

The organization is a social setting in which the members are motivated to discover the hypotheses and expectancies of other members and where evaluation apprehension is aroused in relation to promotion and/or pay. Indeed, at least one prominent organizational theorist has noted that ". . . many of the disfunctions reported between experimenter and subject are similar to the disfunctions between management and employee" (Argyris, 1968, p. 185). Furthermore, Argyris (1968, p. 188) suggests that the "adaptive strategies" described above ". . . are predictable by organizational theory because the relationship between the researcher and the subject is similar to the one between the manager and the employee in formal organizations." Therefore, the operation of motives related to awareness phenomena occurs in many organizational settings and is not restricted to unintended occurrences in standard laboratories. It is wrong to claim that the presence of such artifacts in some standard laboratory research makes the findings of that research inapplicable to organizational problems.

Realism

Although the relationship between resemblance and relevance is the subject of considerable debate, it is frequently claimed that experimental settings are more "realistic" when they resemble organizations. However, there is as much variation of stimuli from one specific applied situation to another as exists between a given laboratory setting and an applied situation. For example, male laughter at an "off-color" joke is more likely to occur in a locker room than at a tea party. Yet, one cannot claim that the behavior in the locker room was more or less "real" than behavior at the tea party, simply because there are few similarities in the two situations. Similarly, it seems quite unjustified to claim that laboratory behavior is less real than organizational behavior, simply because there may be different variables controlling behavior in the two situations. Thus, the argument that "realism" requires multiple similarities in laboratory and organizational settings is ill-founded.

While it is true that experiments vary in the degree of resemblance to organizations, a laboratory event is not endowed with greater generality or less artificiality because it occurs in a setting containing several attributes which are similar to characteristics of organizations. Aronson and Carlsmith (1969, p. 22) refer to such similarities as "mundane realism." It is more likely that only a small number of variables are required to depict organizational phenomena. Weick (1965, pp. 210–226) suggests five attributes which can be varied, without sacrificing experimental control, to increase the degree of correspondence between laboratory and organizational settings: i.e., size of work group, duration of interpersonal contacts, ambiguity of performance feedback, significance of performance outcomes, and task interdependence. However, organizations are different as well as similar! Differences occur between organizations and within organizations (e.g., between subunits or departments, etc.) in the degree to which they are characterized by any combination of the above five attributes. While it is possible that some combinations of all the five attributes may accurately describe a single organization and/or a single subunit within an organization, there is no combination that, if present in the standard experimental laboratory, would make the result of such a lab more generalizable. Validation of the contact hypothesis with large interdependent groups is no more generalizable to other situations than would be results derived from small independent groups of workers. It would be wrong to ignore research on the contact hypothesis on the grounds that it hasn't been tested in all possible combinations of these five organizational variables.

There is little reason to stipulate that any normative list of attributes is important to a large number of organizational situations. The administrator, upon examination and analysis of his organization, relevant subunits within his organization, and the specific problem of interest, must determine which attributes are important. He then must determine whether any existing laboratory studies incorporated these attributes. Realism then, like artificiality, may be reduced to a matter of judgment because "it is not the number of points at which the laboratory and field touch that is crucial, it is the kind of point where correspondence occurs" (Weick, 1965, p. 226). Instead of reinforcing the myth that laboratory settings seldom yield data which are relevant to real-world problems, it is proposed that laboratory settings merely impose identifiable limitations upon the range of situations to which a particular set of laboratory findings may be practically applied. The potential consumer of laboratory-produced information must decide if the laboratory characteristics of any particular study are the critical ones which circumscribe his particular organization and the problem under consideration.

Boundary Variables

As stated earlier, the purpose of the present chapter is to provide potential consumers of laboratory findings with a perspective from which to regard any experiment and make decisions about its relevance for a particular applied problem. The major feature is a concern for the degree of overlap between the number of "critical" elements that influence behavior in a laboratory setting and those present in the applied setting. The identification of similarities and differences between the two environments is the foundation of this perspective. Unfortunately, the task of generalization cannot be solved by simply assuming that the greater the similarity between the two environments (lab setting and applied setting), the greater the likelihood that a stimulus–response relationship will be manifest unaltered in either environment. Rather, it is necessary to restrict focus to just those similarities and differences that make a difference, to those stimulus features that have a real effect on the relationship being considered. Similarities and differences relating only to "mundane realism" (Aronson and Carlsmith, 1969) should be disregarded.

Although the presence (or absence) of a particular characteristic may be essential to the observation of an event, identification of its presence in (or absence from) *both* settings allows it to be dismissed from further attention in the analysis. Certain demand characteristics may be disallowed on this basis. Comparisons will also uncover some differences. Undoubtedly, some of the differences will be trivial. That is, a stimulus event will occur unchanged in either environment in spite of the laboratory presence and organization absence (or vice versa) of a number of specific elements. This judgment can be made on the basis of other research or, more probably, the experience and acumen of the person engaging in the task of generalizing research findings. Characteristics producing these differences can be eliminated from further attention.

In contrast to the above elements, some characteristics will be present in *only one* of the settings and will be, at least in part, responsible for the occurrence of the stimulus–response relationship under consideration. Uncovering these "critical differences" is the first step toward reducing the discrepancy between the laboratory and the applied setting. These critical differences may be conceptualized in the form of "boundary variables"—each varying on an identifiable continuum. It is proposed that the term be used generally[3] to

[3] The more general definition has been also applied to theory development and research strategy by Fromkin and Streufert (1972).

describe a variable which: (a) is common to all laboratory treatment groups, (b) is not present in both the laboratory and the applied settings under consideration, and (c) can alter a stimulus event either by its presence or its absence. In light of the present focus on applying laboratory data to organizational problems, discussion of "boundary variables" will be restricted to their potential for changing a laboratory stimulus event by virtue of its presence in the organizational environment or by virtue of its absence from the organizational environment.

This concept of boundary variable is the central feature of the perspective on generalization presented in this chapter. This concept offers a framework and vocabulary to use in applying the findings of a laboratory study to a particular organizational problem. It should help the applier to be aware of the pitfalls of inappropriate generalization without leading him to discount the usefulness of existing laboratory research. It emphasizes the active role played by the applier in determining the relevance of an experiment to a problem. Lastly, it allows the applier to draw more heavily and with greater confidence on research conducted in standard laboratories.

Table 12-1 presents a summary of some different interactions between a laboratory stimulus event and the presence (or absence) of a boundary variable in an organization. The columns refer to three different laboratory stimulus–response relationships ($Y_{1\ldots3} = f X_{1\ldots3}$).

TABLE 12-1   *Some Possible Boundary Variable and Stimulus–Response Interactions*

	LABORATORY STIMULUS–RESPONSE RELATIONSHIPS		
Organizational Boundary Variables	$Y_1 = f(X_1)$	$Y_2 = f(X_2)$	$Y_3 = f(X_3)$
BV_1 Absent	+	0	0
High Levels of BV_1 Present	0	+	+
Low Levels of BV_1 Present	0	0	+
BV_2 Absent	0	0	0
High Levels of BV_2 Present	+	0	0
Low Levels of BV_2 Present	0	0	+
BV_3 Absent	0	0	+
High Levels of BV_3 Present	0	0	+
Low Levels of BV_3 Present	+	+	0

The rows refer to three different boundary variables ($BV_{1\ldots3}$), each under three levels, e.g., absent, present under high levels, and present under low levels. Plus (+) and zero (0) entries in the cells show some possible interactions: a plus indicates a situation where the boundary variable alters a stimulus event, and a zero indicates a situation where a boundary variable does *not* alter a stimulus event.

The table shows some of the more general interactions between stimulus–response relationships and boundary variables. There are, of course, others. Instead of presenting an encyclopedic listing, the following discussion describes some examples of the most common and facilitates the reader's pursuit of other interactions.

SINGLE BOUNDARY VARIABLE CAN AFFECT MULTIPLE RELATIONSHIPS

Inspection of the first row of Table 12-1 shows three instances where the absence of a boundary variable from the organizational environment influences only one of three different stimulus–response relationships. Three ways in which a third variable (BV_1) can alter a stimulus event $[Y_1=f(X_1)]$ are illustrated in the first three rows. A boundary variable can be influential by virtue of its absence from the organizational setting $Y_1 = f(X_1)$, by virtue of its *presence* under only high levels $Y_2 = f(X_2)$ in the organizational setting, or by virtue of its presence under either high or low levels $Y_3=f(X_3)$ in the organizational setting. Other ways a boundary variable can influence stimulus events are illustrated in the triadic rows for boundary variable two (BV_2) and for boundary variable three (BV_3).

A SINGLE RELATIONSHIP CAN BE AFFECTED BY MULTIPLE BOUNDARY VARIABLES

Examination of column 1 illustrates that a laboratory stimulus event $[Y_1=f(X_1)]$ may be altered by the absence of a third variable (BV_1) from the organizational setting, or by only high levels of a third variable (BV_2) in the organizational setting, or by only low levels of a third variable (BV_3) in the organizational setting. It is also possible that one or more of the boundary variables may, in combination, interact in the organizational environment to alter a laboratory stimulus event in ways even more complicated than those portrayed in Table 12-1. Additional rows could be added that represent the simultaneous presence of two or more boundary variables.

To summarize, the laboratory is seen as neither "artificial," nor "unreal." Instead, differences between laboratory and other environments (e.g., organizations), are regarded as identifiable variables which interact with stimulus events in a lawful and predictable manner. Judgments regarding the applicability of a set of laboratory findings to an organizational problem involve a two-step process. The first step is to descry all the boundary variables which are a source of critical differences between the laboratory and organizational environments. The second step is prediction of the potency and/or direction of the effects of boundary variables upon the laboratory stimulus–response relationship. In many instances, the latter step requires guesses about some (untested or unproven) general laws of behavior. Fortunately, the number of occasions for guesses is constantly being reduced by a usable body of expanding literature describing the operation of artifacts (cf. a recent volume by Rosenthal and Rosnow, 1969) and organizational variables (cf. reviews by Weick, 1965, 1967). It must be emphasized that generalization is not, and can never be, a mechanical activity in which conclusions can be drawn with absolute certainty. Rather, it requires the applier to use his own judgment, tempered by experience, in determining comparability between existing research and the features of the applied setting he is dealing with.

SOME POTENTIAL BOUNDARY VARIABLES IN EXPERIMENTAL RACE RESEARCH

In this section, examples of some common differences between the laboratory and organization are presented that may, for some relationships, become "critical" and thereby attain a temporary status of boundary variables. The coverage is illustrative rather than exhaustive. The variables discussed should not necessarily be considered the most influential. In keeping with the rest of this volume, only race-related boundary variables are discussed. The discussion is organized around two questions: How does laboratory presentation of a particular set of stimuli differ from the same stimuli as they occur in a particular application, and, how do subjects' responses to stimuli in the laboratory differ from the kinds of responses that are of concern in applied settings?

Stimuli

This section focuses on elements of the standard laboratory that compete with the independent variables to influence subjects' response tendencies and thereby become potential boundary variables. It is frequently argued that organizational stimuli are not the same when they are brought into the laboratory. "The very act of bringing a variable into the laboratory usually changes its nature . . . you lose some of the original elements and add some others that were not in the original" (Chapanis, 1967, p. 566). For example, the researcher frequently "purifies" the situation by eliminating the presence of some variables in order to maximize opportunities for the independent variable to be effective. Such strategies may produce significant effects in a purified setting, but such effects could become seriously attenuated when the variable occurs in competition with other variables (or impurities) that may exist in other contexts. What may be impurities in one setting become crucial boundary variables in another.

MODE OF RACIAL CONTACT.   Although there is generally more than one independent variable in most racial studies, the race of one or more of the participants is often a focal stimulus variable. Racial stimuli may be potential boundary variables in a number of ways (cf. Hyman, 1969, p. 10). Methods of introducing newcomers of different races to laboratory subjects vary widely; they also may differ from the nature of interracial encounters in organizations. At one extreme, subjects are introduced to different-race stimulus persons by means of short written descriptions of the stimulus person (e.g., Byrne and

Wong, 1962) or by means of photographs of the stimulus person (e.g., Triandis, Loh, and Levin, 1966). At the other extreme, subjects view videotapes (e.g., Hendrick, Bixenstine, and Hawkins, 1971) or have face-to-face meetings with the stimulus person (Fromkin, Klimoski, and Flanagan, 1971; Katz and Cohen, 1962; Burnstein and McRae, 1962). It is important to notice that written descriptions differ from personal contact on a number of dimensions. Face-to-face interactions yield a greater amount of information about the physical and psychological attributes of the stimulus person as well as conveying a greater number of interpersonal verbal and nonverbal cues (e.g., facial expression, body movements, phonetic variation, etc.).

An interesting demonstration of the effect of differences in modes of stimulus-person presentation is found in a comparison of the findings by Byrne and Wong (1962) with Byrne and McGraw (1964). Byrne and Wong (1962) presented white subjects with a bogus protocol of a stranger who was either similar or dissimilar in attitudes. In addition, the stranger's race was indicated on the protocol by the word "white" or the word "Negro" beside the blank labeled "Race." Subjects exhibited greater attraction for similar strangers and less attraction for dissimilar strangers, regardless of the race of the stranger or the degree of prejudice of the subject. This study was not supported by the first of two experiments by Byrne and McGraw (1964) that showed that similarity of attitudes did not overcome race as a determinant of attraction toward the stranger. This failure to replicate Byrne and Wong (1962) was attributed to a methodological difference in the Byrne and McGraw (1964, p. 207) study: "In this subsequent study, in order to enhance the realism of the stranger, race was additionally indicated by the means of a small yearbook photograph. Possibly more cues to interracial hostility are evoked by a photograph of a Negro than by the word 'Negro'." In the second experiment by Byrne and McGraw (1964), the procedures of Byrne and Wong (1962) were replicated with a yearbook photograph attached to the attitude protocols *of half of* the strangers.

The results indicated that attitude similarity and racial membership each influenced attraction toward the stranger. More relevant to the present discussion is the finding that

> The presence of a photograph exerted a positive rather than a negative effect on attraction ratings. In many respects, this finding is encouraging, if one wishes to generalize beyond the laboratory situation. If there is a realism gradient from the word "Negro" to a photograph of a Negro to the physical presence of a Negro, the present finding would suggest that positive responses increase toward the realistic end of the gradient. Rather than more realistic cues evoking greater hostility from subjects high in prejudice, the reverse is true. Perhaps negative responses toward members of a minority group function best in the abstract (Byrne and McGraw, 1964, p. 209).

More recently, Byrne (1970, personal communication) suggests that the "positive effect" might have been due to the inadvertent selection of stimulus photographs which represented physically attractive blacks. Similarly, when Triandis, Loh, and Levin (1966) presented subjects with white or black stimulus persons represented both on photographic slides and a tape recording, ratings of the stimulus person were influenced by race and grammar variations but not by belief or dress variation. Whatever the reason, it is clear that variations in the mode of stimulus presentation may profoundly alter the intensity and/ or direction of subjects' responses. Consequently, the potential consumer interested in predicting interracial interaction in the real world should give careful attention to the mode of racial interaction in laboratory studies. At first glance, one is tempted *categorically* to define "mode of stimulus presentation" as a boundary variable. However, it is true that modes of interpersonal contact and communication in organizations also vary from personal and telephone contact to written memos through formal and informal channels (Jacoby, 1968; Melcher and Beller, 1967). For example, Guetzkow (1961, p. 199) notes that "organizations are distinguishable from face-to-face groups by virtue of the predominance of indirect, mediated interaction among members, so that the behaviors within the group are relatively inaccessible to any given individual." In applying laboratory findings to such indirect contacts, research based on the abstract modes would be preferable to findings based on fully interactive encounters. Since there is no single mode of interaction which characterizes all organizational life, the consumer of laboratory information must examine particular racial studies and judge if the mode of stimulus contact is similar to or different from the specific organizational context of interest to him.

CHARACTERISTICS OF STIMULUS PERSONS.   Personality and/or physical characteristics of stimulus persons may be potential sources of boundary variables. When the stimulus is a live, responsive person, there are often great differences in the age and maturity of laboratory stimulus persons (usually college students) as compared with members of organizations. Some of the characteristics which vary in prominence among members of the black race, e.g., darkness of skin color, may produce differential responding in white subjects (e.g., Greenwald and Oppenheim, 1968). In order to reduce the opportunity for groups in *identical* treatment conditions to respond to stimulus persons with different racial characteristics, many laboratory studies introduce the same person (usually a confederate of the experimenter) to each of the treatment groups. But when this procedure is adopted laboratory responses to the single stimulus person may be affected by his particular racial characteristic(s). Each unique racial characteristic of the laboratory stimulus person that affects subjects' responses to other independent variables qualifies as a boundary variable. An alternative strategy is to select a number of stimulus persons from the same race and randomly assign them to different treatment groups (cf. Fromkin, Klimoski, and Flanagan, 1971). Results obtained using a number of different persons who share a common attribute of membership in the same race are more likely related to a general racial characteristic (e.g., black) rather than to some idosyncratic characteristic of a single person[4] (e.g., perceived militancy or style of Afro haircut). Use of this latter strategy leads to greater confidence that unique characteristics of the stimulus person are unimportant as potential boundary variables.

ATTRIBUTES OF THE EXPERIMENTER. Of the vast number of stimuli which might be considered when examining any laboratory study, the attributes of the experimenter are an important consideration (cf. Summers and Hammonds, 1966; Rosenthal, 1966, 1969).[5] In the context of race research it must be determined whether the racial attributes of the experimenter are a source of critical differences between the laboratory and organization. The experimental literature provides some information about the effects of experimenter's race on task performance. Sattler has reviewed the effects of experimenter racial attributes upon the task performance of black college students (1970, pp. 142–143):

> White testers in comparison with Negro testers do not necessarily impede the performance of Negro college subjects. Negro testers obtained significantly higher scores than white testers when the probability-of-success conditions informed the college subjects that they had little or an equal chance of equaling the white norm; white testers obtained significantly higher scores than Negro testers under certain conditions and with certain groups (e.g., motor instructions and hard digit-symbol task; digit-letter substitution and mild threat college students with satisfactory high school averages in any probability-of-success condition).

These findings, taken together, suggest that comparisons of black and white laboratory interactions to organizational environments should consider the race of the experimenter (black or white) as it affects how task differences (intellectual or nonintellectual) and the subjects' perceptions of their probability of task success (high or low) influence performance. Race acts as a boundary variable when applying these relationships to improve task performance. What is striking is the absence of data on how these variables affect the performance of mixed racial groups rather than groups composed exclusively of blacks.

More recent studies by Katz and his colleagues (Katz, 1970, pp. 106–112) suggest that the black performance on cognitive tasks is highest with a white supervisor when the probability of success is seen as attainable and based on black norms. Although it is likely to change in the near future, the present situation in most organizations may be described as environments where newcomer black workers will be assigned to nonintellectual tasks under the aegis of white supervisors (cf. King and Bass, in this volume) with work standards based on white norms. The contrasting administrative implication of the research efforts of Katz and his colleagues is that black motivation and per-

[4] Of course, since all stimulus persons were college students, subjects' responses may be attributable to some unknown characteristic common to all college students.

[5] Similar "experimenter" biases have been strikingly demonstrated in survey research by Sherwood and Nataupsky (1968).

formance will be highest under white supervision of nonintellectual tasks with *attainable* performance criteria based on black work standards.

Responses

As mentioned earlier, an occasional catalyst of behavior in the laboratory is the respondent's awareness that he is a participant in research. Although awareness phenomena operate in many laboratory experiments, it need not always be the case (cf. Adams and Jacobsen, 1964; Latané and Darley, 1968; Lowin and Craig, 1968). In general, the effect of awareness is to produce behavior in standard laboratory settings which varies from the ostensibly comparable behavior as it occurs in natural settings.[6] The intrusion of the measuring instrument may heighten this effect. Consider, for example, a measurement obtained by a movie camera. White subjects' responses to black newcomers would be different when the camera bore the sign "property of the Black Panthers" than when the camera bore the sign "property of the K.K.K." or if the camera had been unobtrusively placed or hidden completely from view. Therefore, the measurement procedures or measures themselves may, under some conditions, introduce unwanted additional stimuli into the laboratory experiment that elicit confounding responses. The identification of boundary variables, then, can also be applied to the measurement of the dependent variable or to the manner in which subjects' responses are observed.

AWARENESS OF BEING A SUBJECT. Knowledge of being in an experiment may introduce boundary variables in at least two ways: (a) distortion of private responses in favor of public, socially approved responses to obtain positive evaluation; and, (b) alteration of responses due to a lack of perceived commitment to and/or accountability for any future consequences of his responses. The subject's knowledge of his research participation carries with it, among other cognitions, the idea that his behavior is being observed. This can lead to response biases such as the "guinea pig effect" (e.g., Selltiz, Jahoda, Deutsch, and Cook, 1965) or the "reactive effect" (Campbell, 1957; Campbell and Stanley, 1963; Webb, Campbell, Schwartz, and Sechrest, 1966) that tends to be the result of a reduction in respondent candor. Similarly, subjects may experience a fear of being evaluated or "evaluation apprehension" (cf. Rosenberg, 1969) and be impelled "to put their best foot forward" (Reiken, 1962) by giving the most "socially desirable" response. Interracial responses that place respondents in a favorable light are those that convey an impression of being well adjusted, unprejudiced, rational, open-minded, and democratic.

The dependent variable in many laboratory studies of race relations is a self-report measure which requests subjects to rate the attractiveness, compe-

---

[6] The problem may become exaggerated when the awareness variable interacts with respondent individual differences which are irrelevant to the independent variables.

tency, or desirability as a co-worker of black and white stimulus persons. Self-report measures appear quite susceptible to the influence of these awareness variables[7] (see Cook and Selltiz, 1964, p. 39). First, the purposes of the measures are quite clear, i.e., to measure subject's beliefs, feelings, or orientation toward the stimulus person. Second, the implications of each of his response alternatives are readily apparent to him, i.e., the respondent can create either a favorable or unfavorable impression of himself by responding at the positive or negative ends of the scale, depending upon the circumstances. For example, subjects may be aware that an answer at the positive end of the scale will have the effect of presenting him as unprejudiced, and an answer at the negative end of the scale will have the effect of presenting him as prejudiced. Third, the respondent is able to control consciously his responses. Although a number of experimenters have devised ingenious techniques to disguise the saliency of the purpose and implications of interracial self-rating scales (cf. Cook and Selltiz, 1964, pp. 41–43; Sigall and Page, 1970; Webb, Campbell, Schwartz, and Sechrist, 1966), it is not always desirable to eliminate such determinants of attitudinal response. The contribution of awareness-related stimuli must be considered a possible boundary variable that can be ruled out if common to both lab and application. The tendency to endorse publicly statements discrepant from one's private beliefs in the service of positive self-presentation is a common interpersonal strategy (e.g., Goffman, 1959).

DIMENSIONALITY OF DEPENDENT MEASURE. The nature of the judgments that subjects are asked to make about others is also an important consideration. For example, Rokeach, Smith, and Evans (1960) asked white subjects to rate black and white strangers with similar and dissimilar beliefs on nine-point rating scales with endpoints labeled "I *can't* see myself being friends with such a person" and "I can *very easily* see myself being friends with such a person." The results indicate that subjects' preferences were determined primarily by belief similarity. Triandis (1961) objected to generalizing of findings in the above study because the dependent variable was limited to "friendship choices." Triandis found that race exerted the stronger effect on preferences when measured by a social distance scale which considered other aspects of social interaction such as "admiration of ideas" and "willingness to marry." Later studies by Triandis and his colleagues (e.g., Triandis and Davis, 1965; Triandis, Loh, and Levin, 1966) also confirmed the contention that the various dimensions of social behavior are distinct dependent variables which are differentially influenced by different stimulus variables, e.g., race of person and belief similarity.

The differential effects of stimulus variables on different measures of social discrimination is also shown in an entirely different context. Fromkin, Klimoski, and Flanagan (1971) found that race of newcomer, competency of newcomer, and task success affected preferences for black co-workers in a job context but

---

[7] Again, it should be noted that alternate methods which study individuals *in situ* also employ self-rating scales which are susceptible to the same distortions.

did not affect "liking" for blacks. This, along with the Triandis research, shows that the nature of the response (i.e., the degree of social distance implied by the dependent variable) may become a boundary variable by imposing limitations on the kinds of interpersonal relationships predictable from the data of any particular racial study.

CONSEQUENCES OF BEHAVIOR.   Another way that awareness phenomena can become a source of boundary variables is by eliciting laboratory responses bounded by (a) a shortened time perspective, with (b) fewer expectations of present accountability and (c) fewer expectations of future consequences for behavior. Rarely, in the standard laboratory, does a subject expect to make responses which are likely to affect his behavior beyond the short time he has agreed to be in the experiment (typically only one hour). Any positive or negative consequences of his behavior are not likely to be very long lasting or extent beyond the time he is in the laboratory. Before dismissing all laboratory research with a blanket indictment of irrelevancy, it is important to note that many racial studies circumvent the above limitation by assuming that behavioral acts vary on a continuum of consequentiality ranging from anonymous paper-and-pencil responses to actions that require the performance of effortful and costly tasks over a long period of time.[8] For example, in lieu of asking subjects to circle a point on a scale which indicates how much they like blacks, some researchers have asked subjects to indicate how much time they would be willing to devote to taking black visitors around campus (e.g., Marlowe, Frager, and Nuttall, 1965) or to sign a photographic release statement indicating their willingness to be photographed with blacks for a nationwide publicity campaign advocating racial integration (e.g., DeFleur and Westie, 1968).

The latter "behavioroid" measures (cf. Aronson & Carlsmith, 1969, pp. 54–55) are distinguishable from other measures because they induce an expanded time reference within which subjects commit themselves to consequential action without actually going through with it. The important difference is that subjects expect to honor their commitment by actually carrying out the behavior. In the Marlowe, Frager, and Nuttall (1965) study, subjects' decision to take blacks around campus was a commitment of their future time made with the probable "cost" of eliminating or reducing available time for alternative attractive activities such as a movie or a date, etc. In contrast, merely rating the

---

[8] Some discussions seem to confound three different measurement issues: namely, the accurate measurement of attitudes; the accurate measurement of behavior; and, the accurate measurement of the relationship between attitudes and behavior. Criticisms of the laboratory as artificial often focus on the frequent use of self-rating scales and the rather tenuous argument that proof of a relationship between attitudes (as measured by self reports) and behavior is required to increase confidence in the generality of laboratory findings. The adequacy of self-reported attitudes for predicting future behavior has been justly questioned (cf. Festinger, 1964; Fishbein, 1966; Rokeach, 1966; Wicker, 1970). Indeed, the evidence shows that there is not likely to be any simple relationship between attitudes and behavior, especially for behavior in interracial situations (cf. LaPiere, 1934; Kutner, Wilkins, and Yarrow, 1952; Linn, 1965) where prejudicial attitudes were not acted upon in face-to-face situations.

attractiveness of a black stranger implies little or no commitment to restrictions on their future behavior. Furthermore, behavioroid measures are less susceptible to socially desirable responses than self-report measures, because they may reduce the probability that the individual will modify his behavior in order to present a favorable picture of himself to the experimenter. That is, when responses are expected to have real-life consequences, the anticipation of these consequences may oppose the desire to make a good impression on an experimenter. If a subject is motivated toward positive self-presentation, there is little resistance to saying that he would be willing to work with a black or contribute money to a black cause or have a black as a roommate unless the question is posed in such a way that an affirmative response is seen as actually resulting in his making a financial contribution or acquiring a black co-worker or roommate.

The above examples of behavioroid measures are more convergent with kindred organizational behaviors than simple affective ratings would be. However, the boundary variable perspective reminds us that situations exist in which the response one wishes to alter in the organization has more in common with simple expressions of affect than with interpersonal behavioral decisions. In such cases one would prefer to draw upon research that uses simple rating scales and avoid research that uses behavioroid or behavioral measures.

BOUNDARY VARIABLES IN NONEXPERIMENTAL RACE RESEARCH

The boundary variable approach need not be restricted solely to interpretations of laboratory research. It is also useful for generalizations from nonexperimental data to applied situations. A brief example and some implications for organizational practices may be developed by applying the boundary variable concept to the vast nonexperimental research literature on the "contact hypothesis." It may be remembered that this hypothesis is based on the expectation that contact between members of different races, i.e., the opportunities to interact and communicate, will reduce prejudice. As mentioned earlier, some studies find a positive relationship between interracial contact and interracial attitudes, and others find a negative relationship. In work situations, however, frequency of contact seems to produce little or no attitude change (cf. Amir, 1969, pp. 331–332). Application of boundary variables may provide a means of accounting for the discrepancies between work and other environments.

Comparisons of environments yielding some relationship (either positive or negative) between contact and attitudes with work environments reveal some critical differences between the environments. First, studies of interracial contact in nonwork settings generally occur with minority members of equal or greater status than members of the majority. In work environments, given equal socioeconomic and/or educational status, lower-status jobs are typically allocated to minority members. Therefore, it is likely that "equality of status contact" is a critical difference between work and nonwork interracial contacts. Since equal-status contact occurs more frequently in nonwork than work situations, it qualifies as a boundary variable. Prior to applying the contact hypothesis to work situations, it is necessary to predict how the absence of equal status contacts will affect interracial attitudes in work environments.

Studies of the contact hypothesis have demonstrated that characteristics of the contact situation are important determinants of the nature and magnitude of the relationship. When status is based on factors relevant to the specific contact situation, equal-status contacts tend to produce a positive relationship between frequency of contact and favorable attitudes toward minority members. Increases in status of and contact with minority members tend to increase further the favorability of attitudes toward minority members. Conversely, when contact occurs with blacks of lower status to whites, prejudicial attitudes do not change; and presumably, attitudes become more unfavorable with decreases in status and increases in contact. The rather obvious, albeit simplistic, prediction derivable from the above findings is that the contact hypothesis will not be supported (or will appear as a negative relationship) when minority members are assigned to low-status jobs in work environments. The implications for organizational policy and administration seem patently clear.

A second important characteristic of the contact situation is related to the transpiring interaction. Research evidence (e.g., Amir, 1969, pp. 330–334; Cook, 1963, pp. 41–42; Deutsch and Collins, 1951; Wilner, Walkley, and Cook, 1952; Yarrow, Campbell, and Yarrow, 1958) suggests that casual contact between different ethnic groups, in and of itself, is insufficient to reduce prejudice. In contrast to casual contact, increasing contact of an ego-involving intimate nature tends to reduce prejudice. Comparisons of work to nonwork environments reveal that interracial relationships tend to be more intimate in nonwork situations and more casual in work situations. "Perhaps, in general, work situations involve superficial interethnic contact, and even when the relationship becomes more personal, it is generally confined to the work situation only" (Amir, 1969, p. 332). At least two factors lead to more casual contacts in organizations. Minority members of organizations, at least initially, tend toward voluntary self-segregation in "racial islands" whenever possible. The relatively large size of organizations facilitates maintenance of these contractions in personal space. Therefore, it is likely that the degree of intimacy of interracial contacts is a critical difference. Since interracial contact in work environments tends to be considerably more casual than in nonwork environments, degree of intimacy seems a very likely candidate for a boundary variable. In order to apply the contact hypothesis findings to work situations, it would appear desirable to devise ways to increase the degree of intimacy of interracial contacts in the organization. An implication for administrative policy for integration is that training and work assignments be made in a manner to facilitate more intimate and ego-involving interracial relationships.

A third characteristic which may be an important difference (i.e., a boundary variable) between many nonwork (e.g., housing and academic) and organizational settings is the source of institutional sanctions for interracial contact. Institutional support in organizations usually takes the form of a general impersonal dictum informing employees of an "official policy" favoring impending organizational integration. Organizational support, then, generally exists by virtue of an "administrative policy," custom, or an authority imposed upon the work groups. Racial attitudes in academic and other nonwork environments generally reside in a social atmosphere of *agreement* favoring social integration. Linn (1965, p. 359) notes that

> This role of "racial liberalism" with its associated constellation of attitudes is quite contradictory to the way in which most people have been socialized into our society. Contrary to the university atmosphere, most segments of American society and the norms associated with them do not see racial integration as being socially acceptable; in fact, integration is probably more often viewed as something either to fear or to avoid on a personal level.

This is specifically true when the preferential hiring of blacks implicitly threatens job security. Institutional support can allay such fears and encourage a positive attitude in its workers prior to integrative actions involving increased contact. If confirmation of the contact hypothesis is to be obtained in organizational settings, institutional support might include efforts to reduce prejudicial attitudes by communication of the need for and advantages of integration and substantial incentive for work group acceptance of social norms favoring integration.

SUMMARY

The purpose of the present volume is to build a bridge of some significance between the research and theory of the social scientist and the world of action of the organization administrator. The other papers in this volume recognize the void created by the absence of a relevant body of knowledge based on field data dealing with integrating organizations. There is a need to rely on the cornucopia of laboratory studies which offer two potentially relevant data bases: i.e., studies of race relations and studies of underlying social processes such as social influence, cooperation and conflict, interpersonal attraction, and leadership. The present chapter provides a perspective to bring laboratory findings to bear on organizational applications. Introduction of the "boundary variable" provides a conceptual viewpoint by which this is achieved. The discussions of racial boundary variables illustrate the application of this perspective to problems of organizations. By adopting this perspective, one will not fall prey to the notion that laboratory methods cannot be used to examine practical problems. No progress can be achieved by waiting until the methodology is improved and the laboratory's "artificiality" eliminated.

This boundary variable approach provides a basis for judgmental processes which render data obtained in one domain serviceable in other domains. It is intended that the perspective be applicable as an interface between field or standard laboratory experiments and any number of real-world settings by identifying limitations upon the range of situations to which a particular set of data may be applied. Laboratory research findings are the nucleus and boundary variables are the nexus of the interface that is proposed as an alternative to the widespread notion of absolute restrictions on the use of data beyond the settings in which they were obtained. Instead of ignoring the information accumulated in the laboratory, decision makers must learn the skills of judicious application, an activity requiring both familiarity with existing research and sensitivity to the boundary variables that stand between specific studies and specific applications.

REFERENCES

Adams, J. S., and Jacobsen, P. R. Effects of wage inequities on work quality. *Journal of Abnormal Social Psychology,* 1964, *69,* 19–25.

Adams, R. N., and Preiss, J. J. (eds.) *Human organization research: Field relations and techniques.* Homewood, Ill.: Dorsey Press, 1960.

Amir, Y. Contact hypothesis in ethnic relations. *Psychological Bulletin,* 1969, *71,* 319–342.

Argyris, C. Some unintended consequences of rigorous research. *Psychological Bulletin,* 1968, *70,* 185–197.

Argyris, C. The incompleteness of social psychological theory: Examples from small group, cognitive consistency, and attribution research. *American Psychology,* 1969, *24,* 893–908.

Aronson, E., and Carlsmith, J. M. The social psychology experiment. In G. Lindzey and E. Aronson (eds.), *Handbook of social psychology,* Vol. 1. Reading, Mass.: Addison–Wesley, 1969, pp. 1–79.

Brock, T. C. Communicator–recipient similarity and decision change. *Journal of Personality and Social Psychology,* 1965, *1,* 650–654.

Burnstein, E., and McRae, A. Some effects of shared threat and prejudice in racially mixed groups. *Journal of Applied Social Psychology,* 1962, *64,* 257–263.

Byrne, D., and Wong, T. J. Racial prejudice, interpersonal attraction, and assumed dissimilarity of attitudes. *Journal of Applied Social Psychology,* 1962, *65,* 246–253.

Byrne, D., and McGraw, C. Interpersonal attraction toward Negroes. *Human Relations,* 1964, *17,* 201–213.

Campbell, D. T. Factors relevant to the validity of experiments in social settings. *Psychological Bulletin,* 1957, *54,* 297–312.

Campbell, D. T., and Stanley, J. C. Experimental and quasi-experimental designs for research on teaching. In N. L. Gage (ed.), *Handbook of research on teaching.* Chicago: Rand McNally, 1963.

Cartwright, D., and Zander, A. *Group dynamics: Research and theory,* 3rd ed. New York: Harper, 1968.

Chapanis, A. The relevance of laboratory studies to practical situations. *Ergonomics,* 1967, *10,* 557–577.

Coch, L., and French, J. P., Jr. Overcoming resistance to change. *Human Relations,* 1948, *1,* 512–532.

Cook, S. W. Desegregation: A Psychological analysis. In W. W. Charters, Jr. and N. L. Gage (eds.), *Readings in the social psychology of education*. Boston: Allyn and Bacon, 1963.

Cook, S. W. Motives in a conceptual analysis of attitude-related behavior. In W. J. Arnold and D. Levine (eds.), *Nebraska symposium on motivation*. Lincoln, Neb.: University of Nebraska Press, 1969, pp. 179–231.

Cook, S. W., and Selltiz, C. A multiple-indicator approach to attitude measurement. *Psychological Bulletin*. 1964, *62*, 36–55.

DeFleur, M., and Westie, F. Verbal attitudes and overt acts: An experiment on the salience of attitudes. *American Sociological Review*, 1958, *23*, 667–673.

Deutsch, M., and Collins, M. E. *Interracial housing: A psychological evaluation of a social experiment*. Minneapolis: University of Minnesota Press, 1951.

Elliott, E. Perception and alertness. *Ergonomics*, 1960, *3*, 357–364.

Festinger, L. Behavioral support for opinion change. *Public Opinion Quarterly*, 1964, *28*, 404–417.

Fishbein, M. The relationship between beliefs, attitudes, and behavior. In S. Feldman (ed.), *Cognitive consistency:Motivational antecedents and behavioral consequences*. New York: Academic Press, 1966, pp. 199–223.

Friedman, N. *The social nature of psychological research*. New York: Basic Books, 1967.

Fromkin, H. L. The behavioral science laboratories at Purdue's Krannert School. *Administrative Sciences Quarterly*, 1969, *14*, 171–177.

Fromkin, H. L., and Streufert, S. Laboratory experimentation. In M. D. Dunnette (ed.), *Handbook of industrial and organization psychology*. Chicago: Rand McNally, 1972.

Fromkin, H. L., Klimoski, R. J., and Flanagan, M. F. Race and competence as determinants of acceptance of newcomers in success and failure work groups. *Organizational Behavior and Human Performance*, 1972, 7, No. 1, 25–42.

Goffman, E. *The presentation of self in everyday life*. New York: Doubleday, 1959.

Greenwald, H. J., and Oppenheim, D. B. Reported magnitude of self-identification among Negro children: Artifacts? *Journal of Personality and Social Psychology*, 1968, *8*, 49–52.

Guetzkow, H. Organizational leadership in task-oriented groups. In L. Petrullo and B. M. Bass (eds.), *Leadership and interpersonal behavior*. New York: Holt, 1961, pp. 187–200.

Harding, J., Proshansky, H., Kutner, B., and Chein, I. Prejudice and ethnic relations. In G. Lindzey and E. Aronson, (eds.), *Handbook of social psychology*, Vol. 5. Reading, Mass.: Addison-Wesley, 1969, pp. 1–76.

Hendrick, C., Bixenstine, V. E., and Hawkins, G. Race versus belief similarity as determinants of attraction: A search for a fair test. *Journal of Personality and Social Psychology*, 1971, *17*, 250–258.

Hyman, H. H. Social psychology and race relations. In I. Katz and P. Gurin (eds.), *Race and the social sciences*. New York: Basic Book, 1969, pp. 3–48.

Jacoby, J. Examining the other organization. *Personnel Administration*, 1968, *31*, 36–42.

Kaplan, A. *The conduct of inquiry: Methodology for behavioral science*. San Francisco, Calif.: Chandler, 1964.

Katz, I. Experimental studies of Negro–white relationships. In L. Berkowitz (ed.), *Advances in experimental social psychology*, Vol. 5. New York: Academic Press, 1970, pp. 71–117.

Katz, I., and Cohen, M. The effects of training Negroes upon cooperative problem solving in bi-racial teams. *Journal of Applied Social Psychology*, 1962, *64*, 319–325.

Kibler, A. W. The relevance of vigilance research to aerospace monitoring tasks. *Human Factors,* 1965, 7, 93–99.

Kroger, R. O. The effects of role demands and test-cue properties upon personality performance. *Journal of Consulting Psychology,* 1967, *31,* 304–312.

Kutner, B., Wilkins, C., and Yarrow, P. Verbal attitudes and overt behavior involving racial prejudice. *Journal of Abnormal and Social Psychology,* 1952, 47, 649–652.

LaPiere, R. Attitude versus action. *Social Forces,* 1934, *13,* 230–237.

Latané, B., and Darley, J. Group inhibition of bystander intervention in emergencies. *Journal of Personality and Social Psychology,* 1968, *10,* 215–221.

Lewin, K. The research center for group dynamics at Massachusetts Institute of Technology. *Sociometry,* 1945, 8, 126–136.

Linn, L. S. Verbal attitudes and overt behavior: A study of racial discrimination. *Social Forces,* 1965, *XLIII,* 353–364.

Lowin, A., and Craig, J. R. The influence of level of performance on managerial style: An experimental object-lesson in the ambiguity of correlational data. *Organizational Behavior and Human Performance,* 1968, 3, 440–458.

McGuire, W. J. Theory-oriented research in natural settings: The best of both worlds for social psychology. In M. Sherif and C. W. Sherif (eds.), *Interdisciplinary relationships in the social sciences.* Chicago: Aldine, 1969, pp. 21–51.

MacKie, R. R., and Christensen, R. P. Translation and application of psychological research. Human Factors Research, Inc. (Santa Barbara Research Park, Goleta, California) 1967, Technical Report 716–1.

Marlowe, D., Frager, R., and Nuttall, R. L. Commitment to action taken as a consequence of cognitive dissonance. *Journal of Personality and Social Psychology,* 1965, *2,* 864–868.

Masling, J. M. Role related behavior of the subject and psychologist and its effects upon psychological data. In D. A. Levine (ed.), *Nebraska symposium on motivation.* Lincoln, Neb.: University of Nebraska Press, 1966, *XIV,* 67–103.

Melcher, A. J., and Beller, R. Toward a theory of organizational communication: Consideration in channel selection. *Academy of Management Journal,* 1967, *10,* 39–52.

Morse, N. C., and Reimer, E. The experimental change of a major organizational variable. *Journal of Abnormal and Social Psychology,* 1956, 52, 120–129.

Orne, M. T. Demand characteristics and quasi-controls. In R. Rosenthal and R. L. Rosnow (eds.), *Artifacts in behavioral research.* New York: Academic Press, 1969, pp. 143–179.

Page, M. M., and Lumia, A. R. Cooperation with demand characteristics and the bimodal distribution of verbal conditioning data. *Psychonomic Science,* 1968, *12,* 243–244.

Rieken, H. W. A program for research on experiments in social psychology. In N. F. Washburne (ed.), *Decisions, values and groups.* New York: Macmillan, 1962.

Rokeach, M. Attitude change and behavior change. *Public Opinion Quarterly,* 1966, *30,* 529–550.

Rokeach, M., Smith, Patricia W., and Evans, R. I. Two kinds of prejudice or one? In M. Rokeach, *The open and closed mind.* New York: Basic Books, 1960, pp. 132–168.

Rosen, N. A. Demand characteristics in a field experiment. *Journal of Applied Psychology,* 1970, *54,* 163–168.

Rosen, N. A., and Sales, S. M. Behavior in a nonexperiment: The effects of behavioral field research on the work performance of factory employees. *Journal of Applied Psychology,* 1966, *50,* 165–171.

Rosenberg, M. J. The conditions and consequences of evaluation apprehension. In R. Rosenthal and R. L. Rosnow (eds.), *Artifact in behavioral research.* New York: Academic Press, 1969, pp. 279–349.

Rosenthal, R. *Experimenter effects in behavioral research.* New York: Appleton-Century-Crofts, 1966.

Rosenthal, R. Interpersonal expectations: Effects of the experimenter's hypothesis. In R. Rosenthal and R. L. Rosnow (eds.), *Artifact in behavioral research.* New York: Academic Press, 1969, pp. 181–277.

Rosenthal, R., and Rosnow, R. L. *Artifact in behavioral research.* New York: Academic Press, 1969.

Sapir, R. A shelter. *Megamot,* 1951, 3, 8–36.

Sattler, J. M. Racial "experimenter effects" in experimentation, testing, interviewing and psychotherapy. *Psychological Bulletin,* 1970, 73, 137–160.

Selltiz, C., Jahoda, M., Deutsch, M., and Cook, S. *Research methods in social relations,* rev. ed. New York: Holt, 1965, pp. 480–499.

Sherwood, J. J., and Nataupsky, M. Predicting the conclusion of negro-white intelligence research from biographical characteristics of the investigator. *Journal of Personality and Social Psychology,* 1968, 8, 53–58.

Sidman, M. *Tactics of scientific research: Evaluation of experimental data in psychology.* New York: Basic Books, 1961.

Siegel, A. E., and Siegel, S. Reference groups, membership groups, and attitude change. *Journal of Applied Social Psychology,* 1957, 55, 360–364.

Sigall, H., and Page, R. Two looks at stereo types. Proceedings of the Seventy-eighth Annual Convention of the American Psychological Association, 1970, 335–356.

Simons, J. C. An introduction to surface-free behavior. *Ergonomics,* 1964, 7, 23–36.

Summers, G. F., and Hammonds, A. D. Effect of racial characteristics of investigator on self-enumerated responses to a Negro prejudice scale. *Social Forces,* 1966, 44, 515–518.

Triandis, H. C. A note on Rokeach's theory of prejudice. *Journal of Applied Psychology,* 1961, 62, 184–186.

Triandis, H. C., and Davis, E. E. Race and belief as determinants of behavioral intentions. *Journal of Personality and Social Psychology,* 1965, 2, 715–725.

Triandis, H. C., Loh, W. D., and Levin, L. A. Race, status, quality of spoken English, and opinions about civil rights as determinants of interpersonal attitudes. *Journal of Personality and Social Psychology,* 1966, 4, 468–472.

Webb, E. J., Campbell, D. T., Schwartz, R. D., and Sechrest, L. *Unobtrusive measures: Nonreactive research in social sciences.* Chicago: Rand McNally, 1966.

Weick, K. E. Laboratory experiments with organizations. In J. G. March (ed.), *Handbook of organizations.* Chicago: Rand McNally, 1965, pp. 194–260.

Weick, K. E. Organizations in the laboratory. In V. Vroom (ed.), *Methods of organizational research.* Pittsburgh, Pa.: University of Pittsburgh Press, 1967, pp. 1–56.

Wicker, A. W. Attitude versus actions: The relationship of verbal and overt behavioral responses to attitude objects. *Journal of Social Issues,* 1969, XXV, 41–78.

Williams, R. M., Jr. *Strangers next door.* Englewood Cliffs, N.J.: Prentice-Hall, 1964.

Wilner, D. M., Walkley, R. P., and Cook, S. W. Residential proximity and intergroup relations in public housing projects. *Journal of Social Issues,* 1952, 8, 45–69.

Yarrow, M. R., Campbell, J. P., and Yarrow, L. J. Acquisition of new norms: A study of racial desegregation. *Journal of Social Issues,* 1958, 14, 8–28.

CHAPTER THIRTEEN

Should We Integrate Organizations?

Dalmas A. Taylor

INTRODUCTION BY THE EDITORS

It is, indeed, appropriate that the last word in this volume carries the perspective of a black person and that the concern in conclusion is with power.

While acknowledging the enormity of the tasks set forth in the preceding chapters, Taylor immediately raises questions about whether the dependent position of minorities has been clearly recognized and sufficiently addressed. He challenges both the manager and the society with his statement, ". . . dependent people cannot be integrated into an egalitarian society." Then, he directs our attention to the pervasiveness of institutional racism as uncovered by the 1968 findings of the U.S. Commission on Civil Disorders. It is because of institutional racism that blacks are so skeptical about integration and that redistribution of power is so necessary. Critical to the success of any approach to the integration of organizations is that minorities be represented among the ranks of authority, prestige, power, and control.

Taylor helps correct the imbalance of approaching social change in attitudinal terms, as if the target of change was the individual rather than the organization, within which individuals, of course, play important roles. He suggests that the study of prejudice by psychologists has led to concern with symptoms instead of causes, to an inspection of victims instead of perpetrators, and to a focus on intentions instead of consequences. Taylor's distinction between racism and racial prejudice is a useful one. He argues persuasively that ". . . integration like slavery is an institution devised and defined by whites for blacks—without black input." Where integration is simultaneously given as both the means and the end, then both clarity and strategic thinking are obscured. But more than that, the critical importance of the empowerment of blacks and other minorities is neglected. If equal status is necessary for contact with other people to change men's minds about those other people (minorities), then it is very simple, blacks must have more power for racial justice ever to occur. At least two questions remain: When and how will power be offered and shared, and when and how will power be lost and taken?

Taylor also points out the pressing need to develop a strategy to move us from today's dilemma to the desired goals of racial justice and cultural pluralism.

> *Mislike me not for my complexion,*
> *The shadowed livery of the burnished*
> *sun.*
>
> (*The Merchant of Venice*, Act II)

The question posed in the title of this chapter is more than a mere polemic. The task set down in this volume and carefully elaborated upon in the preceding chapters is indeed a herculean one. Nonetheless, the issue of integration of American institutions is one that immediately provokes skepticism from some—increasingly so on the part of large numbers of blacks. Yet, it should be stated at the outset, no one has worked harder toward the attainment of integration in this society than the black man, and he has done it, in large part, without the help of government, church, or private business (our major institutions!). During the long years of frustration and sustained effort on the part of blacks, at least two factors became evident: (1) dependent people cannot be integrated into an egalitarian society, and (2) the social, political and economic institutions of this country are not being used to reduce the dependency of blacks. To the extent that the objectives of this volume embrace the implications derived from these two observations, there is probable merit in the prescriptions we have been offered.

The group dynamics movement, founded by psychologist Kurt Lewin, has always embraced an interplay between theory, research, and social action. It is, therefore, more than appropriate that scholars, in the context of social–psychological theory and research, have addressed themselves to a pressing social problem—institutional racism. The term "institutional racism" has not been used by any of the authors in this volume; however, I have deliberately introduced it at this point because I think it is critical to the understanding and solution of the issues discussed here. More will be said about racism later; however, for the moment, we can glimpse some understanding of institutional racism by examining the following passage from Carmichael and Hamilton (1967):

> When white terrorists bomb a black church and kill five black children, that is an act of individual racism, widely deplored by most segments of the society. But when in that same city—Birmingham, Alabama—five hundred black babies die each year because of the lack of proper food, shelter and medical facilities, and thousands more are destroyed and maimed physically, emotionally and intellectually because of conditions of poverty and discrimination in the black community, that is a function of institutional racism. When a black family moves into a home in a white neighborhood and is stoned, burned or routed out, they are victims of an overt act of individual racism which many people will condemn —at least in words. But it is institutional racism that keeps black people locked in dilapidated slum tenements, subject to the daily prey of exploitative slumlords, merchants, loan sharks and discriminatory real estate agents. The society either pretends it does not know of this latter situation, or is in fact incapable of doing anything about it (p. 4).

This conceptualization of racism and its concomitant distinction between *individual* and *institutional* racism are the culmination of long years of commitment and subsequent disappointment with the "snail's-pace" progress and ineffectiveness of integration in our society. These disappointments were articulated within the somewhat volatile and controversial rhetoric of black power. The cry for black power represented a shift in emphasis by blacks from a focal concern with assimilation into the "mainstream" and being accepted, to a more assertive posture aimed at the acquisition of power and a change to conditions supporting greater self-acceptance.

A parallel development or shift has occurred within the ranks of psychology. The Society for the Psychological Study of Social Issues (SPSSI), founded in 1936, has typically represented the action-arm of social psychology. As such, one of its approaches to problems of racial prejudice and segregation has been to focus on theories and practices conducive to accomplishing positive or favorable attitude change in housing, education, and employment as a function of desegregation or integration. This approach was actually a challenge to the social thinking of an era influenced by William Graham Sumner's assertion that "stateways cannot change folkways." More simply put, Sumner was suggesting that "you cannot legislate against prejudice." While social scientists took issue with Sumner, it is quite clear that his criticism was in part on target—there was always the secret hope that legislative efforts would ultimately result in attitude change. Consider, for example, Allport's response to Sumner's assertion: "Legislation aims not at controlling prejudice, but only its open expression. But when expression changes, *thoughts* [italics added] too, in the long run, are likely to fall into line" (1958, p. 437). As a secondary consideration, Allport goes on to discuss cogent arguments against the legislative approach (indirect agreement with Sumner):

Laws, especially of the puritan type so common in America, attack symptoms, not causes. To force a hotel manager to accept a Filipino guest is not to strike at the roots of his anti-Oriental bias. To force a child to sit next to a Negro child in school does not remove the economic fear that may lie at the bottom of his family's anti-Negro feelings. People are fashioned by deeper forces, not by surface pressure (pp. 437–438).

Kenneth Clark (1953) has suggested that social scientists are preoccupied with antecedents of social action and social change rather than action and change themselves because these antecedents provide perspective that makes for a comfortable margin of safety, free from the dangers inherent in controversial problems. In proposing a theory of social change, Clark argues:

> The data reveal that desired changes in the behavior of individuals and groups can be brought about by a change in the social situation in which they are required to function. Changes in the social situation are effected and reinforced by individuals with authority, prestige, power and the control over the media of communication and important areas of life. Situationally determined changes in behavior may or may not be accompanied by compatible changes in attitudes or motivation of the individuals involved. Whether or not behavioral changes are accompanied by attitudinal changes does not seem to be related to the observed stability of the behavioral changes. Some of the examined evidence suggest that compatible changes in attitudes and motivation may occur as a consequence of the changed situation and the changed behavior (p. 72).

I am in basic agreement with this sentiment, particularly with the emphasis on the characteristics of the agents of change. I would simply extend this formulation by suggesting that critical to the success of such a model of change is that blacks (or other minorities) be represented among the ranks of those with "authority," "prestige," "power," and "control." In order for this to happen, we obviously cannot believe that these qualities are genetically determined. Recently, youthful insistence among the ranks of psychologists resulted in similar concerns. Psychologists for Social Action (PSA) was founded in 1968 with the intent of pursuing a more activist program than that represented by SPSSI. A focal (and vocal) aspect of this movement was the articulation and encouragement of a more active involvement regarding the problems of prejudice, war, etc. Parallel developments included the establishment of professional caucuses by blacks and by women. In both cases, there was an insistence upon better involvement and representation in the affairs of the American Psychological Association (APA). The chief concerns of black psychologists were abuses in testing and misrepresentation or distortion of research results from black communities by their white colleagues. That this changing emphasis was having some impact within APA was evidenced, in part, by the fact that the convention theme for the annual meeting of APA in 1969 was "Psychology and the Problems of Society." Subsequently, blacks (and women) have played an increasingly larger role in APA conventions and administrative functions.

The most sophisticated translation, in my opinion, of the meaning of these shifts and their relationship to the scholarly pursuit and application of racial prejudice and attitudes can be found in Jones's *Prejudice and Racism* (1972). The argument developed by Jones suggests that social scientists have traditionally reversed the emphasis (or context) in which the study of prejudice should be pursued. By studying prejudice as a departure from egalitarian norms, we have perhaps missed a more important or basic level of analysis—the racism inherent in our social structure (institutions, etc.). After careful analysis of Allport's brief theory of prejudice, Jones develops a model that encompasses three kinds of racism (individual, institutional, and cultural) and reverses the traditional focus represented by the Allport model. Allport explains the causes of prejudice through six approaches that culminate in an emphasis on the object of prejudice. In reversing this model, Jones's model (see Figure 13–1) provides for an analysis that shifts the focus from a concern with the objects or effects of prejudice (i.e., the symptoms) to the underlying conditions that result in some people becoming prejudiced and others not. This shift also minimizes the implications that the victims of prejudice are somehow responsible for their own lot.

FIGURE 13–1.   *Through a Telescope Widely—a Model for the Analysis of Racism*

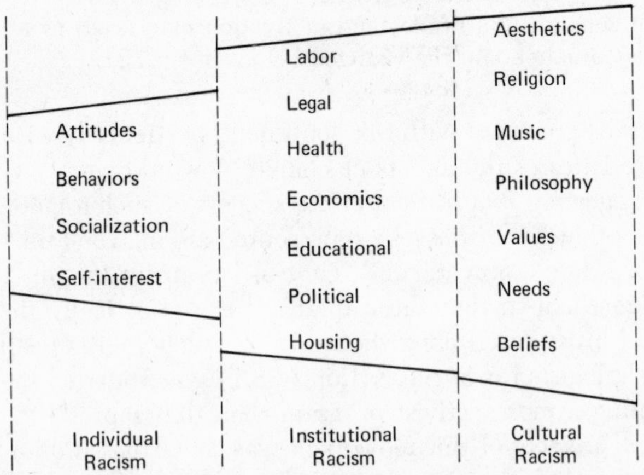

Reprinted by special permission from J. M. Jones, *Prejudice and Racism*, 1972, Addison-Wesley, Reading, Mass.

Implicit in the attitudinal approach to prejudice is that individuals are to blame, and that there is a correlation between attitudes and behavior. This belief persisted despite the work of LaPiere (1934) and others (see Wicker, 1969) which demonstrated that behaviors did not always correspond to prejudice attitudes.

The model developed by Jones reverses the traditional focus of studying attitudes and their sociohistorical antecedents. Additionally, unlike the Allport model, it doesn't make the object person (or victim) of racial prejudice central to the analysis. That approach has too often resulted in the study of or concern with symptoms instead of causes. On the other hand, this new approach begins with the concept of individual racism, which bears some overlap with the concept of racial prejudice. Unlike racial prejudice, however, individual racism emphasizes negative aspects of other groups and positive aspects of one's own group. Further, individuals engage in behaviors designed to maintain group positions of inferiority–superiority. If the analysis stopped here, there would be a good deal of similarity between the two concepts. The second stage in Jones's model, the expansion to institutional racism (as discussed above), had its origin in Carmichael and Hamilton's (1967) thesis on "black power." This expansion, unlike a focus on attitudes, has the advantage of using objective criteria in determining the existence of institutional racism. The evidence of gross racial inequities that flows from institutional policies and practices is all that is needed to substantiate the charge of institutional racism. The objectivity provided by this construct results from its lack of concern with *intentions*. It is the *consequences* of institutional policies or practices that are of importance. If the work force of a company that exists in a predominantly black community is only 4 percent black, and all of those blacks are in low-level job categories, then this is an instance of institutional racism. This definition creates an even greater distinction between racism and racial prejudice. However, as can be seen in Figure 13–1, cultural racism defines a final expansion in which the focus of concern is rooted in the values, traditions, and assumptions upon which institutions are based. Inasmuch as individuals are socialized in institutions, the concept of cultural racism embraces both individuals and institutions. Salient examples of cultural racism are evidences of omissions of achievements and contributions to a culture by a racial group, or when observed differences in a racial group are interpreted as negative or are not rewarded by members of the majority group.

In 1968, a presidential commission on civil disorders attributed racial tension and violence in our society to white racism. The commission's delineation of white racism and its subsequent negative outcomes on blacks and other minorities will not be detailed here. However, the reader is encouraged to join the ranks of the presumably small number of individuals to have read the report from the *U.S. Commission on Civil Disorders*. What is compellingly clear from that document is that we are a long way from solving our racial problems or providing this society a technology for doing so. In 1957, when the Russians launched Sputnik, the United States was out of the space race; yet in the short span of twelve years, we entered that race and successfully landed men on the moon on two different space missions in 1969 (ahead of the Russians). This accomplishment was undoubtedly the outcome of a tremendous effort and cooperation between private industry and government and represented an enormous commitment of fiscal resources to achieve that end. Contrariwise, we have presumably labored for over a hundred years without good solutions or resolve for the problems between races. It is my opinion that, unlike the case of technological advancement, human problem solving or advancement requires that persons responsible for change undergo change themselves. It is perhaps just for this reason that we have not made more progress in solving racial problems. Case in point—white liberals who have advocated civil rights legislation from the comfortable perspective of "North versus South," seem to show diminished passions for integration when it means the house next door or the school where their children are enrolled. The 1973 United States Commission on Civil Rights' report amply documents this diminished commitment by pointing to governmental failures in providing equal educational opportunities, lack of enforcement procedures by the Federal Power Commission, and downgrading of the Office of Federal Contract Compliance by the Labor Department. "In 425 pages of detailed examples, the commission said there has been a failure of leadership at almost every level of every federal agency, including the White House, to live up to its promises on equal rights and equal opportunities" (*Washington Post*, February 10, 1973).

CONTRIBUTIONS FROM PSYCHOLOGY

At least two questions must be addressed in undertaking a volume of this nature. First, it is important to ask—how well can our present knowledge help us to achieve integration in organizations? And secondly, can we do a better job, given this knowledge, than the sophisticated, well-motivated layman? Some quick considerations will help in addressing these issues. Psychology is not an impartial and unemotional discipline. Theories and hypotheses are constructed in the context of tradition, values, *prejudices,* and at times simply out of dissatisfaction with the order of things. Hence, our discipline is as much a value construct, from which the experimenter cannot easily extricate himself, as it is a procedure for pursuing "scientific" data. Given this picture, it is quite significant that very little research on racial prejudice and/or integration has been done by black behavioral scientists. More immediately, with the exception of myself, there are no black authors to the chapters in this volume.

An additional consideration that the reader must be cognizant of is that psychologists in general have not dealt very extensively with the concept of power. The work of French and Raven (1959) is a notable exception to this point. The relevance of this consideration hinges on the assumption that powerlessness is a major factor in the disadvantaged minority that would presumably be helped by integrating organizations. The issue of power was a central concern in a recent compromise between the black leadership of the Atlanta NAACP and an all-white school board. In short, the blacks in Atlanta traded integration for power. In an arrangement that would call for the busing of 3,000 students instead of 30,000 students, the school board agreed that blacks will get nine of seventeen key executive positions in the system, including Superintendent and Assistant Superintendent of Instruction. Implicit in this arrangement was that control, through more power, would provide a better assurance of quality education for black children than would be necessarily accomplished through integrated classrooms. Even though the desired outcome (quality education) might not be achieved via this route, it would be difficult to deny the close relationship between power and the control and allocation of those resources which facilitate quality education. This relationship and its implications generalize to the major organizations in our society. Yet, minorities (and women) are conspicuously absent in top executive or decision-making positions in American organizations.

A coalition of minorities and women's groups recently surveyed executive positions in the sixty-seven largest California corporations. The results indicated that of the corporations' 1,008 directors, not one is black; none is Mexican-American; one is Spanish-surnamed and he holds the Nobel Prize in physics. Six of these directors are women, of which three are married to the company president or chairman, and one is the daughter of the company's founder. There is no reason to believe these data would not generalize to most organizations throughout the country. If the recent thrust taken by the leadership of the Atlanta NAACP is correct, then any solution offered by psychologists or other behavioral scientists that ignores considerations of power would be short-sighted.

Finally, understanding the information presented in the preceding chapters can be faciliated by an awareness of research strategies. The chapter on laboratory research by Fromkin and Ostrom addresses important considerations here. This concern is consistent with the stated objectives in the preface of this volume: "We would like to build a bridge of some significance between the research and theory of the social scientist and the world of action of the organizational administrator (and) . . . to stimulate some experimental research of both laboratory and field varieties which deal directly with this problem" (p. 2). The chapter by Fromkin and Ostrom more than adequately delineates the problems and possible solutions in generalizing from the laboratory to life. However, since a good deal of our information also comes from field studies, it is appropriate to cite additional considerations from that perspective.

Hyman (1969) has noted that a good deal of field research is mainly case studies in which the reader can never be sure whether they represent unusual or typical cases. Additionally, it is not always clear whether a given reference group isn't actually a subgroup of the target population. For example, in an experiment by DeFleur and Westie (1958), subjects who were asked whether or not they would give their permission to have photographs of themselves with blacks shown publicly indicated in making their decisions that they had certain key groups in mind. The forty-six subjects mentioned sixty different reference groups as influencing their decision. Approximately three-fourths invoked some type of reference group, while the remaining fourth based their decisions upon their own feelings. Also, data from Hyman and Sheatsley (1964) reveal that Northerners who move to the South maintain their former reference groups, continuing to favor integration, whereas Southerners who move to the North adopt the new local reference group standards, becoming much less segregationist. Related to this point is the observation that little research, if any, on racial prejudice takes black attitudes into consideration. Consequently, little is known about the reference groups of blacks.

Finally, ethical considerations restrict the range of methodologies that can be employed in investigating prejudice, racism, integration, and related phenomena. Researchers must be concerned about the rights and privacy of human subjects, as well as the conditions to which they are exposed. A president's panel on privacy and behavior research concluded that each individual must decide for himself how much of his thoughts, feelings, and other personal behaviors he wishes to share with others. Obviously, if we allowed ourselves to ignore these considerations, we could more effectively construct situations designed to yield valuable information regarding racial prejudice and discrimination. However, our code of ethics compels regard for the rights of individuals. Consequently, research subjects should never be exposed to conditions that produce lasting changes or stress. These considerations do not prohibit research in this critical area; however, they do challenge the ingenuity of researchers to design experiments that do not violate the rights and privacy of participating subjects.

STATE OF SOCIETY—POLARIZATION/INTEGRATION

The damning indictment of American society as racist, by the Kerner Commission, stops short of demonstrating the psychology of racism and its consequence—racial conflict and violence. Fanon (1966), Comer (1969, 1972), and others have written extensively on how social institutions promote racial practices that not only ensure domination and control by one group but simultaneously abate the anxieties and discomforts inherent in racist practices. As a modal practice then, institutions stage and sustain the drama of conflict between blacks and whites. In the final analysis, it has been the clashing of interests between these two groups that has chipped away at the foundation of this country.

American institutions have proliferated as virtually all-white enterprises. The absence of blacks in our institutional history has made it easier for racist practices to become entrenched. No doubt this entrenchment contributes in large measure to the lack of success of integration. Fortunately or unfortunately, integration, like slavery, is an institution devised and defined by whites for blacks—without black input. It was quite obvious that the system of slavery encouraged as one of its goals, the destruction of the black community. Slave insurrections dramatized the extreme negative reaction to this cruel institution. Now the paucity of evidence to support a genuine desire on the part of whites for a meaningful coexistence (i.e., integration) with blacks and black frustrations with the hypocrisy in American institutions create similar adverse reactions. The Emancipation Proclamation (another white institution) freed the slaves only to expose them to a legal system of segregation and rampant lynchings. Today, many blacks are suspicious of similar outcomes associated with efforts at integration.

James Baldwin has written: "To be a Negro in this country and to be relatively conscious is to be in a rage almost all the time." The rage of which Baldwin speaks mushroomed into the black power movement of the 1960s. However, most of the advocates of black power have been murdered, imprisoned, bought off, or exiled. The void created by their absence will be filled either with meaningful approaches to the goal of racial justice or the crisis of another day is imminent.

Social Responsibility in Organizations

A new breed of executives exists in American organizations today: vice-president for corporate public policy; urban affairs manager; executive vice-president for social policy; director of minority relations and employment; etc. Most of these titles, unheard of a few years ago, reflect a new trend in American industry to address itself to problems of minority and female employment, consumerism, and ecology. Some companies, once boycotted by blacks because of employment practices, now actively recruit minorities and run massive training programs. Yet, in many instances, contradictions still abound. Banks with active minority recruitment programs simultaneously refuse to make mortgage loans in run-down parts of the city—including many minority areas. There are also cases in which companies that are actively engaged in minority recruitment and are providing fiscal support for rebuilding slum housing are also engaged in exploitative business practices that primarily handicap minorities.

Despite these contradictions, a new posture of social responsibility is beginning to characterize American organizations. Whether this change is a function of good citizenship or compliance with federal antibias codes seems less important than an assessment of the effectiveness of the change.

One criterion of effectiveness is the extent to which the changes will create avenues to power for powerless blacks. The NAACP leadership in Atlanta seems to understand this quite well. In other instances in the black community pressures are being directed at the United Givers Fund by creating a separate Black United Fund. In an escalated effort, blacks have threatened to boycott any agency receiving funds from the United Givers Fund that does not have blacks on its board of directors. It should be cautioned, however, that black membership on boards of directors does not automatically produce power. There are several potential problems in this development. Blacks are inexperienced and in many cases do not understand the dynamics of power. Consequently, it is far too easy for whites to use this naiveté to their advantage; namely, the black merely becomes a buffer between the white oppressor and the black oppressed.

More profoundly, however, blacks who serve on boards in white organizations do not have a black constituency supporting them; their positions are usually a result of appointment by whites. Consequently, to advocate points of view favorable to black interests could result in losing the position as board member. If black membership and participation in boards of directors is going to be meaningful and helpful to the black community, then mechanisms must be developed which permit black people themselves to be involved in the selection of those who represent them. When there is an understanding among blacks within organizations that blacks will accept appointments to boards only when the black community is involved in the process, there will be fewer and fewer opportunities for blacks to be used in the further exploitation of their own people. Since there is no power base behind the black board member, it is quite easy for the white majority to ignore him (or her). An example of this involves a rather prominent American firm whose black board member developed a detailed brief as to why the firm should divest its business transactions in South Africa (a country where racial oppression is a matter of explicit government policy). The board patiently listened to the arguments and then voted over-whelmingly to continue business as usual.

Thus far, I have argued that data form psychology and other behavioral sciences in support of the efficacy of integration as a remedy for racial conflict and discord are minimal at best. Additionally, I have suggested that this failure is due perhaps to an oversimplification of the problem—namely, little research if any has distinguished between prejudice and racism. It has been assumed, naively, that a change in attitude would produce behavioral changes. Finally, the research tends to ignore the dynamics of power which characterize any relationship between oppressed and oppressors. Research on Allport's (1954) equal-status contact hypothesis epitomizes this shortcoming in the research literature.

Equal-Status Contact Hypothesis

Allport's (1954) equal-status contact hypothesis derives its conceptual support from the definition of prejudice as a negative attitude. In essence, it presumes that contact between the prejudiced and the objects of the prejudice will reduce the erroneous perceptions thought to be responsible for the prejudice. It is further assumed that this shift will lead to a positive change in attitude and, hopefully, a change in behavior. Heider's balance theory aids somewhat in the theoretical analysis of the possible effects of contact. Heider (1958) postulates unit relationships (things going together) and liking relationships. Contact with another person would establish a unit relationship. If a dislike relationship existed along with the unit relationship, imbalance would be created and pressures would develop to reduce the imbalance. This imbalance could be reduced by changing the liking relationship from dislike to like, producing the effect predicted by Allport's hypothesis. Alternatively, however, the unit relationship could be dissolved with no change in liking. In instances where the contact cannot be terminated, as in school integration, balance theory would predict increased liking as the only option possible. Dissonance theory, however, would make the opposite prediction. In dissonance theory, forced contact is not a condition that produces dissonance. As Brehm and Cohen (1962) note, volition is an important factor in the development of dissonance. Balance theory, then, would predict the result hypothesized by Allport could occur, but not necessarily. Exchange or reinforcement interpretations (Thibaut and Kelley, 1959; Homans, 1961) also bear on the equal-status contact hypothesis. Homans (1961) specifically suggests that if interaction is frequent, sentiments of liking will grow. However, this outcome will obviously be influenced by the rewards and costs in the situation, in which case there would certainly be occasions when liking would not be expected.

The literature on the relationship between proximity and attractiveness indicates that proximity (which increases contact) will lead to increasingly positive attitudes. Festinger, Schachter, and Back (1950), in a study of relationships within a housing project, found that individuals chose to associate with those with whom they were in close proximity and with whom they had the most opportunity to interact. Whyte (1956) found similar results in relationship to voluntary association (presumably based on attraction); those living close together related more than those who were more distant. In a laboratory study, Freedman, Carlsmith, and Suomi (1969) demonstrated that proximity effects are mediated, at least in part, by simple familiarity and that this produces more attraction. Subjects met and sat silently in the same room for differing numbers of sessions. The more frequently the subjects met, the greater their expressed liking for each other.

Proximity is related to attractiveness for several reasons. First, it is easier to interact with people who are close, and this ease positively reinforces the interaction. In addition, when two people are in proximity, there is more opportunity to exchange information, a condition which leads to increased similarity according to the theories of both Newcomb (1953) and Homans (1950). Newcomb points out that proximity increases attraction in two ways. First, proximity and the continued communication it entails increases similarity of beliefs and values. Secondly, with increased similarity, liking increases. Therefore, there appears to be ample theoretical justification for the conceptual validity of the contact hypothesis. Additionally, there is some empirical evidence that such contact can have a positive effect on attitudes.

A second assumption of the hypothesis, however, is that it is necessary for the contact to be on an equal-status level. Evidence on the relationship between perceived similarity and attraction or liking has relevance to the evaluation of this portion of the hypothesis. This analysis is based on the assumption that perceived similarity is greater in two people of equal status than of unequal status. Balance theory can again offer useful insights here. Balance theory would predict that equal status could produce increased attractiveness via perceived similarity. Balance theory notes that if Y is similar to X and Y dislikes X, imbalance and pressures to change are created. Balance may be restored by liking X. It is also clear, however, in line with the above analysis, that balance may also be restored by reducing the perceived similarity. Similarity is based on perception, and the perception can be distorted to achieve balance.

The importance of similarity in race relations is demonstrated by the research derived from Rokeach's belief congruence hypothesis, which argues that negative racial attitudes are based on the dissimilarity of beliefs assumed by whites. Whether belief is more important than race in determining prejudice is still an unclear issue, but the fact is that whites, if given no other information, assume that blacks hold different beliefs and that this is an influential factor in their negative attitudes toward blacks (Byrne and Wong, 1962; Rokeach and Mezei, 1966; Rokeach, Smith, and Evans, 1960; Triandis and Davis, 1965).

Newcomb's (1961) roommate study is the clearest indication of the general relationship between similarity and attractiveness. Newcomb found that roommates originally matched to be similar liked each other more than those who were dissimilar. In this study, the similarity clearly preceded the liking. However, qualification of the effects of similarity must be made in light of findings by Byrne and Wong (1962) and Byrne and McGraw (1964). These authors demonstrated that contact won't increase belief similarity in prejudiced people unless nearly complete similarity exists at the outset.

The importance of status, per se, has been stressed by attribution theorists. Kelley (1967), for example, notes that status has important implications for the type of attribution made, whether positive or negative, since status has implications for whether the behavior was externally or internally caused. Thibaut and Riecken (1955) demonstrated that an individual who complies with a request is liked more if he is of higher status than the person making the request, rather than if he is of lower status. A study such as this, while not dealing directly with equal status, does appear to have implications for equal-status association by showing how status affects the attribution of positive or negative traits. Since it is probably true that most whites have most of their contacts with black people of lower status, attribution of negative traits is most frequent in interpreting the behavior of blacks. Equal-status contact should, therefore, according to attribution theory, change the type of attribution made to black people in a more positive direction. It would appear, then, that research in the area of attribution provides support for the equal-status contact hypothesis.

It is also suggested that the sharing of common goals is essential for the contact to be successful. The requirement for cooperative interdependence, which is also an important aspect of the equal-status contact hypothesis, is closely related to the goal requirement; hence, the two will be treated together. The prediction of the positive effects of a common goal also receives conceptual support from balance theory. If A wants X (goal), B wants X, and A dislikes B, imbalance exists. This may be reduced by a shift in conditions such that A likes B. (Rejection of the goal by A would also restore balance.) Hence, once again balance theory would predict contact with cooperative interdependence and a common goal may result in increased liking, not that it necessarily will.

Reinforcement theory would predict that shared goals under cooperative interdependence should lead to increased liking. Association of another person with positive reinforcement, as would occur in cooperative interdependence, should create increased liking. A study by Festinger and Kelly (1951) demonstrates the potentially positive aspects of creating common goals and goals of a type which require cooperative interdependence for successful achievement. These authors found that subjects who were involved in common goals showed reduced hostility for others who participated in and had favorable attitudes toward the endeavor. Both participation and favorable attitudes would appear to be necessary for the establishment of cooperative interdependence. This study, then, demonstrated the potential efficacy of common or shared goals and cooperative interdependence in the reduction of negative attitudes.

Sherif's studies (1936, 1966) are among the clearest indications that both common goals and cooperative interdependence are necessary for contact to work in the reduction of hostility. After creating conflict and negative attitudes between two groups of boys in a camp, Sherif attempted to reduce the conflict in a number of ways. The only successful method found was to bring the groups together (contact) to obtain something they both wanted (common goal) which they could obtain only by working together (cooperative interdependence).

Then the experimenters tried the equivalent of racial integration. They brought the two groups together for movies, meals, and other social events. But instead of serving to reduce hostility, the events merely provided added opportunity for the two groups to assail each other. Finally, a series of crises were arranged to force cooperation between the groups. For example, water came to the camp in pipes from a tank about a mile away. The experimenters arranged to interrupt it and then called the boys together to inform them of the crisis. Both groups promptly volunteered to search the water line for trouble. They worked together harmoniously, and before the end of the afternoon had located and corrected the difficulty. Similar joint endeavors in response to other experimentally created crises resulted in the cessation of hostility and other negative behaviors. Members of the two groups actively sought opportunities to mingle, entertain, and otherwise socialize with each other.

The general literature on similarity, status, contact, and cooperative interdependence strongly suggests that there is a rational basis for Allport's hypothesis, i.e., there is ample evidence to suggest that it *should* work. Yet, in terms of social policy and practice, there has been little encouragement from results. Concerted efforts in the areas of housing, employment, and education have failed to yield outcomes consistent with Allport's prediction.

The classic study by Deutsch and Collins (1951) examined similar housing projects in which the buildings were either integrated or segregated. In the integrated buildings, the authors found more contact and more positive attitudes toward blacks. This study provides fairly strong support for Allport's hypothesis. Stouffer et al. (1949) found that increased contact among soldiers led to decreased stereotyping, indicating once again the successful outcome of contact.

Other studies have not found such positive effects. A study by Campbell

(1958) indicated that school desegregation which led to increased contact did indeed have a large effect on attitudes, but the effect operated in both directions, with attitudes not only becoming more positive in some individuals, but becoming more negative in others. Other studies have shown that integration may produce more positive attitudes but that the change is limited only to the situation in which the contact takes place and does not represent a more generalized improvement in attitudes toward the group which is the object of the prejudice (Harding and Hogrefe, 1952; Palmore, 1955). Webster (1961) found that whites' attitudes toward blacks became more negative after integration than they had been previously. Negative effects as a result of housing integration have also been found (Kramer, 1950; Hunt, 1959).

The research results appear to be far more negative than would be expected on the basis of the analysis of the general theoretical and empirical information on various subparts of the hypothesis. In addition, examination of the current social situation suggests that the effects of implementation of social policy in line with Allport's hypothesis have not been as successful as one would hope. Although some positive attitude change has probably taken place, racial tension and conflict are still widespread. In addition, there is evidence that attitudes in some instances have become more negative, e.g., the emotional nature of the busing issue.

Several reasons may be suggested for the failure to achieve as great an improvement in attitudes as expected. In the first case, the laws, while increasing contact, may not fulfill all the conditions of the hypothesis. School desegregation often involves bringing lower-class blacks into middle-class white schools. Additionally, it is not always clear whether or not common goals are involved in many of the situations involving integration. More profoundly, however, many of these situations fail to come to grips with the fact that prejudice is deeply rooted in the character structure of most whites. In this respect, the theoretical analysis of attitudes in terms of their functions has implications for the contact hypothesis.

The functional analysis of attitudes as set forth by Smith, Bruner, and White (1956) posits that there are three primary functions that an attitude can serve. The first is the *object-appraisal* function, which permits the individual to evaluate objects and people in order to obtain a stable picture of the world. The second function is the *social-adjustment* function, in which one's attitudes serve to guide behavior in a way that helps the individual to fit in with his social group. Attitudes serving these first two functions would appear to be amenable to change under conditions of the equal-status hypothesis. If the attitude created an incorrect perception of the world in its object-appraisal function, contact should reveal this error and produce attitude change. In addition, changes in the requirements of the social situation could be affected by increased contact leading to changes in attitudes serving the social-adjustment function. The third function is that of *externalization*, in which the attitude serves to solve personal and psychological problems of the individual. For example, an attitude may be formed which projects one's own unacceptable behavior onto the object of prejudice. Integration would not be likely to change attitudes serving this function, since the contact would not alleviate the individual problems underlying the attitude. It is unclear how widespread this function is in prejudiced attitudes, but to the extent that it exists it decreases the likelihood of contact leading to positive attitude change.

Racially Separate or Together?

Pettigrew (1967; 1969) has argued that *only* through contact (integration) can the belief in inferiority and value dissimilarity be eliminated. He further suggests that any separation between the races simply increases forces which support prejudice—including institutional forces. The issues which Pettigrew brings to bear on this argument are delineated in a four-cell model whose dimensions are "contact–separation" and "autonomy" (see Figure 13-2). The four cells in this model are: Cell "A," true integration which includes institutionalized biracial situations with individual and group (biracial) autonomy;

FIGURE 13–2.   *Schematic Diagram of Autonomy and Contact-Separation*

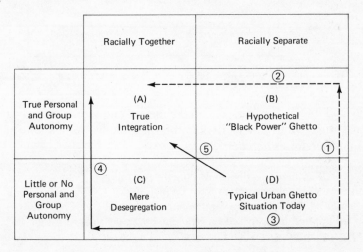

From T. F. Pettigrew, Racially separate or together? *Journal of Social Issues*, 1965, *25*, No. 1, 43–69; revised in 1969.
Note: Dotted lines denote hypothetical paths; solid lines, actual paths.

Cell "B," black power ghetto (hypothetical) independent of society; Cell "C," desegregated situations with little cross-racial acceptance; and Cell "D," today's urban ghetto with little or no personal or group autonomy. Pettigrew suggests that "black separatists" see only one route to integration: from the depressed ghetto to the hypothetical ghetto and then, perhaps, true integration (lines 1 and 2 in Figure 13–2); whereas desegregationists assume the opposite route: mere desegregation, then true integration (lines 3 and 4 in Figure 13–2). Pettigrew argues that the only approach to "true integration" is from Cell D directly to Cell A (line 5).

Since I take exception to this model and its hypothesized outcomes, I will discuss my objections in the context of observations already made and an alternative model (see Figure 13-3). The proposed model takes as its starting point the assertion that the "hypothetical black power ghetto" inadequately depicts the phenomenon which it was devised to explain. Additionally, integration as

FIGURE 13–3.   *Schematic Diagram of Power and Goals*

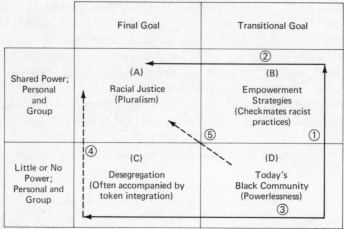

Note: Dotted lines denote paths with low probability of successful outcomes, and solid lines denote paths with high probability of successful outcomes.

a strategy and integration as a goal, in the means–end sense, have always lacked conceptual distinction and clarity. Pettigrew's model suffers this same deficiency. Consider, for example:

> The overall *strategy* needed must contain the following elements: (a) A major effort toward racial integration must be mounted. . . . This effort should envisage by the late 1970's complete attainment of the goal . . . (b) . . . strict criteria must be applied to proposed enrichment programs to insure that they are productive for later dispersal and *integration* (Pettigrew, 1969, p. 64, italics added).

The proposed model in Figure 13–3 provides an analysis that hopefully clarifies this confusion; additionally, its logic evolves from concepts of racism as discussed by Carmichael and Hamilton (1967) and Jones (1972). As indicated above, in the study by Sherif (1936; 1966), the validity of the equal-status contact hypothesis is contingent upon conditions of cooperative interdependence to achieve common goals. However, a precondition to equal status which neither Allport nor Pettigrew acknowledge is *power*. Accordingly, the model proposed here permits an examination of the relationship between power and the ultimate goal in race relations. In Cell "A" racial justice refers to intergroup harmony predicated on concepts of equity and fair play irrespective of racial identification; Cell "B" represents the category of strategies instrumental to achieving racial justice. The advantage here is that this conceptualization does not preclude multiple strategies, nor does it prejudge the character of any strategy. It also acknowledges that some *strategy* is necessary to move from today's situation (Cell D) to the desired goal (Cell A), a feature that is missing in Pettigrew's model. Furthermore, it obviates the usage of the provocative and misleading term "separatist." Cell "C" represents the all-to-familiar practice of desegregation, in which racial barriers are relaxed or substituted by token integration—rarely if ever involving the transmittal of power. Cell "D" typifies today's society, in which most blacks are economically deprived and poorly educated—and powerless to alter these conditions.

Assuming agreement upon the final goal (Cell A), the proposed model in Figure 13-3 allows multiple strategies but only one route to that end. Movement to desegregation and then racial justice (lines 3 and 4) is virtually impossible, as is movement from today's black community to racial justice (line 5), since neither of these efforts comes to terms with the empowerment of blacks (and other minorities). Giving blacks equal education, equal employment, equal income, equal housing, and so on, will never lead to perceived equality in the eyes of whites, without the addition of power. Carmichael and Hamilton (1967) provide a rather detailed analysis of race relations in Tuskegee, Alabama, where blacks have achieved equal socioeconomic status with whites, but still suffer the ill effects of prejudice and discrimination.

> The TCA (Tuskegee Civic Association) held a peculiar position in the black community. Not many people openly supported it (and many wished it would just quiet down), but they recognized that something was wrong with the one-way deferential relationship existing between the races in the community. They knew that it was incongruous for them to have economic and educational achievements and to remain at the political mercy of a white minority. It was, to say the least, embarrassing, and for this reason many black people never talked about it. They withdrew and let the TCA fight their political battles (p. 132).

When the political advantage of the whites became threatened by increases in black voters, whites persuaded the state legislature to pass a law gerrymandering the city of Tuskegee. The result was that only ten black voters were left in the city; no whites were touched by the gerrymandering.

> The blacks had achieved education and economic security—both of which are still projected throughout the nation as cure-alls—but the whites continued to lay and collect taxes, rule over the school system, determine law enforcement practices. The reason is obvious enough: blacks did not have *political* power. Economic security or the promise of it may, as we noted in Chapter V, be vital to the building of a strong political force. But in a vacuum it is of no use to black people working for meaningful change (p. 134).

In light of these events, it seems naive to argue that integration, per se, is the solution to the nation's ills. White liberals have always supported an integrated society as a solution to racial problems. The unchallengeable, overriding goal has been integration. The end was critically considered, means were not; yet, integration has become the means. In fact, the commitment to that particular strategy is so ingrained that it freezes or restricts severely the ability to explore constructive alternatives when considering solutions to racial problems. Blacks have pursued integration strategies by seeking coalitions with the white power structure, rich and upper-class whites, philanthropists, entrepreneurs, middle-class white progressives (liberals), poor whites, and finally radical whites. In all cases, these efforts have met with failure, primarily because (1) internal power relations between blacks and whites were never resolved, (2) hidden conflicts between the interests of poor blacks and middle-class whites were never resolved, and finally, (3) the latent racism of whites has never been adequately confronted.

The 1960s witnessed a crystallization of these issues accompanied by a metamorphosis on the part of many blacks, including members of the black middle class who had separated from their community, divorced themselves from any responsibility to it, yet never gained acceptance by the white community. This marginal class (see E. Franklin Frazier's *Black Bourgeoisie*) is the best evidence of the failure of integration to produce the goals characterized by Cell A in the model in Figure 13-3.

In a recent issue of *Operations Research,* Ackoff (1970) describes a model that is a fair approximation of the strategy implied in Cell B (Figure 13–3). Along with two colleagues, Ackoff developed an untried approach to university aid to the ghetto. It is the assumption behind this approach that is of paramount importance, however: *the best way the white community can help the black community is to enable it to solve its problems in the way it, the black community, wants to.* Therefore, leadership selected from the black community submitted a proposal, which was funded by the Anheuser–Busch Charitable Trust and the Ford Foundation, for $50,000 per year for two years. From this beginning, nine manufacturing firms that grossed more than 1.5 million dollars in 1969 and employed 125 people from the community were established. Through university aid, loans from banks have been secured that have enabled the start-up of additional businesses, including technical and managerial assistance. A credit union which permits community individuals to join for only 25 cents was also established to permit personal loans. The university has developed a program in business education for the disadvantaged in the area, scholarships to private suburban schools have been secured, and an Urban Leadership Training Program has been established.

At the time of his article, Ackoff indicated that the leadership in the black community had established their independence from outer influence. Yet their planning required a sensitivity to potential sources of resources from the larger society of which the black community is a part. This undoubtedly required a skillful utilization of power in bringing about ends compatible with aspirations of the black community and yet not compromising their independence. In conclusion, Ackoff indicates that these ghetto leaders have as an ultimate objective the dissolution of the ghetto by having it absorbed into the main current of the culture of which it is a part.

It is with this final conclusion that I would take some exception. One of my key objections to integration per se is that it typically represents an absorption of the black community—culture, values, and all. The implications of such an outcome are psychologically negative. Implicit in such a process is the indication that blackness is inferior and offers nothing of value—or nothing worth preserving.

Black power advocates represent the most encompassing challenge to these psychologically negative dynamics. Before he died, Whitney Young wrote: "Black power is not a shout of separation. Black power simply means . . . look at me . . . I'm here. I have dignity. I have pride. I have roots. I insist, I demand that I participate in those decisions that affect my life, and the lives of my children. It means that I'm somebody and that's what Black *power* [italics added] means."

A model that can be cited as an example of these dynamics in action was developed within the context of the Unitarian–Universalist Church. In May, 1968, the Unitarian–Universalist Association, at its General Assembly, voted to fund a Black Affairs Council $250,000 a year for four years. These monies are administered solely by blacks, with no strings, in support of innovation within black communities leading to growth in (1) education, (2) economic development, and (3) political empowerment. Through this funding mechanism, curriculum development and special seminars related to the black community have been supported at major educational institutions; a model of economic development which fosters community control and ownership has been initiated through projects in Newark, New Jersey, and Washington, D.C.; finally, notable examples of political empowerment derive from input to the Committee for a Unified Newark, whose voter registration and educational programs created the atmosphere which enabled the election of Mayor Kenneth Gibson. Similar support and involvement with the National Democratic Party of Alabama witnessed its most dramatic success in Green County, Alabama, where the successful challenge to local voting procedures resulted in a majority of blacks being elected to county office—for the first time in the South!

In summary, it is my contention that the most urgent and pressing task facing the managers of today's organizations is to explore ways of creating avenues for the empowerment of neglected minorities. Any careful analysis of organizations would point both to advantages and oppressive outcomes associated with power. Unfortunately, rarely is power shared or transferred without confrontation and struggle. In that light, one of the most useful functions this volume could serve would be to facilitate managers' awareness of the wisdom in sharing and/or relinquishing power gracefully. It is clear to me that black empowerment cannot be realized without the development of new approaches among whites in dealing with their institutions and new modes and models of relationships between blacks and whites.

Only those who have already experienced a revolution within themselves can reach out effectively to help others.

(Malcolm X)

REFERENCES

Ackoff, R. L. A black ghetto's research on a university. *Operations Research*, Sept.–Oct., 1970, *18*, 761–771.

Allport, G. W. *The nature of prejudice*. Reading, Mass.: Addison-Wesley, 1954.

Brehn, J. W., and Cohen, A. R. *Explorations in cognitive dissonance*. New York: Wiley, 1962.

Byrne, D., and McGraw, C. Interpersonal attraction toward Negroes. *Human Relations*, 1964, *17*, 201–213.

Byrne, D., and Wong, T. J. Racial prejudice, interpersonal attraction and assumed dissimilarity of attitudes. *Journal of Abnormal and Social Psychology*, 1962, *65*, 246–253.

Campbell, E. Q. Some social psychological correlates of direction in attitude change. *Social Forces*, 1958, *36*, 335–340.

Carmichael, S., and Hamilton, C. V. *Black power: The politics of liberation in America*. New York: Vintage Books, 1967.

Clark, K. Desegregation: An appraisal of the evidence. *The Journal of Social Issues*, 1953, *IX*, No. 4, 2–76.

Comer, J. P. *Beyond black and white*. Chicago: Quadrangle, 1972.

Comer, J. P. The dynamics of black and white violence. In H. D. Graham and T. R. Gurr (eds.), *Violence in America: Historical and comparative perspectives*. New York: Bantam, 1969.

DeFleur, M. L., and Westie, F. R. Verbal attitudes and overt acts: An experiment on the salience of attitudes. *American Sociological Review*, 1958, *23*, 667–673.

Deutsch, M., and Collins, A. E. *Interracial housing*. Minneapolis: University of Minnesota Press, 1951.

Fanon, F. *The wretched of the earth*. New York: Grove Press, 1966.

Festinger, L., and Kelley, H. H. *Changing attitudes through social contact*. Ann Arbor: University of Michigan, Institute of Social Research, 1951.

Festinger, L., Schachter, S., and Back, K. *Social pressures in informal groups: A study of human factors in housing*. New York: Harper, 1950.

Frazier, E. F. *Black bourgeoisie*. Glencoe, Ill.: Free Press, 1957.

Freedman, J. L., Carlsmith, J. M., and Suomi, S. The effect of familiarity on liking. Unpublished paper. Stanford University, 1969.

French, J. R. P., and Raven, B. H. Group support, legitimate power, and social influence. *Journal of Personality*, 1958, *26*, 400–409.

Fromkin, H. L., and Ostrom, T. M. Laboratory research and the organization: Generalizing from lab to life. In H. L. Fromkin and J. J. Sherwood (eds.), *Integrating the organization: A social psychological analysis*. New York: Free Press, 1974.

Harding, J., and Hogrefe, R. Attitudes of white department store employees toward negro co-workers. *Journal of Social Issues*, 1952, *8*, 18–28.

Heider, F. *The psychology of interpersonal relations*. New York: Wiley, 1958.

Homans, G. C. *Social behavior: Its elementary forms*. New York: Harcourt, 1961.

Homans, G. C. *The human group*. New York: Harcourt, 1950.

Hunt, C. L. Private integrated housing in a medium sized Northern city. *Social Problems*, 1959, *7*, 195–209.

Hyman, H. H. Social psychology and race relations. In I. Katz and P. Gurin (eds.), *Race and the social sciences*. New York: Basic Books, 1969.

Hyman, H. H. and Sheatsley, P. B. Attitudes toward desegregation. *Scientific American*, 1964, July, *211*, 16–23.

Jones, J. M. *Prejudice and racism*. Reading, Mass.: Addison–Wesley, 1972.

Kelley, H. H. Attribution theory in social psychology. *Nebraska Symposium on Motivation*, 1967, *15*, 192–238.

Kerner, O., et al. *Report of the National Advisory Commission on Civil Disorders*. New York: Bantam Books, 1968.

Kramer, B. M. Residential contact as a determinant of attitudes toward negroes. Unpublished paper, Harvard College Library, 1950.

LaPiere, R. T. Attitudes vs. actions. *Social Forces*, 1934, *13*, 230–237.

Newcomb, T. M. An approach to the study of communicative acts. *Psychological Review*, 1953, *60*, 393–404.

Palmore, E. B. The introduction of negroes into white departments. *Human Organizations*, 1955, *14*, 27–28.

Pettigrew, T. F. Racially separate or together? *Journal of Social Issues*, 1969, 25, 43–69.

Pettigrew, T. F. Social evaluation theory: convergences and applications. In D. Levine (ed.), *Nebraska symposium on motivation*. Lincoln, Neb., University of Nebraska Press, 1967.

Rokeach, M., and Mezei, L. Race and shared belief as factors in social choice. *Science*, 1966, *151*, 167–172.

Rokeach, M., Smith, P. W., and Evans, R. I. *Two* kinds of prejudice or one? In I. M. Rokeach (ed.), *The open and closed mind*. New York: Basic Books, 1960.

Sherif, M. *In common predicament*. Boston: Houghton Mifflin, 1966.

Sherif, M. *The psychology of social norms*. New York: Harper, 1936.

Smith, M. B., Bruner, J., and White, R. W. *Opinions and personality*. New York: Wiley, 1956.

Stouffer, S. A., Suchman, E. A., Devinney, C. C., Star, S. A., and Williams, R. M., Jr. Adjustment during army life. In *Studies in social psychology in World War II*. Vol. I: *The American Soldier*. Princeton, N. J.: Princeton University Press, 1949.

Thibaut, J. W., and Kelley, H. H. *The social psychology of groups*. New York: Wiley, 1959.

Thibaut, J. W., and Riecken, H. W. Some determinants and consequences of the perception of social causality. *Journal of Personality*, 1955, *24*, 113–133.

Triandis, H. C., and Davis, E. E. Race and belief as determinants of behavioral intentions. *Journal of Personality and Social Psychology*, 1965, *2*, 715–725.

United States Commission on Civil Disorders. *Racial isolation in the public schools: Report of the U.S. Commission on Civil Rights*, two volumes. Washington, D.C.: U.S. Government Printing Office, 1967.

Washington Post, Feb. 10, 1973.

Webster, S. W. The influence of interracial contact on social acceptance in a newly integrated school. *Journal of Educational Psychology*, 1961, *52*, 292–296.

Whyte, W. H., Jr. *The organization man*. New York: Simon and Schuster, 1956.

Wicker, A. W. Attitudes versus action: The relationship of verbal and overt behavioral responses to attitude objects. *Journal of Social Issues*, 1969, *25* (4), 41–78.

INDEX

Index